Never Look Back

The Jewish Refugee Children in Great Britain, 1938–1945

Shofar Supplements in Jewish Studies

Zev Garber, Editor
Los Angeles Valley College

Never Look Back

The Jewish Refugee Children in Great Britain, 1938–1945

Judith Tydor Baumel-Schwartz

Purdue University Press / West Lafayette, Indiana

Copyright 2012 by Purdue University. All rights reserved.

Printed in the United States of America.

Library of Congress Cataloging-in-Publication Data
Baumel-Schwartz, Judith Tydor, 1959-
  Never Look Back: The Jewish Refugee Children in Great Britain, 1938-1945 / Judith Tydor Baumel-Schwartz.
    p. cm. -- (Shofar Supplements in Jewish Studies)
  Includes bibliographical references and index.
  ISBN 978-1-55753-612-9 (pbk.: alk. paper) -- ISBN 978-1-61249-223-0 (epdf) -- ISBN 978-1-61249-222-3 (epub) 1. Jewish refugees--Great Britain--History--20th century. 2. Kindertransports (Rescue operations)--Great Britain. 3. Refugee children--Great Britain--History--20th century. 4. Jewish children--Great Britain--History--20th century. 5. World War, 1939-1945--Evacuation of civilians--Great Britain. I. Title. II. Title: Jewish Refugee Children in Great Britain, 1938-1945.
  DS135.E5B27 2012
  940.53'18350830941--dc23
                                    2011047678

Front cover photo courtesy of Joseph Haberer.

Dedication

To my beloved husband, Joshua Jay Schwartz, with all my heart.

Contents

Preface		ix
1	Introduction, Rationale, and Sources	1
Part 1: January 1933–August 1939: The Prewar Hitler Era		
2	Laying the Foundations: British Jewry and Refugee Organizations, 1933–38	23
3	The Turning Point: *Kristallnacht*	49
4	Machinery	73
5	Immigration and Resettlement	101
6	Children and Youth Aliyah	137
Part 2: The War Years		
7	War and Evacuation	155
8	Internment and Deportation	181
9	The Guardianship	199
10	Epilogue and Memory	217
Timeline		247
Glossary		249
Discussion Questions		253
Bibliography		255
Index		277

Preface

Every book has at least one mother or father, but is often blessed with a number of midwives and this book is no exception. And while most gestations are counted in months or occasionally even years, the gestation of this book has to be counted in decades.

The nucleus of this book was an MA thesis which I wrote between 1979 and 1981 at the department of Jewish history at Bar Ilan University under the supervision of Dan Michman. Focusing on the Jewish refugee children in Britain, the thesis charted many of the facts known at that time about the Kindertransports and drew upon interviews I had conducted with *Kinder* (refugee children from Central Europe) and wartime refugee activists who were still alive. It lacked, however, the depth of conceptual analysis which would only come through years of historical study in dealing with the refugee problem in general and the intricacies of cultural history in particular.

Aside from three short articles which I culled from the thesis, it basically sat on a bookshelf in my study, superseded by the projects that followed. Throughout the thirty years since I began my thesis I occasionally contemplated reworking my original research into a book, but each time I was sidetracked by yet another project in which I was involved: books about the rescue of children to the United States during the Holocaust; the Holocaust and Prayer; Kibbutz Buchenwald; Gender and the Holocaust; the IZL delegation in the United States; the World War II parachutists from Palestine; and finally, my late father Yechezkel Tydor's biography.

"If a book is supposed to be written, eventually someone will write it," is something I remember my father saying, and it appears that in this case he was correct. About a year ago I received an email from Joseph Haberer, founding editor of *Shofar*, an interdisciplinary journal of Jewish Studies, who had read my thesis and encouraged me to turn it into a book. A former refugee child from England who eventually settled in the United States, Joe's kind words about my original thesis encouraged me to consider the project, and after he put me in touch with Charles Watkinson, Director of Purdue University Press, the present book began to take shape. Insisting that after not having touched the material for thirty years I should be given a chance to rework it into a broader manuscript, Charles and Joe both encouraged me in this desire over the next few months. The result is a book that is very different in most senses from the original thesis, both in its breadth and depth, and of course in its analytical focus. I thank the staff at Purdue University Press and especially Becki Corbin, Dianna Gilroy, Katherine Purple, Joyce Rappaport, and Bryan D. Shaffer for all their assistance in publishing this manuscript.

The list of people who I am pleased to thank for their assistance is quite long, as it basically stretches back over thirty years to the close to one hundred original *Kinder* whom I interviewed or questioned then and those to whom I came back now, and to the staff of the various archives and repositories who assisted me thirty years ago and today: the American Friends Service Committee Archives, Philadelphia; the Central Zionist Archives, Jerusalem; the Franklin Delano Roosevelt Library, Hyde Park, NY; the Imperial War Museum, London; the Labor Party Archives, Beit Berl; the Leo Baeck Institute, New York; the Oral History Division, Institute for Contemporary Jewry, the Hebrew University, Jerusalem; the Public Record Office, Kew; the Religious Kibbutz Archives, Kevutzat Yavneh; Yad Vashem, Jerusalem and Givatayim Branches; and especially to Lilian Levy and the World Jewish Relief, formerly the Jewish Refugees Committee and the Association of Jewish Refugees in London, which was kind enough to allow me to use their administrative files at the Wiener Library, and to Ben Barkow, director, the Wiener Library Institute of Contemporary History in London, who was instrumental in finding me material that had become available since I wrote my original thesis.

My thanks go especially to a select group of people who figurative held my hand throughout my new research, providing me with leads and pertinent information and encouraging me throughout. In particular, to Steffi Birnbaum Schwartz who unstintingly shared her experiences with me, encouraging me with her very special brand of humor; to Walter Laqueur, historian par excellence, witness to the period and incredible friend, who as usual was my mainstay of assistance and information regarding almost anything historical and otherwise; and of course to my close friends who helped me through many important junctures, research and otherwise: Maoz Azaryahu, Adam Ferziger, Baruch Forman, Yoav Gelber, Chanita Goodblatt, Aviva Halamish, Hilda Nissimi, Tali Tadmor Shimony, Eli Tzur, Yechiam Weitz, Hanna Yablonka, and Mira Katzburg Yungman. Of the entire group only Hilda and Mira lived through the writing of the original thesis with me, and all that it entailed at the time, but the entire group of friends shared in encouraging me throughout the writing of the present book and have been there for me through thick and thin.

My family, as always, has been the mainstay of my life that makes it all worthwhile. My very special and one-of-a-kind mother, Shirley K. Tydor, who warned me of a major pitfall connected with my MA thesis over thirty years ago—mother, you have been vindicated!; my loving in-laws Bernice and Dr. Arthur Schwartz; my incredible daughters, Beki and Rina; my terrific step-children and their children—Laya and Alon and their sons Eviatar and Uriah, Chaim and Ayelet and their daughter Halleli Miriam, and Yoni—who have made us into a large and wonderful family for which I am grateful on a daily basis.

Above all, to my one and only, my beloved husband Joshua J. Schwartz, whose first words to me: "Do you ever do anything but write?" still echo laughingly in my ears as we do so much more together today and, I hope, for many, many decades to come. This is the third book I dedicate to him, three being a *hazaka*—a Jewish symbol of possession and continuity—and a testimony to how wonderfully enmeshed we have become in each other's existence and lives.

Judith Tydor Baumel-Schwartz
Ramat Gan
June 2011

Chapter 1

Introduction, Rationale, and Sources

"Of course Berlin is a lovely city, I should know, I was born there!" These were Steffi's opening words to me when we met at a Jerusalem café on the eve of my trip to the German capital in August 2010. With a twinkle in her eye, she recalled events from more than seven decades ago, describing her middle-class German neighborhood, her comfortable home, and her experiences at the Goldschmidt-Schule, the private Jewish school she attended in the Grunewald district of Berlin.[1] As she continued her story, her face took on a more somber look. "I remember when we left Berlin for England right before the war. It was the middle of March and Reenie and I were bundled up against the cold." My sprightly octogenarian friend took a deep breath, paused for a moment, and continued. "My father was ill with Parkinson's and bedridden. Before we left to join the other children at the train station we went in to say goodbye to him at home, and he blessed us, not knowing when he would see us again. My mother accompanied us to the station with our hand luggage. Reenie didn't really register what was happening but I knew what was going on, I remembered *Kristallnacht* and was relieved to be leaving Berlin, except of course for parting from our parents." Steffi leaned back and shook her head, as if to shake off the visions of seventy years past that had suddenly become too vivid to bear. "We left on March 15, 1939, arrived in London on the 16th, and the next day was my birthday. That day I became an adult. I had just turned eleven and Reenie was nine; we were among the lucky ones, we got out on time."[2]

Steffi Birnbaum Schwartz and Reenie Birnbaum were two of almost ten thousand Jewish and "non-Aryan" Christian children (Jewish converts to Christianity or children of mixed marriages) from Central Europe who found refuge in Great Britain between December 1938 and September 1939. Most of the refugee children, the majority of whom were Jewish, came from Germany like the Birnbaum girls; the rest were from Austria or Czechoslovakia. Almost all arrived in the framework of what were known as the Kindertransport Movement—groups of anywhere between ten and five hundred children who were accompanied by caretakers, social workers, and educators, some of whom returned to Nazi Europe time and again in order to bring yet another group of children out to safety. Some of these *Begleiterin*—escorts—ultimately remained in Britain. Others were caught by the outbreak of war in Nazi-controlled territory and remained there throughout the war, if they survived the Second World War.

The Kindertransport children arriving in England fell into two broad categories: those sponsored by individuals who in most cases offered the children an initial home, and those whose upkeep was guaranteed by one of the refugee organizations that needed to find them foster parents. Steffi and Reenie Birnbaum were among the twelve lucky children who were sponsored by Dr. Bernard Schlesinger, chief physician at the Great Ormond Street Children's Hospital in London, who spared them the humiliation of the "slave market": there, newly arrived refugee children were paraded before potential foster parents who usually chose the young, the fair, and the comely girls before all others, leaving behind the other children who wondered for hours if anyone would ever give them a home. Eventually, families were found for the younger children while, due to the lack of potential foster homes, many of the older refugee children were ultimately sent to youth hostels opened for this purpose by the refugee movements.

Steffi and Reenie also ended up in a refugee hostel, but of a very different kind. In their generosity of spirit and funds, Dr. Schlesinger and his wife realized that they had nowhere to house twelve children and decided to open a well-run hostel for their young charges. In addition, they sponsored a number of adult refugees who assisted in this endeavor: a cook, separate supervisors for the boys and girls, a rabbi for the hostel, and a young woman who assisted them with their own children and later married the rabbi. This exemplary hostel was unfortunately not the rule. Many of the older refugee children ended up in places with little supervision and guidance other than occasional visits from social-service organizations.

Originally, the Kindertransport movement was supposed to be an ad hoc solution to what was hoped to be a temporary problem. Children entering Britain on one of the Kinderstransports were given the status of "transmigrants" and were slated to return to Europe once the Nazis would no longer be in power, presumably within a year or two. In practice, however, a very different scenario developed after the autumn of 1939. Following the outbreak of war on 1 September 1939, hundreds of thousands of British children, and along with them, thousands of younger refugee children from Central Europe, were evacuated from the major cities to the Midlands to protect them from the expected German bombings. Suddenly, these children who had barely adjusted to being in England and could speak only a few words of English, found themselves in the British countryside among families who had no idea that they were getting Jewish refugee boarders and had no concept of how to communicate with them.

Some of the children such as Steffi and Reenie settled in well among families taking evacuee boarders and quickly adapted to the change. As Steffi recalled, "They thought they were getting bona fide British children and were a bit surprised to see us, but they were very good people."[3] Other children found themselves facing barely concealed hostility and worse. Some had to be resettled several times as their foster families used them as unpaid farm laborers or tried to convert them to save their souls. For a time, Steffi and Reenie faced such a situation with a proselytizing headmistress in their new boarding school in Cornwall, where Dr. Schlesinger thought they would be safer from the bombs than in the Midlands. As Steffi recalled: "It was absolutely dreadful. I sat in church but never kneeled down and refused to pray to Jesus."[4] For them, rescue ultimately came in the form of a local Jewish woman who took the Jewish girls in the boarding school to her home for the holidays. For others, fear and loneliness and the desire to belong ultimately led Jewish children to convert to Christianity. It was the fear of this process that brought Rabbi Solomon Schonfeld of the Chief Rabbi's Religious Emergency Council to set up kosher canteens for observant evacuee children, including young Orthodox refugees, several hundred of whom had come to Britain under his auspices, and begin to supervise what was happening to the young refugee evacuees.

Meanwhile a group of the older refugee children faced a different form of displacement, having been interned by the British government as "Enemy Aliens" because of their German or Austrian origin. Groups of these refugee boys were even deported to Canada and Australia, where they lived in detention camps, for a time alongside true Nazi sympathizers. Ultimately the Jewish refugee teens were released from internment, in most cases in order to join the Pioneer Corps, the only branch of the armed forces in which refugees were initially permitted to enlist. As the war progressed, older refugee girls also attempted to enlist in the Services to aid the war effort, an experience that young Steffi and Reenie missed as they were both underage.

Toward the latter half of the war, it became clear to the organizers and activists of Refugee Children's Movement (RCM), the organization responsible for most of the refugee children in Britain, that many of the children's parents were no longer alive. Consequently, it was necessary to appoint a legal guardian for the children. Although the Chief Rabbi's Religious Emergency Council (CRREC) lobbied for the British Chief Rabbi, Dr. Joseph Herman Hertz (1872–1946), to be appointed to this position, the choice fell on Lord Gorell (Ronald Gorell Barnes, 1884–1963), chairman of the Refugee Children's Movement. At the time, Steffi was already sixteen and had left school to return to London where she lived in a refugee youth hostel in Belsize Park. News from the war zone was sparse, but what was reaching Britain was dismal. As Steffi recalled, "We were all unhappy there as we knew already what was happening in Europe."[5] Reenie remained in school in

Cornwall until she was sixteen and joined her sister in London where she began to train as a nurse under Dr. Schlesinger at the Great Ormond Street Hospital.

In May 1945, the Second World War ended and for the first time in close to seven years the children could theoretically return to their families. Theoretically, because in many, if not most cases, there were no longer families for them to return to. Having lost their parents in the Holocaust, the majority of the *Kinder* (singular: *Kind*), as they called themselves, remained in Britain after the war, as did young Reenie and Steffi, eventually becoming fully acculturated citizens. But the means by which this came about was at times complex and difficult and there was a world of experiences, not all good or easy, behind the five succinct words—"eventually becoming fully acculturated citizens." The process by which a Jewish refugee child became a productive British citizen was often fraught with tension, discrimination, misunderstandings, and occasionally even religious coercion. Some siblings even chose different paths from each other, such as Reenie and Steffi who will accompany us throughout this book. Yet in view of the xenophobia that punctuated British society, particularly during the war years, most children were willing to do almost anything in order to cease being a refugee, a foreigner, a stranger.

Why Refugee Children?

"A refugee is I, you or they if circumstances decree it. It is a strange survival which is unglamorous, often sordid and has to be made the best of. It is a state to shake off as quickly as possible."[6] This statement, made long after the Second World War by a former refugee child in Great Britain, epitomizes the essence of the refugee experience in general and the child refugee experience in particular: "strange," "sordid," "unglamorous," and, most important, "survival," a word that one usually associates with those who suffered through the Holocaust in occupied Europe, not with refugees who were able to leave Nazi lands before the outbreak of war. The fact that this statement was made by a former refugee child who benefited from what was probably the largest rescue operation that took place during the Holocaust period is telling, in view of the nature of this particular rescue operation, its scope, and its ultimate success. Nevertheless, as seen through the eyes of many of its participants, their refugee-child experience as recipients of His Majesty's beneficence was "strange" and "sordid," even if it did ultimately enable their survival.

During the first decades after the end of the war, the study of refugees from Nazism, both child and adult, was pushed aside in favor of dealing with what were then considered major Holocaust-related topics meriting scholarly—and ultimately public—attention. These included Nazi anti-Jewish policy, concentration camp existence, Jewish leadership and resistance, and, at a later stage, daily life under Nazi rule. Refugees were often considered a "non-issue"; after all, they had left Europe early enough to survive the Nazi onslaught. From the early

1970s onward, when wartime government archives began to be opened in various countries, the refugee issue was raised within the framework of a larger topic of rescue attempts carried out by agencies and individuals in the United States, Great Britain, Palestine, and elsewhere before and during the war. Yet even then, with the exception of scant paragraphs denoting the existence of child-refugee schemes, historians paid little attention to the fact that close to 12,000 unaccompanied Jewish and "non-Aryan" Christian children were saved from Nazism through schemes set up in Great Britain, the United States, Switzerland, and Sweden.[7] Between December 1938 and August 1939, close to 3,000 additional children were moved out of Central Europe to countries later occupied by the Nazis, such as Belgium, France, and the Netherlands; many of them lost their lives during the wartime deportations.[8]

In the earliest studies of the Holocaust period, all Jewish refugees were usually lumped together in a single category—children and adults, men and women—and mentioned only in passing. During the early 1970s, scholars began to turn their attention to topics pertaining to rescue during the Holocaust, giving refugees a somewhat more central focus.[9] But it was only from the latter part of that decade onward that Jewish refugee children became a separate research topic, with initial studies dealing with refugee children in France, Great Britain, and the United States.[10] All of these studies, like those about refugee children which followed,[11] were predicated on a common belief that refugee children were an entity unto themselves, often containing both the best and the worst of the refugee experience.[12] On the one hand, children adapt better to new surroundings, as their facility for learning languages is greater and their chances for successful assimilation far surpass those of any other age group. On the other hand, children can be infinitely crueler than adults, their emotions not yet clothed by the society-imposed but exceedingly thin polite veneer of good manners, propriety, and tact. Consequently, refugee children endured far more at times from their contemporaries than did their refugee parents.

My own introduction to the topic of refugee children was quite personal, as my older half brother and sister had come to the United States as Jewish refugee children from Germany in late 1941. When I began my degree in history I was astounded to find that not a single academic study existed about Jewish refugee children during the Holocaust in any country of refuge. From the outset it was clear to me that I would write my thesis on this topic, but I decided to focus initially on those children who had gone to Great Britain and not the United States, leaving the latter for my doctoral dissertation.

The result was my 1981 MA thesis entitled "The Jewish Refugee Children in Great Britain, 1938–1945."[13] At first I considered publishing it as a book, but I soon got caught up in my dissertation topic and then in additional books that I wrote over the years. As a result, the project got somehow sidetracked, although never forgotten. In 1989 I was the keynote speaker at the Israeli gathering of Kindertransport children that took place at Kibbutz Lavi in the Galilee, and I followed with great interest the creation of the collected volume of memoirs that resulted from the major Kindertransport reunion in London that year. Each television program, film, and book that appeared on the subject during the next decade[14] reminded me of my debt to the *Kinder* who had been so kind as to share their experiences with me and who had concluded almost every interview with the words, "You will write all this up as a book one day, won't you?"

People say that the best things in life often happen out of the blue, and it was true in this case. One Sunday morning in late July 2010 I opened my email and found a note from Dr. Joseph Haberer, founding editor of *Shofar*, an interdisciplinary journal of Jewish studies. Having recently come across a copy of my MA thesis on the Kindertransports and being a former refugee child himself, he asked me, in view of the recent upsurge in interest on the topic, whether I would consider publishing it as a book. Within hours of my answering in the affirmative he connected me with Dr. Charles Watkinson, director of the Purdue University Press. The project which had long been a potential but unachieved desire finally began to take form as a book.

While updating my original writing, I returned time and again to two issues that only someone who had already studied the topic almost a generation ago could address in full. To the best of my knowledge, I was the only such scholar who fit that definition. The first was why those assisting the refugee children in some form—refugee movement activists, Jewish and gentile sponsors, refugee children's foster parents, just to mention a few—chose to do so. Although there is a plethora of theoretical literature that has been written in the past fifty years about what is termed "helping behavior," a broad category of actions ranging from assisting a stranger in an emergency to giving a body part as a donation, only someone who had communicated directly, and in depth, with these activists, volunteers, and sponsors while they were still alive three or more decades ago could accurately employ these theoretical studies to conceptualize why they acted as they did. As none of the existing studies of the Kindertransport Movement had addressed that question in any depth, this issue became one of the theoretical bases for this book.

A second issue was that of the former *Kinder*'s perspective about their experiences. While later scholars who worked on the Kindertransports or collected memoir literature were only able to address how their interviewees viewed their experiences at one specific point in time, I was able to go back to some of my former interviewees to whom I had spoken when they were in their fifties, and could ask them for an additional perspectives now that they were in their eighties. Their responses were fascinating, particularly as some of them had letters or diaries in which they had noted their refugee experiences in "real time" that could be pulled out and used as a starting point to see how their "take" on an issue changed at various junctures in their life over a seventy-year period. For a historian, such an extraordinary situation could only arise because this book was actually more than thirty years in the making, teaching me that at times a delay can metamorphose into a unique advantage. The results of their responses at the forty- and seventy-year benchmarks after their arrival in Great Britain are included in the book you are now reading.

Finally, I noticed an additional inadequacy in the Kindertransport literature that had been published since my initial study: none of the studies actually gave the reader a comprehensive picture of the complete Kindertransport experience. Some books dealt primarily with the scheme's governmental and political aspects, others focused more on the Jewish refugee organizations and their functionaries, a third group "discovered" the activities of the CRREC which I had already written about years earlier, and a fourth group—primarily the individual and collected memoir literature—concentrated almost solely on the children's personal experiences, often mentioned only in passing in the other studies. In some books there was little or no mention of the refugee children's internment and deportation, in others there was little discussion of the Youth Aliyah centers and even less about their activists and young charges, and in a third group the issue of the clergy, Quakers, and Christadelphian activity for the refugee children was nonexistent while children's proselytizing and conversion or the guardianship issue was skimmed over, except in a few scant paragraphs. I have therefore tried to incorporate all of these topics in this book, giving the reader a balanced and well-rounded picture of the refugee children's issue.

Throughout this study, I have concentrated solely on the experiences of unaccompanied Jewish refugee children in Great Britain over a seven-year period, from their arrival on the British shores until the end of the Second World War. In delineating my research subjects I made a deliberate choice not to focus on the fate of accompanied refugee children, a group whose history is more difficult to chart as its members were usually viewed by the British authorities and the refugee organizations as part of a family unit, making it difficult to study the children as a separate entity. As this is a primarily historical study, I have also not dealt in depth with issues stemming from certain refugee children's psychological maladjustment, and mention the interaction between refugee children and their parents who reached Britain after the war only briefly, as this aspect is outside my scope of research. This does not detract from the importance of these topics, and they have been discussed elsewhere.[15]

Who Helped the Refugee Children and Why Did They Do So?

The relocation of almost 10,000 refugee children from Central Europe to Great Britain within a nine-month period prior to the outbreak of the Second World War and the absorption of those children within British society could only have been carried out due to the willingness of thousands, or possibly even tens of thousands, of people who gave of their time, money, homes, services, and abilities to assist these children. Some did it grudgingly, at times for monetary compensations or other benefits, but many did it selflessly, with their full minds and hearts.

Who were these people and why did they do what they did? The first part of the question is easier to answer. Among those who come to mind are those who offered homes to the refugee children, but once we start examining the actual numbers of people involved, the list seems endless. Individuals involved in one-on-one sponsorship of refugee children; previously unconnected individuals involved in a group sponsorship; foster parents; refugee movement administrative volunteers; clerks, telephone operators, secretaries, social service volunteers; volunteer educators; clergy; drivers; food manufacturers; schoolchildren who assisted in compiling or copying lists of refugee children's names from Germany to be given to the Home Office; volunteer canteen workers; policemen who turned a blind eye to somewhat illegal but not harmful actions by young refugee internees; and the list goes on and on.

It is more difficult to formulate a singular response to the second part of the question. Already in his 1975 study of voluntary actions and groups, sociologist David Horton Smith[16] stated that scholars looking to understand voluntary action research must seek out cross-disciplinary input to best comprehend the phenomenon.[17] In order to understand the motives and answers to the question "who does what and why," we must briefly turn to studies from psychology, sociology, and economics that deal with the impetus behind performing or abstaining from voluntary action.

The gamut of activities known as "helping behaviors" has long been studied by social scientists who have tried to formulate a theory to explain why certain people are more likely than others to participate in such activity. David Schroeder et al.[18] and Shalom Schwartz[19] have shown that helping others has been conceptualized as a series of consecutive decisions, the order of which is determined by level of importance. René Bekkers and Pamala Wiepking[20] developed this further in their study of theories relating to philanthropy and voluntary action, and noted the seven mechanisms which are considered the most important forces that drive voluntary action: solicitation, awareness of need, costs, reputation, psychological benefits, changing the world, and confidence. People are more likely to help when they hear that others have done so as well,[21] but are less likely to help if there are more people in the immediate vicinity at the time.[22]

In spite of the aforementioned model, there is no all-encompassing theory of helping behavior and it is difficult to construct one from the seven variables as the theory is a consequence of several principles working at once. Altruism and egoism are not among these principles, and yet altruistic motivation is one of the most important factors in encouraging pro-social and helping behavior.[23] Religious belief,[24] comfortable income and employment,[25] middle age,[26] settled family situation,[27] place of residence,[28] home ownership,[29] major group ethnicity,[30] educational and financial background,[31] parental example,[32] youth group participation,[33] tradition of volunteering,[34] and emotional stability[35] are all variables that affect and increase the amount of helping behavior one finds among various groups.

Sources and Studies

If the search for documentation about the Kindertransport movement were a detective novel, this chapter could possibly be titled "The Case of the Disappearing, or Possibly Reappearing, Sources." Documentation is the make-or-break of any historical study, and this title accurately describes the amount of sleuthing I had to initially undertake when I began my original historical study in the late 1970s. As the British government documents concerning the Kindertransport were already open to the public, my first step was to obtain access to the archives of the refugee organizations responsible for the children's transfer and care. Unfortunately, so I was told, sometime during the late 1950s many of the files and case cards of the Refugee Children's Movement, the main organization responsible for the transfer and care of refugee children in Britain which had disbanded in the late 1940s, had "disappeared," were "lost," or were destroyed. One of the British Youth Aliyah activists who had worked during the war with refugee children later related to me that this appeared to have been a deliberate move, as some of the former *Kinder* had reached powerful and influential positions in Britain and wished to obliterate all traces of their refugee past.[36]

Walter Laqueur describes this state of events in his account of the fate of young Jewish refugees from Nazi Germany. He notes that some of the more influential *Kinder* who later became famous suppressed the place of their birth in reference works such as *Who's Who*. "They had been educated at good schools and at Oxford, but, as Isaiah Berlin once noted, had apparently never been born."[37] The files and case cards that were still in existence, along with the case cards of the Jewish Refugees Committee, were, at the time, all in the possession of the Woburn House Archives and I was told that the material, considered to be confidential, was not permitted to be used by the public or by historians for research.[38]

This, however, was only part of the story, as I began to discover over the years from those who continued to research the refugee issue. In her fascinating book on refugee activist Wilfred Israel, Naomi Shepherd first mentioned that the papers that were supposedly still in the Woburn House Archives were actually being housed elsewhere.[39] Fourteen years later, Amy Zahl Gottlieb, in her study of the Central British Fund for German Jewry, describes how in the late 1980s a number of cabinets filled with files from Woburn House were found in the garage of the Heinrich Stahl Home for Aged Refugees in London, including files relating to unaccompanied children.[40] She and two assistants were asked to compile an archive from what were actually a few cabinets packed with jumbled files. The completed archive was microfilmed in order to be made available to university and national libraries. In his study of "Timespace," Jonathan Boyarin shows us how everything is a matter of chronology and geography, of "when" and "where."[41] Here, too, it became obvious that at various times and in different places "lost" could suddenly be "found" and "confidential" could rapidly become public. Years after my original correspondence with Woburn House, this material, deposited in the Weiner Library and also now part of the National Archives, housed in the London Metropolitan Archives, is no longer "lost," nor is it "confidential," and numerous documents found in these collections have been used for this study.[42]

For research into the legal status of refugee children in Great Britain with regard to adoption, guardianship, and other issues, I made prodigious use of Statutes (The Public General Acts and Church Assembly Measures). Discussions of the British Government's policy toward refugee children and the guardianship Bill are based on the Hansard Parliamentary Debates, 5th Series, an invaluable tool to those interested in the parliamentary history of the period.

The Public Record Office (PRO) in London provided additional material pertaining to British government policy vis-à-vis the entry of refugee children from Nazism. Other important archival collections that I utilized are found at the Leo Baeck Institute in New York,[43] the Central Zionist Archives[44] and the Yad Vashem Archives,[45] both in Jerusalem, and the archives of the Religious Kibbutz Movement, at Kevutzat Yavneh[46] in central Israel. The Yad Vashem archival collections were particularly important as they contained a plethora of material about the workings of the Chief Rabbi's Religious Emergency Council, including administrative material, activists' correspondence, and even personal diaries. Much of this duplicates material found in the archives of Rabbi Dr. Solomon Schonfeld at the University of Southampton and the private papers of CRREC activist Harry Goodman, the first of which is today open to scholars.

An additional source of information was my correspondence with various people involved with the refugee cause, as were unpublished manuscripts, stories, diaries, letters, and relevant documents that I was given by many *Kinder* and refugee activists whom I contacted in the course of my research. Throughout both my bouts of research on the Kindertransports, both during the late 1970s and more recently, in 2010, I utilized oral history collections found at Heichal Wohlyn, the Yad Vashem branch office in Givatayim,[47] and the Division for Oral Documentation at the Hebrew University of Jerusalem.[48] In addition, I distributed questionnaires to former refugee children, interviewed other *Kinder* who preferred not to fill out questionnaires, and questioned both Jewish and non-Jewish foster parents of refugee children in the late 1970s when many were still alive. At that time, I also interviewed a number of refugee movement activists, clergy, and lay religious leaders who had been active in the refugee children's movement. Thirty years later, in 2010, I returned to a number of *Kinder* and recorded retrospective impressions of their experiences, in order to contrast them with the interviews they had granted me when they were in their fifties, thirty years earlier. A full list of interviews and questionnaires can be found at the end of this book.

In addition, I had the privilege of interviewing or corresponding with most Refugee Children's Movement activists, some of the workers of the CRREC, and those Youth Aliyah activists who were still alive in the late 1970s. The hours spent in discussion with them reminded me that only forty years earlier this was not a historical topic but rather a desperate struggle to save the lives of thousands of homeless children. This perspective accompanied me throughout the writing of the initial thesis, and has remained with me thirty years later, as I wrote the story of the Kindertransport movement. Their invaluable comments, criticisms, and encouragements helped shape this book into its present form.

Contemporary newspapers and periodicals, both Anglo-Jewish and general, gave me much insight into the understanding of the problems surrounding the refugee children and the background of the Anglo-Jewish community during the period in question. Pamphlets from the period added to the picture formed by the archival documentation and press survey. Diaries and memoirs of political figures and refugee activists such as Sir Norman Bentwich, Lord Templewood (Sir Samuel Hoare), Lady Eva Reading, and Lord Herbert Samuel provided me with information unobtainable elsewhere.[49] Bentwich in particular was not only one of the chief protagonists in the refugee drama but also a prolific author of more than a dozen books that dealt either entirely or partially with the refugee problem in Great Britain before and during the Second World War.[50] As assistant to the High Commissioner for Refugees (Jewish and other) coming from Germany and as honorary co-chairman of the Council for German Jewry, Bentwich was privy to information withheld from the public and under normal circumstances would have been considered an unsurpassed source for inside information. However, he was also a very biased source, having become actively pro-British in the late 1920s, a bias that was reflected in his writings from this period onward, making their objectivity questionable. Nevertheless, his chapters on the refugee organizations in Great Britain give us insight into the internal workings of the Kindertransport scheme from a personal standpoint.

In his story of Orthodox Jewish Responses in Britain to the Holocaust, Chanan Tomlin writes: "The purpose of historical research and study cannot be merely an academic exercise, although such an exercise may have inherent worth.... Historians of the Holocaust should not be complacent after their theses are published if they have not contributed to the betterment of society."[51] This debatable yet admirable, quasi-religious sentiment can be translated into more historical terms by stating that many of the studies published on the three subjects at whose nexus the Kindertransport Movement is located have already contributed both to our understanding of these important issues in their historical setting and also in some cases to the later treatment of refugees and especially refugee children in extremis. The first subject is the more general issue of children at war, a second is that of British government policy during the Holocaust, and a third is the history of Jewish refugees in Great Britain during the Nazi era.

The earliest volumes on children in war, including Anna Freud and Dorothy T. Burlingham's survey of the psychological reactions stemming from the deprivation of parental care of children in wartime, were published while the Second World War was still raging.[52] Later studies concentrated on children in actual war situations, potential war situations, and particular groups of children in wartime or exile.⁵³ All of these topics served as important grounding studies for trying to understand the experiences the *Kinder* underwent both during their immigration process and during the war years that they spent in Britain. I have utilized these as background material to understand the child refugee experience.

The next group of relevant studies was those about British government policy during the Holocaust; these provided a different focus on the Kindertransport issue. Most of these books began to appear during the early 1970s in response to the change in government documentation policy, which had determined in 1969 that all records of the Second World War should be released by 1972. Consequently, throughout that decade certain record groups pertaining to sensitive topics such as refugees, internment, deportation, and the Palestine Mandate were opened to public scrutiny. Authors writing on these topics in the late 1970s had access to information that their predecessors did not even know existed.⁵⁴

The first serious study of British government policy during the Holocaust was that of Bernard Wasserstein; it appeared in 1979 and focused on what he considered the lack of government concern about Britain's Palestine policy. This, he claimed, could explain what appeared to be Britain's more generous policy toward Jewish refugees from Europe just as it was closing the gates to the British Mandate in the Middle East.⁵⁵ Later studies on the subject, such as those by Meir Sompolinsky⁵⁶ and Louise London, the most recent and most comprehensive study of British government response to the plight of European Jewry,⁵⁷ echoed these conclusions. While mentioning the Kindertransport issue in passing, they give a brief outline of its structure and processes.

The release of government documents also ignited interest in the topics of Anglo-Jewish responses to the Holocaust and the Jewish refugees in Britain during the Hitler era. Six years before Wasserstein's book about Britain and the Jews of Europe appeared, Alan Joshua Sherman had already made use of newly released archives to conclude that British refugee policy was more generous than that of the United States. He praised British refugee organizations in contrast to their American counterparts.⁵⁸ Sixteen years later, Tony Kushner published a pioneering work detailing Anglo-Jewish responses to the Holocaust within the context of domestic antisemitism and Jewish reactions to it.⁵⁹ Soon after, Richard Bolchover published his study of the subject, showing how most of Anglo-Jewry, with a few exceptions such as Rabbi Solomon Schonfeld, restricted its own responses to the Holocaust as a result of how it perceived its own history and fears of antisemitism.⁶⁰

Amy Zahl Gottlieb's study of Anglo-Jewry's role in rescuing European Jewry comes to somewhat different conclusions about this issue.⁶¹ In documenting the work of the Central British Fund for German Jewry, including its involvement in the Kinderstransport movement and the financial upkeep of the refugee children during the war years, she pens an essentially uncritical description of what she sees as "constructive community endeavour."⁶² However, by limiting herself to documentary evidence only, primarily the archives of the Central British Fund, and excluding what she called "anecdotal sources,"⁶³ her historical descriptions tend to turn a blind eye to the problematics of the Anglo-Jewish prewar and wartime leadership, giving readers a one-sided and at times nonanalytical narrative.

Yet another largely uncritical depiction of part of the Anglo-Jewish leadership—the British Orthodox Jewish prewar and wartime leadership—is found in Pamela Shatzkes's study of Britain during the Holocaust, in which she concentrates on a different Anglo-Jewish hero of that period, the Orthodox Rabbi Solomon Schonfeld.⁶⁴ In her fascinating study, Shatzkes focuses on a number of aspects of the Kindertransport issue and particularly on the rescue of children from Czechoslovakia and Schonfeld's activities within the framework of the CRREC regarding the spiritual welfare of the refugee children, a topic I had covered years earlier in my own study.⁶⁵ The most recent study dealing with the response of Orthodox British Jewry in general and Rabbi Schonfeld in particular to the Nazi persecution of European Jewry is that of Chanan Tomlin, who begins his narrative only in 1942.⁶⁶

Additional books focusing on the refugee experiences include those by Marion Berghahn on German Jewish refugees in England;⁶⁷ Peter and Leni Gilman,⁶⁸ Ronald Stent,⁶⁹ Connery Chappell,⁷⁰ Eric Koch,⁷¹ and Maxine Seller⁷² about interned refugees during the war; Helen Fry⁷³ about refugees serving in the British armed forces; and Benzion Patkin⁷⁴ on refugee deportees to Australia. All of these studies make brief mention of the *Kinder* within the framework of their particular topic. Finally, there are the volumes focusing solely on the lives of refugee and Kindertransport movement activists, such as Naomi Shepard's fascinating story of Wilfred Israel,⁷⁵ Muriel Emanuel and Vera Gissing's moving book about Nicholas Winton who was a key figure in rescuing refugee children from Czechoslovakia,⁷⁶ and David Kranzler's two stirring studies of CREEC founder Rabbi Solomon Schonfeld.⁷⁷ As the late historian Tony Judt writes in one of his last short essays, "articulacy is typically regarded as an aggressive talent . . . at times the form so elegantly transcends the content that we accept the latter on trust."⁷⁸ Many of these books are so vehement in their rhetoric against Anglo-Jewish leadership that one loses track of the situation's true complexity, something I have tried to avoid by including the voices of as many groups involved in the various aspects of the Kindertransport scheme as possible in my own study.

This brings us to the existing literature regarding the Kindertransport movement, written over the past few decades by historians and social scientists, and the Kindertransport memoirs, published as individual books and collected volumes. Several books have been published in German, dealing with the Kindertransport experience, some using government and refugee organization documentations and based in part on interviews with former *Kinder*. One was Rebekka Goepfert's study of the Kindertransport, published in 1999, for which she interviewed twenty-six *Kinder* living in Britain, Germany, and the United States.[79] Although this is one of the more comprehensive studies of the topic, it mentions a few of the important topics only in passing, such as the activities of Youth Aliyah; nor did she follow those children who were interned and deported in any detail. A second study is Claudia Curio's interesting reworking of her doctoral dissertation on the Kindertransports and a number of articles she has published on the subject. However, here too, there was little in-depth research and interviewing done on topics such as the inside activities of the CRREC, and on the *Kinder* as internees and deportees.[80] Paula Hill's unpublished dissertation about Anglo-Jewry and refugee children also deals with only a number of these subjects in depth.[81] A collected volume of articles on the Kindertransports, edited by Wolfgang Benz, Claudia Curio, and Andrea Hammel, was published in German in 2003, later appearing in English as a special issue of *Shofar* in 2004. While the volume is a fascinating and important addition to our understanding of the phenomenon, it was not meant to be a comprehensive overview of the entire Kindertransport movement. Consequently, some of the major issues connected with the *Kinder*'s lives in Britain and as deportees are not covered or are dealt with only in passing.[82]

Iris Guske's recent psychological study of trauma and attachment in the Kindertransport context, based on John Bowlby's theories of attachment, is a fascinating psychological addition to the Kindertransport literature but is not a historical study of the movement.[83] One of the most recent unpublished scientific contribution is Jennifer Norton's master's thesis at California State University at Sacramento, titled "The Kindertransport: History and Memory"; the work deals with the different historical narratives and myths that developed from 1938 onward regarding the children's experiences and their historical background.[84] Finally, Vera Fast's most recent history of the Kindertransports gives a comprehensive overview of some issues that other volumes touch on only in brief; however, some of her sweeping conclusions such as those relating to the lack of Jewish homes being offered, the response of Orthodox children to migration, or the sociological background of the British Jewish community are misleading; the full story is in truth much more complex than the picture she paints.[85] While some of these volumes weave the *Kinder*'s voices into the historical or sociological narrative, others concentrate more on the issues than on the protagonists, focusing on processes and not on persons. In this book, I have tried to reach a suitable balance between the two by interspersing the *Kinder*'s recollections into the historical discussion of the incidents that they recall.

In addition to the scientific studies by historians and social scientists, there were a number of popular histories of the Kindertransports written by journalists. The most famous of these was that of Barry Turner, which was commissioned by the Central British Fund (CBF) and was published first in a format for adults and later for children.[86] Turner's book, for which the CBF gave him full access to their archives, is the only one of the histories that includes references and quotations from the children's individual case files that were not opened to other researchers. But in spite of the many quotes and excerpts, the book has no citations and its bibliography makes no reference to archival sources. On the other hand, Turner does draw heavily from the *Kinder*'s memoirs and thus paints a broader picture than many of the scientific studies that concentrate primarily upon parliamentary decisions, organizational activity, and so on. In spite of his attempt at objectivity, one must also remember that Turner's book was commissioned by the CBF, a factor that places his objectivity under question.

Another aspect of Kindertransport literature is the plethora of *Kinder* memoirs that have been published over the past sixty years. The first and probably the most famous was the collective autobiography *We Came as Children*, compiled by a former *Kind*, Karen Gershon, pseudonym of writer Kathleen Tripp, born Kaethe Loewenthal, in 1966.[87] Other collected volumes were the result of the first Kindertransport reunion in London in 1989: *I Came Alone*[88] and the companion volume to the film *Into the Arms of Strangers*.[89] Individual memoirs and volumes of poetry about the Kindertransport experience that I have consulted include those by Harry Avrays, Myra Baram, Klaus Bowers, Martha Blend, Gisele Brand, Valerie Jean Chase, Ruth David, Gertrude Wishnick Dubrovsky, Anne Fox, Vera Gissing, Mona Golabek and Lee Cohen, Eva Heyman, Charles Hannam, Thea Iden, Ingrid Jacoby, Gerd Korman, Frieda Stolzberg Korobkin, Lotte Kramer, Olga Levy, Edith Milton, Otto Newman, Sigfried Ramler, Irene Reti, Bob Rosner, Milena Roth, Steffi Birnbaum Schwartz, Lore Segal, Charles Strasser, Hanus Weber, Dorit Whiteman, Fredric Zeller, and Hannle Zurndorfer.

Although the events described in this book occurred, for the most part, more than seventy years ago, the topic of refugee children is unfortunately all too current. While the world in which these children lived no longer exists, the events of that time had a direct bearing both on these refugee children's futures in particular and on the Western world's policy toward refugee children in general, for example with regard to refugee children from Cuba to the United States in the early 1960s, from Vietnam and Cambodia in the 1970s and 1980s, and with refugee children from Serbia and Croatia in the 1990s, among others. The British government's decision in November 1938 to admit a large mass of unaccompanied refugee children, the organizations formed during this period, the problems and debates surrounding the controversy of hostels versus homes, the difficulties of giving these children a suitable religious upbringing in their own faith—all served as a precedent for similar situations that later arose regarding other refugee children. Asylum migration, which became a topic of great political and media debate during the latter half of the twentieth century, often brought with it great discussions that had an impact on political, social, and educational policies relating to refugee children or forced migrants, as they were often called, trying to rebuild their lives in the United Kingdom and elsewhere.

Over the past fifty years we have seen how dominant discourses about trauma have labeled and homogenized this very diverse group of children, and how policy makers, educators, health workers, sociologists, and religious activists have reacted to these children's special needs.[90] Refugees, as many have stated, are among the most vulnerable and disempowered people in the world, and refugee children are the most vulnerable among the vulnerable.[91] The personal stories of unspeakable violence done to children seeking asylum, the tales of physical and emotional suffering of children sent ahead of their parents to seek refuge or those left behind when parents are forced to flee, are all bleak reminders of the truth behind the statement, *plus ça change, plus c'est la même chose*, the more things change, the more they remain the same.[92] In addition to telling the story of the Kindertransport movement, this book highlights those individuals and groups who during the 1930s reacted unequivocally to offer assistance to the world's youngest dispossessed, illuminating how one can react with humanity. In view of the state of refugee children throughout the world today, this is unfortunately not just a book about a historical episode in the past but one of particular relevance to our time, and a reminder of how a few caring individuals can go a long way to securing these children's uncertain and challenging future.[93]

Notes

1. The bilingual school, which opened in Berlin in 1935, moved to England in the summer of 1939 and was reconvened as the Athelstan School in Folkstone. It existed in various forms until 1941. See Thompson, "The Dr. Leonore Goldschmidt Schule," 301–352.
2. Author's interview with Steffi Birnbaum Schwartz, Jerusalem, 5 August 2010 (henceforth: Schwartz interview).
3. Ibid.
4. Ibid.
5. Ibid.
6. Quoted in Gershon, *We Came as Children*, 150.
7. See Baumel, "The Jewish Refugee Children in Great Britain"; Wischnitzer, *To Dwell in Safety*, 200; Castendyck, "Refugee Children in Europe," 596; Baumel, *Unfulfilled Promise*.
8. Michman, "The Jewish Refugees from Germany in Holland," 248, 529 n. 475; Castendyk, "Refugee Children," 593–96; Tartakower and Grossman, *The Jewish Refugee*, 485.
9. For example: Gutman et al., *Rescue Attempts during the Holocaust*.
10. Papanek and Linn, *Out of the Fire*; Baumel, *Unfulfilled Promise*; Baumel, "Great Britain and the Jewish Refugee Children," 19–25; Baumel, "Twice a Refugee," 174–84.
11. Such as Kadosh, "Jewish Refugee Children in Switzerland 1939-1950," 281–97; Palmer, "Seventeen Children," 88–96; Ansbacher, "Rescue and Return," 433–43.
12. See Kroeger, "Child Exiles," 8–20.
13. Bar Ilan University, Department of Jewish History, 1981.
14. The movies: Mark Jonathan Harris (dir.), *Into the Arms of Strangers: Stories of the Kindertransport* (2000); Melissa Hacker (dir.) *My Knees Were Jumping* (1997); Sue

Read and Jim Goulding, *The Children Who Cheated the Nazis*, British documentary film shown first on channel 4 (2000); Kate Kranz (dir.), *Maybe I Was Lucky* (2002); *Holocaust Day: A Haven in Wales*, a BBC documentary broadcast on BBC2 Wales on Holocaust Day 2005, featuring the reminiscences of some of the two hundred Kindertransport children who found a haven at Gwrych Castle in North East Wales; Nicholas Winton's work was the subject of two films by Slovak Filmmaker Matej Minac: the drama *All My Loved Ones* (*Vsichni moji blzci*; 1999) and the documentary *The Power of Good: Nicholas Winton* (*Sila lidskosti—Nicholas Winton*; 2002), which won an Emmy Award. Plays include *Kindertransport*, by Diana Samuels, which premiered in London in 1993; *Memory*, by Jonathan Lichtenstein, first performed at Clwyd Theatr Cymru in Wales in November 2006 and subsequently produced at the 59E59 Theaters in New York City in 2007; Greg Gunning, *My Heart in a Suitcase*, ArtsPower National Touring Theatre, 2006; *The End of Everything Ever*, NIE (New International Encounter) Theatre, 2008.

15. See, for example, Benz, "Traumatization through Separation," 85–99; Barnett, "The Other Side of the Abyss," 175–94; Newman, *Kinder Transporte*.
16. Smith is the founder of ARNOVA (Association for Research on Non-Profit Organizations and Voluntary Action).
17. Smith, "Voluntary Action and Voluntary Groups," 247–70.
18. Schroeder et al., *The Psychology of Helping and Altruism*.
19. Schwartz, "The Justice of Need," 111–36.
20. Bekkers and Weipking, "Generosity and Philanthropy."
21. Jones and McKee, "Feedback Information," 512–27.
22. Latané and Darley, *The Unresponsive Bystander*.
23. Piliavin and Charg, "Altruism," 27–65.
24. Bekkers and Wiepking, "To Give or Not to Give . . . ," 533–40.
25. Chang, "Determinants of Donations," 217–34.
26. Landry et al., "Towards an Understanding of the Economics of Charity," 747–82.
27. Chang, "Determinants of Donations."
28. Bryant et al., "Participation in Philanthropic Activities," 43–73.
29. Carroll, McCarthy, and Newman, "An Econometric Analysis," 229–49.
30. Bielefeld, Rooney, and Steinberg, in Arthur Brooks (ed.), *Gifts of Time and Money*, 127–58.
31. Brown, "College, Social Capital and Charitable Giving," 185–204.
32. Bekkers, "It's Not All in the Ask."
33. Ibid.
34. Reed and Selbee, "Is There a Distinctive Pattern of Values."
35. Bekkers, "Traditional and Health-Related Philanthropy," 349–66.
36. Author's interview with former Youth Aliyah worker Eva Michaelis-Stern, Jerusalem, 18 February 1980 (henceforth: Michaelis-Stern interview).
37. Laqueur, *Generation Exodus*, 194.
38. Author's correspondence with Woburn House Archives, February 1980; in the author's possession.
39. "The refugee organizations centered on Bloomsbury House destroyed all their files, except a small cache in an old people's home in North London." Shepherd, *Wilfred Israel*, introduction.
40. Gottlieb, *Men of Vision*, xi.
41. Boyarin, *Remapping Memory*.

42. For a full list of sources and secondary literature, biographies, and memoirs used, see the bibliography.
43. For information on the training farm at Gross-Breesen.
44. For material regarding Youth Aliyah training centers in Britain, information on internment and deportation.
45. For information regarding the refugee organizations, Bunce Court School, internment, deportation, and the Chief Rabbi's Religious Emergency Council (CRREC).
46. For information regarding Youth Aliyah centers, evacuation, and internment.
47. These interviews provided a great deal of information on internment and the machinery for transferring the refugee children to Great Britain.
48. Numerous oral interviews at this repository were helpful in creating a total picture of the rescue operation. These included interviews with former social workers, activists of the period in the RCM, and those who were involved in Youth Aliyah activities.
49. Bentwich, *My 77 Years*; Reading, *For the Record*; Samuel, *Memoirs*; Templewood, *Nine Troubled Years*.
50. See, for example, Bentwich's *Jewish Youth Comes Home*; his *Wanderer between Two Worlds*; his *Refugees from Germany*; his *Rescue and Achievement of Refugee Scholars*; and his *Wanderer in War 1939-4*.
51. Tomlin, *Protest and Prayer*, 28.
52. Freud and Burlingham, *War and Children*.
53. Apfel and Simon, *Minefields in their Hearts*; Rosenblatt, *Children of War*; Solantus, *Mental Health of Young People*; Sosnowsky, *The Tragedy of Children under Nazi Rule*; Kroeger, "Child Exiles," 8–20; Bauer and Strickhausen (eds.), "Fuer ein Kind war das anders."
54. Certain files on extremely sensitive topics were not released at the time and the British government decided not to open them until one hundred years past the event in question.
55. Wasserstein, *Britain and the Jews of Europe*.
56. Sompolinsky, *Britain and the Holocaust*.
57. London, *Whitehall and the Jews*.
58. Sherman, *Island Refuge*.
59. Kushner, *The Persistence of Prejudice*.
60. Bolchover, *British Jewry and the Holocaust*.
61. Gottlieb, *Men of Vision*.
62. Ibid., 196.
63. Other than those by Joan Steibel, whom she thanks in the preface for "providing anecdotal accounts that helped to bring some of the players in the story to life." Gottlieb, *Men of Vision*, xiii.
64. Shatzkes, *Holocaust and Rescue*.
65. Baumel, "Twice a Refugee," 174–84.
66. Tomlin, *Protest and Prayer*.
67. Berghahn, *German-Jewish Refugees in England*.
68. Gillman and Gillman, *Collar the Lot*.
69. Stent, *A Bespattered Page*.
70. Chappell, *Island of Barbed Wire*.
71. Koch, *Deemed Suspect*.
72. Seller, *We Built up Our Lives*.
73. Fry, *The King's Most Loyal Enemy Aliens*.

74. Patkin, *The Dunera Internees*.
75. Shepherd, *Wilfred Israel*.
76. Emanuel and Gissing, *Nicholas Winton*.
77. Kranzler and Hirschler, *Solomon Schonfeld*; Kranzler, *Holocaust Hero*.
78. Judt, "Words," 4.
79. Goepfert, *Der Juedische Kindertransport von Deutschland*.
80. Curio, *Verfolgung, Flucht, Rettung*.
81. Hill, "Anglo Jewry and the Refugee Children."
82. Benz, Curio, and Hammel, *Kindertransports*.
83. Guske, *Trauma and Attachment*.
84. Norton, "The Kindertransport."
85. Fast, *Children's Exodus*.
86. Turner, *And the Policeman Smiled*; and his *One Small Suitcase*.
87. Gershon, *We Came as Children*.
88. Leverton and Lowensohn, *I Came Alone*. The book appeared in German in 1994: Goepfert, *Ich Kam Allein*.
89. Harris and Oppenheimer, *Into the Arms of Strangers*.
90. Rutter, *Refugee Children*.
91. Friedman and Klein, *Reluctant Refuge*.
92. Bradman, *Give Me Shelter*.
93. Moorehead, *Human Cargo*; Arbabzadah, *From outside In*.

Part 1

January 1933–August 1939: The Prewar Hitler Era

Chapter 2

Laying the Foundations: British Jewry and Refugee Organizations, 1933–38

Introduction

"Actually, if you wants to stretch a point, you could say that Reenie and I were second-generation British as my father lived in Great Britain before we did," chuckled Steffi as she described her parents' background before talking about her Kindertransport experiences. "My father was born in Silesia and had lost his father at an early age. As his mother wanted him to have a good profession to be able to support the family, she sent him to Glasgow to learn a trade. In those days that wasn't at all uncommon, sending young German Jewish boys to Britain for a few years in order to give them a good education or teach them a profession. My father's family was traditional and there were already lots of Jews in Britain at that time, so he had a community to go to and be part of while he lived in Scotland. After he finished his studies he returned to Germany and that's when he and Oma moved to Berlin, he met and married mother, and we were eventually born."[1]

The Britain to which Steffi's father had been sent was already populated by more than 300,000 Jews at the start of the First World War, and their numbers would swell by an additional 10 percent by the time she and Reenie would arrive over two decades later.[2] To understand the composition of British Jewry that greeted the Kindertransports, let us first go back in time to trace the origins of the many diverse social, economic, and religious groups of which it was composed, stemming from the various immigration waves that had brought Jews of different backgrounds to the British shores.

The Jewish Community in Great Britain

Early Jewish settlement in Britain had been neither continuous nor successful. The first Jews who ventured to the British shores were members of a Jewish delegation bearing gifts for King Tordelbach (Turlough O'Brien) of Munster in 1062. The Annals of Innisfallen note the lack of warm welcome and relate that the bearers of the gifts were dispatched back across the sea.[3] By the end of the eleventh century, Jews had settled in Britain and despite the fluctuations in their economic status, they remained there until All Saints Day 1290 when the 16,000 Jews of England were banished from the British Isles by King Edward I.[4] Despite the banishment, small groups of secret Jews continued to live in London, though unofficial Jewish resettlement of England began once again only in 1656, after the intervention of a Dutch rabbi of Marrano birth, Menashe ben Israel.[5]

The Jewish community in England grew and prospered. By the beginning of the eighteenth century, more than one thousand Jews, both Sefaradi (Oriental) and Ashkenazi (European), resided in London. Growing Jewish communities existed also in the port cities of Leeds, Birmingham, and Manchester. In 1790, the Board of Jewish Deputies was founded as a joint committee for the Sefaradi and Ashkenazi Jewish communities in London, the first major Anglo-Jewish institution to be established after the Jews had officially resettled in Britain. At a later stage, the Board of Deputies became one of the most widely recognized forums representing the views of the different sectors of UK Jewry.

In the mid-nineteenth century, a new wave of Jewish immigrants made its way to the British Isles. Coming from Central Europe, its members settled primarily in the major cities with a small overflow to the provinces, with most Jews working in commerce and textiles.[6] In 1859, another major Jewish institution was founded in Britain: the Jewish Board of Guardians, which evolved to deal primarily with problems of welfare among British Jewry. It appears to have achieved its goal. By the 1880s, the Jewish community in Britain was small but solid and the Jews were well educated, well fed, and successful. Assimilation and intermarriage had begun to penetrate the periphery of the community and those Jews who abandoned the ways of their fathers felt little need to justify their actions in the eyes of their former co-religionists.[7] British Jews considered themselves fully British and assumed that their non-Jewish neighbors completely shared that sentiment. In most cases, little if anything in their lifestyle could remind anyone of the foreign or Orthodox origins of their forbearers. All this, however, was about to change when a new wave of Jewish immigrants reached Britain, whose members were very different from their German Jewish predecessors.

A series of anti-Jewish riots in the Russian Pale of Settlement (1881–82) initiated the mass Jewish exodus westward and Britain became the temporary stop for many immigrants on their way to America. From then until the outbreak of the First World War, more than 120,000 Jewish immigrants from Eastern Europe remained in Britain, many of whom had initially planned to immigrate to

America but were unable to continue their journey due to a lack of funds.⁸ The common denominator of these immigrants, which threatened their health, future, and in some cases, their lives, was their poverty. Despite the initial alarm at seeing the hordes bearing down on "their island," in an act of communal benevolence Anglo-Jewry rose to the occasion, massed forces, and created social services to serve the newcomers, including a shelter for the homeless. In addition, it instituted charitable funds to enable at least some Jews to continue their journey westward. For others, however, Britain was the end of the line, despite the admonition they had received from other immigrants, regarding their journey ahead—"make sure to get off at the second stop!"—in other words, New York.

The immigrants brought with them many customs alien to Anglo-Jewry, a new language, new foods, and a religious revival. A majority of the newcomers crowded into the existing Jewish quarter of Whitechapel in London's East End; the neighborhood rapidly became a crowded, filthy, Orthodox slum. Around the turn of the century, two hundred heders existed in the East End alone, offering Jewish education after school hours. Only later would the Jewish communities of north London (Stamford Hill), north-west London (Hampstead, Golders Green, Southgate, and Edgeware) and east London (Ilford) take shape. Small numbers of newcomers also migrated to Leeds, Manchester, Scotland, or Wales.⁹

In spite of the welfare societies created to aid their newly arrived and often suffering brethren, behind closed doors much of Anglo-Jewry viewed these "uncouth" foreigners with abhorrence. Ostensibly this resulted from the fear of these masses perpetuating ghetto life, but behind this thought stood the apprehension that the actions of their immigrant Jewish brethren would reflect back upon them. Thus, when the Aliens Restriction Act of 1905 was promulgated by the Conservatives, there were those among the Anglo-Jewish old guard who reacted with relief.¹⁰ Intending to stem the influx of Jews from Eastern Europe, the Act introduced highly selective port controls for aliens traveling in steerage class, the method used by most of the Jewish immigrants of that time. Luckily for those immigrants, the terms were implemented under a more Liberal government that interpreted the exemptions very generously.¹¹

The advent of war in 1914 effectively put a halt to immigration. Those who managed to enter Britain in the 1920s were neither numerous nor forceful enough to significantly alter the character of the Anglo-Jewish community. During these years, larger numbers of British Jews migrated from the major cities to provincial communities; many moved up from the working class to the middle class and by the 1930s Jews could be found in virtually every field of life. By 1933, the Jewish immigrants of the 1880s and 1890s had adapted sufficiently to British culture so as to be viewed as the "old guard" by the new waves of foreigners, Jewish refugees from Hitler's Germany who were sweeping towards the British shores. The former immigrants from Eastern Europe had made the full circle.

By the late 1930s, the majority of Anglo-Jewry was concentrated in the Greater London area. Manchester and Leeds were the second- and third-largest

Jewish communities in England. The largest Jewish community in Scotland was in Glasgow, where Steffi and Reenie's father had learned his trade, and the largest in Wales was in Cardiff.[12]

By the twentieth century, Jewish communal life in Britain had become well organized. The Initiation Society (to train ritual circumcisers), the Board of Shechita (ritual slaughtering), the Kashrut Commission, burial societies, and various charitable organizations had become accepted parts of Anglo-Jewish life.[13] Although the majority of Jewish pupils attended British state schools and received their religious education on Sundays and after school hours, by the early 1930s no less than five different bodies were responsible for providing or coordinating Jewish education in Britain.[14]

Jewish education, however, was not always connected with strict religious observance, as was reflected by the religious divisions among British Jewry at the time. By the 1930s, Anglo-Jewry was divided among the Orthodox, Reform, Liberal, and a very small group of Ultra-Orthodox communities. The Orthodox included the members of two synagogue associations: the United Synagogue founded in 1870 by an Act of Parliament, and the traditionally Orthodox umbrella organization known as the Federation of Synagogues founded in 1887 by Samuel Montagu (1832–1911). During the Second World War, the combined membership of the United Synagogue (which included eighty synagogues in London alone) and the Federation of Synagogues accounted for 40 percent of religious affiliation in London where the majority of the Jewish population resided.[15] The power of the United Synagogue was not just numerical but also organizational; its lay leaders were responsible for filling Anglo-Jewry's most prominent religious position, that of the Chief Rabbi of the British Empire. From 1913 to 1946 that position was held by the Slovakian-born, New York-educated Rabbi Dr. Joseph Herman Hertz (1872–1946). The bespectacled Hertz, sporting a long grey goatee and fond of his long black rabbinical robes, was a Zionist-oriented, forceful, and independent personality who would play an important role in the religious life of the Jewish refugee children.

The first Reform congregation, corresponding to the American Jewish Conservative Movement, was founded as a branch of Progressive Judaism in Britain, ultimately metamorphosing into the Movement for Reform Judaism.[16] Following a decade punctuated by demands for changes and decorum in the pre-existing houses of Jewish worship in England, the first Reform Temple, the West London Synagogue, had been founded in 1840. Originally drawing its members from the upper-class Jewish elite, both Sefaradim and Ashkenazim, the British Reform movement limited its innovations to certain ritual modifications, including adopting English as the language of its services. Throughout the nineteenth and early twentieth century, the progressive trend grew in direct proportion to Jewish acculturation to the non-Jewish environment.

In 1902, the Liberal Movement was started by Lily Helen Montagu (1873–1963) and Claude Joseph Goldsmid Montefiore (1858–1938) as the Jewish Religious Union, corresponding to the American Jewish Reform Movement.¹⁷ Montefiore, a great nephew of Sir Moses Montefiore, had been influenced by Liberal Church of England theologians and wished to emulate their enlightened steps in the framework of Judaism. Lily Helen Montagu, daughter of the very Orthodox Samuel Montagu who had founded the Federation of Synagogues, was an ardent social worker and feminist who hoped that the Progressive movement would include women in all facets of religious Jewish life. In 1911, Montefiore established the Liberal Jewish Synagogue where he served as president, erecting educational facilities for the young, notably Sunday and afternoon schools whose purpose was to prepare adolescents for confirmation.

Progressive Judaism appealed to the marginal Jew who identified with the dominant nationality but simultaneously wished to retain ties with Judaism. Although Liberal synagogues opened in North and South London and followed their members to outlying areas, the movement remained centralized in London and attracted few new members during the interwar years. Inconsistent as it may seem, despite their lack of adherence to an Orthodox daily lifestyle, many British Jews, notably those of Eastern European extraction, preferred to frequent Orthodox houses of worship rather than the more progressive temples. Nevertheless, by 1940 the total number of Reform and Liberal temple members had reached 4,000, representing a congregation of 6,000 (including children). The West London Reform congregation alone boasted close to 1,400 members in 1936 while the Liberal St. John's Wood temple had a membership of over 1,600 in 1939.¹⁸

The ultra-Orthodox synagogues, centering around the Stamford Hill "Adath (Adas) Yisroel" congregation, belonged to the Union of Orthodox Hebrew Congregations, an independent Orthodox community founded by Rabbi Avigdor Schonfeld (1880–1930) in 1926. The Hungarian-born Schonfeld, who had received his rabbinical ordination from the strictly Orthodox Sofer Yeshiva in Pressburg (Bratislava) but also held a doctorate in education from the University of Giessen, came to London in 1909 and attempted to establish a "Torah-true" community. Except for a two-year sojourn in Palestine, Schonfeld spent his career building up educational establishments, creating an Orthodox Union that was separate from the existing United Synagogue establishment, similar to the Frankfurt Austrittsgemeinde, the ultra-Orthodox separatist community founded by Rabbi Samson Raphael Hirsch. The Union ultimately maintained its own court of Jewish law, kashrut authority, cemetery, and other services, putting it at odds with the United Synagogue and the Chief Rabbi of the British Empire.¹⁹ In 1929, Schonfeld launched a wave of Orthodox Jewish Day Schools by founding the Jewish Secondary School. After his untimely demise from blood poisoning a year later at the age of forty-nine, his son, Rabbi Solomon Schonfeld (1912–84) continued developing the school, eventually founding four primary schools and expanding the Union of Orthodox Hebrew Congregations to include small Hasidic prayer houses (*shtiblach*) established after 1933 by refugees from Hitler. By 1943, the Union comprised fifty-four affiliated synagogues serving approximately 5,000 families.[20]

Another ultra-Orthodox figure of note during the war years was the prosperous English-born clothing manufacturer, Harry Goodman (1898–1961), who served as political secretary of the British Agudath Israel political movement, a branch of the Agudath Israel World Organization. Goodman's wartime activities among Jewish refugee children mirrored many of those carried out by Solomon Schonfeld; the two often worked in tandem for the spiritual welfare of the refugee children. Goodman was well known for his recalcitrant and at times overbearing personality; friction often developed between the anti-Zionist Goodman and Chief Rabbi Hertz. Only through Solomon Schonfeld's intervention, who in spite of being the Chief Rabbi's son-in-law was ideologically close to Agudath Israel although not bound by its policies, was it possible to bridge the gap between the two segments of Orthodox Anglo-Jewry.[21]

Though active in Jewish philanthropy, these two religious and communal leaders, considered by the larger portion of Anglo-Jewry to be fanatics, moved in a different world than that of the elite group that Chaim Bermant termed the "Cousinhood," the public Jewish figures that controlled most of Anglo-Jewry's philanthropic life.[22] While the "Cousinhood" would be active in caring for the future refugee children's physical welfare, Schonfeld and Goodman were soon to become the self-appointed and not always appreciated guardians of those children's souls, and from 1938 to 1945 were to wage what appeared to be at times a losing battle: attempting to keep the Jewish refugee children Jewish.

The sociological, economic, institutional, and religious composition of Anglo-Jewry in the first decades of the twentieth century was of particular significance in view of the challenges that it was soon to face following the rise of Nazism in Germany and the arrival of the first Jewish refugees from Hitler. What began as a trickle in 1933 would ultimately threaten to become a torrent by 1938 as the Third Reich expanded and its anti-Jewish policies became more vehement and focused. British Jews and their existing institutions would now have to rise to the occasion and decide how best to deal with the plight of their coreligionists both on the Continent and those arriving as refugees at the British shores.

Jewish Children in Hitler's Germany and School Migration to Great Britain, 1933–38

To understand the framework in which Steffi and Reenie Birnbaum and the other Kindertransport children were brought to Britain, let us return to the months following Hitler's rise to power in 1933 and examine the plight of Jewish children in Nazi Germany. At the time, approximately half a million Jews lived in Germany, a bit more than one-fifth of whom were children and teenagers. Nevertheless, the German Jewish population was generally considered an older one, even before the Nazi takeover.[23] Between 1933 and 1938 a combination of a high emigration rate and a low birth rate brought the number of young German Jews down to less than 16 percent of the total Jewish population.[24] This shift was exacerbated by a combination of the general atmosphere of discrimination and the laws targeting Jewish children promulgated soon after Hitler's rise to power.

One of the earliest such laws was the *numerus clausus* legislation enacted on 25 April 1933 limiting the number of Jewish pupils and teachers in German schools to 1.5 percent of the total student body and staff. Exemptions were granted to Jewish children whose fathers had been frontline soldiers or to those whose parents were married prior to the enactment of the law and had one "Aryan" parent or two "Aryan" grandparents.[25] These exemptions, however, did not necessarily alleviate the plight of those receiving them. In his powerful classic novel, *The Last of the Just*, André Schwarz-Bart describes the experiences of Ernie Levy, a Jewish child exempt from the law because of his father's military status, when his new Nazi teacher Herr Geek enters the classroom. After greeting his young charges with the Nazi salute and a roaring "Heil Hitler," Geek cries in a raging tone "*die Hunde, die Neger, und die Juden austreten*! Dogs, Negroes and Jews step forward." Initially attributing this statement to some incomprehensible sense of humor, Levi soon realizes the seriousness of his new teacher's demand when he forces one of the Jewish boys to sing a Nazi anthem about Jewish blood flowing from the knife by throwing him to the floor in a hammerlock until he acquiesces and warbles out the first words.[26]

One solution to the educational discrimination against German Jewish children was to transfer or create German Jewish schools on foreign soil, taking along all the pupils who were able to leave Germany. All in all, more than twenty schools in exile were founded all over the world by teachers and educators who were forced out of Germany after 1933 on political grounds or as a result of their Jewish ancestry. Several of them were founded in or relocated to Great Britain.[27] During the first two years after Hitler's rise to power four such schools—each with a different educational orientation—were relocated from Germany and reestablished in England, enabling several hundred German Jewish children to continue their education in the free world. At the time it was not difficult for these children to leave Germany, as they did not require a visa to enter Britain and even before Hitler's rise to power it was common for teenagers or even preteens from the Continent to travel to Britain for their education. Most of the children came from a comfortable financial background that enabled their parents to pay the school fees and the children's upkeep overseas. Only later in the decade as the economic situation of German Jewry worsened did finances become problematic. As we shall see, at that point the Jewish refugee organizations in Britain stepped into the breach.[28]

The first of the transplanted schools was a progressive German school that placed emphasis on language, science, and character building. Originally it was known as the Herrlingen School near Ulm, founded by Anna Essinger (1879–1960) in 1926; she had received some of her education in America and returned to Germany after the First World War. Unimpressed with the state of German education at the time, the tall and imposing Essinger decided to found a progressive school in which her pupils were encouraged to be independent, self-reliant, creative, and cooperative. Already in early 1933 she recognized that there was no future in Germany and decided to transfer the school, along with many of her staff and pupils, to Kent. Initially renting a seventeenth-century manor house near Faversham and calling her school the New Herrlingen School, in 1936 she purchased the property and renamed the school the Bunce Court School, the name by which it was known until it closed its doors in 1948. Together with her staff, Essinger turned the school into a home for refugee children who had managed to leave Germany and were awaiting their parents in England.[29]

Essinger, a tall and formidable figure with extremely thick glasses ("I was never sure what was going on behind them," remarked one of her former pupils)[30] was a born educator and referred to by both pupils and staff as Tante (Aunt) Anna, usually shortened to "TA." During its early years, Bunce Court had a very high pupil turnover, not only because the students completed their education and moved on but also because the school later provided temporary accommodation for Kindertransport children needing permanent foster homes. Between October 1933 and December 1938, a total of 319 children entered and 195 children left the school. Throughout its existence, more than 900 children passed through the school, some becoming leading figures in their profession ("A remarkable record for an institution which seldom had two pennies to rub together," remarked a former charge).[31] Although Essinger was almost sixty years old when the first groups of *Kinder* reached Britain in December 1938, the Refugee Children's Movement turned to her, asking for assistance in creating a physically and educationally suitable environment in the freezing Dovercourt camp, originally a summer children's resort, where the children had been temporarily placed upon arrival.[32] Essinger would also be instrumental in redirecting the changes in *Kinder*'s selection by potential British foster parents. We will return to her later when describing life at Dovercourt.

In 1933 and 1934, three additional schools followed Essinger's example. The first was an elite institution that put emphasis on social responsibility through public service in order to turn its pupils into productive citizens of the upper classes. Given the name the Gordonstoun School, it was founded near Aberdeen, Scotland by the Oxford- and Heidelberg-educated Dr. Kurt Hahn (1886–1974) on the model of his Schloss Salem School in southern Germany.[33] With a handful of German refugee boys, the gentle-gazed, slightly built Hahn began his school in two historic seventeenth-century buildings designed by the famed eccentric, Sir Robert Gordon, the Wizard of Gordonstoun. The school faced numerous challenges including evacuation to Llandinam in Central Wales during the war and finding a fire-ravaged Gordonstoun House on return from evacuation. But Hahn persevered and managed to turn it into a well-known and honored British educational institution, which few today even connect with its refugee origins. As part of this process, Hahn later converted to Christianity and even preached in the Church of Scotland. Three generations of British royalty were eventually educated at Gordonstoun, granting the former "refugee school" complete respectability in the eyes of the British gentry.³⁴

Another school founded during this period had a more radical left-wing philosophy and educated its pupils in innovative and almost iconoclastic thought. The Beltane School was established in Wimbledon by Ernst (1902–2001) and Ilse Bulova (d. 1987) of Berlin, who continued to teach thirty refugee children through the use of the Montessori Method. The school existed until 1941 when it dissolved following the Bulovas' emigration to the United States with the assistance of his relatives from the famous Bulova watch corporation in Woodside, Queens. In today's world, the left-wing, socialist-leaning Bulova, known for his bright-colored caps and ever-present smile, would be called a "free spirit," the title he was later given in his *New York Times* obituary. He would stress to his students that the process was often more important than the results. "Does a poet finish every poem he begins?" he would ask, driving his students to think independently instead of accepting common axioms. Describing pupil's lives in the institutions he founded, one of his former students remarked that "You couldn't be a conformist because there was nothing to conform to."³⁵

A fourth educational establishment that transferred from Hitler's Germany to Great Britain was a coeducational, nondenominational school that focused on social responsibility and pupils' rights. The Stoatley Rough School at Haslemere in Surrey, some forty-five miles southwest of London, owed its existence to Dr. Hilde Lion (1893–1970), a social scientist and women's-movement adherent who was assisted by Quaker activist Bertha Bracey who wished to alleviate the plight of refugees from Hitler. Unlike most British educational institutions, the school had a policy forbidding any form of corporal punishment and closed its doors only when Lion retired in 1960.³⁶ An important facet of the school's existence was its linguistic and cultural environment that combined an emphasis on German culture with an appreciation of the English surroundings. This was particularly comforting for the transplanted young charges who had left their parents behind in Germany. As Lion wrote in a 1937 speech, "We consider it our foremost duty towards these children to cherish and preserve . . . all the good and great essentials of the German culture whilst teaching them to recognize, appreciate and accept those of their foster country."³⁷

Yet another school to be reestablished in Britain was a unique educational establishment that functioned according to Rudolph Steiner's principles of anthroposophy. Camp Hill House was founded in 1938 by Karl Koenig (1902–66), an Austrian doctor and remedial educator who moved with fifteen colleagues to Aberdeen after the *Anschluss*. At Camp Hill House, the thin, dark-haired, bristly mustached Koenig founded an educational workshop that integrated children with special needs with nonhandicapped children. The workshop's influence spread much further than its local environs; branches of the Camphill Movement were later opened in various locations throughout the world.[38]

Several issues were common to all the educational establishments noted here: finding solutions for ongoing financial difficulties, determining policy on issues of language including sustaining the balance between maintaining German and learning proper English, attempting to foster a good relationship with the neighboring populations, and determining the school's implicit and explicit attitudes toward the Jewish religion and religious teachings.

The children who were educated in these émigré schools were an elite minority, able to gently make the transition from a German to a British environment. But despite their "elite" status, these schools suffered continuously from financial deficit. An official agreement between the Central British Fund (see further) and the Reichsvertretung, the Central Organization of Jews in Germany, enabled parents in Germany to deposit the Deutschmark equivalent of the cost of the children's school fees and maintenance with the German organization that would use it for emigration aid and agricultural training of potential emigrants, and in exchange the Central British Fund would pay those costs in pounds sterling to the schools. However, due to many of the Continental parents' delicate economic situation throughout the 1930s these fees, which all private schools normally depend upon, had to be kept low. Even then, some parents were unable to meet these costs. Only in late 1938 when large numbers of parents had lost their source of income or were forced to leave Germany did the Central British Fund accept the responsibility of paying the children's fees without compensation.[39]

The schools therefore depended upon local financing, including assistance from private and religious groups such as the Society of Friends. Two of the schools—Bunce Court and Stoatley Rough—were in fact greatly influenced and assisted by women of the Quaker movement, echoing not only an issue of religion but also one of gender. As was the case with many of the refugee movement activities, women were often the mainstays of these schools. Anna Essinger was assisted by her qualified sisters, Paula and Bertha, and educator Hanna Bergas.[40] Hilde Lion was assisted by Nora Astfalck and Hanna Nacken, two non-Jewish political exiles from Germany who had been her students at the educational training centers that she had directed in the Weimar Republic. They were later joined by Dr. Emmy Wolff and Dr. Louise Leven, Jewish teachers who like Lion had been dismissed from their posts in Germany in 1933.[41]

While teaching middle and upper school in those days was not necessarily a primarily female profession, time and again we see how the educational and physical care of the Jewish refugee children both in the Reich and in Britain fell most often on the shoulders of women who were willing and able to take up the administrative and educational burden. This appears to have stemmed from a combination of traditional gendered behavior regarding women's roles in childcare and children's education, and the fact that the educational sphere was one of the few socially legitimate vistas for female empowerment during the years prior to the Second World War.[42]

Language, as the verbal representative of culture, was a central focus in all of these schools. German remained the unofficial language for years, despite the teachers' constant reminders and wartime admonishments to speak English. Although almost all teaching was conducted in English, the schools encouraged the study of German, not only for the refugee children but because the schools enrolled British children whose parents wished them to learn German in a "German school."[43]

Mindful of the refugee pupils' language difficulties, Lion's school created ever-shifting English classes to meet their needs. The older children often assisted the younger ones, coming up with innovative definitions for the new words they were learning. "Icicle" was a bicycle with one wheel; a "public conveyance" was a toilet, and so on. One former student remembered what truly got the young boys to switch from reading German to enjoying English, a method that Lion and her staff frowned upon: their discovery of the "penny dreadfuls," inexpensive sensationalist books with Orwellian descriptions of "Martians, death rays, grizzly bears and gangsters."[44] These were much more successful in teaching the young refugees the local language than the phonetic readers from which the children had originally learned English.

Anna Essinger and Hilda Lion were very aware that their schools' success necessitated gaining the goodwill of the neighboring populations. Both schools put on open air performances in English, attended by locals and sometimes even prominent British guests. As soon as the children became proficient in unfamiliar British sports such as cricket, the school arranged sports matches with neighboring British schools. As a result, the local population generally treated the schools to a friendly reception, providing them at holiday time with blankets, mattresses, books, carpets, and various forms of food from scones to soup. One Christmas the children at Stoatley Rough even received a cow through a neighbor's benevolence.

Religion was a sensitive subject in almost all of these schools. While few of the Jewish founders identified themselves publicly with Judaism or felt bound by it (and as noted earlier, one of them later converted to Christianity), a number of them later objected to and publicly criticized any proselytizing of Jewish children. In general, Bunce Court boasted more Jewish pupils than Stoatley Rough or any of the other émigré schools.[45] Consequently, Essinger promised that all children would study biblical and post-biblical Jewish history, and modern Hebrew was offered at the request of parents who were planning to immigrate to Palestine.[46] Hilda Lion also attempted to include several Jewish subjects in the school curriculum.

Although the creation of émigré schools was an innovative educational scheme, it could not solve the problem of tens of thousands of Jewish children looking to leave Nazi Germany. The problem was exacerbated from 1936 onward, when the many exemptions to the *numerus clausus* law were curtailed and Jewish children were legally separated from their "Aryan" counterparts in German schools. Discrimination that had existed previously now became officially sanctioned. Children were subjected to humiliating restrictions, such as being forbidden to join in sports and games and being relegated to sit in the last row of benches. Various forms of mental cruelty were perpetrated by "Aryan" fellow students and teachers alike. Some children were even driven to suicide.[47] As anti-Jewish measures intensified after Minister of Economics Hjalmar Schacht was removed from his post in late 1937, German Jewry was forced to reexamine its plight. As a result, emigration, especially for younger Jews, was often viewed as the only viable option.[48] The result was a growing interest in schemes that would enable Jewish schoolchildren to leave Germany, both in the framework of schools that had migrated, and through other possibilities, even if they could not yet be accompanied by their parents.

Refugee Organizations in Great Britain, 1933–38

"The English are not a people who take easily to foreigners," wrote Neville Laski, president of the Jewish Board of Deputies, in 1939.[49] And yet, between 1933 and 1943 England admitted 63,000 Jewish refugees from Nazism, as many Jewish refugees as did Canada, Australia, South Africa, Uruguay, Spain, and Switzerland combined.[50]

The basic machinery for supporting these refugees, who included thousands of child refugees either with their families, alone, or in organized youth groups, was created between 1933 and 1938. At the time, concerned Jews and non-Jews banded together to aid refugees coming to Britain's shores and created the machinery that was to care for them throughout the war years and for long afterward. The newly founded organizations had a dual purpose: to assist those refugees who reached England and to solve the larger issue of the refugee problem, which included assisting them while still in Germany and finding countries willing to accept them.

By the summer of 1933, the two major Jewish organizations in Great Britain—the Board of Deputies and the Board of Guardians—had become aware that Hitlerism was not an isolated phenomenon and that there was a need to deal with the refugees who were already coming from Germany. Most of the organizations in Britain that cared for the refugees of the Hitler period, both children and adults, were founded between 1933 and 1938. At least one, however, was a preexisting organization that adapted itself in the 1930s to care for refugees from Hitler's Germany.

The Jews' Temporary Shelter in London had been founded prior to the First World War to aid Russian Jewry fleeing from persecution. Between 1914 and 1918, it served as a reception center for Jewish refugees from the European continent.[51] Now in 1933, under the presidency of Otto M. Schiff, the officers of the shelter began meeting trains from the Continent bringing Jewish refugees, singles, couples, and families with children who had neither friends nor relatives to offer them homes in England. Schiff, a nephew of the world-renowned Jewish philanthropist Jacob Schiff, had directed Jewish relief for Continental Jewish refugee in England during the First World War, during which he gained valuable administrative experience and made close contacts with senior British government officials. These contacts would later be of invaluable assistance as the Home Office would consequently be prepared to accept his word when vouching for the financial maintenance of Jewish refugees from Hitler.[52]

In early March 1933, Otto Schiff asked several friends representing different sectors of the British Jewish community, including members of B'nai Brith, to join him for a discussion at the Jews' Temporary Shelter to discuss how they could aid German Jews who sought assistance. As the influx of refugees from Germany grew, Schiff, Neville Laski, and Leonard Montefiore, president of the Anglo-Jewish Association, assured the Home Office that no refugee admitted would fall a charge on public funds.[53] Members of the group, which was now being called the Jewish Refugees Committee, included two members of the board of the Jews' Temporary Shelter (Ernest Mainz and Eric Turk), Bernard Davidson, Frank Lazarus, E. L. Rawson, and three women—Cissie Laski (wife of Neville Laski), Alice Model, who was a pioneer in infant and mother welfare, and Anna Schwab of the Ellern banking family of Frankfurt.

The Jewish Refugees Committee dealt with both individual refugees and family groups, including those who were Jewish and "non-Aryan baptized." As the Christian Council for Refugees headed by the indefatigable philosemitic Anglican minister William W. (Bill) Simpson[54] would only be formed in 1938, at the time the only major voluntary agency dealing with "non-Aryan" refugees was the German Emergency Committee of the Friends Service Committee founded by the Quakers, a group with which Schiff had a sound working relationship. He therefore instructed the Jewish Refugees Committee to aid all refugees regardless of whether or not they were members of the Jewish community.[55]

Committee divisions included a Hospitality Committee, Emigration Committee, Professional Committee to deal with academics and scholars, Retraining Department, Clothing Department, and Free Meal Service at Woburn House. The Emigration Committee in particular, under the leadership of Dennis M. Cohen and with the later chairmanship of Sir Anthony de Rothschild, would later be active, together with Helen Bentwich, wife of Sir Norman Bentwich and niece of Lord Herbert Samuel, in creating the framework allowing the Kindertransports to reach Britain. The Jewish Refugees Committee established various departments for refugees of different nationalities and categorized them according to country of origin. For example, a department was eventually created to deal with refugees from Italy who fled after the imposition of Nazi racial laws in that country in 1939.[56] In addition to the central branch of the Jewish Refugees Committee, local branches were created throughout Britain, some of which would supervise refugee children's hostels after 1939.

The creation of the Jewish Refugees Committee was the first step in Anglo-Jewry's response to the growing influx of Jewish refugees from Germany. During the spring of 1933, a number of prominent Anglo-Jewish leaders began to sense the pressing need for funds to aid those who sought refuge in Britain and came to the conclusion that the necessary sums could only be raised through a nationwide effort that would include all sections of the Jewish community. To coordinate such an effort, they decided to set up a new organization that would synchronize the campaign. In April 1933, a small committee convened at the seat of the banking house of N. M. Rothschild and Sons in London to create such an organization, which they named the Central British Fund for German Jewry. Combining Zionist and non-Zionist organizations, the CBF would act as a fund-raising body for all activities on behalf of German Jews.[57]

Known colloquially by the refugees as "Woburn House," the name given to the refugee center in Bloomsbury that housed much of the bureaucratic machinery that dealt with the refugees, by the end of 1933 the CBF managed to collect almost £250,000 for its refugee work. During that same year, the CBF founded both a fund-raising Women's Appeal Committee and an Allocation Committee that apportioned funds primarily to constructive rather than relief activities. Grants were allocated to the administrative budget of the High Commissioner of the League of Nations for Refugees (Jewish and other) coming from Germany, youth villages in Palestine, and the refugee organization HICEM, an acronym of the combined organizations of HIAS, ICA, and EMIG-Direct, and was instrumental in paying fares of refugees in foreign currency.[58] The Women's Appeal Committee would later raise large amounts for Children and Youth Aliyah, some of which was to be used for maintaining Youth Aliyah centers for refugee children in Britain.[59]

It is difficult to determine how many refugee children received assistance from the existing organizations until the Kindertransports began arriving in December 1938, as most child refugees who arrived in Britain between 1933 and 1938 came with their families; CBF statistics as to their precise number are unavailable. Other statistics as to the number of Germans, including Jews who arrived in Britain during this period are misleading and contradictory as they include a large number of holiday visitors who subsequently returned to Germany.[60]

While the Jewish Refugees Committee continued to care for the arriving refugees and the CBF persevered in raising funds for their upkeep, a number of events that occurred in 1935 made its members realize that it was imperative to create an organization to accelerate emigration of young Jews from Germany. These included the promulgation of the Nuremberg racial laws and the resignation of James G. Macdonald as "High Commissioner for Refugees (Jewish and other) coming from Germany" on 27 December 1935. Subsequently, in early 1936 the CBF formed the Council for German Jewry, incorporating important American, British, and Continental Jewish organizations such as the American Jewish Joint Distribution Committee (JDC), the

CBF, and the United Palestine Appeal, with Sir Herbert Samuel of England and Felix Warburg, founder and honorary chairman of the JDC in the United States, serving as co-chairs.

The two secretaries of the CBF, Meyer Stephany and Lavy Bakstansky, continued their work in the new organization[61] and became secretaries of the Council for German Jewry. Between 1936 and 1939, the Council was the main agency dealing with refugee finances as well as policy and maintained close relations with Jewish groups in Germany, with the High Commissioner for Refugees and with committees in various countries responsible for finding homes for refugees. Sir Wyndham Deedes and Prof. Norman Bentwich, who had been the Deputy High Commissioner for Refugees from Germany from 1933 to 1935, were honorary co-directors in charge of retraining and emigration.[62]

During the pre-*Kristallnacht* period, only one organization was created solely for the purpose of caring for refugee children from Germany: the Children's Inter-Aid Committee. This nonsectarian committee was founded in 1936 by refugee activist Gladys Skelton and Francis Bendit for the purpose of bringing Jewish and "non-Aryan" Christian children to Britain. The Committee was started on a grant of £200 from the Council for German Jewry, £60 from the "Save the Children Fund" (a preexisting English fund that aided groups of children suffering under oppression, such as the Basque or Greek children), and £400 donated anonymously to be used for case work. Between May and July 1936, a total of 124 children were brought to England from Germany, the ratio of whom were 45 percent Christian and 55 percent Jewish. By November 1938, some 471 children had been brought to Britain under its auspices.[63]

This brief survey of the refugee organizations in prewar Britain and their major activists brings us back to the impetus behind "helping behavior" and voluntary action, or put more succinctly, "who does what and why?" It is easy to claim that upon hearing about the plight of German Jewry it was impossible for any of the listeners to stand idly by; unfortunately, this was not true. While there were those who rose to the occasion, others did not, particularly at the formative stage when it was necessary to create the refugee assistance machinery and not just join the already existing organizations. What, then, drove the fifteen men and five women who were mentioned here as active in the refugee movement at its nascent stage to act as they did?

Here we see how several of the mechanisms that Bekkers and Wiepking[64] mention as important forces behind philanthropy and voluntary action come into play. One is, of course, awareness of need, but two others are altruism and egoism, couched more commonly in terms of constant education toward helping behavior and the social expectations regarding voluntary action in a particular society.

The community and culture in which quite a number of the persons mentioned here as leaders and active members of the refugee organizations were raised and later functioned was a homogenous one of the Anglo-Jewish elite. All in this group were part of an insular elite Jewish society with a similar background and upbringing that put great emphasis on communal activity. Who were these activists and leaders and what brought them to the cause?

Neville Jonas Laski (1890–1969), son of a successful Manchester textile merchant, was an energetic dynamo, a jurist with a distinguished reputation at the bar who went on to become the president of the Board of Deputies. The dapper, curly-haired Laski was a son-in-law of Rabbi Dr. Moses Gaster, rabbinical leader of the Sefaradi community, and Laski was an active member of that congregation. Simon Marks (1888–1964) was the only member of the group who could be considered an ardent Zionist, having become one since his meeting and subsequent friendship with Zionist leader Chaim Weizmann in 1913. Marks, recognizable from afar by his trademark dark thick brows, was knighted in 1944 and became the first Baron of Broughton. He was a indefatigable worker who channeled his energy into chairing and managing Marks and Spencer, the highly successful nationwide chair of retail stores that his immigrant father had founded, and his money into institutions and causes he found worthy. Among them were many of the refugee-related causes created during the 1930s in Britain.

Otto M. Schiff (1875–1952), a tireless Frankfurt-born banker who had become a naturalized British citizen in 1901, was recruited by Sir Leonard Cohen to become active in the Jews' Temporary Shelter, of which he ultimately became president. Having made important contacts in the British government while caring for Belgian refugees during the First World War, his name would be enough of a guarantee among certain British Home Office officials to assure their cooperation in opening hitherto closed bureaucratic doors to enable the entry of Jewish refugees.[65] Leonard Nathaniel Goldsmid Montefiore (1889–1961), known for his gentle humor and kindness, was a scholar of independent means who received the OBE for his service in the armed forces during the First World War. Devoting his energies to aiding refugees, he never sought a leadership position in a refugee organization but was always willing to give his time and money to a Jewish cause.[66]

Sir Norman De Mattos Bentwich (1883–1971), a British barrister and legal academic, was the first attorney general of Mandatory Palestine. A professor of law at the Hebrew University who divided his time between Palestine and London, the balding, nearsighted Bentwich, always clutching at his round wire-rimmed spectacles, devoted much energy to the refugee cause, with his travels for the CBF taking him to countries around the world. Lord Herbert Louis, 1st Viscount Samuel (1870–1963), a dedicated Zionist, was a British politician and diplomat who served as the first High Commissioner for Palestine. Although he returned to British politics after his term in the Middle East, Samuel, known for his trademark handlebar mustache, also became active in the Kindertransport movement and led an appeal for homes for the *Kinder*.

Lionel de Rothschild (1882–1942), banker and Conservative politician, was an amateur horticulturalist, best remembered by the non-Jewish public as the creator of Exbury Gardens. A pillar of the Anglo-Jewish community, he and his younger brother Anthony (1887–1961), who later served as chair of the Emigration (Planning) Committee of the CBF, were always ready to cooperate in order to raise funds for the Jewish refugee cause.

As Amy Zahl Gottlieb noted, all of the people mentioned here were Victorians, inculcated with a sense of responsibility toward less fortunate Jews, and traditionally connected to philanthropic Jewish organizations on whose boards of governors they served.[67] Some were actually related by blood and family ties, belonging to "the Cousinhood." Many had studied at the same Jewish private boarding school (Clifton) or were students together at the same university. Almost all of the men had served as officers in the British Expeditionary Forces in the First World War and many retained military ties through their regimental associations. Similar to other men and women of independent means in British society of the time when academic education for social work was still in its infancy in Britain, a few of them, such as Norman Bentwich and Leonard Montefiore, had received "hands-on" social service training in order to be able to work with refugees. Together, they represented the lay and religious leadership of the assimilated Anglo-Jewish establishment.

Those not belonging to the "cousinhood" were on the periphery of the Anglo-Jewish elite, such as Meyer Stephany and Lavy Bakstansky (1904–71), and could step closer to this group by making their voluntary or professional mark in the Jewish organizational world. Stephany, a taciturn accountant, spent most of his professional life working for Anglo-Jewish communal organizations; he was the equivalent of a high-ranking Jewish (civil) communal servant. Bakstansky, described as having a quick clear mind, staccato speech, and steely determination that overwhelmed whomever he dealt with,[68] was a long-time Zionist, secretary of the British Zionist Federation, and general secretary of the Jewish Agency for Palestine who coordinated the CBF's fund-raising efforts. While neither shared the banking and educational background of the others, their actions in the field of refugee work afforded them one of Bekkers and Wiepking's variables—reputation. This is not to state that the only reason or even the main reason for their joining the refugee cause was to better their own professional and personal standing among the Anglo-Jewish elite, but it is an oft overlooked subliminal factor when discussing the overt and covert impetus for voluntary or philanthropic activities.

I have already noted that more people perform voluntary actions if they are considered a positive thing to do in one's society or if one's reputation is damaged if one does not perform that action. This, however, is not enough to explain the participation of non-Jewish activists in the Jewish refugee cause. In many cases, it was an ideological affinity to the Jewish people stemming from a religious basis that was the impetus for non-Jewish activists of a similar elite social background to join forces with these men in the refugee cause. One such activist was Sir Wyndham Henry Deedes (1883–1956), who had served as chief secretary to British High Commissioner for Palestine, Sir Herbert Samuel, retiring from the British army in 1923 as brigadier general. The dark-haired, trim and small-mustached Deedes, a strict Christian who never married, was generally known to have had pro-Zionist leanings since the days of his fighting in Gallipoli during the First World War alongside the Zion Mule Corps, the Jewish volunteers from Palestine who later metamorphosed into the Jewish Legion, led by Joseph Trumpeldor. Upon Deedes's return to England, he occupied himself in London with unpaid social work in one of the city's poorest quarters. In addition, he was always willing to give his name to the Jewish refugee cause. With Norman Bentwich, he later became an honorary co-director in charge of retraining and emigration in the Council for German Jewry.[69]

Did the women who were active in the Jewish refugee cause conform to the same typology as the men discussed here with regard to their pro-social and helping behavior? At first glance, the five women mentioned in this chapter—Cissie Laski, Alice Model, Anna Schwab, Helen Bentwich, and Gladys Skelton—appear to have come from a similar background to the men, and were in some cases related to them; their behavior also corresponds to a similar pattern of voluntary philanthropic action as the one described in relation to the men.

Cissie (Phina Emily) Laski was the wife of Neville Laski and the daughter of Moses Gaster, the Romanian-born British Jewish scholar who served as the Hakham of Bevis Marks, the Spanish-Portuguese synagogue in London. Raised as part of the Anglo-Jewish elite, it was natural that she would become involved in Jewish philanthropic work, not only because of gendered expectations but because of the noblesse oblige expectations of those coming from her background. The same held true for Helen Caroline Bentwich (1892–1972), wife of Norman Bentwich and niece of Sir Herbert Samuel, who was a member of the "cousinhood." A women's-rights activist who tried to fight for the rights of female workers at the Woolwich Arsenal, Bentwich later became an organizer for the Women's Land Army and a politician.

The Frankfurt-born Anna Schwab, active in the Women's Lodge of B'nai Brith, was related to the Ellern banking family of Frankfurt, which made her part of the financial and banking Jewish elite to which many of the aforementioned male group belonged. Alice Model (d. 1943), an active campaigner for mother- and child welfare, founded what would become the Jewish maternity hospital (1895) and the Jewish Day Nursery in London (1901).[70] Her work with refugees was an outgrowth of her previous philanthropic endeavors, corresponding to a variation of what Bekkers and Wiepking term "awareness"; in this case, an awareness of need that translated into traditionally female helping behavior and from which she would ultimately reap the mechanism of psychological benefits that they describe. The one non-Jewish member of this original group of women's activists, Gladys Williams (1885–1975), later known as Gladys Skelton and finally as Gladys Bendit, was driven by a combination of a similar gendered awareness and a religious leaning toward philanthropy, particularly that having to do with children. Williams-Skelton-Bendit was a British and later Australian lecturer, author, novelist, and poet who wrote under the pseudonym John Presland. As an active member of the London-based Save the Children's Fund, she later founded the Inter-Aid Committee and ultimately was active in the Refugee Children's Movement.

These women were in fact archetypes of large numbers of women who would later ensure the success of the refugee organizations and particularly the Refugee Children's Movement. As Sybil Oldfield states in her study of the role of British women in the rescue and care of Kindertransport children, the refugee organizations could not have been created without the backing of "influential English men" who would give the organizations "institutional legitimacy." However, the essential responsibility of ensuring the day-to-day success of the enterprise fell primarily on the shoulders of women such as these.[71] In addition to the variables that came into play in explaining the helping behavior of the male refugee activists such as religious belief, educational and financial background, tradition of volunteering, altruism, and egoism, in the case of women one must take into account additional factors. These include gendered variables such as a traditional social conditioning of women toward a reproduction of mothering, shouldering the responsibilities related to children and family, translating these actions into helping the weak, and the more general gendered ethic of care.[72] All these would come into play in the case of refugee activists on all levels, who would ultimately be dealing with Jewish refugee children in Great Britain.

Anschluss and After

"While Jews were being saved from the Third Reich on a retail basis, the Germans were acquiring new ones wholesale. . . ."[73] At dawn on 12 March 1938, the *Wehrmacht* crossed the German–Austrian border to unite the cities of Adolf Hitler's childhood with the country that ruled most of Europe under his leadership. By 13 March 1938, Austria was officially incorporated into the Reich. At the time of the *Anschluss*, 180,000 Jews lived in Austria, 165,000 of whom lived in Vienna alone; 30,000 of them were schoolchildren under the age of twelve.[74]

In the weeks following the *Anschluss*, mass arrests of Jews were commonplace, homeless children were often seen wandering the streets of Vienna, and terror became part of everyday life.[75] This was aptly expressed by the Viennese saying: "When the bell tolls at 7 AM in the Paris it's the milkman, when it rings at 7 AM in Austria it's the Gestapo."[76] What had taken Hitler several years to achieve in Germany was accomplished in Austria within weeks. The Jews of Austria rapidly became conscious of the urgency to escape, much more so than the German Jews who slowly became accustomed to being treated as less than second-class citizens. The efficiency of the Nazi centralization of the emigration procedure under Adolf Eichmann's leadership was matched in fervor only by

Austrian Jewry's desire to leave their homeland. The dismantling of families became so common that the Viennese Jews had a saying: "From children—letters; from parents—pictures; from houses—lifts; from property (tax) certificates."[77]

By the spring of 1938, the general refugee crisis was finally recognized as an international problem. Within two weeks of the *Anschluss,* Great Britain introduced visa requirements for German and Austrian nationals, fearing an inundation of desperate and impoverished fugitives from the Nazis.[78] In answer to the general crisis, on 23 March 1938 American President Franklin Delano Roosevelt proposed to the governments of more than thirty European and Latin American countries that they send representatives to an international conference to discuss resettlement opportunities for Jews under German jurisdiction.[79] This was the first government initiative taken vis-à-vis European refugees from Nazism. In addition, the refugee question was treated, for the first time, as an international problem that demanded an international solution. However, not all countries responded with enthusiasm to the invitation. Italy flatly refused to attend, while Romania, wishing to rid itself of a "surplus" Jewish population, requested to be categorized with Germany and Austria as a "refugee producer."[80] Not wishing to antagonize Berlin, Switzerland, which had been the first choice as a conference site, requested that it not be held within its borders.[81]

Almost up to the date of the conference it was hoped that the United States, with its forty-one persons per square mile of habitable territory, would offer a viable solution.[82] These hopes, however, remained academic delusions. By late spring 1938, the United States had abdicated all responsibility for the conference preparations and looked to representatives of various world regions, notably Latin America, to sponsor rescue proposals on their own territory. It seemed as if a stalemate was reached three and a half months after invitations were issued. On the sunny afternoon of 6 July 1938, some two hundred delegates convened at the Hotel Royal at Evian, France, overlooking Lake Geneva. The British delegation, larger than that which any other government had sent to Evian, was led by Lord Winterton (Rt. Hon. Edward Turnour), cabinet minister and Chancellor the Duchy of Lancaster. The choice of Winterton, accused by both Jews and a reporter of the *New York Herald Tribune* as being an antisemite, was not a harbinger of success in solving the refugee problem. While his friends referred to him as "a bit of a character," one of his British peers had once called him "the rudest white man he ever met."[83] Only Britain, America, and France sent special delegations; all other countries were represented by regular diplomats of the League of Nations or nearby capitals.

By the date of the conference, two basic approaches to the refugee problem had crystallized—the conservative one such as that of Great Britain, which feared that any helpful arrangement would encourage the German government to accelerate the expulsion of the Jews, and the liberal one, such as that of the United States, aimed at establishing machinery to deal with actual and potential refugees outside Germany.[84]

At the opening of the conference some delegates were apprehensive of American pressure to absorb refugees. However, these fears were proven groundless at the first session, when the American delegate Myron Taylor announced that the United States, in a gesture toward the refugees, would henceforth be willing to fill the German–Austrian quota instead of making the bureaucracy so difficult for potential immigrants that only a portion of the quota was, in practice, filled each year during the early 1930s. The delegates sat stunned: the nations of the world had been mobilized for this? "A collective sigh of relief from the assembly was almost audible as Taylor sat down. For the Jews of Europe, Taylor's speech was a cruel letdown; for everyone at Evian it was a reprieve."[85]

This "collective sigh" was, in fact, translated into collective inaction. If the United States was only willing to fill a preexisting quota, no other national was expected to do more. Thus, by the conference's end, no country aside from the Dominican Republic offered any solution to the refugee problem.[86]

The Evian conference was primarily an American exercise in public relations. Nevertheless, it was also the first time that the Jewish refugee problem was recognized as an international issue affecting those besides Jews. Despite this fact, the gap between realization and action continued to widen. The only tangible result of the nine days of deliberations was the formation of the IGC, the Inter-Government Committee, directed by George S. Rublee. The IGC was to develop "refugee work," persuade countries to permit the entry of a greater number of immigrants, and "undertake negotiations to improve the present conditions of exodus and to replace them by conditions of orderly emigration."[87] Unfortunately, participants were limited to representatives of legitimate governments. This precluded the participation of organizations that had originally been allowed to send representatives to the Evian Conference, such as the Jewish Agency in Palestine.

Among the resolutions of Evian was that no government was to assume obligations for financing of what was termed "involuntary emigration."[88] This resolution was often quoted over the next year by the British government, which, until the outbreak of war, would faithfully keep to the letter of the law. One refugee remarked wryly that "Evian" was merely "naïve" spelled backwards.[89] For the thousands of Jewish refugees seeking asylum, the conference's multitude of resolutions, combined with the absence of solutions, were not only naïve—they were absolutely life threatening.[90]

The "peace in our time" of the Munich Agreement (29 September 1938) heralded the start of Hitler's war on Czechoslovakia. The incident, which became known as Neville Chamberlain's personal Canossa, did not prove that "the umbrella had been mightier than the sword."[91] On 1 October 1938, German troops occupied the Sudetenland. As a result, large numbers of refugees, including communists and Jews, fled to Prague.

Some of the first Jewish refugee children from the annexed areas to reach the shores of Britain were part of a group of eighty-two Jews marooned in the no-man's land between the Sudentenland and the new Czech frontier. This group was among the hundred Czech refugees allowed into Britain whose maintenance was guaranteed by a fund launched by the *News Chronicle*.[92] A new British policy on the question of European refugees began to evolve during the six weeks between the German invasion of Czechoslovakia and *Kristallnacht*. It stemmed, primarily, from British guilty feelings over the results of the "hard-line" appeasement policy which the country had followed during the late summer and early autumn months of 1938. Britain's guilt grew steadily as it watched the German takeover of the Sudentenland and became aware of the fate of the hapless refugees—poignant newspaper articles on the subject appeared almost daily in the British press during these weeks—and was bolstered by the knowledge that despite the purity of British motives, it had aided and abetted selling Czechoslovakia down the river. Thus any change in British refugee policy during this period appears to have been directly connected to British feelings of responsibility over the fate of Czechoslovakia.

The Czechoslovakian tragedy continued to heighten the awareness of the refugee problem in countries outside Continental Europe. However, it was only a harbinger of things to come. At the end of October 1938, Polish nationals in Germany were deported back to Poland in response to the Polish government's claim that it would cancel the citizenship of Poles abroad who had not returned to Poland within the past five years. The hardships which these people had to endure during and after their deportation were often beyond description. In retaliation, the son of one of the deportees entered the German embassy in Paris on 7 November 1938, ostensibly with the intention of shooting the German ambassador. Instead, the shot was fired at Ernst vom Rath—the German third secretary. Vom Rath's death, two days later, gave the green light for a "spontaneous outburst" of the German people, an outburst that was to mark the beginning of the end of Central European Jewry.[93]

Notes

1. Schwartz interview.
2. See Lipman, *A History of the Jews in Britain*, 204–205.
3. Roth, "Economic Life and Population Movements," 48.
4. Bermant, *Troubled Eden*, 6.
5. Roth, *History of the Jews*, 301.
6. Newman, "German Jews in Britain," 31–36.
7. Endelman, *The Jews of Georgian England*, 11, 120, 248–71.
8. Gartner, *The Jewish Immigrant in England*, 85.
9. Alderman, *Modern British Jewry*, 17–18.
10. Gartner, *The Jewish Immigrant in England 1870–1914*, 127.
11. Gainer, *The Alien Invasion*, 55. As early as 1900, the accepted policy was that although Anglo-Jewry was in sympathy with the immigrants, it should not appear to encourage them in order to safeguard itself from antisemitism.

12. *The Jewish Yearbook*, 307–310. The Jewish population of London in 1940 was 385,000 out of a total of 8,575,700 persons in the city (4.49 percent). In 1940, Manchester had 33,000 Jews, Leeds had 25,000 Jews, Glasgow had 15,000 Jews, and Cardiff had 2,300 Jews.
13. Brotman, "Jewish Communal Organizations," 5–17.
14. The Jewish Religious Education Board, founded in 1860, the Talmud Torah Trust (intensive Jewish education), founded in 1905, and the Union of Hebrew and Religious Classes, founded in 1907. In addition, the Association of Non-Provided Schools in London dealt with voluntary Jewish Day Schools under local educational authorities. The Central Committee for Jewish Education, established in London in 1921, coordinated all these bodies and oversaw all Jewish education in Great Britain. See Fishman and Levy, "Jewish Education in Great Britain," 67.
15. Newman, *The United Synagogue 1870–1970*.
16. Kershen and Romain, *Tradition and Change*.
17. Kessler, "Claude Montefiore and Liberal Judaism," 17–32; Umansky, "Liberal Judaism in England," 309–322.
18. Sharot, "Reform and Liberal Judaism in London," 222; Marmur, *Reform Judaism*, 16–41; Liberlas, "The Origins of the Reform Movement in England," 121–50.
19. Kranzler, *Holocaust Hero*, 28–29.
20. Kranzler, *Holocaust Hero*, 30; Shatzkes, *Holocaust and Rescue*, 13.
21. During the war, Goodman published and edited the *Jewish Weekly* and was responsible for weekly broadcasts via the BBC to Jews in occupied Europe. Homa, *Orthodoxy in Anglo-Jewry*; Tomlin, *Protest and Prayer*, 64; Sompolinsky, *The British Government and the Holocaust*, 21.
22. Bermant, *The Cousinhood*.
23. In 1933, more than 40 percent of the German Jewish population was over age forty. See Kulischer, *The Displacement of Population*, 40; Bennathan, "Die demographische und wirtschaftliche struktur der Juden," 94; Stahl, "Vocational Retraining of Jews in Nazi Germany," 171; Rosenthal, "Trends of the Jewish Population in Germany," 272.
24. Tartakower and Grossman, *The Jewish Refugee*, 352.
25. Marcus, *The Rise and Destiny of the German Jew*, 11; Walk, *The Education of the Jewish Child in Germany*, 44, 55.
26. Schwarz-Bart, *The Last of the Just*.
27. Feidel-Mertz, *Schulen im Exil*; Feidel-Mertz, "Integration and Formation of Identity," 71–84.
28. Bentwich, *The Refugees from Germany*, 122.
29. Author's correspondence with Bertha Kahn, May 1980. Mrs. Kahn was a sister of Anna Essinger.
30. Jackson, "Anna's Children." The numbers of children who entered Bunce Court School were as follows: 1933—73, 1934—41, 1935—35, 1936—41, 1937—45, 1938—94, 1939—126. Essinger, *Bunce Court School*, 1, 14–16; Central British Fund Archives, the Wiener Library Microfilm document collection, 27/28/154.
31. Jackson, "Anna's Children."
32. Oldfield, "'It Is Usually She,'" 61–62.
33. http://www.gordonstoun.org.uk/about/school-history (retrieved on 22 August 2010).
34. Roehrs, *Bildung als Wagnis und Bewährung*.
35. Martin, "Ernst Bulova."

36. Feidel-Mertz, "Integration and Formation of Identity," 72; Wolfenden, *Little Holocaust Survivors*.
37. Wolfenden, *Little Holocaust Survivors*, chapter 5.
38. Jackson, "The Camphill Movement," 45-48.
39. Council for German Jewry, minutes of meeting, 27 March 1939. Central British Fund Archives, The Wiener Library Microfilm document collection 27/1/2.
40. Author's correspondence with Bertha Kahn, May 1980.
41. Feidel-Mertz, "Integration and Formation of Identity," 75.
42. Butler, *Gender Trouble*; Mazey and Lee, *Her Space, Her Place*.
43. Essinger, *Bunce Court School*, Central British Fund Archives, the Wiener Library Microfilm document collection, 27/28/154.
44. Wolfenden, *Little Holocaust Survivors*, chapter 5.
45. Between 1933 and 1943, the school had 422 Jewish pupils as opposed to 87 who belonged to the Church of England and 6 who were Roman Catholic.
46. Essinger, *Bunce Court School*, Central British Fund Archives, the Wiener Library Microfilm document collection, 27/28/154.
47. Walk, *The Education of the Jewish Child in Germany*, 44, 55.
48. Presland, *A Great Adventure*, 3. Central British Fund Archives, the Wiener Library Microfilm document collection, 27/28/156. While large numbers of German Jewish youth emigrated due to educational difficulties and restrictions, others, particularly in their late teens, were members of youth movements whose ideology served as the impetus for immigration.
49. Laski, *Jewish Rights and Jewish Wrongs*, 116.
50. Tartakower and Grossman, 343, Table III. Countries of reception for Jewish refugees: England admitted 63,000 refugees (8.1 percent of the total number of Jewish refugees during that period). Canada—8,000; South Africa—8,000; Spain—12,000; Australia—9,000; Uruguay—7,000; Switzerland—16,000. Sherman, however mentions that until November 1938 only 11,000 refugees had been admitted to Britain (4,000-5,000 of whom had subsequently re-emigrated; Sherman, *Island Refuge*, 179.) Only as a result of the Palestine issue (to be dealt with in the next chapter) were the large majority of immigrants permitted to enter Great Britain.
51. Bentwich, *They Found Refuge*, 14-15.
52. London, *Whitehall and the Jews*, 26; Sherman, *Island Refuge*, 25-26.
53. "Proposals of the Jewish Community as regards Jewish Refugees from Germany," n.d., PRO HO 213/1627. See also Cabinet Meeting on Alien Restrictions, 7 April 1933, Appendix PRO CAB 24/239.
54. Weyl, "W. W. Simpson," 22-34; author's interview with the Rev. William W. Simpson, Jerusalem, 22 June 1980 (henceforth: Simpson interview).
55. Bentwich, *They Found Refuge*, 50-51; Gottlieb, *Men of Vision*, 9-12.
56. Bentwich, *They Found Refuge*, 15-16, 50-55; Gottlieb, *Men of Vision*, 103-104.
57. For a history of the Central British Fund see Gottlieb, *Men of Vision*; see also Bentwich, *The Refugees from Germany*, 46. The first appeal was signed by five joint presidents: The Chief Rabbi (Rabbi Hertz), Lord Reading (the first), Dr. Chaim Weizmann, Mr. Lionel de Rothschild, and Mr. Nathan Sokolow (Sokolow and Weizmann were the present and former presidents of the World Zionist Organization).
58. Gottlieb, *Men of Vision*, 32-50.
59. Bentwitch, *They Found Refuge*, 21-27.
60. Sherman, *Island Refuge*, 28, estimates that between 1933 and 1935 between 1,500 and 2,500 Jewish refugees from Germany entered Britain. In comparison, Sir John Hope-

Simpson stated that 3,000 refugees had arrived from Germany by December 1933, an additional 2,400 refugees came between December 1933 and April 1934, and another 2,500 refugees from Germany arrived between April 1934 and June 1935. Simpson, *The Refugee Problem*, 562. Roche adds that from January to December 1936 they were followed by 2,595 refugees from Germany and from January to December 1937 an additional 2,062 refugees from Germany arrived in Britain; Roche, *The Key in the Lock*, 126. Stein states that on the day before *Kristallnacht* there were 5,500 German Jewish refugees in England; Stein, "Britain and the Jews of Europe," 303. Finally, Wischnitzer states that by the end of 1939 Great Britain had absorbed 42,000 refugees from Germany; Wischnitzer, *To Dwell in Safety*, 199.

61. Minutes of Organizing Committee, 16 May 1933. Central British Fund Archives, the Wiener Library Microfilm document collection 27/1/A.
62. Bentwich, *They Found Refuge*, 30–32.
63. *Movement for the Care of Children from Germany, Ltd. First Annual Report*, 3, Central British Fund Archives, The Wiener Library Microfilm document collection 27/28/153 (Henceforth: Movement).
64. Bekkers and Weipking, "Generosity and Philanthropy."
65. Sherman and Shatzkes, "Otto M. Schiff," 243–71.
66. Stein and Aronsfeld, *Leonard G. Montefiore*.
67. Gottlieb, *Men of Vision*, 24–29.
68. Bolchover, *British Jewry*, 34.
69. Elath, Bentwich, and May, *Memories of Sir Wyndham Deedes*. In 1949 Deedes founded the Anglo-Israel Association.
70. Marks, "'Dear Old Mother Levy's,'" 61–88.
71. Oldfield, "It Is Usually She," 57–58.
72. Gilligan, *In a Different Voice*; Chodorow, *The Reproduction of Mothering*.
73. Agar, *The Saving Remnant*.
74. Kulischer, *Europe on the Move*, 199. Sources cite different figures. A second source sets the Jewish population of Austria at 200,000 in March 1938 with 170,000 living in Vienna; Karbach, "The Liquidation of the Jewish Community of Vienna," 259. Yehuda Bauer lists the Jewish population of Austria as 185,246 at the time of the *Anschluss*. See Yehuda Bauer, *My Brother's Keeper*, 223.
75. "Jewish Children in Vienna," 10; author's interview with Boaz Wreschner, Ramat Gan, December 1979.
76. *The Jewish Chronicle*, 17 June 1936: 29.
77. Bentwich, *My 77 Years*, 163.
78. Sherman, *Island Refuge*, 89.
79. Stoessinger, *The Refugees and the World Community*, 39–40. The proposal was possibly initiated by Dorothy Thompson in her article "Refugees: A World Problem," 375–87. Although dated April, the magazine was available to Roosevelt in March and thus may have influenced him. This was stated by the author at the hearings in 1939. The impetus behind FDR's call for the conference has been variously interpreted. See, for example, Friedman, *No Haven for the Oppressed*, 37–55.
80. Wyman, *Paper Walls*, 45.
81. Feingold, *The Politics of Rescue*, 27.
82. Buxton and Angell, *The Economics of the Refugee Problem*, 29.
83. Stewart, "United States Government Policy on Refugees from Nazism," 302; Slyfield, "Earl Winterton."
84. Stewart, "United States Government Policy on Refugees from Nazism," 306–307.

85. Abella and Troper, *None Is Too Many*, 31.
86. Friedman, *No Haven for the Oppressed*, 62–64.
87. Sherman, *Island Refuge*, 119.
88. Adler-Rudel, "The Evian Conference," 272, Appendix II to the resolutions of the IGC adopted by the committee on 14 July 1938, clause 8 section d: "that the governments of the countries of refuge and settlement should not assume any obligations for the financing of involuntary emigration. . . ." The term "involuntary emigration" was substituted for the term "political refugee" that had formerly been in use. Feingold, *The Politics of Rescue*, 337.
89. Sherman, *Island Refuge*, 119.
90. In criticism of the Evian Conference results, the *Daily Herald* wrote: "If this is coming to the help of the refugees, then what would the nations do if they meant to desert them?" Stein, "Great Britain and the Evian Conference," 51–52.
91. Graves and Hodge, *The Long Weekend*, 445.
92. Sherman, *Island Refuge*, 148.
93. Rozien, "Herschel Grynszpan," 217–28.

Chapter 3

The Turning Point: *Kristallnacht*

Introduction

Late in the summer of 1938, the Jewish refugee organizations in Great Britain began to observe an increase in the number of unaccompanied Jewish children arriving in England. The reasons were manifold, ranging from the *Anschluss* of March 1938 to the new wave of antisemitic policies being carried out in Germany from June 1938 onward (*Juni Aktion*). The first of the organizations to sense the change was the Children's Inter-Aid Committee, founded in 1936 for the purpose of bringing Jewish and "non-Aryan" Christian children to Britain.[1] Other British refugee organizations of that period also bore the economic brunt of supporting the handfuls of unaccompanied children who reached British shores during the summer of 1938; these included the Central British Fund for German Jewry, the Jewish Refugees Committee, and the Council for German Jewry.

A few dozen unaccompanied refugee children were but a harbinger of what was to come. In September 1938, the *Jewish Chronicle* carried an appeal by A. Levay Lawrence, president of the First B'nai Brith lodge of England, putting forth suggestions to families willing to aid Jewish refugee children from Germany or Austria: they could serve as foster families for these children for a period of two to three years, donate a monthly contribution to help maintain a refugee child outside their own home (yearly upkeep was estimated at £50 a child), or help the Youth Aliyah movement settle the refugee children in Palestine.[2] In their worst nightmares, however, none of the refugee activists at the time could conceive of the events that were about to take place in the Reich and the consequences they would have for the future of the refugee movement.

The turning point for the organized rescue of unaccompanied refugee children from Central Europe took place in November 1938, in the wake of a massive pogrom against Jews throughout the Third Reich. The carnage of the night of 9–10 November 1938, later called by the Germans *Reichskristallnacht*, sounded the alarm for Central European Jewry. During the uncontrolled riots on this "night of broken glass," over one hundred Jews lost their lives, more than 30,000 were arrested and sent to jails and concentration camps, close to 2,000 synagogues and Jewish community buildings were destroyed, and over 7,500 Jewish stores were looted.[3]

Jews in Germany could no longer delude themselves with the idea that Hitlerism was a passing phenomenon. As one mother wrote to her son who was already studying in England: "I will never forget this . . . night as long as I live. The banging, thunderlike crashing and shouting, was unbelievable. It destroyed something deep inside of me. It destroyed my belief in Humanity. We live amongst savages, my boy. . . ."[4] Norbert Wollheim, who later accompanied numerous transports of children from Germany to England but would be caught in Germany at the war's outbreak, recalled how he walked out of the house the morning after the pogrom to hear someone say "the synagogues are burning." "I couldn't believe it. I went to the synagogue where I was bar mitzvahed, and where I'd been married, and I saw the flames coming from the roof, from the cupola of this beautiful edifice. The fire engines were standing by doing nothing, only protecting the buildings next to it. I still couldn't believe it. I thought, maybe it's the only one, so I went to another major synagogue in West Berlin, and it, too, was burning and already partly in ruins. I thought, this is the people you were brought up with, this is the poets and the thinkers. What happened to German civilization?"[5]

Children who had previously been protected by their parents and families from some of the more appalling events in Germany were now fully exposed to them. Bertha Leverton, who was fifteen years old at the time of the *Kristallnacht* pogrom, described what she saw that night in her hometown of Munich: "When we went to school the next morning, the synagogue was burning. We stood there, absolutely terrified and thunderstruck. The fire engines came, not to help extinguish the fires of the synagogue and the school, which was right next to it, but to prevent it from spreading to the neighboring houses. We ran home, past smashed windows of Jewish shops, past stores and warehouses cleared out and plundered. I can't recall all the details of that day. You try and block something out that is so horrible."[6]

Hedy Epstein heard nothing the night of 9 November and went to school the next morning as usual. "I remember it was a very sunny, but extremely cold day. Classes started punctually at eight. About eight-thirty, the principal walked in and he talked to all of us. Then he suddenly stopped and he pointed his finger at me and he said, 'Get out, you dirty Jew.' I just couldn't believe what I heard because I thought the principal was a good, decent person, and his daughter was one of my classmates. So I asked him to repeat it. And he did. He also came over, and he took me by the elbow and shoved me out the door."[7]

Ursula Rosenfeld remembers being dragged out of her school with a stream of children. "Everybody went to the playground, and I saw, in horror, that the synagogue was alight. The streets were lined with people, and they were all shouting, and jeering, and clapping . . . then two men—I don't think they were uniformed—came out with a Torah and they were dancing around and shouting. Suddenly somebody said, 'Oh, there's a Jew—let's throw her on the fire as well!' I don't know how I got home . . . and when I did, my mother was absolutely shocked. My father had been arrested."[8]

Steffi Birnbaum Schwartz was ten at the time but had no trouble recalling the turning point of German Jewry. "I remember it well, half of the fathers of the girls at the *Mittelschule* [middle school] were taken away. That day the school tried to get us out and all the parents tried to get the children home quickly. On the way home I saw the Reform synagogue which we attended being destroyed. I realized that something terrible was going on and knew that it was only the beginning. . . ."[9]

Until the decisive year of 1938, most Jews in Germany could not think in terms of total catastrophe and the need for rescue. Now, almost overnight, preconceptions were altered.[10] Within days of the pogrom, frantic parents throughout the Third Reich began searching for ways to send their children out of the Nazi clutches in order to save them from what they feared would be next. Although they hoped to ultimately be reunited with their children in a safe haven, many were now willing to send their children out of Germany unaccompanied, to children's homes or foster families. The issue was how to find countries willing to accept such children and places where children's homes or foster families could be found.

The weeks after *Kristallnacht* saw worldwide diplomatic activity on the refugee front. Under pressure to make a statement, but aware of pressures from exclusionist groups to remain within American immigration laws, President Franklin Delano Roosevelt signed an executive order allowing thousands of visitors from Germany then in the United States to remain in the country.[11] Other countries, also placed under moral pressure, preferred targeting refugee children rather than adults and issued declarations about new programs that would allow the entry of unaccompanied persecuted children from the Third Reich. The French government stated that it would admit two hundred refugee children per month, to be cared for by the Oeuvre de Secours aux Enfants (OSE) organization and by the Comité Israélite pour les Enfants venant d'Allemagne et de l'Europe Centrale. Switzerland agreed to take children to be cared for by the Comité Suisse d'aide aux Enfants d'émigrés. The Netherlands also agreed to take an unspecified number of refugee children.[12]

Child refugees were preferred over adults for a number of emotional, psychological, and practical reasons: children evoked a humanitarian response faster than did adults; they would not enter the already problematic job market during the economic depression; they were considered more malleable than adult refugees; and they could be taught local language and customs and could ultimately learn to fit into their new society. But even for child refugees, European countries did not open their doors completely after *Kristallnacht* and kept to a tacit or overt quota that had been set regarding the numbers permitted past their borders.

Almost immediately after *Kristallnacht*, Jewish organizations in Britain mobilized their forces to put political pressure on the government to permit the entry of refugees from the Third Reich. But Great Britain was in a slightly different situation than countries such as France, Switzerland, and the Netherlands in view of the fact that it held a major political key to solving the Jewish refugee problem: the Palestine Mandate. Torn between international pressure to open the gates of Palestine to Jewish refugees and the ongoing Colonial and Foreign Office policy of appeasing Arab anti-Jewish sentiment, His Majesty's Government found itself seeking a refugee compromise that would not serve as a precedent to allow in hordes of Jewish refugees from the Reich, nor would it be willing to divert them to Palestine and jeopardize the tenuous situation in the Middle East.

The direction that the compromise would take became clearer on 15 November 1938, when a delegation from the Council for German Jewry met with Prime Minister Neville Chamberlain at 5 p.m. at the House of Commons. Since *Kristallnacht*, the Council had been bombarded with pleas to assist in saving the lives of German Jewish children. The most poignant of these pleas had come from Wilfred Israel (1899–1943) immediately after *Kristallnacht*, who had described the pogrom to British press correspondents whom he met on the streets of Berlin. Heir to a leading Berlin business and descendant on his mother's side to the first Chief Rabbi of Britain, Hermann Adler, Israel belonged to the Jewish elite of both Britain and Germany and had access to major Jewish organizations in both countries. Five days after *Kristallnacht*, he cabled the Council for German Jewry to propose the immediate rescue of German Jewish children and young people up to the age of seventeen, a proposal that immediately metamorphosed into a more concrete plan to be proposed to the British government. Wilfred Israel would also be instrumental in assisting British Quakers in visiting Jewish communities throughout Germany in order to prove to the British government that parents were indeed willing to part from their children and send them to safety. Some of the Quakers had been instrumental in assisting the transfer of entire schools from Germany to Britain earlier in the decade.[13]

Aware that there were approximately 60,000–70,000 Jewish children in the Third Reich who needed to be brought to safety and building on Israel's proposal, the Council for German Jewry's deputation, led by Viscount Samuel, met with Chamberlain to discuss possible rescue schemes.[14] Acknowledging that neither diplomatic steps vis-à-vis the German government nor an "open-door" policy for all German Jewish refugees was possible, in view of the emergency created by *Kristallnacht*, Samuel urged the British government to consider allowing large numbers of children and adolescents up to the age of seventeen into Britain. He stated that the Jewish organizations would give a collective guarantee that no public funds would be spent on these children, who would be educated and trained with the understanding that eventually they would leave Britain. Chamberlain expressed deep concern and sympathy but made no promises. At the same meeting another participant, Chaim Weizmann, requested the British government to allow the immediate evacuation of 1,500 children to Palestine. Here as well, Chamberlain promised to consider this request sympathetically if the Colonial Secretary raised it with him.

Chamberlain realized that he stood at a crossroads. In view of the changing situation in Germany and the negative response of American public opinion to his appeasement policies, it was imperative to respond in some way to the delegates' requests both in order to regain American support and to prevent being forced to do even more in the future. As a first step, early the next morning his office circulated a record of the meeting, asking the departments whose responsibilities would be affected to consider the points that applied to them.[15] The next step was a discussion that took place at a cabinet meeting held later that day, in which several urgent issues were raised, including what was termed "growing American criticism" of the prime minister's appeasement policy that had earned him the French nickname of Monsieur J'aime Berlin.[16] Throughout that year both the American government and the American people had been singularly unimpressed by British foreign policies, and in his overtures toward appeasing Adolf Hitler, Chamberlain succeeded only in further alienating American public opinion. The existence of the British Mandate in Palestine offered Britain the potential to remove the refugee millstone from other countries' necks, yet it persisted in British policies of limited immigration. Any discussion of using Palestine as a haven for refugees was taboo and it was even one of Britain's conditions of participation in the Evian Conference. America's criticism of British foreign policy toward Germany was therefore compounded by resentment of Britain's unequivocal refusal to consider using the Palestine Mandate as a solution for the rapidly growing refugee problem.

Aware of this dilemma, Chamberlain began by noting that Britain's international position might be restored if it took a positive lead in the refugee issue, and he urged the Home, Foreign, and Colonial Secretaries to draft a statement in that direction. Discussing the various possibilities at hand for large-scale refugee settlement, including a colonial one, the prime minister made his colleagues face the fact that no such settlement could meet the needs of the immediate problem. Instead, he told the home secretary, Sir Samuel Hoare, that it was time to consider the possibility of using Britain as a temporary refuge, a suggestion that the previous day's delegation had raised and a category that was not covered by the existing immigration laws.[17] This was not the first time that the refugee crisis had been discussed in the cabinet, but never before had the prime minister let it be known so forcefully that it would be imperative for Britain to ameliorate the situation by changing its refugee policy in the very near future.

British Immigration Regulations and the Refugee Crisis

Chamberlain's suggestion to use Britain as a temporary refuge was an attempt to circumvent the limitations of existing Alien legislation in Britain. The Alien Restriction Act of 1914, amended by the Aliens Order of 1920, made no distinction between aliens as a class and alien refugees. Aliens were permitted to land if they proved their ability to support themselves and their dependents. Alternatively, they would be employed to fill those positions for which no British labor was available.[18] This was the prevalent immigration statute in Britain during the first years after Hitler's rise to power.

Until 1938, Reich Germans, Austrians, and later Czechoslovakians possessing a valid passport and entering Britain on business, for private visits, or for purposes of study were not required to have visas. Their only restrictions were a prohibition on unauthorized employment and a time limitation. In May 1938, as a result of the *Anschluss*, the German unification with Austria in March of that year, the British government, fearing a deluge of Central European refugees, introduced visa requirements for passport holders of these countries. All aliens, including children, were required to submit visa applications to passport control officers attached to British embassies and consulates; the applications were examined from both financial and security standpoints.[19] This method, while suitable for emigrants under normal circumstances, was tedious and time consuming and therefore obviously unsuitable for the large groups of refugees and especially the children who were now under consideration to be let into Britain.

During the week following the cabinet meeting of 16 November, the Liberal and Labour Parties and the League of Nations Union put organized pressure on the government to take the lead in finding a rapid solution to the refugee problem. This situation was further complicated by an announcement by the Jewish Agency for Palestine that same week regarding a possible solution to the refugee problem. Within days of *Kristallnacht,* the Jewish Agency had demanded the immediate admission of 100,000 Jewish refugees from Germany; now it proposed a plan to bring 10,000 Jewish refugee children from Central Europe to Palestine. The children would be absorbed by the *Yishuv* (the pre-State Jewish community in Palestine), cared for by Jewish families, and supported financially by the Jewish Agency.[20] The *Yishuv*'s demands, promoted as a solution to the acute refugee crisis, received growing publicity in Britain and abroad, making it imperative for the British government to take a vocal public stand on the refugee issue if it didn't want to face American pressure to open the gates of Palestine as a solution to the refugee crisis.

During the five days following the cabinet meeting, the Colonial, Foreign, and Home Secretaries each wrestled with the specific problem of their offices. The Colonial Office headed by Malcolm MacDonald busied itself with Chaim Weizmann's proposal that a group of 1,500 children be permitted to enter Palestine and the subsequent proposal of the Va'ad Haleumi, the National Council in Palestine, to adopt 10,000 refugee children from Germany, 5,000 immediately and 5,000 at a later date.[21] Unwilling to agree to either of the *Yishuv*'s plans, one initially proposed by Weizmann in Britain and the other stemming from the *Yishuv*'s leadership, the Colonial Office turned what was rapidly becoming a heated issue over to the Foreign and Home Offices, asking them to find a solution that would not jeopardize His Majesty's policies. Consequently, the *Yishuv* plans were shelved and were publicly rejected during a House of Commons debate in mid-December.[22]

The Foreign Secretary, Lord Halifax, attempted to appease the growing American displeasure with regard to British immigration policies vis-à-vis Palestine by instructing the British ambassador in Washington to suggest to the State Department that part of the unused British quota for immigration into the United States be used for refugees from Germany. The suggestion was not met with American approval and was consequently inapplicable, as it was legally impossible to move one country's quota over to another sovereign country.[23] The Colonial Office's intransigence on the Palestine issue, combined with the Foreign Office's lack of success in the American arena, returned the ball to the court of the Home Secretary, Sir Samuel Hoare, who realized with dismay that his colleagues expected him to reach a compromise solution that would get them off the hook. As his only option involved making a humanitarian gesture of allowing various refugee groups to enter Britain, they would have to be inoffensive groups such as children and the elderly whose entry would only bend, and not break, the previously existing immigration regulations.

Originally the emphasis had been put on finding a solution for elderly and not youthful refugees. This soon changed, however, to a focus on refugee children due to pressures from the Jewish refugee organizations, including the request that had been made by the Council for German Jewry's delegation.[24] After carefully weighing the alternatives put before him, the Home Secretary concluded that his best alternative was to consider the possibility of allowing large numbers of refugee children from the Reich to enter Britain, albeit temporarily, in order to assuage public opinion regarding what appeared to be British inaction over the new and tragic situation in Germany. The question was how such a program could be put into motion and when it would be announced by the British government.

The Early Refugee Children's Organizational Machinery

As the various cabinet secretaries attempted to reach a compromise that would demand the most of other offices and the least from their own, Jewish organizations began organizing the machinery that would help transfer and care for Central European refugee children in Great Britain. Although the minutes of the executive committee of the Council for German Jewry state that Helen Bentwich initiated a proposal to relocate a thousand children from Central Europe to Britain,²⁵ the German Jewish social worker and refugee activist in London, Solomon Adler-Rudel (1894–1975) claimed to have originated the idea that he then passed on to Helen Bentwich along with two other refugee activists, Cissie Laski and Lola Hahn-Warburg.²⁶

Within two days, Bentwich was joined by a number of people, including Dennis Cohen, chair of the Jewish Refugee's Committee emigration department, in proposing a plan to bring 5,000 refugee children to Britain in groups of 200–500, housing them in summer camps along the English southern coast that were vacant during the winter. Initially they anticipated that the children would mostly be under the age of ten and that the public would be invited to offer them accommodations that would meet the London County Council foster home standards. According to the proposal, the Council for German Jewry would obtain Home Office approval for the children's admission, they would be educated and trained for employment in Britain or their future countries of settlement, and would ideally be accompanied by teachers and social workers from Germany and Austria. The proposal was endorsed by Labour politician James Mac-Coll, Major Geoffrey Langdon, a businessman affiliated with the Jewish Refugee Committee, Viscount Samuel, and Sir Wyndham Deedes, chair of the Inter-Aid Committee for Children.²⁷

The initial idea had been to use the existing machinery of the Inter-Aid Committee for Children from Germany in order to carry out the new rescue scheme. However, the Council for German Jewry questioned whether the framework of this organization would be able to support the large number of refugee children expected. Consequently, Helen Bentwich, Dennis Cohen, Rebecca Sieff, and Gladys Skelton, the secretary to the Inter-Aid Committee, were given the responsibility of forming a new framework for the children's rescue program. Together with a group of refugee activists that included members of parliament, they founded a new organization, the Movement for the Care of Children from Germany.

The creation of any new organization raises a number of questions regardless of its declared objective: how can one explain the need for a new framework when an older one already exists? Why are certain groups that are already active in the organization's objective included in its formation, while others are excluded? Which individuals or bodies make the pivotal decisions regarding the new organization's operative and functional matters, and why were they and not others given or allowed to assume these responsibilities?

In the case of the Movement for the Care of Children from Germany, most sources state that a new organization was needed because the Inter-Aid Committee had neither the organizational nor the financial framework to cope with what was hoped to be an influx of large numbers of unaccompanied refugee children. Why, then, was the older organization not expanded and a new one founded in its stead? The answer appears to be rooted not only in the organizational and financial aspects of the endeavor but also in the nature of the original body—the

Council for German Jewry—dealing with the proposal that Britain host thousands of Central European refugee children. As Amy Zahl Gottlieb states: "It was apparent to all those concerned that the Council was the only organization in Britain with the will and the potential fund-raising ability to shoulder this mammoth task."[28] A less gentle way of phrasing the dynamics would have been to state that as the Council for German Jewry wished to retain its organizational monopoly in dealing with the Jewish refugee issue in Britain, its members realized that any such new and powerful organization would have to begin as an outgrowth of the Council and not an expansion of a preexisting but unrelated body.

This also explains why certain groups and individual dealing with refugees were almost naturally included in the formation of the Movement for the Care of Children from Germany while others were excluded or were not even considered in the first place. Amy Zahl Gottlieb continues: "In its haste to install a plan of action, no attempt appears to have been made to seek out experts or recommend the best means by which so great an undertaking might be handled. Nor was it deemed necessary to convene a committee that included representatives of both the orthodox and non-orthodox Jewish communities, who would participate in the selection of families to host children, especially those from orthodox religious backgrounds."[29] Whether out of haste or not, it seems that little if any thought was given by members of the "Cousinhood," who were long used to dominating and even monopolizing the boards of the major Jewish organizations in Britain, toward involving a larger spectrum of the British Jewish community in the new rescue organization. Although both the Chief Rabbi's Religious Emergency Council and Agudath Israel had already been dealing with the rescue of Jewish children from Vienna since the *Anschluss*, their independence from the Council of German Jewry and their Orthodox orientation marked them as sectarian groups. And as they could not automatically be expected to abide by the Council's policies, they were not even considered as potential partners for the new refugee children's body. For the Bentwiches, Warburgs, Samuels's, Marks's, and Laskis, refugee activists such as Solomon Schonfeld or Harry Goodman were not even on their radar.

Although from their point of view it was understandable that the formative steps of the new organization be taken under the watchful eyes of Helen Bentwich, Dennis Cohen, Rebecca Sieff, and Gladys Skelton, this set the scene for the creation of a relatively homogenous body in terms of the class and background of its major activists. In what later became a nonsectarian organization that included representatives from the Church of England, Nonconformists, Roman Catholics, and Jews, there would be no Orthodox Jewish representatives nor would much thought be given to the special needs of Orthodox refugee children or to questions of foster homes' religious suitability. Consequently, toward the end of the war a number of religious issues involving Jewish refugee children came to the fore and required intervention by the various bodies involved in the refugee scheme.

The Government Announcement and Its Aftermath

While the organizational bureaucracy that would enable the children's resettlement in Britain took shape, the leaders of the Council for German Jewry made behind-the-scenes contacts with representatives of the Home Office regarding the possibility of permitting large numbers of child refugees from the Third Reich to immigrate to or at least temporarily resettle in Great Britain. On the morning of 21 November 1938, Lord Samuel and members of the Council for German Jewry met with the Home Secretary to discuss the rescue machinery being set up to rescue refugee children. Accompanied by a representative of the Inter-Aid Committee and by Bertha Bracey and Ben Greene of the Society of Friends, who had just returned from Berlin where they were helping Christians leave German territory, the group received the first sign that British refugee policy toward children from the Reich was changing. Hearing of their endeavors, Hoare expressed the government's willingness to facilitate the entry of transmigrant children and enumerated the steps that the Home Office was willing to take in order to ensure the children's rapid processing by the visa bureaucracy. These steps were officially announced that evening during a full-scale debate on the refugee question in the House of Commons.[30]

That same morning, the prime minister made the first post-*Kristallnacht* public statement in parliament about British refugee policy, but did not specifically mention children.[31] At 7:33 p.m. that evening, a full-scale debate on the refugee question opened in the House of Commons. Bearing in mind that many non-Jewish MPs would be speaking in favor of relaxed immigration regulations and feeling that their origins required them to be circumspect with regard to the refugee question, the Jewish MPs had agreed in advance not to participate in the debate. This fact epitomizes the general Jewish attitude of the period to keep a low profile with regard both to themselves and their refugee coreligionists. Not only were newly arrived refugees enjoined by Jewish organizations in many countries to speak quietly and never to use their mother tongue in public, but influential Jews the world over also felt that they would jeopardize the refugee cause by pleading for it openly. Thus, the decision of the Jewish MPs was viewed by many British Jews as understandable and by some as being even laudable.

The first speaker, Labor MP Philip Noel-Baker, demanded an immediate clarification of the government refugee policy and advocated permitting great numbers of refugee children to enter Britain. In the course of the debate, the Home Secretary publicly announced that the government was prepared to admit certain refugees who would eventually transmigrate, including all children whose maintenance could be guaranteed either by voluntary organizations or private charitable contributions. Taking the opportunity to commend this effort to his fellow countrymen, he stated that this offered "a chance of taking the young generation of a great people . . . of mitigating to some extent the terrible sufferings of their parents and friends." Asserting the government's willingness to help, he promised "utmost support" for the voluntary organizations' work and vowed to be "at the forefront among the nations of the world in giving relief to these suffering people."³²

The Home Office announcement regarding refugee children from Central Europe did not emerge out of thin air. A precedent for the bold decision had already been created by the case of Basque children. In 1937, during the Spanish Civil War, the British government had allowed 3,800 Basque children, rescued from the bombardment of Bilbao, to seek temporary shelter in Great Britain. British public opinion had been divided on the question of the Spanish Civil War, and the project to bring over Basque children met with a violent press campaign against it.³³ The children were often accused of being "red hooligans," likely to corrupt the "pure English youth."³⁴

All Basque refugee children were guaranteed by private charities and most were kept in reception camps and private homes. By the beginning of 1938, some 3,000 of these children had been repatriated, with the responsibility for the rest being placed in the hands of the National Joint committee for Spanish Relief.³⁵ A second precedent was that of Belgian children taken to Britain during the First World War.³⁶

Now that the official announcement had been made, the rescue machinery began to take shape. The first step was to curtail the existing bureaucracy to expedite the refugee children's paperwork. On 23 November, two days after Hoare's announcement, the House of Commons was informed of an arrangement regarding the substitution of a travel document for visa and passport in the case of children. Expanding upon the matter the next day in his answer to a question by the Quaker refugee activist MP Thomas Edmund Harvey, Geoffrey Lloyd, Under-Secretary of State for the Home Department, reiterated the official government policy on this matter: "It has been decided to waive the requirement of a visa for refugee children brought to this country for educational purposes under the care of the Inter-Aid Committee for Children."³⁷ In his response to Harvey's questioning, Lloyd was basically summarizing official British government policy toward refugee children from the Reich at that time: the children were to be brought for educational purposes; in other words, with a long-range view to their not remaining in Britain, the government would do everything possible to simplify the bureaucracy involved in their transfer. The body responsible for bringing them and caring for them in Britain was the Inter-Aid Committee for Children, and most important, no numbers were mentioned, a reflection of the fact that there was no quantitative government limit to the refugee children scheme.

How many refugee children did the British government actually intend to allow in? No numbers of refugees were mentioned during the House of Commons debate, during which the Home Secretary stated his opposition to any quota in this matter by saying "many people might think it was too big and many people might think it was too small."³⁸ However, even if no official quota existed, long before the refugee child scheme came to an end in late August 1939, various government officials had mentioned 10,000 children as a possible upper limit. This number was doubly reinforced, and possibly also determined, by the fact that the Jewish Agency had proposed to adopt in Palestine a proposal that was turned down by the British government in December 1938. Instead of 10,000 Jewish children being allowed into Palestine, fanning the flames of Arab ire, His Majesty's Government would allow the same number of children into Britain as temporary residents, effectively pulling the carpet out from under the Jewish Agency demands.

The numerical aspect was both connected to and compounded by the deeper motives behind the British government's generous offer of hospitality for refugee children from the Reich. Was the reversal of British government policy, which until then had made entry for refugees from Europe progressively more difficult, the result of Chamberlain's change of heart, having being horrified by the *Kristallnacht* pogrom and moved and impressed by his meeting with the delegation from the Council for German Jewry, as Louise London claims in her study of Whitehall and the Jews?[39] Or was it more an exercise in public relations, a response to the negative feedback Britain had recently received in American public-opinion surveys that also influenced the U.S. government, as others have suggested?

Let us pause momentarily to consider the state in which Neville Chamberlain and his cabinet found themselves in November 1938. It is obvious that they felt a certain degree of responsibility for the results of the Czechoslovakian crisis, to which they felt compelled to add their humanitarian reaction to the plight of post-*Kristallnacht* German Jewry. But there were also additional factors: Colonial Office immigration limitations regarding Palestine, the Jewish Agency proposal of November 1938, and the pressure of political, religious, and social welfare groups in Britain, the United States, and other countries to find a solution to the refugee problem. In view of these factors, by mid-November 1938 Chamberlain and the British government realized that they had to reexamine their previous stand on the refugee question if they wished to retain American goodwill, an economic necessity of the time.[40] All this led to the decision to allow unaccompanied refugee children from Germany to enter as transmigrants, along with certain numbers of other groups such as the elderly, men released from concentration camps (who would be settled in a closed camp in Britain and not allowed to join the labor force), and women who would serve as domestic servants. Aware of the fact that if the British government continued to refuse to consider using Palestine as a possible haven for refugees, it was imperative that it offer an alternative solution in Britain in order to avoid being pressured to compromise its mandate policy by critics of British foreign and colonial policy.[41]

Another factor was the hope that the United States, when confronted with Britain's fait accompli, would find it necessary to follow suit by revising its refugee policies; by doing so, it would cause other countries to take in refugees from

Germany, ultimately taking the pressure off Britain to ultimately open the doors of Palestine to resettle these refugees. This was hinted to by the *London Times* less than five days after the Home Office announcement of 21 November 1938: "If an adequate response is made by the British people to this call, it is to be hoped that in the U.S. and other countries similar steps will be taken so that the duty will be shared."[42]

For the same humanitarian reasons that led British public opinion to rally behind the government's move to save Central European refugee children, British government officials assumed that children would be more palatable to the American public than refugee adults.[43] And if America and other countries did pick up Britain's lead in refugee policy, it would have been worth His Majesty's Government's while to permit the entry of 10,000 transmigrant children if it meant eliminating the 100,000 potential refugee adults knocking at Britain's portals. By reversing its refugee policy, Great Britain effectively turned the tables on its truculent former colonies and their quota system. It was now America's turn to take action on the refugee problem.

Six months later, in the spring of 1939, during the hearings of the Wagner-Rogers Bill in the U.S. Congress, Britain received conclusive proof of how vain its hopes in that direction had been. The bill proposed that 20,000 European children under the age of fourteen be permitted to enter the United States during 1939–40 over and above the numbers stipulated by the immigration quotas.[44] Despite endorsements from the National Council of Churches, Herbert Hoover, Albert Einstein, the AFL, and the CIO, just to mention a few, there were those who during the hearings described potential refugee children as "thousands of motherless, embittered, persecuted foreigners" and "potential leaders of a revolt against our American form of Government."[45] The Bill was amended and in effect buried in Congress and an additional 20,000 children who could have been saved were consigned to remain in Germany.

Britain was naïve in assuming American compliance to the idea of admitting child refugee transmigrants. Although the bill stipulated that the children would be reunited with their parents as soon as conditions were safe, Americans could not conceive of the term *transmigrant*. Where would they transmigrate to? For over one hundred years America had been considered the country to which refugees gravitated. The physical distance between the American and European continents instilled a sense of isolation among Americans that fostered the generally correct assumption that any refugee coming to the United States was likely to stay there. In addition, many of the transmigrant children in Great Britain were actually en route to the United States, marking time until their American quota number would come up. Thus, the concept of America being a stepping stone to elsewhere was ludicrous to most Americans who could not conceive of the fact that an immigrant who had reached the United States would want to go elsewhere.

If the idea had been to build on the vocal protests of the three-and-a-half-million Jews in the United States regarding their German coreligionists, American Jewry remained particularly circumspect during the 1930s with regard to the refugee question. A combination of the economic depression and a rise in rabid antisemitism caused many Jews to feel that a public pro-refugee/anti-quota stance on their part would give antisemites an additional weapon to use against them. Furthermore, they were afraid of the added burden that a mass of immigrants would place upon the American Jewish community. Despite the return to the original immigration restriction in 1937 after additional limitations had been implemented since the early 1930s, all American Jewish leaders, with the exception of the Jewish Labor Committee, remained cautious with regard to the public position they took on the subject of the quotas.[46]

In retrospect, Britain gambled and lost. Its lead was taken up neither by the United States nor by any other nation. The only country that continued throughout the entire period to clamor for refugee children was Palestine—the one place which Britain would not permit them to enter.

While the Zionist organizations fumed at the British rejection of their proposals, the child-rescue organizations in Britain began putting together the necessary machinery to care for the children after their arrival in Britain. Obviously, none of the parties in question was aware that they were, in fact, saving the lives of almost 10,000 Jewish and "non-Aryan" (by Nazi definition) Christian children. For them, it was a matter of removing these children from social, legal, and economic persecution, with only peripheral recognition of issues such as maintaining their religious and national identity. At the time, "rescue" was from poverty and discrimination, not from torture and death. It was this same inability to imagine what the children's ultimate fate would have been that led David Ben-Gurion, the head of the Palestine Labor Zionists (Mapai), to state in 1939 that "if it were possible to save all the Jewish children in Germany by taking them to England but only half of them by taking them to Palestine," he would prefer the second possibility because it is not only the "account of these children but rather the historical account of the Jewish People."[47] However, the matter was not up to Ben-Gurion and the Jewish Agency, but rather to the Movement for the Care of Children from Germany, which was busy raising the funds necessary to guarantee the children's welfare and education during their stay in Britain.

Finances and Legalities

British government conditions presented to the organizations responsible for bringing the refugee children were a major factor that ultimately limited the total number of refugee children who would be permitted to enter the country. Children were allowed to enter on the understanding that the organization under whose auspices they were brought to Britain, in most cases the Movement for the Care of Children from Germany, would assume their financial responsibility until age eighteen. The organization would pay for any vocational training that the children would receive in Britain. Transmigrant children would be prohibited from entering the labor market, and it was expected that these children would emigrate at age eighteen or when their training was concluded.[48] Harsh as they may sound, we should bear in mind that these conditions were laid down in 1938, prior to the outbreak of war, at which time it was not considered a hardship for these children to have to re-emigrate, especially as some of them were eventually expected to join their parents in the United States or South America.

One of the first tasks facing the Movement was to prepare finances for the children's transfer, as it had assured the British government that it would meet all the aforementioned conditions.[49] Initially the funds used to guarantee the children's upkeep and welfare in Britain were raised from private contributions and a grant from the Lord Baldwin Fund (see chapter 4). However, at the end of February 1939 the Home Office insisted that sponsors put up a guarantee of £50 to cover the child's future re-emigration costs if he or she arrived after 1 March 1939. Should the child not re-emigrate for any reason, the guarantee would be returned to the guarantor.[50] Ultimately, the guarantee clause created an element of socioeconomic discrimination among the refugee children, because it gave preference to those from wealthy homes whose families usually had acquaintances or family in Britain who could afford to put up such a guarantee.

During a House of Commons debate on refugee financing in April 1939, refugee activist Josiah Wedgewood, scion of the famous pottery family and Labor MP for Newcastle-Under-Lyme, attacked the guarantee and emigration clauses. Basing his arguments on the humanitarian consideration, he declared that the sponsors of these children, especially orphan children, would eventually wish to adopt them to ensure having them nearby in their old age. This would become logistically impossible when the re-emigration clause would go into effect.[51] Another member of the House of Commons, Daniel Leopold Lipson, Independent Conservative MP from Cheltenham, afterwards publicly criticized the guarantee requirement, using national and demographic arguments. Emphasizing that by being educated in Great Britain the refugee children would be an asset for the nation, he reminded the public that these children would also augment the dwindling British population whose roots were to be found in Britain's low birth rate that was rapidly becoming a cause for concern.[52]

As a result of the furor over this clause, which in practice halted the children's transports for over a month, in April 1939 the Lord Baldwin Fund, created in December 1938 by former prime minister Stanley Earl Baldwin to assist the refugee children's scheme, agreed to pay the guarantee for children without sponsors and those whose sponsors could not afford to pay the sum. Bearing in mind that on 30 September 1938, fewer than 96,000 of the total British population of over 46,000,000, had an annual income of above £2,000, it becomes painfully obvious that a £50 guarantee represented no small sum for the average English family.[53]

The conditions set down by the Home Office were a deciding factor in policymaking for all organizations sponsoring the transfer of refugee children from the Reich and not only for the Refugee Children's Movement. At the time, the Chief Rabbi's Religious Emergency Council (CRREC) under the direction of Rabbi Solomon Schonfeld (see next chapter) was also involved with the rescue of Orthodox Jewish children from Germany and Austria to Great Britain. Having extremely limited financial backing, during this period the CRREC was forced to limit its activities mainly to rescuing children whose families could finance their fares of Britain.[54]

In addition to the financial undertaking, the Movement also dealt with the legalities of the children's transfer to Britain. While it was assumed that most of the children would re-emigrate at the age of 18, their legal position for the duration of their stay had to be examined and secured. Although most of the children were brought to Britain under the Movement's auspices, this organization was not their legal guardian. In fact, they had no legal guardian until Lord Gorell was appointed to this position in 1944 (see chapter 9).[55]

This lack of guardianship, combined with natural humanitarian emotions aroused by the large numbers of orphans arriving in the early transports, raised another issue connected to the children's legal status in Britain: the question of adoption. In February 1939, Home Secretary Hoare stated that the adoption of non-naturalized children was illegal.[56] Because minors could not be naturalized in Britain, Hoare's statement meant, de facto, that no refugee child could be adopted.[57] However, as the war progressed, and information was received about the fate of Jews in occupied Europe, it became obvious that large numbers of children who had left parents behind were now orphaned. Consequently, the adoption issue came under careful scrutiny and reexamination.

One of the first cases (perhaps the very first) to test this law was that of Ruth Hutman, who had come from Vienna as a child in 1938. During the war her foster parents received confirmation from the British Red Cross of her parents' death in Riga. Despite the difficulties involved, her foster parents decided to adopt her. In 1944, after an interview with Home Secretary Herbert Morrison, Hutman was allowed to be naturalized and legally adopted. At the time she was eleven years old.[58]

First Responses

Two important barometers in the Western world that are used to gauge responses to an issue are press coverage and public opinion polls. How did the British press and public opinion respond to the inauguration of the refugee child scheme? Child refugee transmigrants did not pose the same threat to Britain as did refugee adults. Being mostly of school age, there was no question of their ousting British citizens from their places of employment by providing a pool of inexpensive labor; as transmigrants, this German-speaking alien group would not glut the country permanently. As humanitarian and social activist Dorothy Frances Buxton (1881–1963) pointed out, the children coming to Britain were consumers; their needs required services and production, to be paid for from private sources and not the taxpayers' pocket. "The children have to be fed and clothed and housed and warmed and the production of the food, clothing and fuel keeps someone in employment," wrote the wife of Labor MP Charles Roden Buxton, "just as much as the production of shells or armour plate for which we so readily tax ourselves gives employment."[59]

These and other arguments combined with Lord Samuel's emotion-filled appeal to the public to find homes for the refugee children were pivotal in firmly veering public opinion toward supporting the British government's decision to permit the entry of transmigrant refugee children.[60] As the scheme was private, based on the generosity of individuals, and the children were not to be in England permanently, the average Englishman could not be offended, from economic, patriotic, or humanitarian standpoints.

Among the few voices that publicly criticized the scheme was a letter to the editor of the *London Times* expressing a variation of the nationalist ethnic trend that was slowly making itself felt throughout the world. Referring to the fear of the falling birth rate in Britain, the writer stated that if British families would sponsor a refugee children in their home, it would lead to an even more diminished birth rate in that family for obvious economic reasons. The writer was horrified that British MPs could therefore propose such a scheme. "Can it be that the preservation of the island race means nothing to the Government?" the writer concluded.[61]

Apart from this aberration, no negative criticism of the program to aid child refugees appeared in either of the two major London dailies, the independent *London Times* and the Labour-oriented *Daily Herald*. A similarly positive attitude was exhibited by the most widely circulated Anglo-Jewish weekly, the *Jewish Chronicle*.[62] However, negative criticism did point to the meagerness of the entire refugee aid scheme proposed, not specifically to the treatment of children, and was published in the *London Times*, the *Manchester Guardian*, and the *Daily Herald*. Lord Beaverbrook's paper, the *Daily Express*, took a severely anti-refugee position, as did the Rothmere Press of the time—the *Daily Mail*, the *Sunday Dispatch*, and the *Evening Standard*.[63] And in the spirit of religious particularism, the *Catholic Herald* tacitly mentioned the fact that the Catholics would prefer not to assist refugees who did not practice the Catholic faith.[64]

All the papers surveyed reported, as a matter of course, either on the parliamentary debate on refugees during which the scheme was announced or on the scheme itself.[65] It was not surprising that the *Jewish Chronicle* devoted more space to the child refugee problem than did any other paper.[66] Apart from the parliamentary debate coverage, during the week following the debate the *Daily Herald* published several human-interest articles on families in Europe willing to part with their children in order to send them to safety in Britain. The scheme was regarded in a favorable light and readers were urged to sponsor a refugee child if their finances permitted.[67] Similar to the *Daily Herald*, the *London Times* also reported on the scheme, including Lord Samuel's appeal for homes and an editorial making the connection between this scheme and the *Yishuv*'s proposal to adopt 5,000 Jewish refugee children.[68] The similarity between the two papers, however, ended there.

Throughout the entire period during which the refugee child scheme was introduced to the British public, no positive statement, editorial or otherwise, was published by the *Times* with regard to the scheme of sponsoring refugee children. The refugee problem in general was greatly played down by this paper in comparison to its coverage in either the *Jewish Chronicle* or the *Daily Herald*. Although in most papers other than the *Jewish Chronicle* the refugee issue ranked far behind sports, local events, and human-interest stories, the absence of any positive editorial message on the entire refugee subject in the *Times* is striking. Was it an editorial decision to play down the topic in response to the claims that the paper had pro-Jewish leanings? Eighteen months earlier, in a letter to *Times* editor Geoffrey Dawson, their temporary Berlin correspondent H. G. Daniels had written "the German Press has been savage about the Times, in fact worse than at any period I remember. The latest discovery is that if you spell it backwards it spells SEMIT, which leads them to deduce that we are a Jewish-Marxist organization and that nothing else can be expected of us."[69] Other than news coverage of the child refugee debates, no editorials dealt with the topic and even few human-interest stories were devoted to the topic of child refugees.[70]

In the long run, the child refugee scheme was basically considered a Jewish issue and was therefore only found newsworthy on a continuous basis by the *Jewish Chronicle*, which featured articles about and appeals for the children throughout 1939. Ultimately, however, the evacuation of British children from major cities with the outbreak of war pushed the refugee child issue into obscurity even in the *Jewish Chronicle*. Consequently, during the five-and-a-half years of war, the paper carried only thirty-seven articles in total that dealt with various aspects of the refugee children's issue.

Although both the press and public opinion played significant roles in pressuring the British government to alter its refugee policy in November 1938, leading to the decision to permit entry to privately sponsored transmigrant children, apart from documenting the children's arrival in England, little else appeared about them in the press. Only in one other case, about the swing of public opinion and the press against internment in July 1940 (see chapter 8), did these two forces exert sufficient pressure to cause a reversal of previously stated government policy. Apart from these two exceptional cases, it appears that the British press and public opinion played little role in shaping British government policy on refugees.

First Steps

Before bringing the first group of children to England, the refugee organizations decided to assess the general situation of refugee children in the Netherlands, and of potential refugee children in Germany and Austria. Simultaneously, they alerted individuals and organizations in Europe dealing with refugees to begin preparations to transfer the children overland to a friendly port. On 25 November 1938, four days after the Home Office announcement, refugee activist Prof. Norman Bentwich traveled to the Netherlands to meet with Prof. David Cohen, head of the Dutch Refugees' Committee, to discuss the children's travel arrangements. As a result of what he learned during this meeting, Bentwich decided that few of the cases of children already in the Netherlands were urgent, but that it was imperative to begin bringing children out of Germany, Austria, and Czechoslovakia, as German Jewish children were already illegally crossing the border to Holland in an attempt to reach a safe haven.

A week later, Bentwich met with Gertruida Wijsmuller-Meijer, a Dutch Christian long active in the refugee cause, to lay the logistical groundwork for the rescue operation. Immediately following this meeting, Wijsmuller-Meijer left for Austria to arrange for the first group of six hundred children to leave for the Netherlands. Following a meeting with Adolf Eichmann on Monday, 5 December 1938, she received permission for the group to leave Austria. Five hundred of them would eventually sail for England on the *De Praag*.[71] Although this policy was unknown outside the circle of Nazi leaders, following *Kristallnacht* a decision had been made to consolidate the "Jewish question" in the hands of the SS, who were interested in using all avenues available to have Jews leave Europe as soon as possible. In retrospect, Eichmann's decision should be viewed in the light of this change in Nazi policy regarding Jews.

The English press reported that in keeping with the Dutch tradition of offering asylum to refugees from religious and racial persecution, the Dutch prime minister, Dr. Hendrikus Colijn, had announced that his country would be willing to serve as a temporary refuge for children and transmigrants. Although the British press published only a small portion of Colijn's statement, making it sound as if he were opening Holland's doors to refugees in general, which indeed he was not, the arrangement of transferring refugee children via Holland actually took form as the Anglo-Jewish refugee organizations indeed felt that the best route for bringing children out of Germany and Austria was via the Netherlands.[72]

The next step required direct contact with Jewish social welfare organizations in Germany and Austria. For this purpose, Mr. and Mrs. Dennis Cohen, active members of the emigration department of the Jewish Refugees' Committee, traveled to Berlin and Vienna on behalf of the Movement for the Care of Children from Germany. Upon arrival, they contacted the German government and the central Jewish organizations that would be responsible for choosing the children—the *Reichsvertretung* in Germany and the Vienna *Kultusgemeinde* in

Austria. A formal procedure was agreed upon with these organizations and the first transports were arranged.

Thus, the first steps toward bringing almost 10,000 children to Great Britain were taken. Bentwich and the Cohens' trip to the continent laid the basis for the children's transports, which would soon be crossing the border from Germany and Austria to the Netherlands at least twice a week. The Anglo-Jewish refugee organizations enthusiastically engaged in the task of bringing over as many children as was possible under the conditions set down by the British government; so enthusiastically, it seems, that at one time five different Jewish refugee organizations, not to mention various non-Jewish and nonsectarian ones, dealt with the same project.[73]

This proliferation of organizations led to confusion: confusion on the part of the British government, the concerned British gentiles, British Jewry, and the refugees themselves. In the next chapter I will attempt to make order out of what was, at various times, organizational chaos and examine these organizations and the machinery that was created to deal with the child refugee problem.

Notes

1. *Movement for the Care of Children from Germany, Ltd. First Annual Report*, 3.
2. *The Jewish Chronicle*, 16 September 1938, 25.
3. *The Jewish Chronicle*, 25 November 1938, 36. For a summary of the aftermath of *Kristallnacht* and the reaction abroad, see Kochan, *Pogrom, 10 November 1938*; Kley, "Hitler and the Pogrom of November 9–10, 1938," 87–112; Bartrop, "Not a Problem for Australia," 489–99.
4. Fox, *My Heart in a Suitcase*, 40–41.
5. Harris and Oppenheimer, *Into the Arms of Strangers*, 65.
6. Ibid., 63.
7. Ibid., 68.
8. Ibid., 74.
9. Schwartz interview.
10. Margaliot, "The Problem of the Rescue of German Jewry," 247–65.
11. Roosevelt press conference, 18 November 1938, described in Schewe, ed., *Franklin D. Roosevelt*, document 1418.
12. Wischnitzer, *To Dwell in Safety*, 200; Bauer, *My Brother's Keeper*, 273; Tartakower and Grossman, *The Jewish Refugee*, 220, 298, 307, 309, 470, 485; Castendyck, "Refugee Children in Europe," 592–96; Barnard, *The Children You Gave Us*, 97; 124.
13. Shepherd, *Wilfred Israel*, 146.
14. Samuel was accompanied by the chief rabbi, Dr. J. H. Hertz, Viscount Bearsted, Lionel de Rothschild, Neville Laski, and Chaim Weizmann. Samuel, *Memoirs*, 255.
15. Samuel to Chamberlain, record of meeting, 15 November 1938 PRO PREM 1/326. Minutes of the Executive Committee of the Council for German Jewry, 17 November 1938, Central British Fund Archives, the Wiener Library Microfilm document collection 21/1/20. G. C. L. Syers to H. E. Brooks, G. H. Creasy, Pimlott, E. E. Bridges, Makins, 16 November 1938, PRO PREM 1/326.
16. Gilbert and Gott, *The Appeasers*, 51.

17. See Cabinet Conclusions 55(38), 16 Nov. 1938, CAB 23/96.
18. The Aliens Restriction Act 1914 in STATUTES (The Public General Acts and the Church Assembly Measures) LII, 256–57 and the Aliens Restriction (Amendment) Act 1919 in STATUTES LVII, 347–51.
19. Sherman, *Island Refuge*, Appendix 2, 273.
20. Baumel, "The Adoption Plan of Children," 212–29.
21. Record of meeting by Prime Minister's Private Secretary 16 November 1938, FO 371/22536, W 15037/104/98; Telegram sent by Tel Aviv mayor Israel Rokeach to British Colonial Secretary Malcolm McDonald, quoted in *Ha'aretz*, 21 November 1938, 1.
22. 342 HC Deb. 1975–6 (14 December 1938).
23. Welles, memorandum, 17 November 1938, FRUS diplomatic papers, general: 1938 I (Washington: U.S. Government Printing Office, 1938), 829–31.
24. See Lord Halifax's closing remarks at the 16 November cabinet meeting, record of meeting by Prime Minister's Private Secretary 16 November 1938, FO 371/22536, W 15037/104/98.
25. Minutes of the Executive Committee of the Council for German Jewry, 17 November 1938, Central British Fund Archives, the Wiener Library Microfilm document collection 21/1/20.
26. Adler-Rudel, Oral History Division (henceforth: OHD), 17(27), The Institute for Contemporary Jewry, The Hebrew University of Jerusalem.
27. Bentwich, *They Found Refuge*, 65.
28. Gottlieb, *Men of Vision*, 102.
29. Ibid.
30. FO 371/24085 XC/146099. Green was one of the five members of the Society of Friends who had been asked by Wilfred Israel to come to Berlin to work alongside Jewish welfare workers. Bailey, *A Quaker Couple*, 95.
31. 341 HC Deb. 1313–1317 (21 November 1938).
32. 341 HC Deb. 1474 (21 November 1938).
33. Wilson, *They Came as Strangers*, 22. According to Roche, 4,000 Spanish orphans entered Britain; Roche, *The Key in the Lock*, 123.
34. Graves and Hodge, *The Long Weekend*, 415.
35. Simpson, *Refugees*, 76.
36. 341 HC Deb. 1473 (21 November 1938).
37. 341 HC Deb. 1734 (23 November 1938); 341 HC Deb. 1930 (24 November 1938).
38. 341 HC Deb. 1474 (21 November 1938).
39. London, *Whitehall and the Jews*, 109–113.
40. Cabinet meeting, record of meeting by Prime Minister's Private Secretary 16 November 1938, FO 371/22536, W 15037/104/98.
41. See, for example, David Ben-Gurion's statements at a meeting of the Mapai (Labor Party) Center in Palestine, 7 December 1938. Labor Party Archives, 38/23, 41, Beit Berl; Yoav Gelber, "Zionist Policy," 199; Hurewitz, *The Struggle for Palestine*, 96; Yahil, "The Wanderings of the Jews from Germany, Austria and Czechoslovakia," 112–13.
42. *The London Times*, 25 November 1938, 11.
43. See Baumel, *Unfulfilled Promise*, 15–16.
44. Subcommittee of the committee on Immigration of the Senate and House of Representatives, *Admission of German Refugee Children, 20 April 1939 and 24 April 1939*, Washington, D.C. 1939, 3.

45. Feingold, *The Politics of Rescue*, 149; Morse, *While Six Million Died*, 212–19; Szajkowski, "The Attitude of American Jewry," 109; Baumel, *Unfulfilled Promise*, 25–36.
46. The majority of American Jewish activity at the time was outwardly directed (e.g., boycotting German goods) rather than inwardly directed (changing immigration regulations). Brody, "American Jewry," 339–44.
47. Ben-Gurion's speech at the meeting of the Mapai Center, 7 December 1938 (Labor Party Archives, 38/23, Beit Berl).
48. *Movement*, 3; Bentwich, *They Found Refuge*, 68; *The Jewish Chronicle*, 2 December 1938, 20; Lafitte, *The Internment of Aliens*.
49. *Movement*, 3, 16.
50. *The Jewish Chronicle*, 14 April 1939, 17; *Bulletin of the Co-ordinating Committee for Refugees*, April 1939 (London 1939): 7.
51. *The Jewish Chronicle* 14 April 1939, 15; Wedgewood, *The Last of the Radicals*, 230.
52. *The Jewish Chronicle*, 14 April 1939, 16. Population studies made in the 1930s foresaw a heavy population decline in Britain. According to the most hopeful prognosis, the sharp decline would begin in 1949 (population 40,876,000). By 2035 the population would be 19,969,000. The least hopeful prognosis had the decline beginning in 1940 and foresaw a population of 4,426,000 in 2035. (In actuality, by mid-2010 the British population was 61,213,000.) Mowat, *Britain between the Wars*, 519; Angell and Buxton, *You and the Refugee*, 184–205.
53. *Whittaker's Almanach*, 231. It was generally estimated that, during the 1930s, 15–30 percent of the British were poverty-stricken or nearly so. Around 17 percent had no savings. For most working-class families, the purchase of clothes or shoes meant taking credit or a loan. Mowat, *Britain between the Wars*, 499.
54. Interview with Henry Pels, OHD, 35(27).
55. Presland, *A Great Adventure*, 16.
56. *The Jewish Chronicle*, 17 February 1939, 22.
57. This was based on the Adoption of Children Act 1926 (England and Wales) and Adopting of Children Act (Scotland) 1930; in both of them, Section 2, clause 5 states that "an adoption order shall not be made . . . in respect of any infant who is not a British subject and so resident."
58. Author's interview with Lillian Klein, foster mother of Ruth Hutman, Tel Aviv, 22 January 1980 (henceforth: Klein interview).
59. Buxton, *The Economics of the Refugee Problem*, 7.
60. *The London Times*, 25 November 1938, 11
61. *The London Times*, 28 November 1938, 10.
62. The Jewish Chronicle circulation was 20,000 before the Second World War. Bermant, *Troubled Eden*, 160.
63. Sharf, *The British Press*, 207.
64. Shamir, *Before the Holocaust*, 293–94; 302–304.
65. For example, *The London Times*, 22 November 1938, 8; *The Daily Herald*, 23 November 1938, 9; *The Jewish Chronicle*, 25 November 1938, 32.
66. In one issue alone, that of 25 November 1938, the paper carried a total of four full or partial pages including several appeals to sponsor refugee children (30, 31, 32, 36).
67. *The Daily Herald*, 23 November 1938, 9–10.
68. *The London Times*, 23 November 1938, 16; 25 November 1938, 15.
69. Daniels to Dawson, 16 May 1937, quoted in Gannon, *The British Press and Germany*, 116.

70. For example, *The London Times*, 3 December 1938, 14.
71. Wijsmuller-Meijer, Wiener Library Series 02/626. The dates of the various memoirs become very confusing at this point. Bentwich, in *My 77 Years*, 158 and in *Wanderers between Two Worlds*, 283, states that within two days of his return to England, which was immediately following the Home Office announcement of 21 November 1938, he flew to the Netherlands to meet with members of the Dutch Refugees' Committee. *Movement*, 4, corroborates these dates but goes on to state that Bentwich returned to England on 26 November. As for Mrs. Wijsmuller, she recalls having met with Bentwich, Prof. Cohen, Mrs. van Tijn, and important Dutch bankers on 2 December 1938 (Wiener Library Series 02/626). In view of the fact that the first group from Germany was already preparing to cross the border on the night of 1 December 1938, and that logistical arrangements had to be made for the group several days in advance, it is implausible that Bentwich could have made only one trip to Holland around 2 December 1938.
72. *The Jewish Chronicle*, 25 November 1938, 36.
73. *The Jewish Chronicle*, 16 December 1938, 28. The Children's Inter-Aid Committee, B'nai Brith Council for Refugee Children, The Women's Appeal Committee, the Movement for the Care of Children from Germany, and the Chief Rabbi's Religious Emergency Council. This last organization was not listed in the aforementioned article.

Chapter 4

Machinery

Introduction

"Organization will not just 'evolve.' The only things that evolve by themselves in an organization are disorder, friction and malperformance," wrote the Austrian-born professor of management, Peter F. Drucker, who found refuge in England as a young man in 1933.[1] The groups and individuals who were responsible for creating and running the organizational machinery that dealt with the refugee children from the Reich were well aware of the risks of letting organizations "evolve" and therefore did their utmost to make sure that each organization would be run according to suitable standards. What they could not do, however, was set coordinating guidelines that would act as a framework for all the organizations that dealt with the child refugee issue and delineate their bureaucratic, government-related, financial, organizational, and social welfare responsibilities in a way that would avoid overlap and organizational obfuscation. The result was a group of well-meaning organizations that often overrode each other in various matters, creating just what Drucker warned about—disorder, friction and malperformance—all stemming from the best of intentions.

The Child Refugee Organizations

By January 1939, the refugee organizations were enthusiastically engaged in bringing over as many children from the Third Reich as was possible under the conditions set down by the British government—so enthusiastically that at one time five different organizations were dealing with the same project: the B'nai Brith Council for Refugee Children; the Children's Inter-Aid Committee, which never officially disbanded; its successor, the Movement for the Care of Children from Germany; the Women's Appeal Committee; and the Chief Rabbi's Religious Emergency Council.[2] This proliferation of organizations led to confusion and even after the merger of Inter-aid with the Movement, there was still a large amount of overlap between the various organizations.

The B'nai Brith, a Jewish fraternal and service organization, had been dealing with refugee children even before *Kristallnacht* and worked together with Inter-Aid until Inter-Aid merged with the Movement for the Care of Children from Germany.[3] As it was primarily involved in the placement of refugee children after their arrival, B'nai Brith maintained hostels in the London area for that purpose. When the war broke out in September 1939, the organization had a total of 891 children under its care—416 children in these hostels, 85 in subsidized foster homes, and 390 who were living with unsubsidized foster families or their guarantors.[4]

The Children's Inter-Aid Committee, or Inter-Aid as it was popularly referred to, was the major refugee children's organization existing prior to *Kristallnacht*. Under the chairmanship of retired Brigadier General Sir Wyndham Deedes, it united representatives of both Jewish and Christian organizations in the first nonsectarian refugee children's organization in Britain. As such, it was authorized by the Home Office to issue the travel document that took the place of a passport and visa for the young transmigrants. Inter-aid dealt with both Jewish and "non-Aryan" Christian children from Germany and Austria, bringing them to Britain and supervising their placement. The organization was supported by donations from synagogues, private contributions, and funds collected by the Women's Appeal for German and Austrian Women and Children.[5]

Although B'nai Brith and the Inter-Aid committee were the initial existing organizations dealing with refugee children, it is the case that new policies often require new organizations to meet new challenges. At times the challenges are such that the previously existing organizations fall short in their abilities to meet them. In some cases there is already an existing power play; an organizational change enables a new group of activists to come to the fore. In others, the protagonists remain the same but the machinery needs overhauling and the changes allow a new broom to sweep out bureaucratic debris that would bog down the initiative.

In the case of the refugee child scheme, there appears to have been a combination of all the above factors. As none of the organizations would have been able to cope with the numbers of potential refugee children that were mentioned, and large sums of money would be necessary to carry out the scheme, leaders in the refugee cause thought it prudent to broaden the new organization's power base and bring in representatives of a number of groups that would be involved in raising funds for the children's operation and dealing with their resettlement and care. At the same time, they realized that it would be necessary to develop the bureaucratic machinery that could oversee not only the children's transfer but also their placement and supervise their aftercare. Consequently, shortly after the

British government's decision to allow the entry of refugee children from greater Germany, a number of activists in the refugee cause banded together to create a new organization that would take over the bulk of the work involved in dealing with the child refugees, the Movement for the Care for Children from Germany.

On 22 November 1938, the Movement held its first official meeting in the London offices of the Save the Children Fund, whence a number of its founding members had originated. At its inception the Movement, jointly chaired by Lord Samuel and Sir Wyndman Deedes and known originally as the British Movement for the Care of Children, officially amalgamated with Inter-Aid and began the first of several name changes. Initially it was known as the World Movement for the Rescue of Children from Germany; British Inter-Aid Committee, which was too much of a mouthful for daily use and was soon shortened to the Movement for the Care of Children from Germany. In April 1939 it was incorporated and in July was officially renamed the Refugee Children's Movement (RCM), the name by which it was known throughout the war years.[6]

As in the case of many nonsectarian refugee organizations in Britain and the United States, the RCM was not directed by Jewish refugee activists; instead, its board chair was the poet Lord Gorell (Robert Barnes; 1884–1963), editor of *The Cornhill* magazine, a former minister of the Crown, soldier, and educator, who was asked by the Archbishop of Canterbury to assume this task. As Haim Genizi has pointed out in his study of the plight of refugees from Nazism, the reasons for such moves in the case of most nonsectarian refugee organizations were fear of antisemitism, desire for a broader power and popular base than would be possible if the organization were headed by Jews, and the hope that such a move would attract financial supporters and political adherents from various sectors.[7] For the same reasons, another non-Jew, a retired Indian civil servant named Sir Charles Stead, was appointed as the RCM's paid executive director in March 1939. Unhappy with the post, Stead resigned suddenly when the war began and was succeeded by the movement's general secretary, Dorothy Hardisty, who unofficially filled the post of executive director throughout the war years.[8]

Hardisty is a prime example of the often overlooked but invaluable contribution of women to the success of the Kindertransport scheme.[9] In the minutes of meetings of the RCM's executive committee her name appears again and again in various capacities, with her reports about meeting children, committee members, visiting hostels, dealing with religious leaders, giving particulars about numerous schemes, and following children throughout the war years.[10] However, other than mentioning her name and position, neither the official documents of the RCM nor any historical accounts of that period provide any background about the woman who almost singlehandedly kept the RCM together at various junctures.[11]

Who indeed was Dorothy Hardisty? A graduate of Manchester University, she was a sixty-year-old recently widowed civil servant when she took the position of general secretary of the RCM. Having years of experience in the Department of Labor and specializing in youth employment, she now had to work full time in order to pay for her young stepson's medical training. Hardisty had a remarkable memory for names and faces; she kept a file on every child in the RCM and pushed the regional committees to try to understand the children's actions, and especially emotional disturbances, from the perspective of the young people who had undergone persecution, uprooting, and transplanting.[12] Together with Lord Gorell, she often found herself dealing with the critics of the RCM, whether Orthodox organizations who fought the movement for having placed Jewish children in non-Jewish homes, or British non-Jewish critics who could not understand why refugee children would be given advantages over British unemployed youth.

While Hardisty earned a small salary for her labors, other active members were in fact volunteers. Lola Hahn-Warburg (1901–89), who represented the Children's and Youth Aliyah Movement, and Elaine Laski (Blond), representing WIZO, were a pivotal part of the RCM. Both from famous families active in the refugee cause, Hahn-Warburg and Laski were untiring women who ensured that groups arriving in England would be met, and they coordinated the Central Committee. Like Hardisty, these women played a vital role in the smooth running of the organization.

Hahn-Warburg was the oldest daughter of international banker Max Warburg and a sister-in-law of educator Kurt Hahn, founder of the elite Gordonstoun School in Scotland (see chapter 2). Hahn-Warburg had been driven out of Germany in 1938 and understood firsthand how it felt to be a refugee.[13] A unique and energetic young woman and mother of two, she left a deep impression on others. As one of the *Kinder* who arrived in London from Czechoslovakia at age fourteen recalled:

> As I stepped off the train, walking laboriously with the aid of two canes, I spotted the first truly beautiful and elegant woman I saw in my then short life. She was tall, slender, engaged in animated conversation with a tall, pipe-smoking man. When they spotted me, the only child using canes, they rushed toward me and welcomed me. I used canes because Nazi goons fractured my right leg in a refugee camp in central Moravia. The beautiful lady introduced herself as Lola Hahn-Warburg. Her speech was forceful and energetic. She seemed to be in charge of arrangements for the arriving children. Whenever I describe this extraordinary lady . . . I enjoy saying "Had she been born a man, she could have commanded the invasion of Europe on D-Day, June 6, 1944 instead of and just as successful as General Dwight D. Eisenhower did."[14]

Elaine Laski Blond, youngest daughter of the founder of Marks and Spencer, was another full-time volunteer at the RCM who divided her time between meeting the children's transports and checking out prospective foster parents.[15] A member of the "Cousinhood" from all directions, Laski Blond, who was described at her memorial service as "a difficult woman," was "never dull," as her stepson Anthony Blond writes, but rather "autocratic, intelligent and learned."[16] Already separated from her first husband Norman Laski and about to move in with his cousin, Bernard Blond, whom she later married in 1944, Elaine Laski's passionate personal life did not impinge on the time and effort that she continuously devoted to the child refugee cause. Her private life did, however, along with her Liberal Jewish status, affect her relationship with Orthodox Jewish refugee child activists such as Rabbi Schonfeld and Harry Goodman, whom she viewed as fanatics and often clashed with over the issue of transferring Jewish children out of non-Jewish foster homes.[17]

Every organization is only as good as its organizers and members, and every piece of bureaucratic machinery is only as efficient as its workers and volunteers. Hardisty, Hahn-Warburg, and Laski are all examples of women without whom the refugee children's scheme could never have taken off, or continued to exist during the war years. All were middle-aged women with a modicum of background in children's affairs; all devoted a tremendous amount of time to the day-to-day issues of the children's rescue scheme. Hahn-Warburg and Laski were often the first RCM workers, or in this case volunteers, whom the children met upon reaching Britain. Hardisty was familiar with the case files of thousands of children which she had personally opened, and knew many by name. And yet, in the public eye the rescue scheme was usually associated with the names of the men behind it: Lord Samuel, Norman Bentwich, and Lord Gorell. This was typical of many social welfare, educational, or health organizations throughout the Western world, whose figureheads were men while their major activists and daily volunteers were women. The few exceptions were organizations whose figureheads were female members of the nobility or wives of heads of State. Only some thirty years later with the rise of the women's movement would this situation begin to change, at which time women were considered prominent enough figures to use their names to attract members and confer respectability on movements and organizations.[18]

Although the majority of the refugee children rescued through the RCM were Jewish, the organization was nevertheless nonsectarian. Its Central Committee included members from across the spectrum of society: Jews, nonconformists, Roman Catholics, and members of the Church of England.[19] This committee was responsible for meeting the children upon their arrival, helped set up the transit camps to which many were taken, informed the local committees of the time of the children's arrival, and periodically inspected the children's accommodations, whether private homes or hostels. In addition to guaranteeing to the Home Office that the children would not become public charges, it kept a card file on each child with personal data and notes on his or her health, education, and welfare.[20]

While the Central Committee was responsible for the initial steps that the refugee children took in Britain, the local committees received them during their resettlement. As early as November 1938, local committees were set up in

Manchester, Birmingham, Bristol, Cambridge, and Battersea, staffed by volunteers and members of the Jewish Refugees Committee.[21] As greater numbers of children reached Britain throughout 1939, the RCM was forced to decentralize and establish more local committees that took over many of the day-to-day tasks. In addition, the local branches found homes for nonguaranteed children, supervised children in foster homes and hostels, arranged for schooling with the local education committees, set up religious education, by correspondence if necessary, and arranged for teenage vocational training. A list of provincial committees in Great Britain, compiled sometime after the outbreak of the war, shows 65 committees in 45 places in England, Wales, Scotland, Northern Ireland, and the Irish Free State. Many areas had both Jewish and non-Jewish committees; in areas with only one committee, subcommittees were established to organize the children's religious education. At the height of its activity, the RCM included a total of 175 local committees throughout Great Britain and Ireland.[22]

A fourth refugee children's organization, the Women's Appeal Committee, was independently run and dealt mainly with fund raising and placement of children. Functioning financially under the auspices of the Council for German Jewry, between 1936 and 1939 the Committee raised more than £250,000, which was used to finance the expenses of child refugees.[23]

The last of the organizations that dealt with refugee children was the Chief Rabbi's Religious Emergency Council (CRREC). Unlike the other refugee organizations, this group basically concerned itself with only one sector, Orthodox and ultra-Orthodox child refugees from Central Europe. Initially, the organization that assisted Orthodox Jewish refugees immigrating to Britain had been the Emigration Advisory Council of Agudath Israel, a political branch of the ultra-Orthodox anti-Zionist Agudath Israel World Movement, or in short, the "Agudah." However, by early 1938 and certainly after the Austrian *Anschluss*, it became obvious to Rabbi Jacob Rosenheim (1870–1965), head of the Agudath Israel movement, that the London-based offices were incapable of dealing with the potential masses of Orthodox refugees. He therefore recommended that a separate organization be created under the auspices of the Chief Rabbi to deal with this matter, in order to enable the Agudah to concentrate on its other work. After consulting with Viscount Samuel, Agudath Israel's British secretary Harry Goodman (1898–1961) and Dayan (religious judge) Isidore Grunfeld (1900–75), Rosenheim set into motion the bureaucracy that would lead to the creation of the new organization.

In mid-1938, the Chief Rabbi's Religious Emergency Fund was created under the auspices of the Chief Rabbi of Britain, and was rapidly renamed the Chief Rabbi's Religious Emergency Council. Although not intended to become one, the CRREC, which employed between ten and fifteen paid workers, ultimately turned into a conglomerate and a contradiction in itself. While Chief Rabbi Hertz was the nominal head of the CRREC, its executive director and the man who personally oversaw most of its rescue-and-relief efforts was the ultra-Orthodox Rabbi Solomon Schonfeld, an ideological although not official adherent of the Agudath Israel movement. Potential friction between Hertz and Schonfeld stemming from the differences in their organizational allegiance was delicately sidestepped especially after Schoenfeld married Hertz's daughter Judith on New Years Day 1940. In time, Schonfeld actually found himself acting as a bridge between the two groups that supported the CRREC's efforts: members of the United Synagogue and adherents of Rabbi Hertz, and those belonging to the more observant Union of Orthodox Hebrew Congregations, some of whom were Agudath Israel rescue activists, the most vocal of which was Harry Goodman, the British secretary of the Agudath Israel World Organization and the publisher and editor of the *Jewish Weekly*.[24]

How did the Agudist-leaning Schonfeld find himself in the position of representing the Modern Orthodox Chief Rabbi in an organization that leaned heavily toward cooperation with ultra-Orthodox Agudath Israel activists in both Britain and Continental Europe? Schonfeld's personal biography sheds some light on his connections with both groups. As a British-born son of Hungarian parents, during the early 1930s he had followed the path of many children of ultra-Orthodox immigrants with financial resources who were sent to Eastern European yeshivas to continue their religious studies. Schonfeld was initially sent to yeshiva in Nitra, Slovakia, where he studied under Rabbi Michel Dov Ber Weissmandel (1903–57), and then to Slobodka where he received rabbinical ordination and simultaneously obtained his doctorate from the University of Koenigsberg. While studying at Nitra, Schonfeld was greatly influenced by Weissmandel and became an Agudist sympathizer identifying ideologically with the movement.

Nevertheless, after returning to Britain following his father's death and taking his place as principal of the Jewish Secondary Schools, he had to make a practical decision based on finances and not on personal inclination. Now that he headed a Jewish school movement, he could not afford to limit his financial support solely to the Agudah circles. And as most of the Modern Orthodox synagogues were more oriented toward the Religious-Zionist political group the Mizrachi, Schonfeld found it prudent to keep from being labeled an Agudist. He therefore refrained from becoming an official member of the Agudath Israel movement, while at the same time continuing to cooperate with its members and receive financial aid from them for his schools. Simultaneously, he began his cooperation with the United Synagogue in order to request financial assistance from its members for his educational institutions. This cooperation sowed the seeds for his eventual cooperation with the Chief Rabbi, leader of the United Synagogue movement, in his rescue activities.[25]

As a rescue activist, Schonfeld was a consummate politician and pragmatist, knowing how and when to bend before government pressure or to manipulate bureaucratic situations to his advantage, but also when to stand fast on an issue, even when it meant not taking a stand. Just as he had refrained from becoming an official member of the Agudah in order not to alienate potential Orthodox supporters for his schools who were Mizrachi sympathizers, during the war years the CRREC took no position on Zionist issues, as it was jointly supported by the religious-Zionist Mizrachi organization and the anti-Zionist Agudath Israel. Here, too, Schonfeld saw removing what could be a volatile bone of contention as one of the ways of ensuring cooperation between groups with diametrically opposed positions on a central issue in the Jewish world. His goal was not to further the political issues of either of his major supporting political groups but to ensure the CRREC's success in the field of rescue, and later to strengthen its religious activities among Jewish children, both refugee and British, after their evacuation.

This, however, was long in the future. The CRREC had initially been created to provide kosher food for Jewish hospitals and orphanages in Germany via the Chief Rabbi's Emergency Fund. Immediately after *Kristallnacht*, when these activities were curtailed, the CRREC began to concentrate on a number of new ventures, many of which were connected to ameliorating the plight of Jewish children in Central Europe.[26]

One of these ventures involved bringing religious German and Austrian children to England. Bypassing the existing child refugee organizations, the CRREC's secretary, Henry Pels, received lists of urgent cases from Germany and negotiated with the Home Office for entry permits. Unlike the RCM, which tried to bring over only guaranteed children and later had a blanket guarantee given to them by the Home Office, the CRREC brought over children who did not always have guarantors and was therefore responsible for them. In view of the CRREC's financial status, which did not enable it to pay for both the children's guarantees and their fares, its policy was to deal almost exclusively with children whose families could finance their fares.[27]

Another group of children whom Schonfeld brought to Britain came from Austria through lists compiled by the CRREC's contact person in Vienna, the head of the Vienna branch of Agudath Israel, Julius Steinfeld (1884–1974), known as the "*shtadlan* [interceder, advocate] from Vienna." Like Schonfeld, Steinfeld was of Hungarian descent and similar in personality to the British rescue activist who brazenly negotiated with the authorities to obtain entry visas. In this case, however, the authorities in question were not His Majesty's officials but Nazi leaders including Adolf Eichmann who even incarcerated Steinfeld once when he appeared to overstep his bounds. Learning of the plight of Orthodox Jewish children in Vienna, Rabbi Weissmandel of Nitra suggested to Steinfeld that he should put together a children's transport. As Steinfeld was acquainted with Schonfeld's Viennese family, he telephoned Weissmandel's former student in London shortly after *Kristallnacht* with his list in the hope of obtaining assistance. Children's groups leaving Austria were being selected by the Jewish community offices in Vienna, the Vienna *Kultusgemeinde*, which was ignoring Orthodox children. Schonfeld, already working on rescuing a group of German rabbis and scholars with their families, stepped up to the challenge. Calling a meeting with Rabbi Jacob Rosenheim and Harry Goodman, Schonfeld made his way to Vienna the following day and met with Steinfeld. Taking Steinfeld's list compiled from names of children from Agudah families belonging to the Viennese synagogue, the Schiffschul, Schonfeld returned to Britain and negotiated directly with the Home Office in order to allow in transports of children. They began to arrive from Germany and Austria in December 1938.[28]

The method used by the CRREC to choose and bring over refugee children to Britain was different from that employed by the RCM. As a rule, individual cases were not handled. Lists of children were forwarded to London by Agudath Israel communities or by Steinfeld, who acted as the official CRREC representative in Vienna. Once the names were received, CRREC representatives in London would arrange for the children's visas and their transportation. Although it worked independently from the RCM, the CRREC had to follow the same criteria and therefore established its own Children's Department headed by Judith Hertz, daughter of the Chief Rabbi. One of Schonfeld's unique successes was his ability to convince Hasidic parents who did not commonly send their children out of Austria with any but all-Hasidic groups, to allow their children to join his transports. In order to enable this, Schonfeld personally led a number of children's transports to Britain, traveling the continent and back to meet the parents personally and vouch for their children's future.[29]

As was the case with the RCM, one of the CRREC's biggest worries was the financial aspect of the enterprise—the assurance of sufficient financial guarantees for refugee children—on which the promise British government visas rested. By and large, donations to the refugee organizations provided the funds for the children's upkeep and later guarantees. Fearing that the CRREC would begin making its own appeals and divide the small number of donors between groups, the Council for German Jewry allotted them two financial grants in the prewar period. Nevertheless, the CRREC began making its own appeals during this period and published several requests for financial assistance in the Jewish press, particularly in the *Jewish Chronicle*.[30]

The funds that were raised, however, were far from able to cover the CRREC's expenses. Unlike the RCM and other refugee groups that feared governmental repercussions for bringing over unguaranteed children and even temporarily halted the transfer of refugee children during late February 1939 for that reason, during the spring of 1939 Schonfeld brought over a number of unsubsidized and unguaranteed cases, undaunted by the problems that would unfold after their arrival, along with larger number of unsubsidized older refugees and refugee clergy. Unwilling to let the financial and administrative difficulties stop him from bringing over what he considered to be "a few urgent cases" of refugee children without financial backing, his relationship with the Council for German Jewry, which feared that they would have to underwrite the cases, became strained. Nevertheless, time and again Schonfeld managed to find funds to cover the children's costs, even if it meant traveling to cities where he would speak to Orthodox families and practically coerce them to take in refugee children and provide guarantees for them.³¹

Ultimately, all the Orthodox children whom Schonfeld brought over from Europe were housed either in the hostel that he had set up in his own school, in his mother's home, or with Orthodox families who had pledged to house and care for the children. Wherever they were, Schonfeld was, in the flowery words of Dr. Judith Gruenfeld, administrator and headmistress of the Jewish Secondary School, "their conquering hero, the Pied Piper, a fatherly youngster, and at the same time a gifted organizer. He seemed to them a messenger from that corner of the heavens whence our salvation cometh."³²

Apart from its rescue activities, the CRREC also assumed responsibility for the Jewish education of all refugee children. It provided religious instruction in hostels in Willesden, Ealing, Stamford Hill, Manchester, and many other areas.³³ It was this overlap between the CRREC's own rescue activities for Orthodox children and its having been charged with the Jewish education of all refugee children that gave Schonfeld and Goodman the initial opening to complain that the RCM was accepting offers of homes from non-Jewish foster parents and that even the few Orthodox Jewish children that the organization was bringing over were at times being sent to non-Jewish foster homes. Throughout the spring and summer of 1939, Schonfeld refused to accept the RCM's statement that not enough Jewish homes could be found for the Jewish refugee children, but despite the fact that the Jewish press carried requests for Jewish foster homes, few families responded. Time and again, Schonfeld pointed out that he had taken the time to travel to areas where there were Orthodox communities and personally convince their members to take on the responsibility of Orthodox refugee children. Why, then, could the RCM not send its Jewish members to Jewish communities in order to find Jewish, not even Orthodox, families willing to do the same for Jewish refugee children?³⁴

Schonfeld and Goodman were convinced that this was the result of the fact that the boards of various Jewish and nonsectarian refugee organizations were composed of only secular Jewish or non-Jewish members, stemming from the fact that the "cousinhood" who had put together the original membership of the Council for German Jewry, the RCM, and other bodies was not used to even considering potential cooperation with Orthodox Jewish organizations and their leadership. Had there been an Orthodox representative on these boards, so they claimed, that person would have felt responsible for the Jewish refugee children's spiritual future and not only their physical circumstances. Consequently, Jewish children would only have been sent to Jewish foster homes. In February 1939, Harry Goodman lodged a formal complaint with the Council for German Jewry, stating that no representative of Orthodox Jewry was included on the Council.³⁵ As a result, he claimed, Jewish children were being sent to non-Jewish homes and were open to the influence of missionary societies. This marked the first overt sign of religious friction between the CRREC and other groups dealing with child refugees in Britain, friction that continued throughout the war years, particularly with those responsible for child placement like Dorothy Hardisty. The situation came to a head in late 1943 and early 1944 with the reawakening of the "placement furor" regarding the resettlement of Jewish children in non-Jewish homes. Liberal and secular Jewish activists and RCM volunteers such as Hahn-Warburg and Elaine Blond were for the most part aware of the possibility of missionary influence on Jewish refugee children. However, this was not one of the uppermost problems in their mind when they sought immediate child placements during the spring and summer of 1939.

Unlike their secular and non-Jewish refugee activist contemporaries, Schonfeld and Goodman were not only quite aware of this issue but were greatly troubled by it. Although Goodman reiterated his fear of the problem in numerous forums of refugee activists, in view of the urgency to remove persecuted children from Central Europe and find them foster homes in Britain, the RCM and its coordinators turned a blind eye to the issue of religious compatibility between foster family and refugee child. This was a stark contrast to the situation in the United States, where, by law, all refugee children had to be placed with foster families professing the same religion even if it meant that an Orthodox Jewish child would be placed with a Conservative or Reform Jewish family.[36] Due to a combination of his personality and militant Orthodoxy, the intractable Goodman, more than the congenial Schonfeld, was considered by his secular contemporaries to be a difficult partner in any endeavor, particularly as he would constantly complain about their spiritual and moral laxity in the care of refugee children. In an attempt at typical British understatement, the Reverend William W. Simpson, member of the RCM's executive committee, once described Goodman with a deep sigh as "one of the more difficult brethren to deal with."[37]

Goodman and Schonfeld were not only afraid that Jewish refugee children placed with gentile foster parents would have difficulty in practicing their religion; they greatly feared that some families would also take the opportunity to attempt to convert the young charges to Christianity. In July 1939 at an emergency meeting that took place at Woburn House on the subject of missionaries, Goodman brought up the example of the Christian–Jewish Alliance, represented on the Coordinating Committee, showing how the Alliance was a front for a missionary organization that proselytized Jewish refugee children. Nothing, however, was done about this matter, and it later came to a head with the Guardianship issue in 1944.[38]

The Coordinating Committee for Refugees

Goodman's bone of contention stemmed not only from the composition of the RCM's executive committee but also from that of other organizations, primarily the Coordinating Committee for Refugees. Created in May 1938 on the initiative of the British Home Office to cope with the post-*Anschluss* influx of refugees and to serve as a link between the various refugee organizations, the Coordinating Committee underwent reorganization in December 1938 following the change in British government refugee policy. A former governor of the Punjab province in India, Lord William Malcolm Hailey (1872–1969) was appointed committee chair and Thomas Robbins served as honorary organizer.[39] On 2 January 1939, the organization's executive committee was formed and, apart from Hailey and Robbins, included Col. F. D. Samuel; Sir Henry Bunbury (1876–1968), a retired senior civil servant and authority on public expenditure;[40] Ernest Bell; and Society of Friends activist S. Ormerod as public relations officer.[41]

The purpose of the Coordinating Committee was to assist the refugee organizations in consulting each other on matters of policy, creating a channel of communication between the refugee organizations and government departments, and distributing pertinent information to refugee organizations. Quaker activist Mary Ormerod, who served as secretary of the committee, was particularly forceful in her dealings with government entities. The committee was also responsible for Czech children coming with their families through the British Committee for Refugees from Czechoslovakia and children from Germany coming with their parents through the German-Jewish Aid Committee.[42]

Initially, eight refugee organizations comprised the Coordinating Committee, only one of which was nominally Jewish, the German-Jewish Aid Committee. Other organizations were either outright Christian or nonsectarian: the Catholic Committee for Refugees from Germany, the Church of England Committee for Non-Aryan Christians, the Inter-Aid Committee for Children Coming from Germany, the International Student Service, the Society of Friends, the Society for the Protection of Science and Learning, and the Trades Union Congress and Labour Party (the International Solidarity Fund). Following its reorganization, additional organizations joined the Coordinating Committee, including the aforementioned Christian–Jewish Alliance.[43]

Finances and bureaucracy are the make and break of all refugee organizations. Attempting to create order out of bureaucratic chaos and in view of Sir Bunbury's field of expertise, the Coordinating Committee undertook to prepare a report on the financial liabilities of the World Movement for the Care of Children from Germany, with the aid of a well-known London firm of chartered accountants, Gibson, Harris, Prince and Co., who offered their services free of charge.[44] Even this, however, did not mitigate the group's difficulties in dealing with the bureaucratic monolith of guarantees, visas, and transports, causing Norman Bentwich to remark: "the blessed word for a time was coordinating, until it lost its blessedness."[45] According to one version of events, Lord Hailey eventually resigned his post in protest while others recall that he was politely asked to resign due to his disapproval of the way the Coordinating Committee was being run.[46]

One important step in coordinating the refugee organizations was to locate them together under one roof. In February 1939, the organizations purchased

Bloomsbury House, a former hotel, as their headquarters in the hope that the physical centralization of the refugee organizations would lessen the confusion created by their overlapping responsibilities. While the organizations were now physically more accessible to each other, the bureaucratic problems involved in bringing Jewish refugee children to Britain were not always lessened.

Other Methods of Bringing Jewish Refugee Children to Britain

In addition to the organizations that dealt with the transfer of Jewish refugee children from Central Europe to Great Britain, there were three alternate methods for the refugee children to come to the country. The first consisted of individuals who brought over groups of children, the second was composed of individuals who brought over individual children, and the third were children who came as members of a family group.

As early as 1938, a number of concerned and financially comfortable English men and women, on their own initiative, put up guarantees for large numbers of child refugees, arranged for visas, chartered planes, and flew in groups of children. One of the best known was Jean Hoare, a Quaker and the cousin of Sir Samuel Hoare. Although she had long been active in the refugee cause, she was especially moved by the plight of Czechoslovakian children. Funded by the Royal Institute of British Architects, she flew to Prague and arranged to bring a planeload of children to England. Her flat in Bloomsbury was constantly full of young refugees. She was only one of a number of Quaker activists who brought groups of refugee children to England.[47]

British MKs Philip Noel-Baker and Sir Samuel Hoare were two other Quakers whose beliefs played a vital role in their attitude toward refugees. Several groups of children were brought to England under the auspices of the Society of Friends. Members of the society were encouraged to sponsor these children, and Quaker families opened their homes and hearts to the young transmigrants.[48]

Throughout the prewar and war years, the Society of Friends, known colloquially as the Quakers, were of great aid to refugees of all faiths. A Christian sect that had been formed in mid-seventeenth-century England, the Friends were a pacifist group that believed in no creed, clergy, or other ecclesiastical forma and demanded plain speech and dress, refusal of tithes, oaths, and other worldly courtesies from its members. From the time of the American Revolution onward, the Quakers developed a tradition of ministering to refugees of all ethnic backgrounds, religious persuasions, and national origins. Despite their meager numbers—in 1944 there were 20,269 Quakers in England and only 160,000 in the entire world, 110,000 of whom were in the United States and Canada—the assistance they offered refugees went far beyond their numerical strength. Because of their program to provide milk to undernourished German children in post–World War I Europe, during the 1930s and early 1940s the Nazis gave the Quakers special status in both occupied and nonoccupied Europe. Remembering these earlier relief activities, the Nazis allowed them a certain amount of freedom of movement; this position eventually led them to become middlemen for various Jewish rescue organizations both before and during the war.[49]

It was not only Quakers who sponsored the rescue of children's groups from Central Europe. One of the most famous individual rescue attempts was organized by Nicholas Winton (b. 1909), who organized Czech children's transports throughout the spring and summer of 1939. The British-born stockbroker had been born two years after his German Jewish parents had moved to England, were baptized, and changed their name from Wertheim to the more English-sounding Winton. Winton, raised as a Christian, was not particularly religious and only later in life did he even learn about his family's Jewish origins which, by his own admission, played little if any role in his actions.

Many years after his rescue exploits, Winton recalled how his one-man rescue operation began: "It all happened during a short telephone conversation one Friday evening in December 1938. I was due to leave for Switzerland on the following Monday, for a skiing holiday with my friend, Martin Black . . . he rang me and simply said 'I have cancelled my holiday and I hope you'll do the same. I am off to Prague. I have the most interesting assignment and I need your help. . . . come as soon as you can.'"[50]

When Winton arrived in Prague, his friend told him about the refugees from the Sudentenland in Czechoslovakia who had fled to Prague ahead of Hitler's army. Black was an emissary from the British Committee for Refugees from Czechoslovakia, a committee on which a number of Quakers such as Mary Ormerod were also active. Explaining how they were trying to get endangered adults out of the country, Black turned to Winton and told him that the major problem, as yet unresolved, was the children: children whose parents had left them behind, orphaned children, children whose parents were desperate to get them to safety even though they themselves were unable to leave.

On the spur of the moment, Winton decided to take over organizing the immigration of refugee children from Czechoslovakia who had often fallen through the cracks of the rescue scheme. While in Germany and Austria the central Jewish organizations—the Berlin-based Reichsvertretung and the Vienna Kultusgemeinde—had been responsible for putting together lists of children for immigration purposes, checking their particulars, making sure that they would fit the Home Office specifications, in Prague there was at the time no working equivalent of these central organizations that could coordinate the bureaucracy involved in the rescue scheme. Instead, when Winton began his endeavor in Prague there were five different refugee committees at work in the city, each of which dealt with a different section of refugees. Setting up an office in his hotel room, Winton was joined by a young teacher from Britain, Trevor Chadwick, who had heard of the young refugees' plight and decided to leave his job and travel to Prague in order to help.

Chadwick, who became Winton's right hand man in the rescue venture, came to it completely by chance, having been sent initially to Prague on a very different mission. Two years older than Winton, with a degree in jurisprudence and a year's experience in the Colonial Service in Nigeria, Chadwick was a born-and-bred Briton who had returned to England to marry a farmer's daughter and teach at the preparatory school that his late father had founded in Dorset. Chadwick's uncle, now the school headmaster, had originally planned for his nephew to succeed him but he soon realized that the tall, witty, and handsome young man may have been an excellent teacher but was too much of a nonconformist to become a headmaster. Chadwick preferred sailing, fishing, gambling, and drinking at the local pub to school administrative work. To break up the monotony of his days, he once turned up in school with his head shaven, another time posing as an ice-cream man selling from a cart to school visitors, often coming to teach in his fisherman's jersey after a night of fishing until dawn. A father of two young boys, he had been sent with another teacher to Prague in late 1938 to bring back two refugee boys for the school to adopt. Realizing the urgency of the refugee crisis after he reached the city, he heard of Winton's presence in Prague, sought him out, and volunteered his services. Chadwick ultimately took a leave of absence from his job in order to return to Prague and head the rescue scheme on that end, ultimately becoming the honorary secretary of the Children's Section of the British Committee for Refugees from Czechoslovakia. Unlike Winton, Chadwick had no Jewish roots, nor was he a Quaker, but he saw himself as a humanitarian who responded to people in need. In addition, he was an adventurer who took on the task as a challenge to his wit, nerves, and skills.[51]

Winton returned to London with lists and photographs of children. Being a stockbroker, he said, meant finishing work at 3:30 when the stock exchange closed, and he had enough time in the afternoons to do his "real" work of preparing the basis for the children's transfer to Britain. When he turned to the RCM in the hope that they would adopt the scheme, he was told that they were financially overextended with their attempts to bring over children from Germany and Austria and could not take on additional groups of refugee children from Czechoslovakia. By then, Winton had realized that for the most part he would be working without assistance from the existing child refugee organizations in Britain and would need to do almost everything on his own. As a first step he printed up stationery and business cards for contacting guarantors for the children he wished to bring over. At that point he contacted the Home Office to learn the bureaucratic procedure he would need to go through to bring the children to Britain: he would be required to submit their forms and medical certificates, and provide proof that he had a foster home for them to go to. A guarantor or he himself would put up a £50 guarantee for each child.[52]

How does one go about getting prospective foster parents to choose refugee children? Winton grappled with this question and eventually decided to print cards with photographs of six children, their names and ages, from which potential guarantors could choose their young charges. Some objected to what they considered crass commercialism, but Winston's gamble paid off: seeing the photos made the children real to potential foster parents and helped them commit to the rescue scheme. Along with four volunteers who worked in the mornings and early afternoons until he could join them after the stock exchange closed for the day, Winton put together lists of guaranteed children, submitted them to the Home Office, and waited for entry permits. At times, the permits were so slow in coming that Trevor Chadwick in Prague would forge similar documents that would be submitted to the Czechs and later the Germans in order obtain the children's exit and transit permits. Surprisingly, the Nazis and their collaborators appeared unaware that the documents were not genuine and stamped them without delay. However, needless to say that as soon as the children reached Britain, Winton always sent someone to the port of entry to unobtrusively substitute genuine permits for the false ones that had been submitted in Prague.

Early in March 1939, Winton submitted the first list of twenty children for which foster homes and sponsors had been found. The group left Prague on 14 March 1939, one day before German troops invaded what remained of Czechoslovakia. Fearing that war was imminent, Winton's group stepped up their pace, attempting to reach as many members of the public as possible in order to find guarantees for the endangered children. Working with a number of British voluntary missions and goodwill agencies, Winton placed ads in newspapers and magazines, and spoke on the radio, in synagogues, churches, and schools in order to keep up the steady flow of offers for homes and sponsors.

Similar to the RCM's policy, Winton placed the children in whatever homes were available, regardless of the families' religion. Recalling that a delegation of Orthodox rabbis came to him to lodge a personal protest against this policy, possibly even consisting of Schonfeld and Goodman, he stated: "I took no notice of their objections. It may seem terrible from the Jewish point of view but, on the other hand, the children are alive! I was after saving lives, not souls. I told them: 'I've got my work to do, you've got yours. If you prefer a dead Jew to a proselytized one, that's your business.'"[53] Yet he was also the first to admit that there were a number of Christian organizations, such as the Barbican mission, whose aim was to raise Jewish refugee children as Christians and ultimately convert them. To combat this trend, Winton tried to place as many children as possible through B'nai Brith and Youth Aliyah, groups that put a premium on helping the refugee children maintain their Jewish identity.

All in all, throughout the spring and summer of 1939, Winton and his friends managed to bring 669 refugee children, most of whom were Jewish, to Britain, finding a home for each of them. Like many of the rescue protagonists, once the war began Winton's story faded into the background and for over four decades his friends and family knew nothing about his prewar activities. However, a chance encounter with a suitcase of documents in the late 1980s gave the continuation of his story an interesting twist; we will return to him in our final chapter, to show what occurred when he neared his ninth and tenth decades.[54]

In addition, other lesser-known individuals organized similar "rescue missions." However, this was probably the least common method used for saving refugee children.

What made individuals such as Jean Hoare, Nicholas Winton, and Trevor Chadwick invest their time, money, and strength to give over months of their lives to help refugee children? Despite Winton's origins, none was Jewish by birth, none a professional philanthropist or social worker, and none had been associated with refugee organizations before that time. It appears, however, that Hoare's religious beliefs as a Quaker, her educational and financial background, group ethnicity, and family tradition of volunteering all played a role in her actions.[55]

In comparison, it appears that neither Winton nor Chadwick's religious beliefs guided them to give up a portion of their hours or lives to rescue persecuted children. Both had comfortable income and employment, Chadwick had a settled family situation, while Winton was as yet unmarried. Neither was middle aged, nor did they have parental examples of volunteering or a youth group tradition of such. If we, however, adopt Bekkers and Wiepking's list of the mechanisms that drive voluntary action, in both cases there was an immediate recognition and awareness of need that had grown out of an unplanned situation—Winton was asked by his friend to join him in Prague, and Chadwick was chosen to travel there with another teacher in order to bring back refugee students that his school would adopt. Here correct solicitation also played a role. Jean Hoare was asked by another Quaker woman, Bertha Bracey, to join the cause. Winton had been asked by his Quaker friend, Martin Black, to come to Prague to see whether he wanted to help. Chadwick had been sent to Prague by his uncle the headmaster for a particular mission that developed far beyond its original goal, due to a combination of Chadwick's adventurism and discontent with his present form of employment.

In all cases, volunteering to further the child refugee scheme appears to have answered a deep-set need in the protagonists, giving them immediate positive feedback that their actions were making a difference to the cause they were supporting. To this one must add their unique personalities. All were adventurers to one degree or another while simultaneously being altruistic and empathetic. And finally, they were the right persons in the right places at the right times, without which these characteristics and needs might not have found their outlet.

Apart from the groups brought over by individuals, individual children were also sponsored and brought to England by concerned British citizens. Even before the refugee organizations began to seek sponsors for the children, private individuals in Germany and Austria placed advertisements in the Anglo-Jewish paper asking for families to take in their children. Sometimes the advertisements were placed by British acquaintances of the family or by relatives in England who could not afford to fully support or house a child.

From the middle of 1938 on, these advertisements were common enough that entire columns of them ran in a special section in the *Jewish Chronicle*. "Please help me bring out of Berlin two children (boy and girl), ten years, best family, very urgent case"; "Which family would like to take over Jewish boy, 15 years, from first-class orthodox Viennese family and give him the chance to be taught a trade. Father was in the jewelry trade, now penniless, very urgent. Pocket money and clothes will be provided."[56]

In both advertisements emphasis was placed on the high quality of the child's family. This was often a sign that the advertisement was placed by Continental Europeans, who often hoped that the emphasis on family background would be more appealing to the English potential foster parents than many other qualities. The words *very urgent* appeared in most advertisements of this type and were the key to understanding the exigency felt by Central European Jewry following *Kristallnacht*. Never before had parents or relatives faced such a tragedy—having to place classified advertisements in the newspapers in order to find a shelter for their children.

As experience showed, the children in the first advertisement probably had a better chance of finding a sponsor than the boy in the second one, as both his gender and age were against him. By and large, potential foster parents preferred younger children to older ones and girls to boys. And as we will see in the next chapter, during the months when one needed a guarantor before being allowed to join a Kindertransport, additional preferences such as looks, coloring, and docile personality could make the difference between remaining in Germany, Austria, or Czechoslovakia and being sent to safety.[57]

A third group of children, albeit not unaccompanied, who reached Britain were those coming with their families. As opposed to children arriving on the Kindertransports, these young people no longer had to fear for their parents' safety, as their whereabouts were known. Apart from the regulations pertaining to minors, such children were treated no differently than their families with regard to their legal status in Britain. Czechoslovakian and German children arriving with their families through their respective country of origin's representative came under the responsibility of the Coordinating Committee. Most of these families, children included, were considered transmigrants as they were waiting for their American quota number to come up.[58]

In many cases, children who did not come with their entire families actually came only with their mothers, who were allowed into Britain as domestic servants. In all, 14,000 Central European refugee women came to Great Britain employed as domestic servants, bringing over 1,000 children with them.[59] But even those children fortunate enough to come to Britain with one of their parents were not always lucky enough to remain with them. After they arrived in Britain, some refugee families were unable to care for their children adequately at home due to their impoverished state. During the 1930s and 1940s, British immigration laws prohibited the employment of aliens in jobs that were not specifically created for them and that could not be taken by British citizens. Women could usually find employment in housework or sewing, but men found it more difficult to find employment. This could lead both to psychological demoralization and financial inability to care for children. Such children were placed in foster homes by the Jewish Refugee Committee in Bloomsbury House.[60] After long hours of queuing at the Welfare Office, seekers would usually find home for these children, although not necessarily Jewish ones. Most of these preadolescent and adolescent refugees rapidly adapted to their English environment, more rapidly than their parents who tended to remain within the cloistered refugee community. Tragically, their eventual reunion with their parents whose refugee mentality often embarrassed and alienated them was not always a joyful one.[61]

Covering the Costs

When it comes to organizational planning, two questions materialize time and again: "Who will do the work?" and "Who will pay the bills?" While it is usually easier to find volunteers willing to divide up the tasks at hand, the financial aspect of covering continuous expenses is often the make-or-break issue of many organizations.

In planning the transfer to and resettlement of the refugee children, the Kindertransport associations faced both of these questions again and again. While it was possible to find goodhearted and able volunteers to take over the organizational aspect, the financial issues were harder to solve. As early as 24 November 1938, the Undersecretary of State for the Home Office, Mr. Geoffrey Lloyd, announced that following the decision of the Evian Conference, His Majesty's Government would not offer financial assistance to refugee children in Britain for education and training.[62] Thus, from the start of the rescue operations it was clear that funds would have to be raised from private sources to cover a number of ongoing expenses. These including covering costs of the children's fares, which usually had to be paid in foreign currency, purchasing hostels and paying their upkeep including furnishing them, paying the salaries of a matron and cook, and providing children's clothing, subsidizing children living with foster families who were unable to undertake the children's total support, and as of March 1939, paying the £50 guarantee required by the British government.

How would these funds be found? While most individuals who sponsored children paid for their guarantee and upkeep out of their own pocket, it was still necessary to find additional funds to sponsor children brought over by the RCM. The most obvious solution was to utilize the existing fund-raising bodies such as the Council for German Jewry (discussed in previous chapters). Created originally to help young people emigrate from Germany, the Council contained representatives of British, Continental, and American Jewish organizations. In February 1939, the Council president, Sir Herbert Samuel, resigned and was replaced by Lord Reading (Gerald Rufus Isaacs, 1889–1960), marking the end of the pretense that the Council represented both American and British organizations. Henceforth, the Council for German Jewry was a British institution that cooperated with the American Jewish Joint Distribution Committee (JDC). The Joint and the British Council for German Jewry were among the organizations that supplied the rescue operation with foreign currency to help pay the children's fares.[63]

A second source of finance was the Lord Baldwin Fund. Knowing that public figures and politicians had a better chance of galvanizing public financial support than organizational heads, soon after the British government had come to its decision, the refugee organizations turned to former Prime Minister Stanley Earl Baldwin (1867–1947) to enlist his support for the refugee scheme. On Thursday, 8 December 1938 Baldwin turned to the British public in a radio appeal for refugees beginning with the words: "I have to ask you to come to the aid of the victims not of any catastrophe in the natural world, not of earthquake nor of flood nor of famine, but of an explosion of man's inhumanity to men. . . ."[64] The speech was recorded on 12-inch records and sold at 8s each, post-free with all profits going to the refugee fund.

In April 1939, following the British government's requirement to show a £50 guarantee for each refugee child and in an apparent reversal of policy, Lord Baldwin and the Appointments Committee decided to apportion £200,000 for child refugees. The sum was given to the RCM to help pay guarantees and maintenance costs for refugee children. Maintenance alone was estimated at £40–£50 a year per child. During the same month, Christie's auction house organized a sale to aid the Lord Baldwin Fund.[65]

The Lord Baldwin Fund acted as a magnet to draw contributions from people of all ages, from all walks of society. Storekeepers, day laborers, housewives, and even refugees who were already in England donated to the fund. The most poignant letters accompanied donations from children, and even a number of refugee children sent in possessions to be auctioned off at the Christie's sale. One example was a letter received from a little German Jewish girl in London: "Right Honorable Lord Baldwin, I have English from my oncle in Frankfurt a/M gelernt. He was oncet a haircutter in London. I am ten year old and am in England since Januar. I send you a very old dolli for your Christie sale for refugees. It is very old and was from my great mama gegiven. In England I have no fear and all peoples are kind. Thank you best. Lisa Wolf." The letter was accompanied by an old German wooden doll dressed in a green robe with a green cape. The Lord Baldwin Fund closed in the summer of 1939, having collected more than £500,000. It was estimated that 90 percent of the fund's contributors were Jews.[66]

In spite of the generous contributions to the Fund, there was still not enough to truly cover the costs of transferring and resettling the refugee children. For that, it was necessary to tap into additional forms of appeals, receive donations, and find innovative ways of raising the needed funds. During the spring and summer of 1939, several appeals for donations both in money and in kind appeared in the press and were broadcasted on the radio following Lord Baldwin's speech. A BBC broadcast during the winter of 1938–39, entitled "Children in Captivity," requested gifts in kind for the refugee children who had been brought directly from Europe to the reception camps. The appeal resulted in an offer of free food from neighborhood tradesmen, free shoes for all the children from Marks and Spencer, and two boxing gloves which the National Sporting Club at Earl's Court sent to the children at the Dovercourt camp. Many of the later appeals appeared in connection with a Jewish holiday. For example, an appeal appearing in a February issue of the *Jewish Chronicle* requested that fruit and sweets be sent to the children at Dovercourt for the upcoming Purim holiday.[67]

Yet another method of raising funds for refugee child expenses came from school "adoptions" of such children. Just as many circles at work "adopted" refugee children, entire schools followed suit and offered to pay for the upkeep of several refugee children and to educate them free of charge in their school. Many schools, including several special educational institutions, announced their intentions to take in children in order to both support and educate them. Paradoxically, after a year or so, there were schools that requested permission from the RCM to remove the refugee children and place them elsewhere. Being so advanced educationally, the children were creating envy and friction among their fellow classmates.[68]

Even these varied fund-raising schemes were not enough to cover the children's resettlement costs. Throughout 1939, a number of pamphlets were published that dealt with the child refugee problem and proposed various means of raising additional funds.[69] These included collecting money in shops, offices, at cinema and theater performances, supporting agricultural training for a boy refugee for a year, supporting a year's schools of a refugee child in Britain or Palestine, granting hospitality to refugee children living in boarding schools during the school holidays, holding benefit performances and sales, and using Workers Circle Contributions in a particular location or area to further a project related to child refugees.[70]

Ultimately, Charity Benefits and Workers Circle Contributions became the most common fund-raising mechanism in most areas, probably because they were both well-known methods of fund raising long before the child refugee scheme began. In November 1938, a ball was held for the Inter-Aid Committee and the Save the Children Fund under the patronage of Marquess and Marchioness Reading. A boxing tournament held in December 1938 for the refugee fund raised £80. Concerts were given for the children's fund and a pastel exhibition donated 50 percent of its proceeds toward the support of refugee children.[71]

Not only did organized Workers Circles adopt the refugee children's cause, but even groups of previously unrelated professionals would get together in order to purchase a child refugee hostel, pay for the guarantees or upkeep of a group of refugee children, and cover their medical fees, clothing, and pocket money. One of the first "worker's circles" to do so was composed of a number of doctors and dentists who purchased a home at Ramsgate in January 1939 to be used as a hotel for twenty-five refugee teenage boys. A different worker's circle cared for a group of nineteen refugee children aged eleven and twelve from June 1939 onward by donating 2s each per quarter for their upkeep.[72]

Assorted suggestions for aid to the refugee cause appeared in the press during the latter part of 1938 and the early months of 1939. One of the best-known ones was the suggestion to issue a refugee postage stamp to cover the costs of immigration and support.[73] This suggestion was raised in a House of Commons debate on refugee financing in April 1939, as was the possibility of demanding a payment to renew the Nansen passports issued by the League of Nations to stateless persons. There seems to have been no practical outcome for either suggestion.[74]

This, however, brings us to the other side of the financial coin, the British government's attitude toward refugee finance in general and child refugee finance in particular. In an attempt to lighten the financial burden of families offering the children homes, the British government granted a tax allowance to persons maintaining refugee children. Upon giving proof to the inspector of taxes, a taxpayer maintaining a child under the age of sixteen was eligible for a tax allowance of £60 annually. This allowance was also granted to people supporting a child over the age of sixteen who was studying in school full time.[75]

The British government's attitude toward refugee financing changed drastically between 1938 and 1945. Initially, the child refugee organizations had to assure the government that the children would not become a public burden and that these organizations would not request government financial assistance. This assurance was identical to the one that all Jewish refugee organizations gave the British government starting from 1933. Nevertheless, as early as 14 November 1938, MP Daniel L. Lipson directed a question to Undersecretary of State Geoffrey Lloyd about the possibility of government financial assistance to "responsible private agencies." Not all MPs were as sympathetically disposed toward the refugee problem as was Lipson, the Jewish independent representative for Cheltenham. Before allowing Lloyd to reply to Lipson's questions, his fellow conservative MP Lieutenant-Colonel Gilbert John Acland-Troyte interjected with "Will my Right Honorable Friend consider the interests of the British taxpayer!" reminding his listeners that they were first and foremost British representatives who had been elected to protect their constituent's interests.[76]

Nevertheless, by July 1939 the British government began to examine methods of financially supporting the refugee cause, despite the fact that this would be contrary to the principles set down at the Evian Conference.[77] The prewar estimate of the cost of maintaining, educating, and training the children brought to Britain by the RCM alone, and then funding their re-emigration, was approximately £250,000. Many other factors not covered in this estimate had to be taken into consideration when calculating the RCM's total expenditures including transportation to Britain, guarantees for unguaranteed children, employee salaries, and administrative costs for items such as stamps, paper, advertisements, rent, utilities, and taxes. Like the other refugee organizations, the RCM received no government assistance, a factor that placed an almost unbearable burden upon the child refugee organization, a state of events that did not go unnoticed by the British government. Once war was declared, however, and it was obvious that the refugee children were not going to return to Europe in the near future, the government realized that in order to ensure the refugee organization's continued efforts it would be necessary to change its financial policies in that direction.

After due deliberation, the British government agreed to pay £100,000 to maintain the refugees in Britain. From the end of 1939 it had agreed to pay half the cost of their maintenance and administration. The government agreed to a £ by £ grant of the amount expended by the voluntary refugee agencies. Ultimately, the British government became responsible for three-quarters of the cost of welfare and administration and all maintenance costs of needy refugees.[78]

Conclusions

"Bureaucracy is a giant mechanism operated by pygmies," stated French author Honoré de Balzac, articulating his somewhat sardonic view of one of the major systems that regulate much of our lives.[79] Others have been even more caustic about the nature of bureaucracy and bureaucrats.[80] Nevertheless, bureaucratic machinery is necessary in order to organize and regulate society, execute tasks in what is supposed to be a more efficient manner, and tackle new challenges through a mechanism that provides a priori solutions to the difficulties that might arise. The key to keeping the machinery from overwhelming the task at hand is found within the area of a triangle bordered by three crucial questions, two of which were mentioned earlier—"Who does the work?" and "Who pays the bills?"—to which one must add, "Who makes the rules?"

An important factor in the success of any bureaucratic machinery is not only defining its goals but also understanding the nature of the greater framework in which it functions. In this case, the greater framework in which the refugee child machinery functioned was shaped by a combination of factors: the nature of the Continental European organizations, Nazi, Jewish and other, which had bearing on the refugee children's status and possibility of emigration, the legal mandate which the British government allotted the child refugee organizations and the amount of government intervention, or interference in their activities.

In all cases, the child rescue bureaucracy found itself in relatively propitious circumstances. Once the British government declared its willingness to allow in an unspecified number of refugee children, its intervention in the bureaucratic wheels that would bring these children to Britain was almost standardized. Apart from the necessary paperwork and an explicit individual or organizational guarantee that the children would not become public charges (and later the £50 guarantee required to bring a refugee child to Britain), the only other requirement was that the potential homes would meet a set of long-existing welfare standards.

The Nazis, too, were interested in having the Jews leave Europe as soon as possible. Their negative general attitude toward Jews notwithstanding, following *Kristallnacht* the declared Nazi policy was to encourage Jewish emigration from the Reich, which might explain the superficiality with which Nazi bureaucrats in Prague examined the forged visas with which Winton and Chadwick often presented them. The problems began when necessary paperwork was delayed in other countries and one was relying upon more rigid Jewish emigration agencies, such as the *Auswanderungsabteilung* (Emigration Department) of the *Reichsvertretung* in Germany, which would not consider forging or altering documents as did the intrepid Chadwick and Winton over and over. Although this difference may have stemmed from the German Jewish bureaucrats' fears over their fate if such a ruse were to be discovered, it might also have been a by-product of their more rigid upbringing and personalities.

The problems began when there were urgent cases of refugee children who required guarantees that had not yet been issued or paperwork that hadn't been processed on time. Under such circumstances, one of the other two questions—"Who does the work?"—was of paramount importance. While members of the "cousinhood" who were active members of the refugee committees might occasionally have the ear of a particular MP, they were hard pressed to move the bureaucratic wheels faster than they were already moving, and their background would never allow them to "misrepresent" a situation in order to obtain the necessary permits. In contrast, Solomon Schonfeld of the CRREC did not feel himself under any such constraints. Time and again, in discussions with British immigration bureaucrats he bent the truth regarding the existence of financial backing for the children's resettlement or a place for them to stay, even when it meant moving beds into the classroom of his school which had suddenly turned into a "refugee children's hostel" or turning his mother's home into an extension of a hostel.

Why was Schonfeld capable of altering the truth when dealing with British officials and then creating a concrete situation which mirrored his fictional promises in order to bring more refugee children to Britain? Why were the RCM activists incapable of doing the same thing in order to achieve that goal? Two explanations are background and personality. Like other ultra-Orthodox rescue activists during the Holocaust, such as the Vaad Hatzala in the United States or the Sternbuch group in Switzerland, it appears that Schonfeld was guided by one principle, that of rescuing as many Jews, in this case Jewish refugee children, as possible. His overriding law was that of saving lives, something that transcended any local ordinance. In contrast to many others of the "cousinhood," he also had no desire to assimilate into British society and had no problem manipulating a system to his advantage.[81]

In addition, his personality was that of a person who rose to a challenge and was used to fighting authority. When his father died and he was supposed to take over his father's communal position and institutions, some tried to block his appointment, citing his youth and the fact that his father had not left precise stipulations about the identity of his successor. Schonfeld forged on, undaunted, in spite of the fact that the substitute rabbi founded his own synagogue and took many of the community's members with him, and found additional supporters for his schools and synagogue movement from the Hasidic Jewish communities and new synagogues established by refugees after 1933. These two factors, his ultra-Orthodox orientation and his fighting personality, combined to enable him to do whatever he saw necessary, including occasionally bending the truth when dealing with British officials in order to save Jewish refugee children from the Nazis.[82]

Unlike Schonfeld, Winton and Chadwick were not Orthodox Jews, yet they were willing to bend and break every rule in the book in order to bring refugee children, primarily Jewish, from Czechoslovakia to safety in Britain. Why? The answer can probably be found in a combination of their adventurous and nonconformist personalities and in the fact that they worked as free agents, unencumbered by not being attached to a large refugee organization headed by public figures, often former military men or government figures, some of those belonging to the peerage or former civil servants.

It seems, therefore, that the two major considerations for being able to "buck convention," bend rules, and even lie to authority when necessary (and get away with it) when it came to refugee work, was having a certain type of personality and not being co-opted by a major refugee organization. These facets gave one much more leeway in action than otherwise. It is interesting to note that having more freedom in the case of "who makes the rules?" may have cut Schonfeld and Winton off from the established sources of revenue in terms of "who pays the bills?" but also cut them slack in allowing them to tap into innovative funding sources, using very unconventional methods frowned upon by the refugee establishment.

The Roman satirical writer Petronius (d. 66) is quoted to have said: "We tend to meet any new situation by reorganizing . . . and a wonderful method it can be for creating the illusion of progress while producing inefficiency and demoralization."[83] Aware of the pitfalls of bureaucracy, most of the figures behind the machinery surrounding the refugee children's rescue scheme did their utmost to ensure that their progress would be as efficient as possible within the existing legal and administrative limitations. Others, as we have seen, occasionally even ignored or transcended these limitations in order to achieve incredible successes in bringing children out of the Third Reich. These activists were not only involved in the children's transfer from Europe but also followed many of them during in their initial resettlement in Britain up to and including the outbreak of war.

Notes

1. Drucker, *Management*, 444.
2. *The Jewish Chronicle*, 16 December 1938, 28.
3. Bentwich, *They Found Refuge*, 65.
4. *The Jewish Chronicle*, 11 August 1939, 21.
5. Presland, *A Great Adventure*, 2, Central British Fund Archives, The Wiener Library Microfilm document collection 27/28/156.
6. Refugee Children's movement, Articles of Association, Central British Fund Archives, The Wiener Library Microfilm document collection 27/28/164. Refugee Children's Movement official change of names, in: Movement for the Care of Children from Germany Ltd, Annual General Meeting, 3 July 1940, Central British Fund Archives, The Wiener Library Microfilm document collection 27/28/161.
7. Genizi, "American Non-sectarian Refugee Relief Organizations," 164–220.
8. Bentwich, *They Found Refuge*, 81.
9. Oldfield, "It is Usually She," 57–70.
10. Executive Committee meetings of the Movement of the Care of Children from Germany, Central British Fund Archives, The Wiener Library Microfilm document collection 27/28/166, 27/29/167.
11. Such as Bentwich, *They Found Refuge*, 81.
12. Blond, *Marks of Distinction*, 76.
13. Kaye, *Burning for the Cause*, 2001.
14. Friedenfeld, "Lola Hahn-Warburg," *The Jewish Chronicle*, 29 March 2010.
15. Blond, *Marks of Distinction*, 87.
16. Blond, *Jew Made in England*, 37–38.
17. Blond, *Marks of Distinction*, 88.
18. Mikula, *Women, Activism and Social Change*.
19. Members included Lord Gorell as chair, Lady Eva Reading as deputy chair, Elaine Laski, Lola Hahn-Warburg, Maurice Gestetner, and Rabbi Maurice Swift as the Jewish representatives, Rev. Monsignor Canon George L. Craven representing the Roman Catholics and the Rev. William W. Simpson representing the Nonconformists. Simpson interview.
20. *The Jewish Chronicle*, 2 December 1938, 20; *Bulletin of the Co-ordinating Committee for Refugees*, April 1939, 7.
21. *The Jewish Chronicle*, 25 November 1938, 30–31.
22. List of Provincial Committees, The Munk Collection, P/15/9, Yad Vashem Archives, Jerusalem. Author's interview with Joan Barash, daughter of the coordinator of the Manchester hostel for refugee children, Tel Aviv, 22 March 1980 (henceforth: Barash interview); Stefan K. Schimansky, "Refugee Children," 27.
23. *The Jewish Chronicle*, 9 December 1938, 17.
24. Interview with Henry Pels (OHD), 35(27).
25. See Marcus Retter's testimony in Kranzler, *Holocaust Hero*, 10. Retter, a young Orthodox refugee from Austria, was secretary to the Union of Orthodox Hebrew Congregations and assistant to Rabbi Schonfeld in his rescue activities.
26. *The Jewish Chronicle*, 9 December 1938, 17.
27. Interview with Henry Pels, OHD, 35(27).
28. General memorandum on rescue from Austria, 2 March 1939, The Munk Archives, P/15/2, Yad Vashem, Jerusalem. Steinfeld managed to leave Vienna in May 1941 and found refuge in Cuba. In 1942, after the American State Department was convinced

29. Judith Gruenfeld, *Shefford*, 9.
30. *The Jewish Chronicle,* 24 March 1939, 25.
31. Letter Rabbi Hertz to Lord Samuel, 22 March 1939, The Munk Archives, P/15/2, Yad Vashem, Jerusalem.
32. Gruenfeld, *Shefford,* 10.
33. *The Jewish Chronicle,* 11 August 1939, 21.
34. *The Jewish Chronicle,* 12 May 1939, 35; *The Jewish Weekly,* 23 June 1939, vol. IV, no 178, 1.
35. *The Jewish Chronicle,* 24 February 1939, 16.
36. Baumel, *Unfulfilled Promise.*
37. Simpson interview.
38. *The Jewish Chronicle,* 14 July 1939, 23.
39. Pearce, *The Turning Point in Africa,* 43.
40. Obituary, *The London Times,* 7 September 1968.
41. *Bulletin of the Coordinating Committee for Refugees,* London, February 1939, 3–4.
42. M. Ormerod to Makins, 10 June 1938, PRO FO 371/22527, W7582/104/98, f.82.
43. *Bulletin of the Coordinating Committee for Refugees,* London, February 1939, 10.
44. Ibid., 5.
45. Bentwich, *Wanderer between Two Worlds,* 284.
46. Simpson interview.
47. Author's interview with Boaz Wreschner, Ramat Gan, 5 December 1979 (henceforth: Wreschner interview).
48. Questionnaire: Ruth Finch.
49. *Whittaker's Almanach* 1944, 445. For more on Quaker work with refugees during the First World War, see Jones, *A Service of Love in Wartime.* See also American Friends Service Committee programme in France, 1940–41, Foreign service, France. Relief general, 1940, American Friends Service Committee Archives, Philadelphia. The American Friends Service Committee was the American relief work arm of the Society of Friends, who during the 1930s had established centers in Berlin, Vienna, Paris, and Geneva to assist victims of Nazism.
50. Emanuel and Gissing, *Nicholas Winton,* 66.
51. Ibid., 92–103.
52. Ibid., 72–76.
53. Ibid., 83.
54. Nir Hasson and Yehuda Lahav, "Jews Saved by U.K. Stockbroker to Reenact 1939 Journey," *Haaretz,* 9 September 2009 http://www.haaretz.com/jewish-world/news/jews-saved-by-u-k-stockbroker-to-reenact-1939-journey-to-safety-1.283126.
55. Bekkers and Wiepking, "To Give or Not to Give," 533–40; Bielefeld, Rooney, and Steinberg, *Gifts of Time and Money,* 127–58; Bekkers, "Its Not All in the Ask"; Brown, "College, Social Capital and Charitable Giving," 185–204; Reed and Selbee, "Is There a Distinctive Pattern of Values."
56. *The Jewish Chronicle,* 23 Dec. 1938, 3.
57. Eva Reading, *For the Record,* 166.
58. *Bulletin of the Coordinating Committee for Refugees,* London, February 1939, 10.
59. Lafitte, *The Internment of Aliens,* 48.

60. Barash interview.
61. Singer, *Children of the Apocalypse*, 186.
62. 341 HC Deb. 1930.
63. Bauer, *My Brother's Keeper*, 271; Lotan (OHD) 49 (27).
64. *The Jewish Chronicle*, 16 December 1938, 30.
65. *The Jewish Chronicle*, 7 April 1939, 19.
66. *The Jewish Chronicle*, 31 March 1939, 18; 14 July 1939, 22; Bauer, *My Brother's Keeper*, 271.
67. Gershon, *We Came as Children*, 33; *The Jewish Chronicle*, 13 January 1939, 13; 24 February 1939, 26.
68. Hanna Bergas E/188, Yad Vashem Archives. Bergas was a teacher at the Bunce Court School. *The Jewish Chronicle*, 7 July 1938, 29; S. Adler-Rudel (OHD) 17 (27); Eva Michaelis-Stern (OHD) 16 (27).
69. Cohen, *Salvaging German Jewry*; Buxton, *The Economics of the Refugee Problem*; *The Caring for Child Refugees*.
70. Cohen, *Salvaging German Jewry*, 18; Buxton, *The Economics of the Refugee Problem*, 44.
71. *The Jewish Chronicle*, 11 November 1939, 33; 9 December 1938, 47; 23 December 1938, 55; 16 June 1939, 28.
72. *The Jewish Chronicle*, 13 January 1939, 13; Pearce, "The Fascist Threat," 22.
73. *The Jewish Chronicle*, 2 December 1938, 43.
74. *The Jewish Chronicle*, 14 April 1939, 15.
75. *The Jewish Chronicle*, 30 December 1938, 18.
76. 341 HC Deb. 1930 (14 November 1938).
77. *The Jewish Chronicle*, 21 July 1939, 17.
78. Special financial arrangements made with the RCM will be dealt with in chapter 7.
79. Honore de Balzac, cited in Peter, *Peter's Quotations*, 58.
80. Goldwyn, "The Indestructible Bacillus Bureaucraticus," 46–48.
81. Zuroff, *Response of Orthodox Jewry in the United States*; Baumel, "Strange Bedfellows," 465–92; Friedenson, *Heroine of Rescue*.
82. Kranzler, *Holocaust Hero*, 30.
83. Peter, *Peter's Quotations*, 57.

Chapter 5

Immigration and Resettlement

Introduction

"Sometime after *Kristallnacht* my parents saw a notice in a Jewish newspaper in Berlin in which Dr. Bernard Schlesinger from London said he would guarantee twelve Jewish children coming to England. As soon as my parents saw the paper they turned to me and said: 'You are going first and we will come later (*Wir kamen nach*).' They kept saying it over and over as if they were trying to convince themselves that it was the right thing to do or that things would actually work out that way at the end. Reenie was younger and didn't register what was going on as much as I did, but I knew what was happening as the fathers of my schoolmates were being taken away. 'You will be immigrants!' my mother said trying to cheer us up, but soon after we reached London we realized that we were really something else, we were refugees."[1] With these words, Steffi Birnbaum Schwartz continued the account of her odyssey and that of her younger sister Reenie to Britain.

When referring to refugees and refugee children, the use of the term *immigration* often appears incongruous. While an emigrant voluntarily leaves a country and chooses his or her own destination and a deportee leaves involuntarily at a time and for a destination chosen by another, a refugee is forced to leave but may choose both time and destination.[2] European children from the Third Reich arriving in England after *Kristallnacht* were certainly refugees—forced to leave their mother country as a result of religious and racial persecution—but they were often called by a new term coined for those leaving Central Europe, a term meant to sound less harsh at that time: *involuntary immigrants*.[3]

Where could they go? As a former German refugee once remarked, the list of countries willing to accept refugees or "involuntary immigrants" from Germany in 1938 was much shorter than that of the countries refusing them entry. As the waiting list for certificates to enter Palestine grew steadily longer, the American quota system created queues for immigration visas that began several years before the immigrant even received a quota number. Apart from Australia, which had promised in December 1938 to take 15,000 refugees over a three-year period, the British Dominions offered little help. Switzerland had closed its borders in August 1938 and put up barbed wire along the frontier. Most of Latin America was still open to refugees—if they were professional agriculturalists in the possession of £500 each in addition to their fares. Mexico stipulated that all immigrants had to be willing and able to marry local Indian women and thus speed up their own assimilation. During the Evian Conference, the Dominican Republic had offered to take 100,000 refugees but by the end of November 1939 it had issued visas to only twenty of the 2,000 who applied.[4] There was also British Guyana which might have been utilized if not for the U.S. refusal to match British financing. In light of this situation, the Home Secretary's announcement opening the doors of Britain to any refugee child whose maintenance could be guaranteed was a heaven-sent opportunity for parents in Central Europe.

Immigration Procedure

Steffi and Reenie were among the lucky refugee children with a personal guarantor and sponsor who met all the British government requirements necessary to host refugee children. These included not only putting up the £50 but also being able to provide the children with minimum living conditions such as their own bed and toilet articles, adequate food, and other material necessities. To assure that the children would be well cared for, from the onset of the refugee child scheme the British Government stipulated that all children had to be guaranteed either by private individuals or by the refugee organizations. A guarantee involved an assurance that the guarantor would totally support the child in question until age eighteen or until that child finished his or her professional training. To distinguish between children guaranteed by private individuals and those guaranteed solely by the RCM, the former category was referred to as *guaranteed* children, while the latter group was called *unguaranteed*. Guarantors were often relatives and acquaintances of the refugee child in Britain who also provided the Home Office with the child's picture and particulars. To ensure that these children would not run into a legal problem in the future if their guarantor ran out of funds, such guarantees were also financially underwritten by the RCM.[5]

Most refugee children, however, were unguaranteed. And as they lacked personal sponsors, the Refugee Children's Movement assumed responsibility for meeting the Home Office stipulations. Thousands of letters sent both by parents in Europe and by social-welfare organizations trying to find guarantors for children were directed towards the RCM's head office in London. Most read along the following lines: "This is Heidi, who is twelve, she is lame but very cheerful . . . " or, "Martin is nine, he has a gentle nature and I know you would like him. . . ."[6] Numerous children could not find guarantors, and for lack of funds the RCM was unable to bring over many of the applicants in unguaranteed groups. The stacks of letters still unanswered in the RCM's head office at the start of the war was a harsh reminder of the organization's financial difficulties at a number of junctures throughout 1939.

Bureaucracy was one of the most dominant factors in the first stages of the unguaranteed refugee children's transfer to Britain. The long checklist of organizations through which the children's applications had to pass included more than a few refugee agencies both in the children's country of origin and in Great Britain, local governmental offices in Central Europe, Nazi administrative bureaus, and finally, British government offices. The process was time-consuming and nerve-wracking, and there was no guarantee that in the end the child in question would indeed receive the longed-for emigration papers.

The Reichsvertretung der Juden in Deutschland (the Central Organization of Jews in Germany), headquartered in Berlin, was responsible for selecting the unguaranteed Jewish children in Germany. When potential sponsors in England specified requirements for the children they wished to take, the RCM passed this information on to the Kinderauswanderung Abteilung (Children's Emigration Department) of the Reichsvertretung (later, in 1939, to the same department in the Reichsvereinigung, which replaced the Reichsvertretung) and the case in question then became its responsibility. Local committees of the Reichsvertretung then looked for suitable Jewish children, while non-Jewish children were selected by the Paulusbund (a covenant of "non-Aryan" Christians created in 1936) in Berlin. Although Jewish social-welfare agencies in Germany received numerous requests from desperate parents, the Children's Emigration Department was responsible for making the final selection of the children who composed each transport.

Despite its position as nerve center for emigration of Jewish children from Germany from the mid-1930s on, the Children's Emigration Department, headed by Kaethe Rosenheim, was seriously understaffed. The cultured, elderly, highly educated, and hard-of-hearing Rosenheim, affectionately known by some as "Rosie," was less respectfully nicknamed *Taubschen* ("little dove," also "little deaf one") by her youthful coworkers. Rosenheim was the guiding force behind the Kinderauswanderungs Abteilung until her eleventh-hour departure to the United States in 1940. The daughter of a famous Berlin surgeon and herself a trained social worker, Rosenheim had been dismissed from her position in the civil service after Hitler's rise to power, at which time she joined the Reichsvertretung. Extremely social, even after she and her exhausted staff had worked continuously for several days running to send off a children's transport successfully, she was known to turn to them late in the evening and delightedly exclaim, "Let's have a party!"[7]

Although this department had been in existence for several years prior to the Kindertransport scheme, the large influx of applications in late 1938 necessitated hiring additional workers. Apart from Rosenheim, the staff consisted of Norbert Wollheim, Herta Souhami, and a Miss Springer, who assisted with various tasks. Wollheim, who had recently lost his job at a Jewish import–export business, joined the Kinderauswanderungs Abteilung after *Kristallnacht*, having been asked to do so by Otto Hirsch, one of the heads of the Central Organization of Jews in Germany. Years later, Wollheim described the scene he encountered upon first entering the department:

> When I went there I almost fainted when I saw the disorder. There was a big conference room in the office and a big table covered with heaps of cards and a desk which was covered with papers, and the telephone was constantly ringing. The staff were mostly social workers and although they were doing their very best, they had no experience in technical matters like the transports. . . . The first thing I did was to try and organize the cards into alphabetical and geographical order. These were the permits which gave the young people a license to enter England. Then we had to put together the transports. Lists had to be submitted to England and lists submitted to the Gestapo. Then you had to organize the people from places outside Berlin to come to Berlin and assemble on a certain day, at a certain time. There was also a lot of technical work at the last moment. Children got sick, or parents said, "No, we can't afford to let our children go," and the lists had to be changed; we had to be in constant contact with London . . . this wasn't a nine-to-five job. We worked deep into the night . . . but it was work that had to be done.[8]

Preference was given to two categories of children whose removal from Germany was considered urgent: young boys in concentration camps and children for whom one or both parents were in such a camp or had been deported. Similar criteria were applied by the children's committee of the Jewish Refugee's Committee in the Netherlands when dealing with refugee children.[9]

Herta Souhami, a former Westphalian Jewish social worker who worked in the Children's Emigration Department even prior to *Kristallnacht*, described the procedure used to select unguaranteed children in Germany: the children's parents would submit applications and pictures to the provincial social worker, who would evaluate the urgency of the case. The paperwork, including health certificates, school certificates, pictures, statements about the parents' health, geographical, and financial situation and other related documentation would then be forwarded to the Central Office in Berlin, which received thousands of applications each month. As the combination of huge volumes of applications received daily and the lack of help in the social work offices precluded the possibility of reading them all, irate and desperate parents often came directly to the Central Office, complaining that they had not received replies. Perseverance often paid off. In such cases, the social worker would frequently sift through the pile of applications from that parent's district, and having found the application would deal with it as soon as possible. This system was not the most efficient, but under the circumstances there appeared to be little alternative.[10]

At that point, the British bureaucracy took over. When children were chosen for a transport, their particulars and health certificates were sent to the RCM's main office in London, as were lists of cases that were particular urgent due to danger of incarceration, parental death, and absence of livelihood. All documents were then transferred to the Home Office, which issued the children's entry permits. These were then returned to Germany via airmail and submitted to the German police for clearance. Inexplicably, some were always withheld by the German authorities while the rest were returned to the Jewish organizations that distributed them to the transport leaders.

A wide variety of escorts accompanied the transports, ranging from former youth-group leaders to unemployed Jewish professionals. Wollheim accompanied the first of more than twenty children's transports leaving from Berlin, but because the escorting procedure had not yet been approved by the Gestapo he was forbidden to cross the border to Holland along with his young charges. Only after he convinced the German authorities that it was in their interest to have the escorts accompany the children to London to ensure that none would be turned back and forced to return to Germany, did the Nazis allow the escorts of future transports beyond the German border. Their one condition, however, was that all escorts would return to Berlin; otherwise, the transports would come to an end. During the summer of 1939, one transport was even led by Rabbi Leo Baeck and Otto Hirsch, leaders of the Reichsvereinigung.[11]

Parents of children chosen for a transport were notified of the time and place of departure and the amount of luggage permitted per child, usually one suitcase. Most children brought clothes, books, family photographs, diaries, dolls, and other cherished possessions. Parents also tried to outfit children for the future, as they had no idea how long the separation would last. Anne Fox described how her mother prepared the clothing she was to take to England: "Everything was bought or made with future growth in mind, as the clothes had to last for a while. The hems were huge and the sleeves had tucks. *Mutti* also prepared me for my impending womanhood by packing sanitary napkins and explaining their use when the need would arise."[12] Vera Gissing, who left for England from Czechoslovakia with her sister Eva, recalled the opposite behavior: "We didn't have much time to prepare for our departure. We only had about three weeks. Our mother bought loads of material and had the local dressmaker working hard so she would send us both to England with a decent wardrobe. All the clothes were made to fit. There was no allowance for growth. It was my parents' way of coping with the forlorn thought that our departure was only a temporary one."[13]

Children leaving the Third Reich were subject to the same currency limitations as adult emigrants who were permitted to take no more than ten *Reichsmark* per person out of the country. Occasionally, a child succeeded in smuggling out small sums of currency hidden in hollowed-out articles such as clothes brushes, shoe-polish containers, and the like. Even after being warned that such action could endanger an entire transport's leaving Germany, there were parents who continued to try to smuggle currency out with their children, sewn into their toys or even in one case as a gold piece placed under loose powder in a teenage girl's compact.

Others who wished to keep within the law but still provide for their children's financial future gave their emigrating children possessions that could later be converted into currency from which the children would eventually be able to support themselves if necessary. What possessions, however, can one give a child and not arouse suspicion? Gold and silver family heirlooms or religious objects were a poor choice, as were gold-plated music boxes or anything that could be taken away by zealous Nazi guards on the train. Some parents gave children valuable musical instruments to carry, as it was feasible in German eyes that the emigrating child was indeed a young musician.

Not only were Nazi guards on the lookout for contraband when the children left Germany; the British customs officials were equally wary of what the children might be trying to smuggle into the British Isles. That same child carrying a musical instrument was viewed differently by the British customs authorities who were not used to the continental European emphasis placed on music lessons or the existence of young musical prodigies. One refugee boy who arrived in Britain carrying a Stradivarius violin almost endangered all subsequent transports. Enraged by yet another said-to-be "poor refugee child" arriving with such a valuable object, the British customs official turned to the transport escort Norbert Wollheim, asking whether the boy could in reality play the violin. "I had no idea whether or not he could actually play but I had no choice and so I turned to him and asked him to play something. Hearing nothing but the blood pounding in my ears, I watched incredulously as all the customs officials jumped up and stood at rapt attention until the boy finished." Later that day, Wollheim found out that the eleven-year-old Jewish refugee boy from Berlin had played the only song in his repertoire that his parents had taught him just in case such a situation would arise—"God Save the King!"[14]

Berlin and Frankfurt served as Kindertransport collection points in Germany. Parents of young children often told them that they were going to England together and only immediately prior to departure did they inform their children of the truth—that they would be going alone as part of a children's transport. Bertha Leverton from Munich remembered how children had to say goodbye to their parents in an anteroom because parents were barred from the platform after some had fainted there. "Now we were the big children. We had a background. We knew where we came from. But how do you get a little one—a five-, a six-, a seven-year-old—onto a train? Every parent promised their child, we will soon come and follow. How otherwise did the parents get the little children on to the trains? 'Give us a few weeks, when either things will blow over, and you'll come back again, or we'll come and join you.' That was a promise every parent made to their child."[15] Some children reacted stoically; others became enraged. There were children who burst into tears, and more than a few clung to their parents and initially refused to leave. Only after the parents promised them over and over that they would soon be reunited in Britain did these young children agree to part from their parents and board the train taking them to safety.

For most children, the parting process was unforgettable. Steffi Birnbaum Schwartz, leaving with her younger sister, remembered it more as a transition stage. "I was relieved to leave Berlin except for parting from my parents. I wasn't concentrating on leaving but on getting away; it all sort of went over Reenie's head. I don't remember my mother telling me to take care of her especially because the tone was that soon they [my parents] would be coming to England to be with us."[16] She was not the only one who was told that the separation would be just temporary. Olga Levy Drucker recalled being told something similar by her parents. "Mama said that she and Papa thought they would get to England in about six weeks, 'God willing.' The way she said it, I was not sure whether I believed her. A thought kept coming into my head: What if we never see each other again? I tried not to think about this."[17]

For the parents, the moment of parting was equally traumatic, but most of them tried to keep their fears to themselves. Steffi and Reenie Birnbaum were not the only children who were leaving a very sick parent. Charlotte Levy, who sent her son Hans to England, remained in Germany to care for her dying husband Berthold. "I knew my husband had just a very short time to live, and I did not know whether I should tell Hans the truth about his father's condition. I must say, thanks to my sister Martha, I didn't do it. She said to me, 'Let him go with a light heart. Don't let him go with a heavy heart.' England would be a difficult change anyway, so I didn't tell him anything about it. When Hans took leave from his father early in the morning of 15 March [1939], it was a terrible thing to know the two wouldn't see each other again."[18] And indeed, Berthold Levy died five-and-a-half weeks later on 23 April 1939.

In a large hall at the railway station, the transport leader read out names from a list and checked the children's documents. Parents were not permitted onto the platform, so the parting took place in this hall. Some parents were very demonstrative; others made great efforts to keep their emotions under control. A few even followed the train from station to station in order to wave goodbye to their children. Special coaches or compartments were reserved for children of a Kindertransport, with Nazi guards stationed in each compartment.[19]

Franzi Groszman, who sent her young daughter Lore to England, remembered the emptiness when she returned home from the train station. "There were many, many children there, and they came and hung this number on her. The children in front of her were all crowded together saying, 'Don't push! Don't push!' And suddenly someone came and said, 'Now, everybody go take your suitcase.' In no time, the suitcase was gone, the child was gone, the other children were gone—just emptiness. Then we turned around and went home. I did not talk. It was awful. People have asked me, 'What did you feel?' Nothing. This was such a shock. When we came home, we didn't talk to each other. My parents, my husband and I, we did not talk, we didn't look at each other."[20]

Apart from those children whose parents or close family came to see them off, there were also children who left on their own, without anyone accompanying them. One was Alexander Gordon, whose father had died when he was an infant and whose mother had been deported to Zbąszyń in October 1938 as a Polish citizen. Gordon, who had been raised in an orphanage and had a short stint as a young teenager in a *hachshara* (pioneer training) kibbutz in Germany, registered himself for a Kindertransport at the advice of Jewish community officials. "I reported to the train at six o'clock in the morning with one suitcase, ten marks, and very skimpy clothing. The station was crowded with children of all ages, from four to seventeen, and their parents. I think there must have been three hundred of us. I got on the train, went into one of the compartments and looked out the window. The people were behind gates and the parents were telling the small children to get onto the train. The children didn't want to leave. The parents said, 'We'll see you in England in a few weeks,' and there was crying and it was bedlam. I was sitting all by myself. I had no parents—nobody. I was one of the oldest, and there was nobody whose shoulder I could cry on. All I knew was, I was going away. I was going to England. Whatever would happen, would happen."[21]

For many of the groups, the journey through Germany was difficult. An eleven-year-old refugee child remembered: "I recall vividly our arrival at the German–Dutch frontier, when the Nazis boarded the train for a last inspection, before it crossed into another country. One Nazi per compartment.... The one in our compartment pulled down the blind, made us stand in the gangway, pulled down all the suitcases from the racks, opening them and throwing everything onto the floor. He took one or two small items, really of no value, except a sentimental one. He also asked us for our money, taking the equivalent of nine shillings from each child, and so we left the fatherland with a shilling in our pockets.... Fear was in all of us, until the moment the whistle blew, the Nazis left and the train passed over the frontier. At this moment we opened the windows, shouting abuse and spitting at them...."[22]

In addition to the groups of Jewish and "non-Aryan" Christian refugee children who came to Britain directly from Germany, other groups originated in Austria. Although the bureaucratic procedure used for Austrian refugee children was similar to that for those of Germany, the emigration operation commenced differently in the two countries. While the Nazis permitted the first groups of refugee children to leave Germany without tremendous difficulty, the Austrian group left only after direct and tense negotiations between SS officer Adolf Eichmann and Dutch refugee activist Gertuida Wijsmuller-Meier. On Monday, 5 December 1938, Eichmann granted Wijsmuller-Meier an audience and at the end of the meeting he extended permission to begin the exodus of Jewish and "non-Aryan" Christian refugee children from Austria. There was, however a caveat. To ensure that the emigration scheme would take place under pressure, he demanded that the first group of six hundred children leave within five days, by Saturday afternoon, 1 December 1938. Working against the clock, Wijsmuller-Meier and members of the Jewish community arranged for the children's departure and despite the great logistical difficulties involved the group left Vienna before the deadline.[23]

This was the first of dozens of groups of refugee children who left Vienna under the auspices of the RCM or that of Rabbi Schonfeld and the CRREC in the following months. Other than the Schonfeld children who usually came via the intermediation of Julius Steinfeld and the Schiff Schul, most Jewish children in Austria were selected by the *Kultusgemeinde* in Vienna and non-Jewish children by the local branch of the Society of Friends (Quakers). Groups of Austrian refugee children ranged in size from thirty to five hundred or more, as did the groups from Germany. The route they used to England was almost always via Holland, whence they followed the same course as the groups from Germany.

As there was no central Jewish organization in Czechoslovakia that could arrange children's transports, logistics were handled on the most part by the Winton-Chadwick committee in Prague, who contacted the Gestapo and made arrangements for the transports. Chadwick, in particular, endeared himself to the children whom he dealt with personally. Ingeborg Wohlmann met Chadwick when she and her sister (aged nine and six) were taken by their mother for an interview before being chosen to leave for England. "My memory is of a smiling man who put my very nervous mother at ease. At one point, he mimed that he needed the help of a big book, but pulled out the smallest book I had ever seen—it must have been a dictionary. He made us all laugh. We left on the last plane."[24] The rest of the procedure, including the route via the Netherlands, was the same for groups from all three countries. Although several groups of Jewish children from Prague were taken out by air, this mode of transportation was abandoned after the total Nazi takeover of Czechoslovakia on 15 March 1939.[25]

In addition to the children who came directly from the Reich, a small group of German Jewish refugee children also reached Britain from Zbąszyń, Poland. On 28 October 1938, some 15,000 Jews of Polish extraction were deported from Germany and dumped at the Polish border. The Polish government, claiming that these Jews had forfeited their Polish nationality, refused to admit most of them and sent them back to the no-man's land on the Polish-German border. Eventually, more than 7,000 Jews made their way to the small town on the Polish border named Zbąszyń, where they lived in disused stables and subsisted on food smuggled to them by charitable organizations. Early in January 1939, the Polish Refugee Fund in Britain announced that £5,000 had been earmarked for bringing children from Zbąszyń to Britain and guaranteeing their eventual re-emigration.²⁶

On Wednesday, 5 February 1939, the first group of fifty-four children, aged six to sixteen, arrived from Zbąszyń, accompanied by Elsley Zeytlyn, treasurer of the Polish Refugee Fund. All of the children were Orthodox; many were ill, one severely enough to be taken to a hospital. After landing in Gravesend, the children were sent to London and shortly after were taken to their guarantors. Nearly all the children voiced the hope that they would eventually be allowed to go to Palestine.²⁷ One recalled his experiences in Poland: "We were ditched at the frontier and, together with a large number of other people, we were taken to an old deserted army barracks in Zbonszyn [Zbąszyń], Poland, where we were given temporary accommodations in terrible conditions. From there we were sent to a hotel near Warsaw where we spent some weeks before sailing for England. My brother was thirteen and I was ten years old."²⁸ Another, Theo Verderber (Mordechai Vered), recalled how the group parted from their parents and traveled to Warsaw, where they were sent to a vacant summer camp called Valencia: "A week later we were taken to Gdynia to board the *S.S. Warszawa*. We were allotted small cabins with six bunks in each . . . there was nothing for a boy of ten to do but roam around and explore . . . the friendly cook let me come in and even offered me some tasty bits. We sailed through the Kiel Canal. It was frightening to see those mighty German warships flying huge red flags with black swastikas on white round patches . . . we arrived on 15 February 1939. Already I missed my mother, sister and brothers. On leaving the ship we were taken to a restaurant in Whitechapel where good Jewish people waited to take children into their homes."²⁹

A second group of children, the youngest of whom was nine years old, arrived in early August 1939, again under the auspices of the Polish Refugee Fund. After being taken to a hotel in London for breakfast, eleven of the children were sent to Leeds and the rest were divided up among foster homes and hotels in the area.³⁰ The last group of seventy children from Zbąszyń reached Britain on 29 August, three days before the outbreak of war, accompanied by three Jewish nurses from Poland. Most of these children, too, were religious; ten were immediately taken into the care of the Orthodox Mizrachi movement. The rest were divided among foster families in eleven cities. At a certain point Jonah Machover, an active executive member of the Jewish Relief Organization, traveled to Australia to find permanent homes for the Zbąszyń children. However, the submarine warfare during the Battle of Britain made it unsafe to transfer the children and the plan was abandoned.³¹

A final group of Jewish Kindertransport children was brought to Britain from the free port city of Danzig via organized communal transports. In all, four children's transports comprising a total of 124 children left Danzig during the spring and summer of 1939. Their route was similar to that taken by the children from Germany: by bus to Marienburg, by train via Berlin, Bentheim, Rotterdam, and from there to the Hoek van Holland where they sailed to Harwich by ferry.

Two Gestapo agents accompanied each transport to the German–Dutch border. The outbreak of war in September 1939 prevented the departure of a fifth transport that was to include seventy-one children, but half of them ultimately succeeded in reaching England through various routes. By December 1939, two hundred Jewish refugee children from Danzig had arrived in Great Britain and had been placed in hostels, on agricultural training farms, with a Quaker family in Birmingham, and with private families in Stroud.[32]

The most common route taken by all Kindertransports was by boat from Hoek van Holland to Harwich. Groups of children were often met at the German-Dutch border by Wijsmuller, who placed them on a bus. After the children showed their papers at the checkpoint, the bus took them to the port where they boarded a ferry to England.[33] In other cases, the children remained on an international train that crossed the German–Dutch border. Often the children burst into song when the first Dutch guards entered the train. Edith Bloomberg, who escorted a children's transport recalled: "I have very strong memories of that moment, some folk song was sung, but it sounded like Beethoven's *Ninth Symphony* in its jubilation."[34]

Many of the children had never traveled by boat before. Some became seasick, others worried about how they would find the bathrooms, but for all it was a form of adventure. One refugee who had been a teenager recalled: "Not only had I never been on a large ocean-going ship but I had never even seen the sea . . . the ship had been specially chartered for us. The only adults on board were the crew and those in charge of us. While they were busy I explored the ship, top to bottom, bow to stern . . . everything I saw was new to me, it was fascinating. . . . I spent the night in one of the saloons which had been improvised into a dormitory. Not much sleeping was done there that night. There were about forty or fifty boys, all about fifteen or sixteen years old, in that room . . . we were all a little over-excited and for the next hours we exchanged, in the dark, all the political jokes which we had picked up. They were mostly variations of 'Hitler, Goebbels and Goering . . . ' The jokes, as such, were not memorable but the occasion was. We did not need to look over our shoulders or lower our voices and the realization that we could say what we liked with impunity engendered an atmosphere of enormous gaiety."[35]

When the children reached Harwich, the RCM's representative boarded the ferry and placed a label around each child's neck, bearing his or her name and number. Immigration authorities stamped the Home Office permit and the medical officer stamped the children's labels. The children were then permitted to disembark and their luggage was searched. After they completed immigration formalities, unguaranteed children were taken by train or bus to a reception camp; guaranteed children were taken to Victoria Station in London to be met by their guarantors. Before taking custody of the children, guarantors were expected to sign a form assuming responsibility for their young charges. Guaranteed children whose sponsors lived far away and could not meet them in London were placed on a train by a representative of the RCM and met at the local station by a member of the local committee in the foster parent's area or by their sponsor.[36]

Although the guaranteed children knew that they were going to a specific family and to a specific address, this did not always give them a feeling of security. Steffi Birnbaum Schwartz and her sister Reenie were again among the lucky children who knew not only to whom and to where they were going, but had already met the other Jewish children from Berlin who were to be sponsored by the Schlesingers. Steffi recalled: "We went together in a group, all the children who were being guaranteed for the Schlesinger school. We arrived in Liverpool station and there were hundreds of children there. But even though the Jewish guides tried to keep us together, when I got off the train at the Liverpool Street Station I was still stunned by all that was happening."[37]

Another refugee child recalled meeting her sponsors as the high point of the journey: "It was not until the train pulled in at Liverpool Street Station and we were met by our 'uncle' and 'aunt' that I felt just a little excited and conscious of the fact that the journey was over; that I was with strange people in a strange land, my mother would not be there to tuck me up in bed, and the house I was going to was just a house and not a home. But I did not feel sad. It was like being on holiday; everything was new and exciting and the sense of fear and hurry—which I'd almost grown accustomed to—left me for the first time that night. I was seven years old."[38]

Resettlement

Contrary to the Dutch practice of placing children in group settlements and hostels, the RCM decided that placing the children in foster homes would be the most effective way to facilitate their absorption into British society. Compiling a list of potential foster homes became a matter of paramount importance. As soon as the planned rescue operation became known, both Jews and non-Jews offered their hospitality. Appeals were made in churches; many members of religious communities, notably Christadelphians (also known as Biblical Unitarians) and Quakers, offered their homes. The lower middle class was usually most generous toward refugee children. Among the foster parents were large numbers of schoolmistresses, widows, and couples whose own children were grown.[39]

The procedure for approving foster homes was standard. Local committees interviewed potential foster parents, checked out their homes, inspected the living quarters, and examined the possibilities for Jewish education and observance in the area. One Jewish family who offered hospitality to a relative was refused because the sanitary facilities in their home included only an outhouse and not an indoor toilet. Committees also examined potential foster parents' motives, fearing that families might request to return a child after maintaining him or her for several weeks and discovering how much work it entailed. In their social history of England between the two World Wars, Graves and Hodge state that despite the depression, Britain of the 1930s was a country of temporary crazes—hiking, nudism, the Loch Ness Monster, and the Talking Mongoose. The organizations dealing with refugee children fervently hoped that "take a refugee child" would not join the list of such fads.[40]

Reception Camps, Hostels and Foster Homes

As the first groups of children arriving from Europe were mainly unguaranteed because of their rapid emigration process, the RCM had to find them accommodations until they were placed with foster parents. It was early December, frost was on the ground, and the obvious solution was to temporarily open an uninhabited holiday camp for their use until the refugee organization could find enough foster families for all the children. Thus, the Dovercourt Bay Holiday Camp near Harwich and the Pakefield Holiday Camp near Lowestoft became "reception centers" for the unguaranteed refugee children who would come over from the first transport onward. J. A. Berger of London was appointed chair of a special supplies group dealing with clothing and supplies for these camps. Some of the supplies were donated as a result of the BBC broadcast "Children in Captivity," others were from firms such as Marks and Spencer that donated surplus shoes, local butchers who donated meat, and a greengrocer who sent a dozen cases of fruit every week for months. Rabbi Schonfeld of the CRREC, acting on behalf of Chief Rabbi Hertz, made a supply of kosher food available to the children.[41] Hertz also published a letter that was handed to every arriving child, wishing them happiness and telling them to be on their best behavior, to show gratitude, and not to congregate together in public or talk loudly in public places.[42]

The first group of 196 children from Germany arrived in England on 2 December 1938; two of the children originally scheduled for the transport were left behind due to high fever.[43] Half the children were from a number of Berlin orphanages (the Fehrbellinerstrasse Children's home, Ahawah, Auerbach, and Reichenheim orphanages) burnt during *Kristallnacht*. The rest were from Hamburg and Breslau, mostly unguaranteed older boys in immediate danger of incarceration.[44] Such unguaranteed groups arrived regularly during the first months of 1939 until it became financially impossible for the RCM to bring them over in unlimited numbers. In April 1939 it became impossible for more than 300 unguaranteed children to come to Britain until the previous ones were placed.[45]

A second group, 502 in all, including 100 non-Jewish children, arrived from Vienna on Monday, 12 December 1938. The youngest were taken to Dovercourt and the older ones to Pakefield. By Thursday, 15 December when another group of 350 arrived, 60 of the children already at Dovercourt had found homes and another 30 were scheduled to leave the following week.[46] In certain cases the children's arrival was used as a method of acquiring donations for their upkeep. Newsreels were made of the children at the time of their arrival and were shown around the world. Moved by the children's ragged clothes in the films, one group of women in Johannesburg set out to knit them warm clothing with wool supplied by a wholesale firm. The completed packages of clothing, knitted by both Jewish and non-Jewish women who had worked diligently for several months, were shipped without charge to Lord and Lady Marley in England, whose address served as a depot for their collection and distribution.[47]

The next group of children from Germany, who were supposed to leave on Saturday, 10 December, actually left two days later due to the intervention of Chief Rabbi Hertz, who protested having the Orthodox children travel on the Sabbath if not absolutely necessary to save their lives. As the group's situation at the time was not considered life threatening, the Council for German Jewry advised those dealing with the transport's logistics on the German end that the group should not leave before Monday, 12 December in order to enable the Orthodox children not to have to desecrate the Sabbath.[48]

The Holiday Camp reception centers may have been an innovative ad hoc solution to an urgent problem, but it was not a solution completely free of difficulties. The first problem involved the physical conditions. As the camps were meant for summer use, the buildings were unheated and often physically unsuitable for the winter. It was therefore not uncommon to see the children bundled up in their warmest clothing all day long. Children would pass the time playing games, playing the piano, cleaning, or talking. Three refugee doctors were always on premises. The second impediment concerned the finances necessary to bring the camps up to standard. Although the camps had the bare necessary facilities for the children they offered little more. To fill in the gaps, neighborhood people were extremely generous. One man drove twenty miles each way to bring the children sweets; another, a dentist, offered his services to the refugee children without payment. Chief Rabbi Hertz came down from London to visit the children at the camp in Dovercourt, and he planted a tree to mark the occasion. To enable all the refugee children including the Orthodox to eat, all the food in the camps was kosher and each child was budgeted at a shilling a day for food expenses.[49]

But even with kind and generous neighbors, the conditions were far from ideal. Alexander Gordon recalls being taken to the holiday camp at Lowestoft upon arrival. There was no heat and "it was raining, freezing cold, and we were in these little huts. I was with all boys who were my age. After sitting there a couple of days, a notice came: They are looking for fifty Orthodox volunteers to go to Leeds. Everything comes back to religion. I said, 'Anything—let's get out of here because it's winter.' It was cold, and we were freezing."[50]

Lore Segal ended up at Dovercourt. "You waited to be processed. You waited to find the suitcase. You waited for the buses to come. They were big double-decker buses and took us to Dovercourt Camp, a summer holiday camp that had little streets of huts. The children were assigned to these different huts, four little ones and one older one to each cottage as I remember. The memorable part of this camp experience was that at night the temperatures dropped radically. It was one of the coldest winters in history. The water froze in our sink so that we couldn't wash and couldn't clean our teeth. In the morning we went for breakfast to this big hall made out of glass, and the snow seeped in between the panes, which was very exciting."[51]

The refugee children could not stay at the camps for a long period of time, and the Movement for the Care of Children from Germany did its utmost to arrange their placement with foster parents. Potential foster parents would travel to the reception camp to choose their refugee children. The process of choosing the children by this method was spoken of derogatorily as "the market," as the comely children would be chosen while the plain ones would be left behind week after week. This procedure repeated the scenario that had happened several years earlier with Basque refugee children who had come to Britain and had been lined up on the stage of the Kent Academy to be chosen. OSE activist Ernst Papanek described the situation as follows: "The bright active children were snatched up and fought over and you could just see the leftover children, those who were not taken until the very end, shrivel up and die inside themselves."[52]

Bertha Leverton remembered "the market" well. "Every Saturday and Sunday, they had what we called the 'cattle market.' We were told to put on our best clothes and we'd sit around the table and visitors used to come. We felt a bit like monkeys in the zoo. We were being stared at and evaluated and people were chosen and taken away from the tables and interviewed. Prospective host families would interview you to see if you were suitable to be taken into their families . . . most people in England expected refugees to look like refugees. I think it was a minus for us that we didn't look bedraggled, ragged, in old and torn clothes. . . . Most families wanted little blue-eyes and blond girls from about three to seven. Little boys were accepted as well. The older children found it a bit more difficult to find foster-parents. They hastily established hostels to take a big influx of the children who weren't chosen quickly because we had to be chosen fast, in and out."[53]

Another refugee girl remembered the rumors at Dovercourt about why certain children were being chosen while others were not. "There were rumors that if you were lucky in your adoption the people might help your parents—but it was also said that girls of fifteen like myself were only wanted by English families as servants. What frightened me was the thought that I would be giving strangers absolute power over me, I didn't know if the Committee would still care what became of me once I had left the camp."[54]

The system in which potential foster parents would look at the various children, and then spend a few minutes alone with them was likened by more than one child to selecting a pet in an animal store. There were risks of incompatibility between the refugee child and foster family as it was impossible to judge a child's character in the short interview permitted. Fortunately, during the first year only fifty children had to be removed from foster homes due to incompatibility. Teenagers were difficult to place in foster homes as sponsors preferred to take young children, preferably those who were fair. At one point, refugee movement activists even suggested that children over the age of sixteen not be brought into Britain.⁵⁵

When the first groups of children reached Dovercourt, the leaders of the Movement for the Care of Children from Germany had not truly considered how the system would work. Focusing on the rapid need to move the children into foster homes, they had not taken into account that children might remain in Dovercourt for several weeks until the matchings occurred. In the meanwhile they would need someone on the spot who had experience with refugee children, could organize the freezing camp, create some kind of educational framework for the children, and serve as an adult figure to whom they could turn. Despite the fact that she was almost sixty years old, their choice fell on Anna Essinger of the New Herrlingen (Bunce Court) School. Together with a number of teachers, a kitchen coordinator, ten of her oldest high school students, and a few volunteers, Essinger created a framework in which the children could pass their time while waiting to be chosen by foster parents. Although only pencils and paper were available, she started a learning program so that they would not lose the educational opportunity. At the same time, the Movement for the Care of Children from Germany published appeals for volunteers, notably English teachers, to work with the children, in the press. Volunteers were promised free board and lodgings, fare to and from London, and pocket money if necessary.⁵⁶

Essinger also made sure that the children would remain in touch with their parents in Europe. Children in Dovercourt were encouraged to send one letter and two postcards a week to their parents through the camp post office. Fiercely opposed to the "cattle market," Essinger's protests influenced the RCM policy, which ultimately did away with the selection system and assigned children to homes before their new foster parents even met them.⁵⁷

During their stay in the holiday camps some of the older refugee children, who had often taken on adult tasks after the *Kristallnacht* carnage, slowly returned to being children. As soon as several transports of children were situated together in the camp, local rivalries emerged, the most common of which were friendly altercations between children from different cities trying to prove that "my hometown is better than yours."⁵⁸ Seeing these discussions as a healthy outlet for the frustration the children were undergoing, those running the camp did not try to repress these feelings, but did try to keep their expression within socially accepted limits.

Some of the children remember Dovercourt as the place where they learned their first English songs: "There were attempts through songs like *Swanee River, Tipperary,* etc. and some desultory lessons to inculcate some basic English. We did a lot of circular dancing, with arms linked, to Hebrew melodies which I remember to this day."⁵⁹ But the basic idea of the reception camp was its temporary nature, with the goal of getting children into foster homes as soon as possible. Once a week foster parents traveled to the camp to choose the children. In the evening lists of names of children were read over the loudspeaker. These children would report to the head office to be informed of their new destination, and would usually leave the next morning.

In late December 1938, the 550 children in the Pakefield camp were evacuated due to the extreme cold. Two hundred and fifty were taken to St. Felix girls school in Southwold; the teaching staff gave up their Christmas holidays to care for them. Some were moved to the Samuel Lewis Convalescent Home at Walton, others to a hostel in Norwich. By Tuesday, 21 December, only 320 children were left in the camp which was eventually evacuated.[60]

At the end of March 1939, the Dovercourt camp was also closed. The remaining children, mostly older boys, were moved to two hostels: Orthodox boys to the hostel at Westgate and non-Orthodox boys to Barham house in Claydon near Ipswich. At the end of 1939, the Westgate hostel closed as all the Orthodox boys had found training positions or homes. Barham House, no longer needed as a clearinghouse, became a permanent agricultural training center for two hundred refugee boys.[61]

Although the preferred form of refugee child resettlement was in foster homes, hostels ultimately became the most common place of resettlement for older refugee children, particularly for older boys who were the hardest to place. As early as mid-December 1938, the RCM realized that it would be necessary to create quite a number of hostels, as the first groups being brought over from Germany included large numbers of older boys, either from orphanages or whose parents were incarcerated or deported by the Nazis. These were boys such as Alexander Gordon, for whom offers of hospitality were not that forthcoming. Not only did the refugee organizations recognize this situation, but other sectors including real estate agents seemed to become rapidly aware of it as well. By late December 1938, property was advertised in the Jewish press as being fit for a hostel: "Upper Clapton, large freehold property containing 24 rooms, suitable for housing 50 children. Price £3,250."[62]

These collective homes for large numbers of refugee children were established in many communities, and were staffed either by volunteers, members of the Jewish Refugees Committee, or members of the local committee of the RCM, which often worked together. Hostels were initially formed in London, Bristol, Leeds, and Manchester, and later in other cities such as Southport, Birmingham, and Sunderland.[63] By early 1939, appeals began to appear regularly in the *Jewish Chronicle*, asking for a donation of one pound a week to support a refugee child in a hostel.[64] Quite a number of hostels were furnished through donations in kind. In one religious boys' hostel in London, a shopping company provided mattresses, another firm donated blankets, and food was donated by the Deserving Charities Organization. Boaz Wreschner, who had worked with refugee children in London, remembered the generosity of certain storekeepers to the children living in hostels: "The East End traders were often the most generous. I remember how they used to come to the hostel loaded with food, clothing, and other gifts for the children. They truly took them under their wing and made sure that they would lack for nothing tangible as they realized that they couldn't give them what they truly needed, their parents."[65]

As they were not standardized, there was a great difference in conditions among the various hostels, even in the same city. In certain hostels conditions changed when there was a change in administration. An eleven-year-old refugee boy recalled how when he and his older brother reached England he was sent to a boys' hostel in Leeds while his brother was sent elsewhere. "At first there were about eighty boys, but the number slowly decreased as boys left for various reasons . . . at the beginning it was all right but later it got worse mainly through a change in the management. But of course children and young men were there from different countries and different types of homes and it would have been a miracle had we all blended together in harmony."[66] Another refugee boy recalled how many children who ultimately left their foster homes ended up in hostels for older refugee children: "When I left my foster home I was sent to a hostel in London. There were about thirty or forty boys, most of whom I had known at Dovercourt. The hostel was situated in a large house but not large enough for such a crowd. In the two dormitories the beds were no more than two feet apart. There was a good deal of grumbling about conditions and the discipline."[67]

Depending on what they received in donations, other hostels were set up with more luxurious conditions. A fourteen-year-old refugee girl recalled her surprise at seeing the conditions at the hostel that she was sent to after a brief stay in a foster home: "This [hostel] was beautifully furnished and kept and I remember thinking even then that a few luxuries less would have enabled a few more children to be taken in."[68]

While the hostels provided a place to sleep, food to eat, and some sort of framework for the children, their fears or emotional needs were not always taken into consideration. One refugee girl who came to Britain at age ten recalled life for her at the hostel: "A local committee provided the money and I think on a physical level we were generously catered for and well looked after. I feel, however, that mentally many of us suffered greatly in that atmosphere for such a long period during our adolescence. This was in part due to war circumstances, to the desperate homesickness we experienced, but also because the people who looked after us were not really suited to the task. Neither of them had any experience of dealing with young girls, and both were in the same unhappy position as we were, having left members of their families behind. Consequently the atmosphere in the hostel was more often than not very unhappy."[69]

Orthodox and non-Orthodox children were usually accommodated in separate hostels to avoid conflict and friction, as religious observance was unfamiliar to children of nonobservant backgrounds. The religious hostels, notably in East London and Manchester, were in constant contact with or partially run by the CRREC. Periodically, appeals from these hostels, seeking Orthodox foster families, would appear in the press.[70]

Foster families were undoubtedly the preferred method of resettlement, although only guaranteed children went directly to such families and bypassed the reception centers. Initially there was no coordinating body that listed the offers of foster homes, and this caused some confusion among the various organizations. Consequently, in December 1938 the *Jewish Chronicle* published a letter from a member of the B'nai Brith Care Committee for Refugee Children, requesting that people wishing to offer their homes to refugee children do so through a central fund in order to prevent duplication of offers. The author stated that the homes had to be investigated and educational facilities for Jewish upbringing considered before any offers of hospitality could be considered. Additional consideration also had to be given to the number of children who could be placed in one district so as not to create German-speaking enclaves.[71]

The "enclave issue" involved more than the fear of creating German-speaking children's groups, as this was the prewar period during which Germany had not yet been branded as "the enemy." Throughout the placement procedure, the RCM adopted its guiding policy to avoid forming conspicuous Jewish enclaves that they feared would fuel antisemitism and raise an outcry against the scheme. Offers of homes came from all over the country, often from districts where there were no Jewish residents, and its placement committee made it a policy to distribute the Jewish refugee children as far and wide as possible instead of resettling all or even most of them in cities with large Jewish population such as London, Manchester, and Leeds. In dispersing the children widely, the RCM also claimed that they were obeying a tacit request of the Home Office which urged that "in their own interest" the children not be placed together.[72]

Yet another resettlement issue facing the RCM was that of religious placement. Should Jewish refugee children be placed with Christian foster families? When the RCM was established in 1939, its representatives were initially divided on the question of accepting non-Jewish hospitality. There were those, such as Eva, the Marchioness of Reading, who felt that all hospitality was welcome; this opinion prevailed primarily among the Liberal members of the RCM. One or two members raised the question of whether taking advantage of such hospitality might lead to proselytizing; however, the possibility was not considered a substantial threat and the lack of sufficient offers of Jewish homes ended any serious discussion of refusing non-Jewish offers of hospitality. The final decision was made to accept all homes, Jewish and non-Jewish, that met the necessary requirements.[73]

The result of this decision was that although no Jewish family offering hospitality that met the necessary requirements was ever turned down, they were not necessarily given priority in placement, particularly if the family lived in a Jewish enclave. Were gentile families preferred over Jewish ones? The RCM ascribed to no such overt policy at any time; however, if a Jewish refugee child, particularly a non-Orthodox one, had to be placed, and both a Jewish and non-Jewish offer of hospitality existed, the child would not automatically be sent to the Jewish potential foster home. This appears to have partly resulted from the RCM placement committee's nondenominational composition and stemmed, at least according to Rabbi Schonfeld, from the fact that there was no Orthodox representative on the RCM board.⁷⁴

Schonfeld was indeed the fly in the ointment for the RCM members on this issue, and remained as such throughout the entire period, constantly chiding them for sending Jewish children to non-Jewish foster homes and warning them of the dangers of proselytizing. From the early weeks of the Kindertransports onward, he insisted that there were enough Jewish offers of hospitality for every single Jewish refugee child from the Continent, if not in the form of families than at least in the form of Jewish-run hostels. Throughout its entire existence, however, and in spite of the placement difficulties in terms of foster care, the RCM refused to consider hostels as beneficial for the children as foster homes, even after learning of cases in which the children were pressured to convert. Writing to another member of the RCM board in the middle of the war, Lord Gorell referred to what he considered as "Schonfeld's obsession," stating "I don't like at all this undue association of Rabbi Schonfeld who seems to be to be unmindful of the real interests of the Children's Movement."⁷⁵

Although the RCM's resettlement policy allowed large numbers of Jewish refugee children to be placed with families instead of in hostels, the fear of religious pressure from the foster families was indeed realized during the war years, when significant numbers of Jewish refugee children, billeted in Christian homes, requested to convert. And as this danger had already been noted in early 1939, why, then, were Christian offers of hospitality accepted and encouraged, and why was there no overt policy to only place Jewish refugee children with Jewish families (as was the law in the United States) or in hostels, leaving the non-Jewish offers of homes for the "non-Aryan" Christian refugee children whom the RCM was bringing over? One answer was a form of political correctness of that time, or in the words of one of the committee members, "to have refused all these [gentile offers] would have resulted in affronting the humanity and chilling the benevolence of those Christians who had at last recognized the ineluctable claims on them of all childhood, no matter what its creed."⁷⁶

Another answer had to do with the "head-in-the-sand syndrome." By the time the refugee authorities became aware of the dimensions of the proselytizing that had gone on, the war was at its zenith and in many cases it was too late to rectify the situation. Large numbers of non-Orthodox children who had been sent to gentile foster homes had little or no knowledge of Jewish observances and therefore found it easy to naturally adapt to their environment. And after living in such an environment for years, even if they did not officially convert to Christianity, many of these children eventually married non-Jews and their children were lost to the Jewish communities.⁷⁷

Asked about this phenomenon long after the war, one former Jewish refugee girl described the process that Schonfeld had feared: "As a girl of six I went into a Christian family, the father being an English master in a Grammar school and a conscientious objector. The transition from being a Jewish to being a Christian—and I am now a convinced Christian and a member of a church—was not difficult. My adoptive parents attended church regularly, prayed and taught me at home so that I grew up in this atmosphere and imbibed it."[78] Another refugee girl placed in a non-Jewish foster home recalled that by the time the RCM got around to trying to remove her and the two other Jewish refugee girls from the vicarage that was their foster home, they refused to be moved: "We fought like mad to stay and were eventually left alone. Having at last found some security in our lives we were reluctant to give it up. I was fourteen when we were all three baptized."[79] As time progressed and the CRREC began to intervene in such situations, the RCM made attempts to deal with what was rapidly becoming a growing problem, particularly following the evacuation of many refugee children to the Midlands after the outbreak of war. The result was the Guardianship Furor, to be discussed in a later chapter.

Apart from reception camps, hostels, and foster homes, another form of resettlement was agricultural training. In addition to the children who were ultimately sent for agricultural training after reaching age sixteen, a large group of children were brought to Britain as part of an organized agricultural training scheme. This scheme, initiated by philanthropist Rebecca Sieff, and later run under the chairmanship of Col. Charles Waley-Cohen and finally Siegfried Gestetner, was originally designed to bring 1,000 and later 1,500 young people to Britain for agricultural training.[80] The children under consideration had begun their training in Germany and Austria and would continue in Britain with a view to subsequent emigration to Palestine. This agricultural training developed parallel to the implementation of the *Auslandshachshara* scheme in England, discussed in the next chapter. Refugee teenagers coming to Britain under this scheme were sent to one of sixteen training centers in Britain in England, Scotland, Wales, and Ireland, some of which were used jointly by the Jewish Agricultural Committee and by Youth Aliyah.

Among the famous training farms were the David Eder Farm in Kent, which served to train German and Austrian refugee youth together with members of Hechalutz, and Manor Farm, one of the first to be created in early 1939, serving groups from agricultural training and those from the Habonim and Netzach Zionist movements from Czechoslovakia.[81]

Twenty-eight members of the Gross-Breesen agricultural training farm, which had been opened in Germany in early 1936, came to Britain in 1939, many of whom continued their agricultural training at one of the various centers. A total of 120 non-Zionist youth were permitted to train in Oxfordshire until their emigration. Jewish refugee youth in the Cotswolds were trained by members of the Christian pacifist Bruderhof, themselves refugees from Germany.[82]

Of the 1,350 youths who entered Britain as agricultural trainees, 475 were placed in these centers, while 615 trained with private farmers. The 250 not fit for agricultural work were accommodated in seven hostels in London.[83] The outbreak of war and internment of enemy aliens disrupted the plans of the Agricultural Committee, which established additional training centers to provide temporary employment for released internees. Of the 227 agricultural trainees of all ages, including refugee teenagers who had been "evacuated" (in other words, deported, see chapter eight) overseas by the British government as enemy aliens, 84 remained in Canada and Australia.

During the war years, the Agricultural Committee of the Central British Fund took over the obligations of the smaller agricultural committees. The Jewish Agricultural Committee worked in close conjunction with the War Executive Agricultural Committee (see chapter 6) in supplying agricultural workers for urgent food production. In addition, according to the Central British Fund report produced when the agricultural committee ended its work in 1950, more than six hundred children who had come to Britain under the auspices of the RCM ended up joining an agricultural center after leaving school at age fourteen.[84]

A final resettlement method for refugee children was one that had actually started before *Kristallnacht*: schools that had moved en masse from the Continent to Britain. After the mass exodus of Jewish refugee children from Central Europe began, it was not uncommon for entire classes or even entire Jewish schools to be part of a Kindertransport to Britain.[85] This mass transfer of schools occurred frequently in May–June 1939. One example was a branch of the Jüdische Privatschule in Berlin, which was founded in Folkestone, Kent, in 1939, and took the name Athelstan School (the former school whose buildings it had occupied). Instruction was bilingual (German and English); Hebrew was also taught in the framework of general religious instruction, with "crash courses" provided for those children wishing to immigrate to Palestine. The school existed until the compulsory evacuation of Kent in May 1940 and the simultaneous internment of many of the teachers, themselves refugees, as enemy aliens. The children were evacuated to Wales, where they were boarded out to individual families and received into the local schools.[86] The last school to move en masse was the Berlin ORT technical school. Soon after the outbreak of war, 106 boys and 6 instructors were temporarily transferred to the Kitchener Camp in Richborough, after spending their first night in England at an East London hotel. The school was eventually resituated in the Leeds area.[87]

Adaptation

> Between March and September 1939 we lived in the hostel which the Schlesingers had set up for the twelve children they brought to England. I shared a room with Reenie. We brought hand luggage with us but had been informed that we should prepare clothing for when we get bigger and older as we will be there for a long time. And so our suitcases went by sea.

> We felt very much at home at the hostel in London where we spoke German among each other but also learned English to speak to everyone else. There was a cook, and both the boys and the girls had *metaplot* [Hebrew for "caretakers"] to care for them. The hostel even had a refugee Rabbi which Dr. Schlesinger had guaranteed and the rabbi's future wife was a refugee girl who had been taken over from Germany to look after Dr. Schlesinger's five children in Hampstead. All in all we were like one large Jewish family. The big changes would only come later, when we were evacuated from London at the beginning of the war.

With these words, Steffi Birnbaum Schwartz continued the story of her odyssey from Germany to Britain, describing the first steps in her resettlement.[88]

Wartime diaries and postwar compositions of former refugee children,[89] and interviews with them about their encounters, provide us with insight into the experiences and psyches of refugee children during their period of transfer and adaptation to their new homes. The readings indicate that in many ways, Steffi and Reenie's experiences were similar to those of other refugee children; however, in other ways they were very different. As comely young girls, they fit into the preferred category of most guarantors. As sisters they were extremely lucky to have been placed together, as the choice of accommodations was limited by the type of hospitality offered; at times it was necessary to separate siblings.[90] When Kindertransport children accompanied by siblings could not be placed in the same homes as their brothers and sisters, their comfort was tempered by the longing not only for family members still in occupied Europe, but also for those living in the same country and even city with whom they could not meet on a daily or sometimes even weekly basis.

Some children begged their foster parents to take both them and a brother or sister. Ten-year-old Freida Mertzbach, who had come to Britain with her fifteen-year-old sister Hilda, remembered constantly asking her foster mother if the family would be willing to take in her sister who had been sent to a refugee hostel in London. "I promised to eat less food, to help clean the house, to do anything to make it possible for them to take in Hilda, but they refused, saying that they only had place for one child and didn't want to take a teenager who would be harder for them as an older couple."[91] Infrequently siblings were placed in the same neighborhood and managed to maintain a close relationship. Others, separated by great distances, did not see each other for long periods of time.[92]

Because Steffi and Reenie were in a hostel, surrounded by other Jewish refugee children, their transition to life in England, even linguistically, was slower and easier than it was for those thrown into a foster family where they had to communicate in English almost immediately. Most refugee children had little or no knowledge of English at the time of their arrival but within a short period, ranging from between two weeks to two months, could understand the language to some extent. Of a random survey of thirty-one Jewish refugee children at a

Kindertransport gathering in the late 1980s, thirteen had no knowledge of English upon arrival in Britain, twelve had some knowledge, and six knew some English from school.[93]

Understandably, their command of the language depended upon the refugee child's age and level of schooling. Children usually achieved fluency within six months to a year of reaching England. Certain youngsters, not having the opportunity to speak German, forgot their mother tongue in time. Others felt themselves forced by social pressure to speak English, especially after the outbreak of war, and some refused to speak German as soon as they had some command of the English language.[94] Those children billeted with distant relatives who spoke German found the immediate transition easier than those in solely English-speaking foster homes. But after a while even those children commonly made English into their main language of communication, even among themselves.[95] A typical example of this linguistic transition was German Jewish refugee teenager Susi Adler's decision, early in 1941, to switch over in her personal diary from German to English. Nevertheless, within two months she still made diaries entries in German, testimony to the fact that she still felt more at home in that language than in her newly adopted tongue.[96]

One of the stranger things for refugee children to adapt to in England was British cooking. Although there were refugee children who found English food palatable and at times even similar to what they had eaten at home, other children noted that a number of foods such as Yorkshire pudding, porridge, and tea were especially trying. Many stated in retrospect that they found the food inedible except for Cadbury chocolate, which they preferred to the German brands. As Walter Laqueur states in his overview of the fate of young Jewish refugees from Nazi Germany, "What passed for bread at the time in Britain tasted horrible and they thought Marmite and macaroni sandwiches unfit for consumption even by animals."[97] One refugee girl was even given a prize for finishing her porridge each morning. In contrast, Orthodox refugee children usually found the food in observant Jewish houses to be identical to that which they had eaten in Central Europe and thus had little trouble adapting gastronomically to their new arrangements.[98]

All refugee children were given free elementary school education up to the age of fourteen. After that age, they were allowed to enter secondary school on condition that they qualified and that a vacancy existed. Small numbers of children were placed in fee-paying schools that offered free places to refugee children. However, it was generally expected that by age sixteen most of the children would have entered some sort of vocational training program to prepare them for the future. Refugee children were usually discouraged from considering intellectual or white-collar professions even if they showed the aptitude. The general attitude of the RCM was that "few of them will have the opportunity, either in this country or elsewhere, to enter the liberal professions and though this bears hardly on some, especially in view of the aptitude of Jewish children for intellectual pursuits, it is wise to take a realist attitude as to their future careers."[99]

Older refugee children faced different bureaucratic problems than younger ones. The initial government rationale for allowing the entry of older refugee children was to provide them vocational training as long as this would not be prejudicial to British labor. However, who would determine which type of training would be offered? The Coordinating Committee for Refugees argued that the choice of training must be left to the discretion of the foster parents. The Movement for the Care of Children from Germany argued that under those conditions most children would become blue-collar workers, something seen as unfair to children from professional and commercial backgrounds in Europe.[100] Ultimately, the largest numbers of children were either sent to work in agriculture or in factories; only a small number actually received any type of white-collar vocational training.

A random survey of an average group of refugee children produced the following findings. In a group of 582 boys, 99 were sent to agriculture, 54 to factory work, 83 to engineering, 45 to the metal industry, 24 to furriery, 57 to tailoring, 25 to woodworking, 25 to leatherworking, and 27 to domestic service. The rest were being taught to be draftsmen, painters, printers, motorcar mechanics, salesmen, shoemakers, opticians, textile workers, art workers, hairdressers, upholsterers, dental mechanics, watchmakers, builders, jewelry makers, clerical workers, chemical workers, and butchers. One was being trained as a seaman. Among a survey of 168 girls, 50 were working in a factory, 21 were training as domestics, 45 worked in dressmaking, 25 in hairdressing, 18 were nursery assistants, 6 were being taught tailoring, 2 were being trained as dental nurses, and 1 was studying to be a teacher.[101]

Two groups of refugee children faced special problems unique to their group: the "non-Aryan" Christian and the Orthodox. Most of the children in the first category were *Mischlinge*, products of mixed marriages having no Jewish upbringing of any kind who considered themselves as "true" Germans, Austrians, and Czechs. Often they had been told by their parents that they were being sent of holiday to England; upon hearing the truth when they arrived, some suffered psychological breakdown and trauma. These children, now classified as refugees from Nazism due to religious persecution, were the same children who, the previous day, had goose-stepped with their friends and shouted "*Heil Hitler.*" Indeed, many of them continued to use the Nazi salute in the reception camps.[102]

The other group of children to face special difficulties were the Orthodox refugees; the problem stemmed from requirements concerning their religious observance. As fewer Orthodox homes were offered than the number of Orthodox refugee children needing hospitality, the RCM decided to place some of these children in non-Orthodox and even non-Jewish foster homes. This policy, and the letters that some of these children sent to their parents in Germany about the problems they were experiencing, caused more than one Orthodox family in Germany to reexamine the possibility of sending their children to England under such circumstances. In an attempt to reassure these parents, the Berlin-based Jewish newspaper *Jüdisches Nachrichtenblatt* published an article about the refugee children's successful resettlement in England.[103]

Because of their religious requirements, unguaranteed Orthodox children were the most difficult to place and were usually the last children to leave the reception camps and "transit" hostels. At one point it was even suggested that a residential club house in London be opened for older Orthodox children or trainees to solve their problems of lodging. However, little was done before the war began to help in this direction.[104] The concrete problems began when Orthodox children were sent to non-Orthodox or non-Jewish homes. At that point, some Orthodox children voluntarily adapted to their immediate surroundings by eating non-kosher food and desecrating the Sabbath, a few having been told by their parents before leaving Europe that they should consider the situation *pikuach nefesh* (a life-threatening situation in which one does anything necessary to survive as long as it is not immoral). Totally cut off from their refugee peer group and the local Jewish community, these children saw adaptation as the one solution to their insecurity stemming from strange and unfamiliar surroundings.[105]

As opposed to the Orthodox children who adapted voluntarily to their non-Orthodox surroundings, other children were forced to violate their religious precepts by their non-Jewish or nonobservant Jewish foster family. "I remember being fed pork over and over by my foster family until I was quite violently ill," wrote one Orthodox former refugee girl. "It was so common that they tried to force us to work on the Sabbath in spite of our explaining that it was our religious day of rest," wrote several Orthodox former refugee children when describing problems that they had in their religious observance. Others were forced to resort to subterfuge in order to have any type of Jewish connection. An Orthodox former refugee girl recalled her battle to take Hebrew classes that were offered free of charge to refugee children. "I wanted to attend Hebrew classes which were given at the local synagogue but my Gentile foster family refused to let me attend. Each time when I would raise the subject they would find me different chores which just 'had' to be done at that moment so that I would not make it to the classes on time. One day when I finished the chores and wanted to go to class they even locked me in my room to make sure that I would not go out. That's when I decided that I would not put up with this any more and climbed out of the window and down the side of the house in order to get to the synagogue on time for the Hebrew classes."[106] These clashes over religious observance, which were only seen before the war among some of the Orthodox refugee children sent to non-Orthodox foster homes, became more frequent after the war's outbreak when thousands of Jewish refugee children, evacuated from urban areas to the Midlands, were billeted with families that had never met a Jew before and had no understanding of Jewish religious observances.

But almost all refugee children, whether Orthodox or secular, found that social issues were often of greater difficulty than either technical or ideological–religious concerns, particularly in the case of their relationships with British children. Most refugee children first met their British contemporaries in school, and the initial language barrier between the groups was overcome in time. At that point, large numbers of children developed pleasant but superficial relationships with their British contemporaries, which never deepened into friendship. After the outbreak of war, some children felt hostility directed toward them by schoolmates who emphasized the refugee child's foreignness and German origins. "I remember them calling me 'little Miss Hitler' in school," said one former refugee girl.[107] Other children, particularly those not yet in their teens, ultimately developed a good social relationship with their schoolmates.

Refugee teenagers often had a harder time making friends and being accepted by their peer group. Oddly enough, Orthodox teenagers had the least difficulty adapting to life in England. Accustomed to the differences between themselves and their neighbors in Europe, it appears that they took their new surroundings in more stride. Referring to his relationship with his non-Jewish counterparts, one Orthodox former refugee child summed up the general attitude of many Orthodox children by stating ironically that "our relationship was normal under the circumstances. They were English *Goyim* [Gentiles]. . . . We were German Jewish refugees!"[108]

Coming not only from a different country but at times from cultural climates that were far removed from those of the homes of their foster parents, the first impressions of some refugee children was that England was a peculiar, if not indeed primitive, country. Not only were refugee children dealing with the traumas of separation and homesickness, but they were also facing some degree of culture shock. Many were used to basic amenities not yet known in middle-class, and certainly not in working-class Britain, such as central heating. Those being fostered in a working-class home often had to cope with outdoor toilets. The winter of 1938–39 was one of the most severe in years; it seemed to rain without interruption, making the children feel like they would never see sunshine again. The bullying in English schools was foreign to them and the educational idea of becoming nice English boys and girls did not appeal to many of the refugee teenagers. Many complained about exploitation, a few about sexual harassment, and more frequently about beating. Some stated that at school they were treated as outcasts. In other cases, local Jews appeared to resent the secular culture of the Jewish children from Central Europe, and even Jewish children in school did not always befriend them and were at times standoffish.[109]

One former refugee boy recalled his own first impressions of his new home:
1. The English lived in funny flimsy houses.
2. They had never heard of double-glazing of windows.
3. They let 90% of the heat of their fires go up the chimney.
4. They did not have telephones with automatic dialing outside of London.
5. Even respectable middle-aged men smoked cigarettes and not cigars.

6. They drank a peculiar liquid that looked like coffee, tasted like poison, and was said to be tea![110]

The cultural barrier between many refugee children and their foster parents can be illustrated by an incident related by Elisabeth Singer in her fictionalized account of a Jewish refugee girl whose parents, unable to keep her with them in London, place her temporarily with a Christadelphian family. Despite his impoverished state, her father, once a famous doctor, sends her tea roses for her birthday, as he had done every year in Germany. While to the daughter this gesture serves as reassurance and evokes nostalgic memories of happier days, it irritates her foster parents as a needless waste, particularly in view of the fact that the girl was with them on sufferance, her parents ostensibly being unable to care for her properly at home.[111]

This brings us to the question of foster parents and their attitude toward the refugee children. Despite the later claim that there were insufficient numbers of Jewish families that offered to sponsor Jewish children and that consequently it was necessary to send these children to non-Jewish foster homes, large numbers of British Jews did enthusiastically open their homes. Nevertheless, although they were generous in their contributions to the refugee cause, there was a constant shortage of Jewish families offering hospitality compared to the number of Jewish refugee children seeking it, simply because there were many families, particularly among East European and Orthodox immigrants, who could not meet the Home Office standards and provide the children with the physical necessities required, or put up the financial guarantee.[112] As for the Jewish families who did sponsor refugee children, with all good intentions there were families who treated the children as an "exhibit," with one Jewish housewife saying to another "come see my refugee child" as it were a status symbol.[113]

British non-Jews, too, responded warmly to the appeals for hospitality and opened their homes to refugee children. Members of two Christian sects, the Quakers and the Christadelphians, were particularly hospitable to refugee children. Nevertheless, there were older children and trainees who felt the brunt of public hostility after war was declared. It was difficult for certain British gentiles to understand "Germans" who had run away from Germany and wished to fight other Germans, but many of these were countered by non-Jews who went out of their way to be kind to Jewish refugee children. One Jewish refugee girl recalled how after hearing that she loved music, a local music teacher offered his services to teach her free of charge. Edgar and Marjorie Hall, a Christadelphian couple who came from a community that had been active in caring for refugee children, remembered how on Sunday mornings, many churches made appeals from the pulpit for homes and sponsors for refugee children.[114]

Although the Church of England and other Christian denominations in Britain concerned themselves primarily with the plight of "non-Aryan" baptized refugee children, they generally regarded the efforts to aid Jewish refugee children quite favorably. Various churches sponsored projects whose ultimate goal was to collect funds for the child refugee scheme. Although the mass evacuation of Jewish refugee children from Central Europe was not regarded by the church as an opportunity for proselytizing, there were religious communities that expected the children to "behave as Christians," to attend church, read the Bible, and eventually, if they felt the "inner spark," to convert.[115]

The difficulties that unaccompanied Jewish refugee children faced, whether sponsored by Jewish or non-Jewish families, were often different than those of children who came with members of their families. On the one hand, they were indeed with their families, and did not have to worry about their physical well-being as did those children whose parents were still in Europe. On the other hand, while unaccompanied refugee children had to cope with their own fears and difficulties, those living with their refugee parents had the added difficulty of having to cope with their parents' fears as well as their own.

For most families, finding lodgings was of primary importance. Once this problem was overcome it became a daily fear that they would displease their landlord or landlady and be asked to leave. Parents would continuously enjoin their children to be on their best behavior. As stated in the tenth-anniversary booklet of the Association of Jewish Refugees: "Children grew up with the nerve racking order, repeated a hundred times a day 'Be quiet, for G-d's sake, be quiet, she will give us notice!'"[116]

As was the case with children brought to Britain by organizations, these children faced their new surroundings, food, and language in isolation and bewilderment. Some were treated condescendingly as "poor relations" who had to be helped and pitied but were, above all, a source of embarrassment to their sponsors. One of the deepest blows for most refugee children was often the psychological one of seeing their parents, usually confident adults, now suddenly as bewildered and unable to cope as they were themselves. For the bewildered refugee child, parents were often the last bastion of normality in a strange and unfamiliar world. The first sight of a parent subject to external authorities (i.e., Home Office regulations and limitations) served to undermine parental authority in the child's eyes.

In addition, children often found themselves in a role-reversal situation, "parenting" their parents. As children often learned English more rapidly than their parents, they were forced at times to translate for them, assist them in filling out forms, go shopping with them, or accompany them to meetings. Until child and parent had attained sufficient fluency in the language to make themselves understood, both existed in a state of uncertainly, bewilderment, and fear. The early discovery of a parent's helplessness, vulnerability, and hitherto-unsuspected fallibility was a crushing blow for the refugee child who was, at times, forced into such a realization before he or she had the emotional maturity to cope with its results.

Throughout the months of 1939, the Kindertransports continued to reach Britain from Germany, Austria, Czechoslovakia, and Zbąszyń. The last prewar transport arrived in Britain on the morning of Friday, 1 September 1939. Initially the transport was supposed to consist of thirty-one children of Youth Aliyah and thirty-five children traveling under the auspices of the RCM. However, when the number of children allowed to leave was limited to sixty, the youngest ones had to be left behind.[117]

On Thursday, 31 August 1939, the offices of Youth Aliyah in London had received word that the transport would not be allowed to leave Berlin as war was expected to be declared and the German–Dutch border was closed. Frantic telephone calls went back and forth between London and Berlin. Finally, a call was received from the Dutch Refugee's Committee advising that the transport would be allowed to cross the border into Holland on the condition that the Dutch would receive assurance that the transport would be admitted into England. This assurance was obtained in record time with the aid of the Council for German Jewry.[118]

As was customary, the train carrying the children traveled from Berlin to Cologne and then to Cleve, at which point the children were met by Mrs. Wijsmuller, who was waiting there with a Dutch bus. With her assistance the group was allowed through the checkpoint and across the border. The bus driver, who was unfamiliar with the route from the border to Hoek van Holland, had to ask directions from people along the route. Hearing that this was a bus of *Joodische Kinderen*, many insisted on joining the bus to personally direct the driver, completely disregarding the fact that they would have no transportation home.

Representatives of Youth Aliyah and the RCM met the children upon their arrival at Harwich. Youth Aliyah Children were taken to Gwrych Castle in Wales on the 5:30 p.m. train from Euston Station in London, while those traveling under the auspices of the RCM were taken to London to be met by their guarantors and then be transported to foster homes. As this involved traveling on the Sabbath the Orthodox children protested; however, they acquiesced upon hearing of the outbreak of war.[119]

Summary of Prewar Immigration Figures

Between 2 December 1938 and 1 September 1939, a total of 9,354 refugee children were brought to Britain through the Refugee Children's Movement.[120] Of these, 7,482 were Jewish; of them, more than 700 arrived under the auspices of the Chief Rabbi's Religious Emergency Council.[121] Among the Jewish children who made up 79 percent of the total number of children brought to Britain, 45 percent were Liberal, 20 percent Orthodox, and 14 percent nonpracticing. Another 431 children were brought to Britain from Central Europe by Inter-Aid prior to *Kristallnacht*, and several groups came from Austria under the auspices of individuals and organizations during the summer and autumn of 1938. The total number of unaccompanied refugee children in Britain was therefore more than 10,000. As of 1 September 1939, three of the children brought to Britain by the RCM had married and four had died.

Before the end of 1939, a total of 331 children arriving under the auspices of the RCM had re-emigrated, 93 to join their parents and 23 to join other relatives. Another 107 left with their parents, while 108 left to join distant relatives in Palestine and Australia. A total of £4,604 was spent by the RCM to assist 276 children in their re-emigration. In addition, five hundred children from Central Europe came to Britain under the auspices of Youth Aliyah. In the next chapter we will examine the Youth Aliyah rescue scheme in greater detail and chart the differences between these children and those coming to Britain under the auspices of other organizations.

Notes

1. Schwartz interview.
2. Tartakower and Grossman, *The Jewish Refugee*, 2–3. See also introduction.
3. See, for example, appendix to resolutions of the Inter-Government Committee, appearing in Adler-Rudel, "The Evian Conference," 272, Appendix II.
4. Stewart, "United States Government Policy, 304; 342–45.
5. Presland, *A Great Adventure*, 5, Central British Fund Archives, The Wiener Library Microfilm document collection 27/28/156; *Movement*, 7; Refugee Children's Movement, Second Annual Report 1939–1940, 3, Central British Fund Archives, The Wiener Library Microfilm document collection 27/28/153.
6. Stevens, *The Dispossessed*, 150.
7. Author's interview with Norbert Wollheim, New York, 11 April 1981 (henceforth: Wollheim interview); author's interview with Hilda Matzdorf, Jerusalem, 3 December 1981 (henceforth: Matzdorf interview).
8. Harris and Oppenheimer, *Into the Arms of Strangers*, 77–78.
9. Interview with Kathe Rosenheim, head of the Children's Emigration Department, OHD 63(27); interview with Adolphine Bernstein, president of the Council of Jewish Women in the Netherlands, OHD 18(27).
10. Herta Souhami, OHD 50(27).
11. Harris and Oppenheimer, *Into the Arms of Strangers*, 112; Baker, *Days of Sorrow and Pain*, 246.
12. Fox, *My Heart in a Suitcase*, 41.
13. Harris and Oppenheimer, *Into the Arms of Strangers*, 95.
14. Wollheim interview.
15. Harris and Oppenheimer, *Into the Arms of Strangers*, 103.
16. Schwartz interview.
17. Drucker, *Kindertransport*, 34.
18. Harris and Oppenheimer, *Into the Arms of Strangers*, 105–06.
19. Gershon, *We Came as Children*, 19–27.
20. Harris and Oppenheimer, *Into the Arms of Strangers*, 102.
21. Ibid., 107.
22. Gershon, *We Came as Children*, 27.
23. Wijsmuller-Meijer, Wiener Library series 02/626. Only 500 of the 600 refugee children in that group traveled under the RCM's auspices.
24. Emanuel and Gissing, *Nicholas Winton*, 101.
25. Wreschner interview.

26. *The Jewish Chronicle,* 13 January 1939, 24.
27. *The Jewish Chronicle,* 17 February 1939, 32.
28. Gershon, *We Came as Children,* 25.
29. Testimony in *Kindertransport: A Special Interest Group of the Association of Jewish Refugees,* April 2010, 10. http://www.ajr.org.uk/documents/KT_Newsletter_Ap_2010.pdf.
30. *The Jewish Chronicle,* 14 August 1939, 21.
31. Machover, *Towards Rescue,* 7–8.
32. Echt, *Die Geschichte der Juden in Danzig,* 215–16; Lichtenstein, *Die Juden der Freien Stadt Danzig,* 103.
33. Raanan Malitz (OHD), 21(27).
34. Author's correspondence with Edith Bloomberg, 22 May 1980.
35. Gershon, *We Came as Children,* 30.
36. Author's interview with Edgar and Marjorie Hall, Tel Aviv, 30 April 1980 (henceforth: Hall interview).
37. Schwartz interview.
38. Gershon, *We Came as Children,* 46.
39. Hall interview; *The Jewish Chronicle,* 2 December 1938, 10.
40. Author's interview with Hilda Schmerler, Ramat-Gan, 18 July 1980 (henceforth: Schmerler interview). *Bulletin of the Coordinating Committee for Refugees,* London: February 1939; Graves and Hodge, *The Long Weekend,* 265–304.
41. *The Jewish Chronicle,* 16 December 1938, 32.
42. Laqueur, *Generation Exodus,* 191.
43. *The New York Times,* 3 December 1938, 8. There are conflicting sources on this point. In *Contemporary Jewish Record* 2:1 (January 1939): 93 it states that the first group of 200 children from Germany arrived on December 2, 1938. The *Daily Herald* of London, 3 December 1938, 7 cites the number of children as 208. Gershon, *We Came as Children* (21) and Presland, *A Great Adventure* (5) put the number of children as 320.
44. *The London Times,* 3 December 1938, 14.
45. *Movement,* 6.
46. *The Jewish Chronicle,* 16 December 1938, 32.
47. Sichel, *From Refugee to Citizen,* 43–44.
48. Council for German Jewry Executive Meeting, 1 December 1938, Central British Fund Archives, The Wiener Library Microfilm document collection 27/1/2.
49. *The Jewish Chronicle,* 9 December 1938, 17.
50. Harris and Oppenheimer, *Into the Arms of Strangers,* 140.
51. Ibid., 141.
52. Papanek and Linn, *Out of the Fire,* 243. OSE (Oeuvre de Secours aux Enfants—"Undertaking for Saving Children") was an organization active in health care and child care both during and after the First World War. During the Holocaust, the OSE was involved in rescuing Jewish refugee children in France, running children's homes, and, with the Quakers, rescuing Jewish refugee children to the United States. See Baumel, *Unfulfilled Promise,* 61–64. Author's interview with Eva Michaelis, Jerusalem, 2 February 1980 (henceforth: Michaelis interview).
53. Harris and Oppenheimer, *Into the Arms of Strangers,* 145–46.
54. Gershon, *We Came as Children,* 39.
55. *Movement,* 13.

56. Essinger, "Bunce Court School 1933–1943," pamphlet, n.p., n.d., 1, 14–16, Central British Fund Archives, the Wiener Library Microfilm document collection, 27/28/154; Testimony Hanna Bergas E/188, Yad Vashem Archives (Bergas was a teacher in the Bunce Court School); *The Jewish Chronicle,* 9 December 1938, 14; 16 December 1938, 32.
57. *The Jewish Chronicle,* 6 January 1939, 24.
58. Testimony Hannah Bergas, E/188, Yad Vashem Archives.
59. Gershon, *We Came as Children,* 36.
60. *The Jewish Chronicle,* 23 December 1938, 18.
61. *Movement,* 9.
62. *The Jewish Chronicle,* 23 December 1938, 4.
63. *The Jewish Chronicle,* 13 January 1939, 20.
64. *The Jewish Chronicle,* 24 February 1939, 25.
65. Wreschner interview.
66. Gershon, *We Came as Children,* 80.
67. Ibid., 81.
68. Ibid., 80.
69. Ibid., 82.
70. *The Jewish Chronicle,* 14 July 1939, p. 23; 21 July 1939, 20.
71. *The Jewish Chronicle,* 2 December 1938, 22, letter by I. Kestenbaum.
72. Simpson interview, Presland, *A Great Adventure,* 8, Central British Fund Archives, The Wiener Library Microfilm document collection 27/28/156.
73. Movement for the Care of Children from Germany, Ltd. First Annual Report, Central British Fund Archives, The Wiener Library Microfilm document collection 27/28/153.
74. *The Child Estranging Movement: An Expose on the Alienation of Jewish Refugee Children in Great Britain from Judaism,* Central British Fund Archives, The Wiener Library Microfilm document collection 27/29/167.
75. Letter Gorell to Gestetner 21 June 1943, Executive Committee Minutes and Papers, Central British Fund Archives, The Wiener Library Microfilm document collection 27/28/166.
76. Presland, *A Great Adventure,* 8, Central British Fund Archives, The Wiener Library Microfilm document collection 27/28/156.
77. Former refugee children's questionnaires: Hannelore Bergenthal, Hetty Raz, Naomi Peritz. All questionnaires are in the author's possession. Hall interview.
78. Gershon, *We Came as Children,* 66.
79. Ibid.
80. Waley-Cohen also served as chair of the Jewish Agricultural Committee sponsored by the Central British Fund. Bentwich, *They Found Refuge,* 94. The members of the Committee consisted of representatives of the Jewish and non-Jewish refugee organizations and representatives of the National Farmers' Union and of the Union of Agricultural Workers. In addition, the committee dealt with the agricultural training of trainees ages eighteen to thirty-five, ex-concentration camp inmates who were forced to leave Germany. Letter to the Marquess of Reading, 15 June 1939, Central Zionist Archives (henceforth: CZA) L/13/147, Jerusalem.
81. Circular of the Histadrut of Hechalutz in London, Iyar 1939, CZA, S7/782; testimony of S. Adler-Rudel, OHD 17(27). Below is a table showing the numbers of trainees in various agricultural centers (circular, 16):

Name of Center	By 16 May 39	Plan for 28 May 39	to be placed	project	Total
East Grinstead	47	-	75	-	122
David Eder Farm	18	20	35	-	73
Salvation Army	32	45	-	-	77
Manor Farm	54	6	45	50	155
Glasgow	6	18	-	-	24
Cambridge	-	11	-	-	11
Liverpool	24	-	-	-	24
Manchester	40	-	-	-	40
Cheshire	-	3	2	-	27
Richborough	20	-	-	-	20
Cottwold	-	-	-	15	15
Goleigh Farm	-	-	-	80	80
Einzei Platze	36	20	-	100	156
Tythrop House	-	-	-	60	60

82. *Fünfter Brief an die Alten Gross-Breesener*, 1 (found in the archives of the Leo Baeck Institute, New York, AR A.1068/3686). Gross Breesen in Germany had been directed by Prof. Curt Bondy to provide non-Zionist oriented agricultural training for Jewish youth aged fifteen to seventeen. Despite its agricultural success, Gross-Breesen failed to generate a positive affirmation of Judaism. Angress, "Auswanderlehrgut Gross-Breesen," 170–79.
83. Bentwich, *They Found Refuge*, 95–97. Another source cites 2,500 teenagers as having been brought to Britain through this agricultural resettlement scheme. However, this may include older trainees, which could explain the discrepancy in the numbers. Wischnitzer, *To Dwell In Safety*, 200.
84. Bentwich, *They Found Refuge*, 98–101.
85. Joseph Heinemann (OHD) 52(27), Erwin Lichtenstein 1895/127 d. Yad Vashem Oral History Division, Heichal Yahadut Wohlyn, Givatayim.
86. Private correspondence between Dr. Leonore Goldschmidt and Dr. Joseph Walk, 20 January 1967. Dr. Goldschmidt and her husband were cofounders of the Kent branch of the school.
87. *The Jewish Chronicle*, 15 September 1939, 22; 24 November 1939, 21.
88. Schwartz interview.
89. For example: Baumel, *Loving and Beloved*.
90. Author's interview with Lillian Klein, Tel Aviv, 16 January 1980 (henceforth: Klein interview).
91. Author's interview with Freida Mertzbach, Tel Aviv, 22 January 1980 (henceforth: Mertzbach interview).
92. Questionnaires: Ellen R. Alexander, Ursula Mandell, Klein interview, Hall interview. Singer, "My First Year in England."
93. From an informal survey that I took of former Jewish refugee children at the Israeli Kindertransport reunion, Kibbutz Lavi, 1989.
94. Questionnaires: Zeev Berkley, Gertrude Urman, Sonja Kupferschmid, Gabrielle Ben-Ron, Ruth Golan, Ursula H. Mendell, Edith H. Visni, Ellen R. Alexander, Klara Scheck, Augusta Shifrin, Chava Markowitz. Signs in the street read "Refugees, we are at war with Germany, speak broken English instead of fluent German," Gershon, *We Came as Children*, 86–87.

95. Information about refugee children's language preferences comes from a study that I conducted of several hundred refugee children who reached the United States and Great Britain during the Holocaust. See Baumel, *Unfulfilled Promise*.
96. See Baumel, *Loving and Beloved*.
97. Laqueur, *Generation Exodus*, 194.
98. Questionnaires: Augusta Shifrin, Eva Levy, Noemi Kalisch, Ursula H. Mendell, Ruth Berkley, Ilsa Schatkin. Edith H. Visni, H. Raz, Gabriella Ben-Ron, Gertrude Urman, Nehemia Markowitz, Klara Scheck, Chava Markowitz.
99. Presland, *A Great Adventure*, 12, Central British Fund Archives, The Wiener Library Microfilm document collection 27/28/156.
100. *Bulletin of the Coordinating Committee for Refugees*, March 1939 (London 1939), 14; *Movement*, 15.
101. *Movement*, 18.
102. Reading, *For the Record*, 168.
103. "Jüdisches Hilfswerk in England," 1.
104. Letter from A. Horovitz esq. to Rabbi Munk, n.d., P/15/9, the Munk collection, Yad Vashem Archives.
105. Questionnaires: Naomi Kalisch, Ruth Weinbach, G.G., Nehemia Markowitz, Chava Markowitz, Gabrielle Ben-Ron.
106. Questionnaires: Gertrude Urman, Klara Scheck.
107. Questionnaires: Naomi Peritz, Getty Batya Rabin, Zeev Berkley. Stevens, *The Dispossessed*, 263-67.
108. Questionnaire: Mordechai Goldfaden.
109. Laqueur, *Generation Exodus*, 194-95.
110. Author's correspondence with Nachman Schaeffer, 22 May 1980 (henceforth: Schaeffer correspondence.
111. Singer, *Children of the Apocalypse*, 49.
112. Questionnaire: Ernst Valfer.
113. Questionnaires: Chava Markowitz, Augusta Shifrin.
114. Questionnaires; Hannelore Bergenthal, Naomi Peritz, Gabrielle Ben-Ron, Getty Batya Rabin.
115. Hall interview; Simpson interview.
116. Association of Jewish Refugees in Great Britain, *Britain's New Citizens*.
117. Raanan Malitz (OHD) 21(27).
118. Youth Aliyah Training Centres in England, n.d. (Autumn, 1939?), CZA, S 75-1173.
119. Habbas, *Sefer Aliyat Hanoar*, 182; Raanan Malitz (OHD) 21 (27).
120. *Movement*, 17.
121. Author's interview with Arieh Handler, Tel Aviv, 21 June 1980 (henceforth: Handler interview).

Chapter 6

Children and Youth Aliyah

Introduction

On a rounded hill above Abergele in North Wales, one can see the towering battlements of what remains of Gwrych Castle, a mock castle built in 1819 by a wealthy Lancashire industrialist. In its heyday, the castle boasted 120 rooms including 28 bedrooms, an enormous dining room, billiard room, music room, library, and 8 bathrooms as well as an ice house and a dynamo and battery room that provided a private electric supply as the castle was not connected to the local grid. Over the years, the castle changed hands numerous times, and from 1948 to 1968 it was opened to the public, attracting more than 10 million visitors and earning the nickname "the showplace of Wales." In 1968 the castle once again changed ownership, first becoming a restaurant-bar lounge, then a medieval market center, and finally a site for jousting tournaments. In 1985 Gwrych Castle was closed to the public, not to open again.

Today those towers and turrets, which peek out of the hillside overlooking the sea, are part of a derelict ruin that has little in common with its glorious past. At the end of the twentieth and the beginning of the twenty-first century there were a number of unsuccessful attempts to sell the castle to the highest bidder. In the interim, a Gwrych Castle Preservation Trust was established as a registered charity in order to bring it back to its former glory with a state-of-the-art website encouraging interested parties to donate to this cause with the click of their mouse. Alongside a description of the castle's condition, a virtual tour, memories of Gwrych, and a guestbook, the official Trust site has a sidebar entitled "Operation *Kindertransport*" which states that during the war hundreds of Jewish children were given refuge at the castle and remained there until after the war ended, "when land in the newly created State of Israel became available."[1]

The somewhat imprecise description appearing on the Preservation Trust site nevertheless delineates the basic series of events connecting Jewish refugee children, many of whom had come to Britain on the Youth Aliyah scheme, with Gwrych Castle, albeit with more than a few almost humorous historical gaps in the narrative. Gwrych Castle was one of a number of *hachshara* (agricultural pioneering) centers (pl. *hachsharot*) used by Jewish refugee children who had come to Britain within the framework of Youth Aliyah shortly before the Second World War, with an eye to eventually immigrating to Palestine, their original goal, as soon as it would become possible.

A multitude of differences existed between Youth Aliyah trainees and RCM children in Britain, although all were categorized by the authorities as "refugees from Nazi oppression." The reasons behind these differences can be better understood by examining the history and ideology of the Youth Aliyah movement that guided its young members during the Nazi years, through their wartime experiences in Britain and for many long years afterward.

What Was Youth Aliyah?

Youth Aliyah, or *Aliyat Hanoar* as it was known in Hebrew, was created by Recha Freier (1892–1984), wife of a Berlin rabbi, in 1932. Combining productive agricultural training with educational and Zionist values, it gave many teenage Jewish boys and girls a purpose and occupation during the mass unemployment time that resulted from the breakdown of the German economy during the Great Depression. The final goal was, as the name implied, *aliyah*—immigration to Palestine, to youth villages or agricultural settlements.

As Youth Aliyah developed in Germany, it also became politicized. All Zionist youth movements in Germany maintained some type of political orientation. Some of the more active Zionist youth groups in Germany during the 1930s were Bachad (Brit Halutzim Dati'im; "Covenant of Religious Zionist Pioneers"), a modern Orthodox-oriented group, Hashomer Hatzair ("The Young Guard"), a Marxist left-wing-oriented movement, and Maccabi Hatzair ("Young Maccabee"), a social-democrat-oriented undertaking. From the early 1920s, all such movements had been organized under a central umbrella organization called Hechalutz ("The Pioneer"), which later also coordinated the various agricultural training centers on which the young pioneers prepared for life in Palestine. Despite the fact that in 1935 Hechalutz in Germany was described as a unified Zionist body boasting almost 15,000 members, the groups composing it were highly distinct from each other, maintaining separate *hachsharot* where youngsters would receive similar agricultural training but separate ideological indoctrination.[2]

By late 1938, it became imperative to send Jewish children out of Central Europe; however, there were an insufficient number of available immigration certificates to Palestine, and additional alternate transit countries had to be found. In early 1933, Youth Aliyah had already initiated the concept of *Aus-*

landhachshara (agricultural training outside Germany) and by 1939 *hachshara* centers existed in European countries such as Denmark, France, Holland, Luxembourg, Italy, Sweden, Yugoslavia, and Switzerland. England was added to the list of *Auslandhachshara* countries after *Kristallnacht* when Youth Aliyah activists proposed to bring one thousand younger *hachshara* candidates to England and three hundred to Ireland.[3] The *hachshara* scheme for these younger children was known as Miha, short for *Mittlernhachshara* (Middle *hachshara*) and involved educating and training Jewish youth ages fourteen to sixteen who had completed nine years of school but were nevertheless still too young to join the official Hechalutz training programs geared to older teens. Instead, these youngsters were offered a combined half-day study plan with half a day of agricultural training.[4] Children sent to Britain in the framework of Auslandhachshara/Miha in order to await their immigration certificates to Palestine would meanwhile continue their education, learn English, and be trained in basic agricultural skills.

The procedure for sending these children to Britain was similar to that which the RCM used to bring over refugee children from Central Europe. With letters from the Youth Aliyah office in London confirming that the children whose names were included in the letter would leave for England, a Youth Aliyah representative would approach the German government and receive passports for the children. Until July 1939, the children traveled only with their *madrichim* (group counselors), most of whom returned to the Continent at the end of the transport. After July, their transports were combined with those of the RCM using the Hoek van Holland–Harwich route and RCM escorts.[5]

Lists of children had to be revised constantly as families seeking to leave Germany made contingency plans and at times received visas out of the country on which their children were included. However, before the outbreak of war more than five hundred children and their *madrichim* reached England.[6] In order to coordinate the various groups, the Youth Aliyah offices in Palestine sent representatives to London and the London office gradually became the largest Youth Aliyah center outside of Palestine. Zionist refugee activists in London formed an advisory committee with the rather bombastic title of "Children and Youth Aliyah for Rescue Work, International Relations, Negotiations and Fund Raising," consisting of Zionist activists, functionaries, and public figures such as Vera Weizmann (wife of Israel's future president Chaim Weizmann), Eva Michaelis Stern, Solomon Adler-Rudel, and Lola Hahn-Warburg in order to act in practice as a public-policy and fund-raising body.[7]

Two main problems faced the Children and Youth Aliyah offices, which was the movement's official name in Britain, once the children reached England. The first was finding accommodations for the children. Unlike the RCM, Youth Aliyah principally opposed placing children in foster homes, even Jewish ones, as this would not prepare them for the collective way of life that the organization hoped they would be leading in Palestine. Sending them to non-Jewish families was, of course, out of the question as it was feared that there they would be exposed to assimilationist influences. The two solutions were either to place the children on special *hachshara* farms purchased, leased or given as a gift to Youth Aliyah, or to place them as "hands" on farms in certain districts in order to concentrate them geographically, enabling them to meet with their *madrichim* in the evenings for cultural activities.[8]

Another problem facing the Youth Aliyah offices was that of obtaining immigration certificates to Palestine for the children before they passed the age of seventeen, at which time they would no longer be eligible for special "Youth Aliyah certificates."[9] The bureaucratic difficulties began when the children, having left Germany, were no longer considered "children in danger" and were removed from the priority list for such certificates. Once the war began and it was physically impossible for children in Germany to leave for Palestine (which as a British Mandate country was automatically in a state of war with Germany), the refugee children in Britain were put nearer to the top of the list for Youth Aliyah certificates and a few even managed to make *aliyah* (move to Palestine) during the war years.

For most of the children, however, the situation was not that simple. Much of the bureaucratic endeavor surrounding the questions of who would or would not get immigration certificates was the result of political pressures; the *hachshara* centers were no exception. The central Zionist movement in England, known as Hechalutz BeAnglia (Hechalutz in England) was responsible for distributing immigration certificates among the various youth movements such as Habonim, Young Maccabi, Hashomer Hatzair and Bachad, which had been transferred from Germany and began to become active among religious Zionist Jews in England at the time. Miha children coming on *Auslandhachshara* to England had already aligned themselves with one of these various ideological groups in Germany, and their choice of movement often determined whether they would receive an immigration certificate or remain in England. This was a cause of friction between members of the various youth movement, and between Youth Aliyah and Hechalutz. For the same reason, Youth Aliyah tried to keep the various groups in *hachshara* centers as homogenous as possible.[10]

Orders for all groups came from their respective central offices in London. The friction existing among the members in a movement's higher echelons often filtered down to the *hachshara* centers, where it was echoed among the trainees of "rival" movements. Movement leaders noted this rapid politicization of Youth Aliyah trainees with great sadness, causing one of them to wryly remark that it was a "good start" to introducing them to the mass politicization of Jewish life in Palestine at that time.[11]

Youth Aliyah *Hachsharot* and Training Centers

Throughout the prewar and war years, close to twenty *hachsharot* and Youth Aliyah centers functioned throughout the British isles. Some were small and existed only for a short time, while others continued to operate for longer intervals. Here I will discuss a few of them in an attempt to create a composite picture of the various Youth Aliyah training centers for Jewish refugee children that functioned in Britain during the prewar and war years.

A major problem in trying to reconstruct a picture of life on the *hachsharot* is the nature of the sources at our disposal that describe life at the various training centers during the prewar and wartime period. Much of the information that we have today about the state of the early *hachsharot* in Britain comes from Youth Aliyah publications of the period or the Youth Aliyah circulars of the early war years. While such circulars usually gave precise information regarding the physical specifications of a *hachshara*, the movement's intentions regarding the center's future, the number of refugee trainees placed there, and its work-training schedule, it is difficult to know whether they accurately represented the state of events regarding the young refugees' attitudes toward their *madrichim*, the way the *hachshara* was run in practice, or the true nature of the relationship between the Youth Aliyah trainees and their Jewish and gentile neighbors.

The most famous of the *hachsharot* was an estate in Scotland that had belonged to former British Prime Minister Lord Arthur James Balfour (1848–1930). Balfour was best known for the Balfour Declaration, the letter he sent to Baron Rothschild in 1917 in his capacity as British Foreign Secretary, declaring that the British favored the creation of a Jewish homeland in Palestine. In December 1938, Viscount Traprain (Robert Arthur Lytton Balfour), the former prime minister's nephew, offered his late uncle's residence in Scotland for the agricultural training of two hundred Jewish refugee children. The residence, known as Whittingehame House, was situated twenty miles from Edinburgh and its many acres were to be used for teaching the children skills of agriculture, horticulture, and forestry. Both children from Youth Aliyah and the RCM were housed at the estate.[12]

Whittingehame House came with sleeping and eating quarters, forests and farmlands, but without some of the necessities for running a home for Jewish refugee youth. In February 1939, the *Jewish Chronicle* published an appeal for goods required for Whittingehame House, such as typewriters, clocks, bicycles, a piano, a wireless, and English and Hebrew books. The response was heartening and Jews and gentiles alike generously donated to the cause. As the upkeep of each of the two hundred children at Whittingehame House cost £50 per year, various groups such as the London Women's Society, the South East London Refugee Children's Committee, the Hampstead Synagogue Ladies Aid Society, and others each gave "covenants," which were promises of support for groups ranging from ten to twenty refugee children. Once these promises were finalized, R. C. Maxwell was appointed as headmaster of the Estate school and 166 Jewish refugee children, two-thirds of whom were boys and one-third girls, moved in. Due to the large number of children who were placed at the estate it was impossible to form an ideologically homogenous group and children from various Zionist youth movements were all sent to Whittingehame.[13]

Although Whittingehame House was lyrically described by Norman Bentwich as "a little Jerusalem in Britain's green and pleasant land," an inquiry by Youth Aliyah in the autumn of 1939 following the dismissal of Jacob Schwartzman, a Hebrew teacher sent from Palestine, uncovered gross mismanagement.[14] The Committee of Inquiry's impressions were generally unfavorable about the way the school was being run. According to the inquiry report, Whittingehame's headmaster was not Jewish, nor was half the staff, many of whom had no previous experiences in dealing with Jewish children, leading to frequent clashes with the refugee youngsters. Both field and housework were not well organized: lessons were given for only two hours a day. Zionist zeal was sadly lacking: 30 of the 166 children no longer wished to immigrate to Palestine. Friction existed between the various groups at Whittingehame, and only the Orthodox children managed to maintain a good relationship with the other children and the staff.[15]

Confronted with the inquiry results, the Youth Aliyah offices in London could no longer be fobbed off with promises of future implementation of cultural and Zionist activities. Three items were scheduled for immediate reappraisal and change in the school. The first was curriculum: a new timetable for studies was to be made with a viable curriculum suited to the children. Two new teachers chosen by Youth Aliyah would be engaged, one for Hebrew and one for general studies, with both teachers preferably fluent in English and Hebrew. Six *madrichim*, preferably all male, would be sent by Youth Aliyah to organize cultural work in the evenings.[16]

Everyone—Youth Aliyah, the school administration, and the various Zionist youth movement leaders—agreed that the school should be given the right to expel "unsuitable" children. However, who was to decide which children were "unsuitable"? Youth Aliyah considered itself to be *in loco parentis* and therefore wished to be allowed to choose which children would be sent to Whittingehame School and, if necessary, which to remove. The school administration, on the other hand, wanted unchecked discretionary powers of expulsion. Although negotiations on this subject continued for quite some time, the two parties never reached an agreement.

Due to its proximity to Edinburgh, the Whittingehame Farm School was adopted by the Edinburgh Jewish community.[17] Despite this close relationship, or possibly because of it, a number of misunderstandings arose that caused friction between the two. Some stemmed from the gap between the psychological expectations of English Jewry regarding what they considered proper refugee behavior, a case of "knowing one's place," and the more normal life that the *madrichim* wished the children to lead. One of the young refugees recalled how Whittingehame Farm School ordered cake for Sabbath morning breakfast from a bakery in Edinburgh, something which the Edinburgh Jewish community considered an unnecessary luxury in view of the fact that they considered the children at Whittengehame as living on their charity. "We were shocked when we heard what the Jews of Edinburgh were saying about the one piece of cake each that we were permitted on Saturday morning: 'How dare charity cases spend someone else's money on *Kiddush* cake for *Shabbat*?! It was unheard of!' In their minds, Jewish refugee children, even if they were part of Youth Aliyah, always had to remember that they were refugees, and that they were there because of the beneficence of the British and particularly the British Jews."[18]

The community and farm school management eventually worked the issue through, but like a number of other situations, it left an indelible mark on the relationship between the two groups. This story echoed some of the incidents that refugee children experienced not only in England but also in other countries regarding the perception of how a refugee child was supposed to look or act, and the misunderstandings that occurred as a result of their true situation. As the American uncle of a Jewish refugee girl from Germany remarked upon her arrival: "How can you pretend to be a poor immigrant when you arrive here with three suitcases?!"[19]

Although the children's physical scars from Nazi oppression, if existing, vanished quickly, their mental scars took much longer to disappear. Things that meant little to the British Jews or even the British Youth Aliyah activists took on added significance for the refugee children as they reminded them of the horrors of the Nazi regime and what they had been through. A small example was their reaction when shown the school uniforms they were supposed to wear. Gerda Margulies, who had been at Whittengehame, recalled the children's reaction to the brown-colored shirts they were supposed to wear: "Brown shirts? Immediately we thought of the Nazi SA thugs who would march around in brown uniform shirts, the ones who came into our houses during *Kristallnacht* to take away our fathers and brothers."[20] In early March 1939, the matron of Whittingehame School requested an exchange of the uniform's brown shirts for navy blue ones, thus solving the delicate problem.[21]

Already in 1941, there were vacancies at the Whittingehame Farm School, as children left when they reached the age of eighteen. In 1942, the school was closed due to the lack of newcomers. The remaining children were transferred to Dalton House near Edinburgh.[22]

The Great Engham Farm *hachshara* center near Kent was established by Youth Aliyah to house twenty-five children from Czechoslovakia who were registered for, but unable to be housed at, the Whittengehame Farm School. They were assisted financially by the RCM, which placed fifty RCM children at the Farm School and by the Agricultural Committee of the Council for German Jewry, which placed another thirty children on the farm. A group of Jewish refugee children from Poland were also placed there under the auspices of the Women's Appeal Committee. The farm served primarily as a transit camp for Miha; during the summer of 1939 between 300 and 350 children aged thirteen to sixteen spent some time learning and working there. In the words of Jewish Agency representative Peretz Leshem (Fritz Lichtenstein), "the Great Engham farm was a busy as a beehive" with children coming and going, throughout the middle of 1939.[23]

Most of the children at Great Engham started their agricultural training by working as "hands" on neighboring farms. Due to the labor shortage, they were even asked to assist in an extended agricultural endeavor, the local hops' picking. Along with the agricultural work, they were also active in the ARP (Air Raid Protection) scheme that was put into effect throughout Britain. The ARP began in 1945 when the Home Office began to train doctors, policemen, and air-raid wardens in preparation for air raids in time of war. In 1938, the Lord Privy Seal (John Anderson) gave orders to prepare 400,000 small air-raid shelters for the general population; these were nicknamed "Anderson Shelters." By January 1939, the government was circulating the "Guide to National Service," and people of all ages throughout Britain were urged to volunteer their time toward preparing Britain for what was to come.

It was in this context that Youth Aliyah young refugees contributed their first efforts to aid the British war effort. The children at Great Engham were no exception. As one of them recalled, "We were all very serious about getting Britain ready to fight the Nazis. Most of us felt that it was the least we could do, especially as we were too young to actually join the military."[24] The children at Great Engham threw themselves into the task, filling almost two thousand sandbags in the time allotted them to fill half that number. Although the work was difficult, the *madrichim* considered it good training for physical labor in Palestine and preparation for what the children would inevitably experience there.[25]

A third Youth Aliyah *hachshara* was named "Pine Trees." The seventeen acres of Pine Trees in Ashford, Kent, were rented from the widow and son of MP Kenwood and were opened in late summer 1939. Housing forty children, most from the Berlin Hashomer Hatzair movement, several girls from Vienna, and nine *madrichim,* Youth Aliyah intended eventually to place ninety children in all on the estate. Initially the children worked on neighboring farms with the intention of their beginning work at Pine Trees later in the year; however, it took much longer for the plan to be carried out and Pine Trees never became a self-supporting *hachshara*. On the other hand, the children's arrival stimulated trade in the nearby village of Ashford. According to the circular of Youth Aliyah training centers in Britain, a good relationship consequently developed between the children and the townspeople.[26]

Hale Nurseries was another Youth Aliyah *hachshara*, located between Salisbury and Bournemouth. The twenty-one boys who were placed there adapted quickly to their surroundings and, according to a semi-official publication of Youth Aliyah, developed a close relationship with the non-Jewish proprietor. After overcoming the initial language barrier, the children were also reported to have blended well with the local workers. Eventually, fifty young people, including twenty belonging to the left-wing Hashomer Hatzair movement, worked at the Hale Nurseries and became entirely self-supporting.[27]

Refugee children from yet another set of Zionist youth movements—Gordonia (a socialist-pacifist movement based on the teachings of A. D. Gordon),

Young Maccabees, Zionist Youth, and Brith Kodesh (youth movements connected with the General Zionists)—were placed in Laudough Castle near Cardiff, which was donated to Youth Aliyah by the YMCA. In an attempt to give the young trainees a taste of what their future was supposed to be, the castle's manager was a young Zionist emissary (*shaliach*) sent from Palestine who had trained in Germany.

As in most of the Youth Aliyah centers, the children at Laudough Castle divided their day between work and study. Teachers at the *hachshara* placed great emphasis on the children's language lessons, both English and Hebrew, to prepare them for their temporary sojourn in England and their permanent life in Palestine. In addition, the children were given science and Jewish studies classes to bring them up to par with their Zionist contemporaries in terms of Jewish knowledge. The work at Loudough Castle was primarily agricultural and included a large amount of housework to keep the castle in shape. Forty-three of the children from Laudough were evacuated to Gwrych Castle at the outbreak of war.[28]

Bydown was an additional *hachshara,* founded in Devon by a group from Great Engham who were forced to move there in November 1939 when Kent became a proscribed area to aliens. Its headmaster, Dr. Fridolin M. Friedmann, had been the former headmaster of the Landschulheim of Caputh near Berlin and had led several Kindertransports prior to his own emigration. As he ran Bydown with an iron hand, many of the young trainees who were unhappy with the way the *hachshara* was run expressed their subversive and almost revolutionary streak in a wall newspaper that they posted for all to read. By 1941, all of the children at Bydown had been placed at self-supporting centers. Bydon's lease was not renewed when it ended in October 1941.[29]

One of the most colorful and well-known *hachsharot* was set up at Gwrych Castle in Northern Wales. On 28 August 1939, the castle's owner, Lord Dundonald, offered it rent-free for use by Jewish refugee children. Lord Dundonald supplied a grant toward the rates and taxes on the castle and even took it upon himself to pay half the cost of repairs. As the castle had been uninhabited for over fifteen years, these repairs were extensive and of the utmost urgency. He also expressed hope that the five hundred acres of land accompanying the castle would compensate the children for the building's derelict condition.[30]

As soon as the war broke out, Gwrych Castle's location took on a double significance for the refugee children. The castle was situated in an area of Wales designated for receiving evacuated children. Knowing that war was imminent, the first group of Youth Aliyah children was sent there from Kent on the night of Thursday, 31 August 1939 to avoid being caught in the mass evacuation beginning the next day. A second group of thirty-one children, the last transport to arrive from Germany, was also sent there on the first day of the war. In all, the castle, which in peacetime was supposed to house the Orthodox English *hachshara Bachad,* accommodated 172 children, 129 of whom were Youth Aliyah candidates.

Like the children at Great Engham, those at Gwrych Castle did ARP volunteer work by painting white linen and filling sandbags. According to the Youth Aliyah circulars, as was the case in a number of *hachsharot*, the nearby village of Abergele was economically stimulated by the youngsters' arrival; the children substantially augmented the village population and required various services. Consequently, it was reported that as with other *hachsharot*, the castle's young inhabitants got on well with the villagers of Abergele.[31]

Sixty of the children at Gwrych Castle belonged to Bachad and were under the supervision of Eliezer (Erwin) Seligman. A yeshiva was started at the castle by Rabbi Samuel Sperber, who taught fifteen boys at a time, giving them a short but extensive course in Jewish learning. The Transylvanian-born Sperber, educated at the Hungarian yeshiva of Vishov, had moved to England soon after Hitler's rise to power and began organizing Jewish education classes until he started his work with Jewish refugee children. Although he became active in the Zionist Federation only later, he was already a staunch Zionist and simultaneously imbued the children with both a love of Judaism and a love for the Land of Israel. At the same time, not wanting to discriminate against female refugee trainees, Bachad took the first steps in opening a girl's seminar for religious studies at Gwrych Castle.[32]

In 1941, the *hachshara* center at Gwrych Castle was abandoned due to the lack of agricultural work in the area. Before it closed, the BBC visited the castle and taped records for a program broadcast on Passover eve of that year entitled "Refugees in Flight." The remaining children at Gwrych Castle were sent to Youth Aliyah Centers at Ruthin, Nantclwyd, Sealand, Donnington, Kynnersley, and St. Asaph.[33]

Apart from the Youth Aliyah *hachsharot* in England, Scotland, and Wales, a number of Youth Aliyah centers were set up in Northern Ireland. Refugee trainees there were housed either in Clonin Castle or Millisle Farm near Belfast, which by midwar had thirty-five trainees. However, due to travel restrictions in Northern Ireland, it became exceedingly difficult to maintain adequate communication between these groups and the central Youth Aliyah office in London. Despite the fact that the *hachsharot* were flourishing agriculturally, the central office decided that these centers would no longer be developed and that they would gradually be closed down.[34]

Education, Communication, and Finances

One of the major problems facing Youth Aliyah was how to continue to develop the refugee trainees' Jewish and Zionist education while preparing them for immigration to Palestine. The problem became exacerbated after evacuation, when certain groups had to leave their *hachsharot* and join other training centers. Each movement grappled with this issue separately, but it appears to have bothered the Orthodox Zionists more than the secular, as Bachad was the only one to address the issue in practice by setting up a *mercaz limud* (study center) in Manchester. The center, which consisted of a yeshiva, girls' seminar, and seminar for *madrichim*, was directed by Hans Heinemann, assisted by Rabbi Samuel Sperber, Rabbi Isser Yehuda Unterman of Liverpool, Rabbi Yaakov Kopul Rosen of Manchester, and Rabbi Alexander Altman.

Groups coming to the *mercaz limud* would spend six months in intensive study in order to enrich their Jewish knowledge. The center, which had no parallel at that time among British Jews, was a widely acclaimed success and it received requests to join from a number of British children and refugees who had not been connected previously with a Zionist youth movement.[35]

The great physical distance between the central Youth Aliyah office in London and the widely flung *hachsharot* meant that lines of formal and informal communication had to be kept open in order to keep everyone in contact. As a result, the Central Youth Aliyah office tried to publish frequent newsletters that were circulated among the various training centers throughout Britain. In addition, the Miha group in Bydown published a monthly bulletin entitled *Hamachreisha* (The Plough), which later merged with a Bachad publication to form *Zeraim* (Seeds). Bachad, too, published its own newsletter entitled *Chayenu* (Our Lives). At first, these newsletters were written in German and Hebrew. Later, when the children became fluent in English, and some had even forgotten their German, they were written primarily in English. In addition to passing on news from the various *hachsharot*, after 1943 when news of the fate of European Jewry began to filter into Britain, these newsletters took on the added task of morally strengthening the young refugees who understood that there was a good chance that their families who had remained in Europe were no longer alive and that the world that they had known had been totally destroyed.[36]

As was the case with the RCM, finance was one of the make-or-break issues in determining how well Children and Youth Aliyah could function in Britain. Prior to the outbreak of the war, Youth Aliyah in Great Britain was supported by donations received from a number of sources. One was the Women's Appeal Committee headed by Rebecca Sieff and Yvonne de Rothschild (wife of Anthony de Rothschild), which aided Jewish refugees in Britain, specifically women and children. Another was a series of private grants and donations raised through the Eddie Cantor Appeal, formed when American Jewish actor Eddie Cantor toured England for sixteen days in July 1939 and raised more than £100,000 for Youth Aliyah. A third source was the British Council of the Young Pioneers Movement for Palestine. As it became apparent that the refugee children would be forced to stay in Britain for much longer than had been initially assumed, Youth Aliyah leaders realized that it would be necessary to raise larger sums for their upkeep than had originally been planned.[37]

As a partial solution, members of the Youth Aliyah executive suggested that refugee boys and girls could live on collective farms but be self-supporting by working elsewhere. During a 1940 interview with Lola Hahn-Warburg and Elaine Laski, Meyer Stephany of the Council for German Jewry announced that he was ready to approach the British government for a grant on behalf of Children and Youth Aliyah. The RCM also promised the Council a sum equal to that raised by the Women's Appeal Committee to cover the refugee trainee children's maintenance costs in England during 1941. Negotiations with the RCM continued in the hope that the grant could be extended to cover the maintenance costs for the children during November and December 1940 as well, but the extra sum was not forthcoming.[38]

As a result, Youth Aliyah found itself financially dependent upon the goodwill of a number of refugee organizations that basically passed them back and forth like a hot potato, each time wishing for someone else to take charge. De facto, the Council for German Jewry's financial responsibility toward Youth Aliyah had ended in 1940. As the Council did not have the means to continue this support, they requested a loan for this purpose from the RCM to cover Youth Aliyah's expenses until March 1941, setting the goal of making most of the children self-supporting by then.[39] Despite this plan, it took much longer to reach the goal of making most of the Youth Aliyah refugee trainees financially independent. Some of the youngest trainees received assistance from Jewish sources until close to the war's end.

The most welcome means of no longer having to support the young refugee trainees was to have them immigrate to Palestine. Prior to the outbreak of the war, Central European children who had been evacuated to Britain were eligible for immigration certificates. Indeed, one group of fifteen children from Great Engham and Whittengehame Farm School left for Palestine in July 1939. After the outbreak of war, the central offices of Youth Aliyah in Palestine decided to use all available immigration certificates for children in Nazi-occupied countries only, as those in Britain were considered to be living in relative safety. While understandable under the circumstances, this policy had both technical and psychological repercussions on the lives of the Jewish refugee trainees in Britain.

The technical aspect was based on the refugee trainees' ages and their eligibility for Youth Aliyah immigration certificates. As only children up to age seventeen were eligible for such certificates, and most refugee trainees had come to Britain in 1939 between age fourteen and sixteen, by 1943 they were ineligible for Youth Aliyah immigration certificates and were therefore forced to remain in Britain to wait for adult immigration certificates, which at the time were almost unavailable. The psychological aspect was based on the refugee youngsters' expectation that shortly after coming to Britain they would be immigrating to Palestine. Upon realizing that they would have to remain in Britain for an indefinite period, many became depressed and eventually left the *hachsharot*.[40]

Conclusions

How are the various motivations for "helping behavior" reflected in the story of the Youth Aliyah *hachsharot* for Jewish refugee children in Britain? Unlike the

RCM children who were dependent upon individual sponsors, the Youth Aliyah children came in groups and their main direct or indirect interface with the British Jewish and non-Jewish population was through group sponsorship and contact with locals at or near the agricultural estates on which they were placed.

Sponsors were usually solicited from a cohesive group and the children's sponsoring came about as a group act. The costs to the individual, both financial and in terms of time devoted to the scheme, were minimal as it was a group sponsorship. There were definite psychological benefits connected to the act of group sponsorship, both for the individual on his or her own and for the individual as part of a group interface. The factor of having a sense of changing the world as part of altruistic action appears also to have come into play with group sponsorship. The final factor—confidence—was doubly strengthened both by a moral identification with the act being performed and by the awareness of taking part in a positively viewed group effort.[41]

As for the helping behavior of those who came into direct contact with the Youth Aliyah children on *hachsharot,* several of the additional factors cited as being supportive of such behavior were evident. Many, if not most, of the townspeople who developed a relationship with the Youth Aliyah trainees had firm religious beliefs, were in a settled family situation, were middle aged, emotionally stable, and while not necessarily having a tradition of volunteering, certainly had a tradition of mutual assistance in a rural or agricultural setting.[42] Consequently, although the nature of the Youth Aliyah trainees' contact with British society was often different than that of their RCM-sponsored contemporaries, the mechanism of helping behavior that came into effect with regard to this group appears to have followed a similar pattern to that already charted with regard to the majority of the *Kinder.*

And what of the "helping behavior" of Youth Aliyah activists in Britain toward the refugee children? On the group level, the basis for the assistance offered was undoubtedly a combination of religion and ideology: the desire to keep the trainees Jewish and to make them into Zionists while preparing them for life in Palestine, the Jewish homeland. Looking at the individual British Jewish activists who were supportive of the Youth Aliyah activities for Jewish refugee children, including women like Rebecca Sieff, it appears that they were propelled by a number of factors mentioned previously. These, in particular included a sense of noblesse oblige, group cohesion, and a tradition of volunteering and helping.

As for the Youth Aliyah balance sheet in terms of their work with the refugee trainees, on the most part, it appears that Youth Aliyah's efforts to train and prepare Jewish refugee children for life in Palestine were successful. While the RCM's policy was to promote integration and assimilation among Jewish refugee children in Great Britain, Youth Aliyah did everything in its power to keep the children under its auspices together. Fearing that placing the children with foster families would expose them to non-Zionist and possibly assimilationist influences, Youth Aliyah created *hachshara* centers throughout Britain to assure that the children would live collectively, learn collectively, and work together as a group. A former worker in Youth Aliyah's London office in wartime summarized the situation by saying: "While the Refugee Children's Movement cared mostly for the children's physical well-being, we (Youth Aliyah) cared also for their values and gave them a purpose in life, a goal to work towards."[43]

This policy of centralization was initially frowned upon by Bloomsbury House, seat of the organizations caring for Jewish refugees in Great Britain, which believed that only by scattering the Jewish refugee children throughout Britain could they ultimately blend into British society, and that only by not concentrating the young refugees together could Anglo Jewry protect itself from an outburst of antisemitism and discrimination. Youth Aliyah, on the other hand, had no desire for the children to blend into British society, nor did it believe that keeping the children together on agricultural training centers and having them aid the British agricultural battle for self-sufficiency during the war would lead to heightened antisemitic sentiments. In a sense they were correct. During the war years when food and manpower shortages were acutely felt, the agricultural contributions of youth Aliyah groups on the various *hachsharot* appear to have been greatly valued by the townspeople among whom they worked.

Another proof of Youth Aliyah's contribution to the Jewish refugee cause had much to do with what they offered their refugee trainees as opposed to what the RCM was providing the Jewish refugee children that it had brought to Britain under its auspices. During the war years, significant numbers of adolescents brought to Britain by the RCM requested to join the Youth Aliyah *hachsharot* seeking the companionship and values that Youth Aliyah, provided that they could not get through the RCM. Foster parents were a matter of luck. Some were wonderful to the refugee children while others were out to exploit them in various ways. Hostels were also a gamble. Some could be cold and unfriendly while others had warm and caring administrators. But even if the *hachsharot* administration was not always the finest, the *madrichim* were usually close with the young trainees, only a few years older than they were, and most important, exhibited shared values that coalesced the children into a cohesive group. It was that warmth and togetherness that the Jewish refugee children craved, and the reason that they asked to join the *hachsharot* even if the hostels and foster homes in which they were living provided them with greater amenities.

Despite the fact that many of the young refugee trainees never actually immigrated to Palestine, their years on the Youth Aliyah *hachsharot* stood them in good stead. The values that Youth Aliyah instilled in them developed their Jewish identity; the companionship that they had in the training centers gave them a social basis of belonging. Together these two factors served as a successful bulwark against assimilation and conversion that, as we will soon see, were so rampant during the war years among Jewish refugee children who were moving chronologically away from their childhood, their European origins, and their refugee past.[44]

Notes

1. http://www.gwrychtrust.co.uk/html/operation_kindertransport.html, retrieved on 19 September 2011.
2. Bentwich, *Jewish Youth Comes Home*, 35; Shatzker, "The Jewish Youth Movement in Germany," 301–25.
3. Eva Michaelis (OHD) 16 (27). The Youth Aliyah children actually arrived in Denmark only on the day war was declared, unlike other countries that had set up active training programs several months earlier. Yahil, *The Rescue of Danish Jewry*, 21. Letter S. Adler-Rudel, 8 December 1938, CZA S7/782.
4. Leshem, *Strasse zur Rettung 1933–1939*, 18, 24. Yocheved Bar Rachel (PHD) 38 (27).
5. Raanan Malitz (OHD) 21 (27).
6. Habbas, *Sefer Aliyat Hanoar*, 164.
7. Leshem, *Strasse zur Rettung*, 183, Eva Michaelis (OHD) 16 (27).
8. *The Jewish Chronicle*, 2 December 1938, 10.
9. Michaelis-Stern interview.
10. Solomon Adler-Rudel (OHD) 17 (27).
11. Eva Michaelis (OHD) 16 (27).
12. Michaelis-Stern interview; *The Jewish Chronicle*, 9 December 1938, 17; Bentwich, *Jewish Youth Comes Home*, 89; Bentwich, *My 77 Years*, 177.
13. *The Jewish Chronicle*, 17 February 1939, 31; 7 July 1939, 29.
14. Bentwich, *My 77 Years*, 178, letter Marduk Shattner to Henrietta Szold and Hans Beyth, 29 October 1929, CZA S75/1173; Report of the Board of Guardians of Whittingehame House, 10 October 1939, CZA S75/1173.
15. Letter Marduk Shattner to Henrietta Szold and Hans Beyth, 29 October 1939, CZA S75/1173.
16. Report of the Board of Guardians of Whittingehame House, 10 October 1939, CZA S 75/1173.
17. Yocheved Bat-Rachel (OHD) 38 (27).
18. Author's interview with Gerda Margulies, Tel Aviv, 16 December 1979 (henceforth: Margulies interview).
19. Gershon, *We Came as Children*, 78; Saenger, *Today's Refugees*, 64.
20. Margulies interview.
21. Whittingehame Farm School, Ltd. First Annual Report, 31 January 1940.
22. Letter from Eva Michaelis to Henrietta Szold on the conditions of former *hachshara* centers, 19 June 1941, CZA S75/1639. *The Jewish Chronicle*, 6 February 1945, 5.
23. Youth Aliyah Training Centres in England (n.d., Autumn 1939), CZA S75/1173. Leshem, *Strasse zur Rettung*, 199.
24. Author's interview with David Heinemann, Jerusalem, 22 December 2010 (henceforth: Heinemann interview).
25. Mowat, *Britain between the Wars*, 631–32; Bennett, *John Anderson*, 222; author's correspondence with Fred Dunston (formerly Fritz Deutsch, *madrich* at the Great Engham Farm), 20 June 1980.
26. Youth Aliyah Training Centres in England, CZA S75/1173.
27. Habbas, *Sefer Aliyat Hanoar*, 170.
28. Ibid., 178–79; Leshem, *Strasse zur Rettung*, 201.
29. Mandel, *In Memory of F. M. Friedmann*; letter from Eva Michaelis to Henrietta Szold, 19 June 1941, CZA S75/1639.
30. *Chayenu* (Bachad Bulletin) 1:1, November–December 1939.

31. Youth Aliyah Training Centres in England, CZA S75/1638.
32. Michaelis-Stern interview. Leshem states that 160 of the children belonged to Bachad. Leshem, *Strasse zur Rettung*, 201. Youth Aliyah Newsletter by Anita Engle, "Youth Influences in Palestine's Development (n.d.) CZA S75/1638. Author's interview with Prof. Daniel Sperber, Ramat Gan, 22 April 1981 (henceforth: Sperber interview).
33. Letter Eva Michaelis to Henrietta Szold, 19 June 1941, CZA S 75/1639. Survey of Progress and activities of Bachad since the Pegisha meeting of December 1940 (January 1941), Religious Kibbutz Archives (henceforth: RKA) 933.68(42)-1, Kevutzat Yavneh.
34. Letter to Religious Kibbutz, September 1939, RKA 15-83. Handler interview.
35. Handler interview; undated report, RKA 15-84.
36. Michaelis-Stern interview.
37. Raanan Malitz ODH 21 (27), Meeting of the Executive committee of Children and Youth Aliyah, 5 November 1940, CZA S75/1637.
38. Meeting of the Executive committee of Children and Youth Aliyah, 5 November 1940, CZA S75/1637.
39. Executive meeting of children and Youth Aliyah, 14 October 1940, 2, CZA S75/1637.
40. *The Jewish Chronicle*, 28 July 1939, 16; letter from Eva Michaelis to Henrietta Szold, 14 October 1940, CZA S75/1637.
41. Bekkers and Weipking, "Generosity and Philanthropy: A Literature Review."
42. Ibid., "To Give or Not to Give . . . that is the Question," 533–40; Landry et al., "Towards an Understanding of the Economics of Charity," 747–82; Reed and Selbee, "Is There a Distinctive Pattern of Values Associated with Giving and Volunteering? The Canadian Case"; Bekkers, "Traditional and Health-Related Philanthropy," 349–66.
43. Michaelis-Stern interview.
44. Ibid.; and author's correspondence with Eva Michaelis-Stern, February 1980.

Part 2

The War Years

Chapter 7

War and Evacuation

Introduction

"Pied Piper Tomorrow."[1]

Those fateful words relayed over the British wireless on the afternoon of Thursday, 31 August 1939 heralded the evacuation of 1,473,000 mothers, schoolchildren, teachers, blind persons, and handicapped persons from the vulnerable areas of Britain.[2] With the outbreak of war, months before a single enemy aircraft would be seen in British skies, the Jewish refugee children entered a new phase of their absorption, which lasted throughout the so-called "phony war," until the invasion of Scandinavia in April 1940. During the early morning hours of 1 September 1939, thousands of younger refugee children were evacuated, along with 826,959 unaccompanied schoolchildren in England and Scotland, to areas deemed safe from German bombing. After a journey of six or seven hours, the children reached evacuation centers, where they were billeted with households.

Enemy bombs had constituted a major threat in Britain since the First World War when during one raid in 1918 German planes dropped three tons of bombs on Britain.[3] During the 1920s and 1930s, calculations as to the number of German airplanes and effectiveness of bombing created the statistic that 100,000 bombs could be dropped on London in fourteen days.[4] Such calculations, or rather miscalculations, were the impetus behind the evacuation plan presented to parliament by the Committee of Imperial Defense on 26 July 1938. Priority classes for evacuation included schoolchildren in units with their teachers, younger children and their mothers, pregnant women, and blind and crippled adults. Refugee children residing in official evacuation areas were therefore eligible for evacuation.[5]

By January 1939, plans were being made in earnest. Local councils began seeking reception homes for potential evacuees where local and national bodies agreed upon housing standards. As the threat of war grew nearer, there were rehearsals both for blackout and evacuation; for the former on 10 August 1938 and for the latter on 28 August. Thus when the 826,959 unaccompanied schoolchildren in England and Scotland assembled in their schoolyards in the early morning hours of Friday, 1 September 1939 complete with gas masks, rucksacks, and labels it seemed as if it were only another one of the innumerable drills. As the day progressed, however, and children were sent on six- and seven-hour journeys to strange households and strange beds, what had started as a game became very serious. By the end of the day many children had broken down both emotionally and physically.[6]

The outbreak of war itself was a very difficult moment for most refugee children. Fifteen-year-old Lorraine Allard from Fürth remembered hearing war being announced on the radio. "I just felt the world's come to an end. Terrible. Shattering if I think about it, because everything was built around the hope of reunion with my parents and my temporary stay in England. Everything we'd ever talked about, or written about, and thought about, it had all collapsed."[7]

There were refugee children who felt that the declaration of war shattered their newly found sense of security. As one stated: "The final blow was the news that we were on the move again. We'd hardly been a year at our presents address and now we were to be evacuated. My feelings in the car as it drove out of London and into the country lanes were exactly the same, I remember, as on the train out of Germany: A sort of frustrated anger at being forced to move and bewildered despair at not knowing quite why we were moving."[8]

Steffi Birnbaum Schwartz was one of the lucky children who remembered the first stage of evacuation, that lasting until the beginning of the Battle of Britain in late spring 1940, as an upheaval, but as a particularly unpleasant one: "In September we were evacuated from the hostel along with the other children from London. Five of us from the hostel got to Cuffley in Middlesex. We were sent, Reenie and I, to a young Protestant couple who were called Mr. and Mrs. Kelley, who thought they were getting bona fide British children and were a bit surprised to see us. But they were very good people. They asked us to say the Hebrew prayers at meals as there was no synagogue and they wanted us to keep our religion. They never made the slightest intention to try and turn us into Christians. We even celebrated Christmas with them, but as a social holiday and not a religious one."[9]

Other children, both British and refugee, were not as lucky. Vera Gissing remembered the upheaval:

> I was just getting used to the Rainfords and their way of life when, barely two months after my arrival in England, I was evacuated to a little town outside Southport. I was placed in another Methodist family with a lady I called

"Aunty Margery." Aunty Margery was very kind but she wanted the whole world to know about it... every Wednesday she had the ladies of the church come to tea... she would make me stand on a pedestal, and she would say to her ladies, "This little Czech refugee, if it wasn't for me, she'd stand here naked. If it wasn't for me, she'd go hungry," and so forth. I hated to be on show, and I thought, how dare she? What about all the beautiful clothes my mother sent? What about all the wonderful dishes my mother cooked? I really felt like a poor little refugee. But I got back at her after all that. They always said prayers before we ate, and one day Aunty Margery said, "Vera, why don't you say a prayer in Czech?" Without a moment's hesitation, I said in Czech, "Dear God, please, can't you stop this woman from being so bossy and such a show-off? Amen." I said this prayer day-in and day-out for the rest of the year that I was there, and it made me feel much better.[10]

Upon reaching the evacuation centers, all children were billeted to households, including many younger refugee children like Steffi who had previously been in hostels. The two most common methods of billeting were haphazard allotment and direct selection by the householders. While haphazard allotment had its challenges and there were frequent mismatches, the other possibility was initially much more traumatic. Children were often paraded around while householders looked, examined, and finally took their pick. As British social researcher Richard Titmuss wrote, during the selection process, "Scenes reminiscent of a cross between an early Roman slave market and Selfridge's bargain basement ensued."[11]

For a goodly number of English children this was the final traumatic experience, the pathetic culmination of a strange and threatening day. For many refugee children, a "market" was a known quantity, bringing with it memories of Dovercourt and Victoria Station in London. This time, however, refugee children were only a small portion of the total number up for selection. For some of those refugee children, evacuation was an added trauma. For others, it was a major step in their integration, as it was the first time they were being treated exactly like their British counterparts.[12]

The RCM in Wartime

With the outbreak of war, the RCM's bureaucratic system underwent a number of abrupt changes. If until now the child refugee organization had not managed to decentralize its bureaucratic system, the new military situation in Britain galvanized it into action. Understanding that if the country would be bombed there would be a good chance that communications with London would be cut and it would be extremely difficult to visit the refugee children in wartime, the RCM executives realized that it was in their interests to create a system whereby children in various regions would not be dependent upon the central RCM office in

London for all their needs. In addition, the war situation heightened the need to economize the head office's payroll, giving another impetus to farming out tasks to regional and local bodies.[13]

Consequently, soon after war was declared the RCM formed twelve regional committees, each with their own office and organizer, corresponding to the twelve regional defense areas into which the country had been divided: Leeds, Nottingham, Cambridge, Cambridge region, London region, Oxford, Gloucester, Cardiff, Birmingham, Manchester, Edinburgh, and Tunbridge Wells. Preexisting local committees were grouped under the appropriate regional committee, and eventually 163 local committees functioned under the various regions.[14] Regional committees fulfilled a double purpose: to act both as liaisons and as clearing houses. Their first task was to serve as a liaison both between local committees and Civil Defense Commissioners and between local committees and the RCM head office in London. At the same time, they were to encourage the formation of suitable local committees, investigate offers of hospitality, and receive and pass on offers that could not be filled locally, to other districts.

Local committees were also given instructions about their responsibilities to the regional committees. They were to refer all cases of serious illness, physical or mental, to the regional committee office, which was then to notify the RCM head office in London. They were to assist children in finding employment, do follow-up work pertaining to employment, notify them of a billeting or job transfer of any child, frequently visit the children under their care, report on their health, welfare, and progress to the regional committee twice a year, and ensure that financial obligations to the movement were met.[15]

While looking so precise and organized on paper, all of these instructions and stipulations underwent changes throughout the war years depending upon the number of refugee children billeted in a particular area, the number of times that these children were transferred from home to home or from school to school, the size of the staff working or volunteering at any particular time for the local or regional committee, and the British government regulations at a particular moment, vis-à-vis aliens in general, which had its repercussions on the legal status of refugee children as well. As Lorraine Allard, the refugee child from Fürth who was evacuated to Lincoln recalled: "I was the first refugee to arrive in Lincoln, so I was like a novelty to the town. . . . While I was in Lincoln, I was never contacted by anyone from Bloomsbury House, or any refugee committee, or anyone who arranged the place for me in Lincoln. I was completely on my own. I think I just slipped through the net."

In addition to the aforementioned bureaucratic upheavals caused by war, the fear that irreplaceable records would be destroyed through bombing caused the RCM head office to rethink the original idea of retaining all the refugee children's main records in the Movement's London central office. Consequently, early in the war its executive committee decided to remove the aftercare records from London to a rented Hindhead country house, later named "The Grange."

A staff of fifteen lived there on a permanent basis—three refugee girls and two refugee boys maintained the house, and were responsible for housework and gardening respectively. For the same reason, a duplicate file for each child in the form of a roneodex card existed in the regional committees. Each card gave the child's name, age, address, religion, place of birth, and address of parents. The reverse side listed information about the child's health, training, and proposed re-emigration plans. Only toward the end of the war, in late 1944, did the Jewish Refugees Committee at Bloomsbury house prepare a complete index of refugees, including refugee children.[16]

Although these were the weeks when the Aliens tribunals were established throughout Britain, and all aliens over the age of sixteen were required to register and receive notification of status (to be discussed in the next chapter), at this point refugee children were not considered a menace to the tribunals, but merely an annoyance. This phase lasted less than eight months and came to an abrupt close with Hitler's renewed offensive in the West in the spring of 1940.

Reception Communities and the Evacuated Children

To understand the experiences of the Jewish refugee children in Britain during evacuation, we first have to locate them within the larger story, that of the hundreds of thousands of British children together with whom they were evacuated from the major cities to the midlands and the outlying areas. And to understand the experiences of these children, we first have to understand their dynamics with the reception communities and the families taking them in.

By law, all families in the evacuation areas who had one or more spare rooms in their homes were required to take in children. Thus, as Gertrude Dubrowsky rightly notes in her study of a group of children from Leipzig absorbed in the Cambridge area, "the potential of child abuse existed from host families who did not want to have children imposed upon them."[17] However, there were many cases of families without a spare room who offered hospitality, who put them in with their own children or took more than one evacuated child.

The motives of such families offering hospitality to evacuated children in reception communities were very similar to those who had agreed to sponsor or host refugee children during the previous months. However, in this case there was an added factor: national burden and collective British responsibility. Returning to Bekkers and Wiepking's theories of philanthropy and voluntary action, the helping behavior toward evacuated children, refugee and British, expressed by individuals in the reception communities was a direct result of national solicitation for individuals and families willing to take evacuated children to come forward, with national benefits, both in terms of financial remuneration and social status, attached to the request.[18] No separate requests were made initially to find homes for Jewish refugee children, and the households usually had no idea that they were not getting British citizens as their evacuees.

In practice, the evacuation, when it finally took place, was often bureaucratic and organizational chaos. Local population were not always given sufficient warnings regarding the possible outcome of mass evacuations, and not enough people of all classes were involved in receiving children. As Richard Titmuss writes, "the more well-to-do people, the superior artisans and clerk classes tended to shirk their responsibilities."[19] Consequently, the refugee child evacuees were often boarded with relatively uneducated lower-middle-class householders who had received little or no explanatory information about the children.[20]

How did the reception families treat the evacuee children? Two child psychoanalysts—Anna Freud and Dorothy Burlingham—studied the psychological implications of evacuation as early as 1942, examining the result of wartime stress and the deprivation of parental care on children. In their study entitled "War and Children," the two concluded that foster families who billeted evacuated children in their homes either treated them as members of their own families, immediately drawing them close to their hearts, or as indifferent outsiders, giving them the minimum necessary but with little emotional warmth or even connection. This corroborated the conclusions of an earlier study conducted in 1940 by Amy St. Loe Strachey almost a year after the British children were first uprooted.[21] Religious, cultural, and language barriers notwithstanding, the householders' attitude toward refugee children seems to have been expressed along these two similar lines.

Jewish Refugee Children during Evacuation: Stage One (September 1939–April 1940)

Jewish refugee children were evacuated from major British cities using the exact same procedure as all other British children. All children aged five to fourteen were evacuated with their schools. Other children, such as those in Youth Aliyah centers, were evacuated as a group, as were fourteen hostels evacuated en masse.[22] For some of the refugee children this was a major step in their integration, as it was the first time they were treated exactly as their British counterparts. In other cases, the strange environment served to create a feeling of solidarity among quite a number of refugee children. For those refugee evacuees who had already begun to integrate, their experiences and adjustment problems were similar, if not identical, to those experienced by British children.[23]

Refugee children nevertheless experienced additional difficulties during their initial reception that were unique to their group, particularly because of the cultural and language barriers. In certain cases, families who attempted to show their evacuated refugee boarders caring and closeness lacked basic information or were misinformed about their needs. Consequently, they were misguided in their actions toward the children. This was particularly true regarding religiously observant refugee children.

Judith Gruenfeld described what happened when Orthodox children of the Jewish Secondary School from London, a great number of whom were refugees brought by the CRREC with little command of English, were evacuated to Shefford and welcomed by their hosts: "Everywhere a welcoming meal with some especially nice things had been prepared for them. Foster-parents . . . had joyfully anticipated how they would relish the first meal, a ham omelette, that token of welcome that had been so lovingly prepared for them. And everywhere it had been the same story. The children, shy and tired, had not touched the meal, had shaken their heads and hardly sipped a few drops of tea. . . . Some had been able to say a few words of 'thank you' that obviously came from their hearts, but they had all succeeded in creating . . . an atmosphere of disappointment and frustration. What on earth was the matter with those children? Were they just awkward, ungrateful and troublesome?"[24]

Only after a number of teachers visited the various homes and explained the Jewish dietary laws were the hosts' minds set at ease. But in cases where the refugee children had come alone and not within the framework of an Orthodox school group such as that at Shefford, the first difficult impressions were not so easily corrected. Seeing the children's incomprehensible reactions to their attempts at kindness, the hosts' patriotic ardor and motherly love cooled abruptly. By the next day there were householders whose attitudes had undergone a 180-degree turn; some even submitted a request to have the refugee child re-billeted. Most householders certainly attempted to give their evacuee boarder a period of grace during which they were to acclimatize themselves to their new surroundings. However, as time passed, voluntary return to the city on the part of certain older evacuees and transfer to a different billet of younger and difficult evacuees solved many of the problems.

Despite the RCM's attempts to maintain contact with the several thousand refugee children evacuated from urban areas, it was difficult, if not impossible, to solve the problems that arose for some children as a result of the evacuation. One, as we have already seen, was the issue of language. Most of the more recently arrived refugee children, as opposed to those who had already been in the country several months, knew very little English and were therefore unable to communicate with members of the household in which they were billeted. Trying to communicate with each other in the only way they knew, refugee children were chided for speaking German—the enemy tongue—and were unable to even explain why they did not know how to express themselves in any other language.[25]

One refugee boy recalled how his fellow schoolmates would laugh at his attempts to speak English. "They surrounded me in the playground and forced me to say something in German, and then ran giggling to their friends to try and repeat what I'd said."[26] Another remembered his feeling of shame toward his mother tongue: "I used to feel terribly embarrassed when people asked me to 'say something in German' and always refused to oblige."[27]

Even those children who had arrived in the early months of 1939 did not as yet have complete command of the English language by autumn of that year. Having gotten used to urban English accents, refugee children abruptly found themselves without communication abilities, because they could barely understand the rural accents in their new homes.[28] Eventually, however, they all learned enough English to communicate, many of them even excelling in the language.

"I appeared to learn English fairly quickly. This was probably due to necessity rather than skill as I knew absolutely no one who could understand German and I became desperate to make myself understood," stated one refugee girl.[29] Another child recalled that he was the only member of his class to be able to spell the world "beautiful" correctly: "The teacher said that she thought it remarkable that the only pupil to spell the word correctly was a foreigner."[30] Joseph Haberer from Villingen, Germany recalled studying in the Paddington Technical Institute, which had been moved from London to Northampton during the Blitz. "I very quickly caught up with them in learning the English language, however. I began to read voraciously, all sorts—fiction and nonfiction. Everything I could get my hands on. I read books by Freud and Adler, especially Adler who wrote about the inferiority complex. That resonated with me. I read *Robinson Crusoe* and other children's literature classics."[31]

As time went on, some of the children who had no opportunity to speak their mother tongue forgot their German; others made the choice to speak English in order to assimilate into English society. That choice became a serious problem for children reunited with German-speaking family members after the war. Inge Sadan remembers how over the war years she, the youngest of three siblings saved to England, forgot her German and had no way of communicating with her parents after the war, a not infrequent situation that arose and will be discussed in the epilogue.[32]

Another problem involved economic adjustment. As Freud and Burlingham wrote, "children who are billeted on householders who are either above or below the social and financial status of their parents will be very conscious of the difference."[33] This was painfully true for many refugee children who for the second time were undergoing a change of living standards from those to which they were accustomed to in Europe. For understandable reasons, it was often impossible to duplicate a child's Continental living standards when placing him or her through the RCM. This second drop in living standards within a few short months often had a disheartening effect on many refugee children, which led to acute depression.

"The family that I was billeted with after evacuation had only an outdoor privy," recalled Manfred Kirsch, who had come from a middle-class Jewish family in Berlin. "It was definitely a new experience for me. My sponsors in London were not as comfortably off as my own family had been, but my new foster family was definitely much poorer."[34] Another former refugee girl spoke of being surprised that she was given so many chores to do after school. "In my new foster family there was no question of an eleven-year-old being treated as a child. After I came home from school I was to do the washing up, the mucking out, the serving and even some of the cooking, as if were a hired hand. For the first time in my life I realized how lucky I had been at my first foster home where all I had to do was go to school, come home and be homesick for my parents."[35]

Orthodox refugee children faced special problems, as there were almost no Orthodox families in the areas where they were billeted. While this was true for British Orthodox children as well, the refugee children's lack of English heightened their difficulties. Householders confronted for the first time in their lives with Orthodox children, especially refugees with whom they could barely communicate, were at a loss as to how to treat them. These children's dietary regulations, Sabbath observances, and educational requirements were alien both in concept and in deed to most of the householders. The vicars of many towns, who had hoped for young voices to augment the church choirs, were in for a disappointment when the young refugee evacuees arrived.

Judith Gruenfeld lyrically described the householders' situation at Shefford:

> They had been cheated in the fulfillment of their national duty. They had wanted to take little evacuees to their homes, to their hearts, to their churches and Sunday Schools. They had intended to make them a part of their own family. But with these children this was simply unthinkable. They were so totally different from what they had expected them to be and some of the little ones cried all the time . . . they could not communicate but had the look of haunted animals. The bigger ones, many of them charming and polite, spoke and laughed in a different language and did not eat anything but bread and drank only lemonade. They did not join in prayers, they had strange boxes in their luggage, had strange cotton squares with fringes under their shirts.[36]

Evacuation commenced on Friday, 1 September. Orthodox Jewish children, both refugee and British, were faced with their first spiritual crisis on that Friday evening. Jewish schools that had been evacuated en masse organized a makeshift communal meal—in Shefford, for example, each child received one piece of bread and one piece of kosher sausage to eat that night—and communal Sabbath observance, but householders, unaware of the Sabbath regulations, unwittingly caused much discomfort for Orthodox children until the families became better informed about Jewish religious observances.

The question of kosher food was the first and most common issue that observant and traditional Jewish children—refugees and British—had to face during evacuation. With regard to religious dietary laws, on the morning of Monday, 3 September 1939, two days after evacuation, the Chief Rabbi requested an announcement in his name that only a minimum of necessary dietary laws should be observed in view of the war situation. That day the following message was broadcast over the B.B.C. radio: "The Chief Rabbi has been informed that some difficulties have arisen as a result of the strong desire of Jewish children brought up in religious homes to carry out their observances in regard to food in their new surroundings. He wishes to draw the attention of all Jewish parents and children in the reception areas to the fact that in a national emergency such as the present, all that is required of them is to refrain from eating forbidden meats and shellfish."[37] The only problem was that in many of the lower economic status reception households a radio was a nonexistent luxury and there were significant numbers of Jewish children who never heard the broadcast nor made aware of it.

In spite of the fact that the evacuation had been practiced for weeks and prepared for months in advance, the official religious authorities, and first and foremost the Chief Rabbi, appeared to have made no efforts to prepare the religious groundwork for the evacuation. With the exception of this radio broadcast by the Chief Rabbi and of several printed information sheets that were to be given to evacuated Jewish teachers and communal leaders, there was no preparation or explanatory information directed toward potential or actual householders who received refugee children of any Jewish denomination. This supports Titmuss's claim that householders and communal leaders were not prepared for reception, nor were they offered any explanatory information or assistance once evacuation and resettlement were underway.[38] Local RCM committees were to supply such information to householders after evacuation. However, the extent of their success in this task was directly connected to subjective factors such as the amount of understanding and patience these workers had for the particular problems of the observant or traditional refugee child, the funds at their disposal, and, of course, intermovement friction between the local members of the Jewish Refugees Committee and the RCM.[39]

As for other religious bodies, evacuation had not taken Rabbi Schonfeld and the CRREC by surprise. However, it took several weeks before they could reorganize their activities to cope with the changes that had taken place. Primary activities were directed toward Jewish education of evacuated children, and the CRREC paid particular attention to the plight of the Jewish Secondary School that had been evacuated to Shefford. Other than that, it appears that at this first stage the CRREC made few explanatory overtures if any toward householders in reception communities who took in traditional Jewish or observant children, refugee or British. Other than its activities at Shefford, the CRREC's main refugee child-related activities involved being responsible for the kosher canteens that were opened in three evacuation centers and four hostels.[40] This was a response to reports that had reached the Anglo-Jewish press in September and October 1939 regarding the lack of provisions for organized kosher food in the reception areas.[41]

As a first step, the CRREC, through the Chief Rabbi's Kosher Canteen Committee, attempted to arrange one communal hot kosher meal for the refugee children, usually at noontime. In fact, the communal meal system had been suggested as a general measure for all evacuees by the home secretary, Sir John

Anderson, but was not implemented as local authorities were on the most part apathetic.[42] The committee also offered assistance to Jewish families in the reception areas, to enable them to house Jewish evacuee children.[43] For breakfast and dinner, children adhering to Jewish dietary laws had to either compromise their observances or suffice with bread and cold vegetables. There were householders who understood the problem and made every effort for their refugee boarders to be able to partake of the food at their home. There were a few who even refrained from eating meat or shellfish for weeks on end so as to enable their young observant Jewish boarder to partake of food with the family.[44]

Jewish Refugee Children during Evacuation: Stage Two (May–December 1940)

During the first six months following the outbreak of war—the period known as the "phony war" (also known as the "twilight war"), marked by the absence of military operations in Continental Europe and Britain—quite a few city parents concluded that the dangers of war had been exaggerated and decided to take their children home from the reception areas. These included certain Jewish parents who were distressed at having their children billeted with gentile families and older refugee children who were unhappy with their situation after evacuation and who returned of their own choice to refugee hostels that were still functioning in the major cities. In some areas such as Cambridge, the Jewish children who remained were refugee children who had no parents to ask for their return and no homes to return to. These children would later become the focus of an intense battle between Chief Rabbi Hertz (who was also evacuated to Cambridge at the time and spent part of the war years there), the CRREC, and the RCM.[45]

After May 1940, the attitude toward the children's evacuation once again changed. The fall of the Netherlands and the battles in France during the spring of 1940 heralded a second phase of the war in Britain, characterized by a fifth column scare, the internment and deportation of various categories of aliens including quite a number of older refugee children (a topic dealt with in the next chapter), and finally the Blitz, the sustained bombing of Britain between September 1940 and May 1941. This led to a second round of evacuation in which certain children, including refugees, were removed from their initial reception families and sent further afield so as to be physically removed from the bombing. Consequently, there were refugee children who had settled into a comfortable routine with their householders, who now had to adjust to a new pattern of existence.

Some refugee children found themselves living under better physical conditions than before; others were moved to families experiencing worse economic circumstances. And while language was usually no longer a problem after close to a year of living in Britain, the religious issue was at times exacerbated by the move. Some of the children came to an understanding with their new hosts about their religious requirements. Other refugee children were not as lucky.

Steffi Birnbaum Schwartz recalled how the Kelleys, her initial host family, had been quite understanding and supportive when it came to anything having to do with the Jewish religion. But when their sponsor, Dr. Schlesinger, thought that they weren't getting a good enough education in the local school and now wished them to be further away from the bombing, Steffi and her sister, along with several other "Schlesinger" refugee girls, had to move to a more distant location: the Kingsley boarding school in Cornwall, thirteen hours travel away from London.

"We were completely bewildered in this new school. The first Sunday an older girl came up to me and asked why I wasn't getting ready to go to church. I answered that I am Jewish and that we don't go to church and she answered that a lot of the other girls were Jewish and they do go to church so why shouldn't I go as well? This was all engineered by the headmistress who was a beast and antisemitic and wanted to turn us into Christians." Steffi ended up going to church in order to get along with the other girls. "It was absolutely dreadful. I sat in church, never kneeled down or prayed to Jesus, but the headmistress was there all the time helping the priest who was half blind and she saw everything. After many months of this, two of the Jewish girls from the hostel went all the way and converted."[46]

Refugee children tended to gravitate toward people who showed them kindness and warmth. Lacking family in England to serve as a balance, they were often susceptible to proselytizing by their Christian hosts. Because a large percentage of families hosting evacuated refugee children were not Jewish, the problem that had arisen in only a few cases before the outbreak of war now became a broader phenomenon. There were householders who demanded conversion as the price of their hospitality.[47] Other families required the children to attend some type of religious service, be it synagogue or church. Hungry for a "family feeling," refugee children at times elected to attend church services with their foster families, even when a synagogue existed in the vicinity.[48]

Some children were torn between wanting to fit in and the fear of rejecting their own religion. Anne Fox recalls having been asked to participate in the local Christmas pageant. "When one of the teachers asked me if I wanted to represent Mary in the play, I thought long and hard about it. I reasoned that Mary was Jewish, so I felt justified in playing the part. I made a dignified Virgin Mary, wearing a blue flannel bathrobe and an old lace curtain draped over my head."[49]

Olga Levy Drucker, who was also reassigned during the war to a second reception family after her first was considered by the RCM to be "too Christian," recalled her own feelings on the subject: "I liked going to church and prayer meetings, and hearing missionaries and singing hymns. What else was reliable and constant in my life? . . . but suddenly I had a new insight . . . the Jewish Refugee Committee had wanted me to move again because they thought I was getting too much church. Funny that they had waited so long."[50]

Even when the second reception family was Jewish, the non Jewish-help who worked there often had an interesting "take" on Judaism when dealing with the refugee children. Steffi Birnbaum Schwartz recalls how a wonderful Jewish woman from Cornwall, Mrs. Dorothy Singer, heard about her headmistress and went to all the schools in Cornwall to find Jewish evacuees and refugee children. Having faced down the conversionist headmistress, she stated that from now on all Jewish girls who had nowhere to go would come to her for the Jewish holidays and threatened to report the headmistress to the Jewish Refugees Committee and to the government. From then on, Steffi, Reenie, and the other Jewish girls would come to her for Rosh Hashanah and the Yom Kippur fast when Mrs. Singer's husband, Dr. Singer would read to them from the Bible to give them a feeling of it being a special day. The serving maids, however, were another story.

"That morning [of Yom Kippur] we were asleep upstairs and one of the maids came up to the second floor and opened our door and offered us a cup of morning tea. When the girls stated that they can't have tea as it is a fast day, Yom Kippur, and that we were fasting, the maid informed them of her understanding of the holy day: "Oh that's all right, you only fast after breakfast!"[51]

Jewish Refugee Children during Evacuation: Stage Three (January 1941–December 1943)

A third evacuation stage began for the Jewish refugee children in Britain in early 1941, when the RCM realized that the existing methods of Jewish education for refugee children were not having their desired effect. In its second annual report from 1939–40, the Movement had already made statements pertaining to the religious education of the children under its auspices who had been registered as Jewish: "The basic principle of the Movement with regard to the religious welfare of these children is that each child should receive religious instruction in the faith in which it was brought up and that no child should be allowed to change its religion without every possible effort being made to ascertain the views of the parents or some near relative."[52] This seemingly innocuous statement came in the wake of a series of events related to the religious status of groups of Jewish refugee children that had become obvious at the end of the second state of evacuation: misbehavior, proselytizing, and children's requests to convert.

Even before the outbreak of war, one way that Jewish organizations tried to ensure that Jewish evacuees, including Jewish refugee children, would have access to Jewish frameworks that could act as a bulwark against assimilation and conversionist groups was to provide them with ongoing Jewish education. These frameworks were not only to be provided to Orthodox evacuees but to all Jewish children, refugee and native, Orthodox, Traditional, Liberal, and Reform. As early as May 1939, the Central Committee for Jewish Education, the Jewish Religious Education Board, the Union of Hebrew and Religious Classes, and the Talmud Torah Trust met and drew up plans for religious education after evacuation.[53] Although the impressive plans were implemented shortly after the war broke out, in practice, Jewish education after evacuation followed the typical organizational pattern of disintegration, recuperation, adaption, and ferment.

By December 1939, the Joint Emergency Committee for Jewish Education, formed earlier that year, had created ninety centers for Jewish education (another fourteen were in the planning stages), employing 107 teachers and serving 3,000 Jewish children in Britain, some in London, others in evacuation centers. By March 1940, 129 such centers were functioning. By December 1940, it was reported that 4,500 children were receiving Jewish education in old reception centers, in addition to 1,000 children in new centers established in Cornwall and South Wales and an additional 600 children studying in London.[54] The education offered to many Jewish children, including refugee children, prior to the war, was not regulated, teachers were not qualified, and education was not centralized. After the evacuation it was discovered among all religious groups, including Jewish children, that "large numbers of town children are being brought up with no religious knowledge at all."[55]

Despite the massive efforts of the Joint Emergency Committee even after evacuation, many Jewish children received no religious education whatsoever, for various reasons.[56] Lack of teachers, disinterest of children, return of children to the cities despite evacuation orders, lack of suitable premises for education, and early curfew limiting the number of available after-school hours for Jewish education were all factors limiting the effectiveness of post-evacuation Jewish religious education.[57]

In comparison, it is interesting to note the attitude of the Catholic Church toward religious observance and education after evacuation. In 1939, the Archbishop of Edinburgh issued an encyclical urging that evacuated Catholic children be fetched home if no facilities for religious teaching existed in the reception areas. The attitude was often taken that children should run the risk of being bombed rather than be educated at non-Catholic schools in the receptions areas. "What many people in the reception areas failed to appreciate was that in the eyes of the Roman Catholic Church spiritual health was more important than physical safety."[58] No corresponding attitude existed among Jewish communal leaders.

The months leading up to January 1941 were not the most successful for the bodies dealing with Jewish refugee children in Great Britain. The initial excitement of caring for the children had subsided; after evacuation they constituted only a minute fraction of the total number of temporarily homeless children. In addition, while rapidly making the transition when it came to caring for the children's physical welfare under the changing conditions, the RCM did not do so with regard to their spiritual welfare. By 1941, when the RCM requested that Jewish education be provided to refugee children, contact had been lost with many children; in other cases, their spiritual alienation had already taken place.

Until 1941, the Jewish refugee children in Britain had been cared for in the existing religious educational framework and no special measures were enacted to ensure their spiritual welfare, other than the CRREC's efforts to maintain the

Jewish secondary school that had been reestablished at Shefford. However, the disintegration of social structure and family life in rural areas, due to the second stage of drafting into the army that occurred during 1941–42, created severe delinquency problems among various groups of evacuated refugee children who were left without any form of supervision. As a result, the RCM felt that the need for religious guidance and education among these children had become acute. Jewish education boards began paying special attention to the spiritual guidance and religious education of the younger refugees who had in many cases been neglected in these spheres since evacuation at the beginning of the war.[59]

For several months, the subject had been raised in meetings of a number of major Jewish institutions in Britain. In late May 1941, Harry Goodman, the Agudath Israel's representative on the board of deputies, spoke with great concern about the religious welfare of Jewish refugee children, asking that the board try to obtain statistics on the number of cases of refugee children asking to be baptized.[60]

Having called this "a difficult problem" in their internal meetings for quite a while, the RCM decided that stronger steps would be necessary than those that had thus far been taken. In the late spring of 1941, the RCM approached the Joint Emergency Committee for the Religious Education of Jewish Evacuated Children and the Liberal Jewish and Reform organizations to set up a special committee that would arrange for Jewish education to be provided to refugee children.[61] The organizations compiled lists of children, with 1,800 refugee children registered in London and 4,000 in the provinces.

To counter accusations of having neglected the refugee children's spiritual education by placing them with non-Jewish foster families, and compounding this by not having given them Jewish education following the evacuation, the RCM then set up a new and separate Religious Teaching Sub-committee that included RCM members such as Lola Hahn Warburg, Elaine Laski, Lili Montagu, and Dorothy Hardisty, Board of Jewish Deputies Adolf Brotman and Rabbi Schonfeld. As part of the subcommittee's work, it appointed regional secretaries to deal with the care of these children's spiritual well-being and Jewish religious education throughout Britain. In areas where no Jewish religious leader lived and no educational center existed, the organizations arranged for the child to correspond with a rabbi or teacher.

In July 1941, the RCM's committee on Jewish education began bringing up cases of children who were wishing to be baptized. In one case, it was stated, the father, who had been contacted about the issue, had objected to any such action. In another, it had been impossible to reach the parents. In a third the refugee girl was so happy in her evacuation home that she threatened to run away if she were forced to leave and her baptism request would be refused.[62] Seeing little movement and no progress in the committee, in September 1941 Rabbi Schonfeld resigned in protest from the subcommittee, preferring to concentrate his efforts within a more separatist framework.[63]

Another problem leading to separatist action was the RCM's decision to appoint Rabbi Dr. Werner Van der Zyl, former religious director of the Kitchener Camp at Richborough, to be responsible for the religious education of Jewish refugee children in the London area from 1941 on. The German-born rabbi (b. Schwerte, Westphalia, 1902) had been raised in an Orthodox family before joining the Reform movement. Van der Zyl had arrived in England accompanying a children's transport in 1939; from that time on, he was active in Jewish education in Britain.[64]

How did the Orthodox bodies in London respond to this state of events and particularly to the appointment of a Reform rabbi responsible for the religious education of such a large group of Jewish refugee children? Having seen the deplorable and inadequate results of having one educational committee serving the entire Jewish community—the Joint Emergency Committee for Jewish Education in which the Liberal and Reform movements participated—in early 1941, Rabbi Hertz had already decided that it was time for separatist action. In April of that year, he initiated the formation of the Chief Rabbi's National Council for Jewish Religious Education as a "vigilance body" to improve the standards of Jewish education, ostensibly for all children in Britain but, in practice, primarily for the refugee children distributed in the counties. The RCM was represented on its board and for a period of time was also supported by the CRREC in its campaign to strengthen the forces of Jewish education.[65]

If the events that British children, and among them, Jewish refugee children, underwent in the autumn of 1939 could be called "evacuation by committee," the spiritual care that many Jewish refugee children underwent during 1941 and 1942 could be called "education by committee." The plethora of committees formed to deal with Jewish education in Britain in general and the spiritual education and care of Jewish refugee children in Britain in particular during the war years far surpassed the scope of actual activities that most of these committees engaged in during the months in question. Was the overwhelming desire to form yet another committee to deal with the problem a genuine response to the acknowledgment of a growing problem or a knee-jerk bureaucratic response to what was tacitly agreed to be an insolvable situation? Was it an effort to deal in a forthright matter with an implicit spiritual disaster in the making or an attempt to divide the responsibility for this disaster up among as many persons as possible? It is impossible to say.

In August 1942, the Central Council for Jewish Refugees formed the Joint Committee for Religious Education and Welfare of Jewish Refugee children, which similar to the RCM subcommittee had been formed solely to deal with the religious educational problems of Jewish refugee children.[66] Unlike the RCM subcommittee that dealt in practice with all Jewish refugee children, this one cared primarily for Orthodox children and functioned in conjunction with the Joint Emergency Committee and local religious subcommittees. It also attempted to combat the conversionist overtures that had been made toward Jewish refugee children in general, and which by and large were succeeding.[67]

In addition to religious education, Zionist national education, supplied mainly by the Hechalutz movement to *hachsharot* in Britain, was offered during the 1940s to Jewish refugee children. Hechalutz frameworks had offered the children courses in English and Hebrew since shortly after their arrival in England. Such courses became more intensive, and widened their scope from 1940 onward, to include Jewish history, philosophy, art, and other topics. In addition, Hechalutz created a library of more than a thousand volumes and periodicals dealing with Judaica and additional themes (history, philosophy, religion, ethics, Zionism, mathematics, botany, health, zoology, and sport, to mention a few) to serve the Jewish refugee children who were on the *hachsharot*.

In July 1941, four three-day nationalist-oriented seminars were sponsored by Hechalutz. Within a short period of time the movement held over forty-two weekend seminars dealing with various subjects ranging from Jewish literature to biology. By publishing their Hebrew journal, the *Alon Le-Ivrit* (Hebrew pamphlet) the movement encouraged the study and use of the Hebrew language among members of the *hachsharot*. However, only toward the end of the war did Hechalutz note an upsurge of interest in Jewish culture and Hebrew language among all Jewish refugee children in Britain.[68]

By 1942, the refugee children, like other evacuated children, had passed through the "settling-down process" of being shifted from billet to billet, no longer had a language barrier, and were often comfortable with their foster or evacuation families. Other refugee children used their new linguistic and cultural familiarity in order to move to different circumstances, leave school, change places of employment, and begin bettering themselves.

Nevertheless, despite the efforts of the CRREC, Rabbis Hertz, Shonfeld, and Harry Goodman, even many local religious leaders, both prior to and after the evacuation, preferred to ignore the Jewish refugee children in their midst. Yitzchak Talmon, an Orthodox refugee teenager, recalled what happened when a group of Orthodox refugee boys approached a certain communal leader in Margate as to the possibility of a twice weekly *shiur* (religious study lecture) in Talmud. "He was very unhappy with the idea, to put it mildly and it was only under duress that he agreed to meet with us and learn with us as a group."[69] The CRREC was accused of caring mainly for their own, namely the Orthodox, while for a long time traditional, Liberal, and Reform Jewish refugee children had no "vigilance body" to protect their spiritual interests. On a personal level, former refugee child stated a different level of attitudes that they encountered vis-à-vis placement with gentile versus Jewish families. While there were many non-Jewish foster families who treated their refugee children with compassion and understanding, there were Jewish foster families for whom older or stronger children were seen as little more than unpaid labor. Reiterating a common motif among refugee children, former refugee child Chava Markowitz recalled that while girls in her area who were placed with Jewish families were referred to as "our refugee girl" and became an exhibit in the family, there was more chance for children placed with non-Jewish families to be referred to as "our little girl" and treated more naturally as a family member.[70]

Older Refugee Children

Many of the older refugee children and trainees who had not been evacuated but remained in the major urban centers and danger zones found themselves in unexpected situations as the war progressed. Through the Home Office order of 27 November 1939, many refugee children were forced to leave their places of employment.[71] The large number of older British children abruptly leaving school glutted the teenage labor market; refugee children were considered a superfluous drain on the economy. Expecting to win the war in a few months, Britain continued to tolerate foreigners, including refugee children, but was no longer lenient in providing them with employment.

Upon reaching the age of eighteen, large numbers of refugee children were employed at work of national importance as a result of new regulations placing these young people under the direction of the Ministry of Labour. This assisted their social as well as their economic integration into British society as they were now aiding the collective war efforts. However, it was the fifteen- to eighteen-year-olds who met with the greatest difficulties. In spite of the fact that older refugee youth were invited to join the Jewish youth organizations and Zionist movements such as Bachad, Agudah Youth, Ezra, Hashomer Hatzair, Hanoar, Hechalutz, Otto Hirsch Youth, Maccabi, Mishmar, Habonim, New Liberal Jewish Association (a social youth group), which wanted to aid them in their social integration with British Jewish youth of their own ages, there were many who preferred to turn their back on Jewish organizations and saw their best chances of integration as coming from fully merging into non-Jewish British society.

Others preferred to seek their fortune by flouting convention and adopting a totally different lifestyle than that to which they had been educated.[72] As a result, there were refugee girls who married quite young while others became unwed mothers out of unhappiness and loneliness.[73] During the war years, a high rate of juvenile delinquency existed in Britain, and there were major rises in offenses against property.[74] Much of this was attributed not to poverty and need but to a general breakdown of the moral code in the time of war. Certain refugee children, looking for acceptance by their peers, turned to street gangs or petty crime during those years, and some continued in this way of life even after the war was over.[75]

Financing the RCM during Wartime

With the outbreak of war, the RCM activists realized that many of the refugee children's re-emigration plans would have to be abandoned. Children who were supposed to join parents and family who did not have a chance to leave Continental Europe would be remaining in Britain throughout the war years. Those who had planned to immigrate to Palestine would not necessarily be eligible for immigration certificates.

Nevertheless, some children did manage to join their families abroad, often in Latin America or the United States, during the war years. Between 1939 and 1941, some 1,500 children who had come to Britain under the RCM's auspices—over 16 percent of the total number of RCM sponsored refugee children—re-emigrated.[76] By 1942, however, the numbers had dropped sharply, as few additional families had been able to get out of Europe since the war began; just twenty-six refugee children re-emigrated from Britain. In 1943, the numbers rose once again to 138, testimony to the availability of larger numbers of U.S. immigration, and to a number of families who had found refuge in Spain and Portugal and could now immigrate elsewhere, joined by their children.[77] The organization therefore recognized that it would need more funds that had been thought of initially in order to maintain the children in Britain until general re-emigration plans could be put into effect at some later date, or in the words of American journalist and anti-Nazi activist Dorothy Thompson, "For settling people successfully in new homes, one needs money and again money."[78]

In view of the influx of refugees from Nazism into Britain after *Kristallnacht*, in December 1939 the cabinet committee on refugees discussed granting financial aid to the collapsing refugee organizations in that country. Despite the tight financial budget and the meager allotments available, the government realized that by not granting aid to refugee organizations it would be promoting economic and social chaos. Due to these extenuating circumstances, in 1940 the British Government granted £533,000 to the Central Council for Jewish Refugees. There was a great deal of controversy over the question of whether the RCM was entitled to separate financial assistance; however, after a closer examination into the organization's work the assistance was granted.[79]

In addition to the lump sum granted to the refugee organizations, beginning in 1941 the British government, through the Central Committee for Refugees, paid a government grant-in-aid of up to 18s a week toward the maintenance of refugee children living with foster parents.[80] Refugee children in hostels also received a maintenance payment at the rate allowed for English children under the same circumstances. The young trainees or working people not earning enough to cover their expenses were granted maintenance subsidies based on need assessments made by the Assistance Board. Eventually the RCM, like all refugee organizations, received 75 percent of its administrative costs and approved welfare payments from the British Government.[81]

The War Transport

Only one organized group of refugee children managed to reach England from the Continent during the war. On 14 May 1940, four days after the German invasion of the Netherlands, Gertruida Wijsmuller-Meijer procured five cars and drove a group of forty German and Austrian children from the Amsterdam Municipal orphanage (Burgerweeshuis) to the port of Ijmuiden. There she placed them on the *Bodegraven* before it sailed for England at 7:50 p.m..[82]

Having reached the English shores, the boat attempted to land at Cornwall; however, the British, assuming it to be an enemy vessel, fired upon it and forced it to turn away. Only after hours of circling the British coast was the boat permitted to land at Liverpool. When asked about the circumstances leading to their daring escape from wartorn Holland, the children, ranging in age from infancy to age sixteen, all repeated the name "Mrs. Wijsmuller, Mrs. Wijsmuller." After careful questioning the story of the rescue was pieced together. The children were eventually brought to Manchester, where they settled in hostels and foster homes. For propaganda purposes, the Nazis reported that the boat carrying the children had been sunk. To counter this attempt, an intelligence worker of the BBC requested that Mrs. Rae Barash, an active member of the Jewish Refugees Committee in Manchester, relate the story of the children's successful arrival in Britain on the BBC program "Women and War Work."[83] With the exception of a handful of children who crossed individually or with families from Bordeaux in 1940, no other Jewish refugee children managed to escape from Continental Europe to Britain during the war years.[84]

The Evacuation of British Children to the Dominions

In spite of the pressures and problems that Jewish refugee children in Britain faced regarding their education and adjustment, as a rule it was rare to encounter discrimination on the administrative and governmental level. One exception to that rule was the Dominions evacuation scheme of late spring and early summer 1940. The Nazi invasion of Western Europe and the possible threat of invasion to England put an end to the "phony war" that had characterized the period until mid-April 1940 and raised the specter of a possible threat of invasion to England. Consequently, various groups both in Britain and abroad began discussing the possibility of evacuating British children between the ages of five and sixteen to the Dominions and the United States in order to ensure their safely. The project began in earnest in June 1940 with the creation of the Children's Overseas Reception Board. The first country to respond was Canada, when in early June 1940 the Canadian Minister of Resources, Thomas Alexander Crerar, announced that Canada would soon shelter thousands of child evacuees from Britain, Holland, France, and other invaded countries. The children, aged sixteen and under, would be sheltered by private families until the end of the war and would enter Canada as non-immigrants. A public cry soon arose within the United States to offer similar humanitarian assistance. Editorials in major dailies called for a change in American immigration laws to permit the entry of unaccompanied children under age fifteen.[85]

Impatient at what appeared to be government foot dragging, some decided to respond quickly. On 20 June 1940, following a two-day meeting convened by Eleanor Roosevelt, the United States Committee for the Care of European Children (USC) was formed to assist in providing sponsorship for British children brought to the United States and to assure high standards for their care.[86]

The evacuation of British children to the United States began in late June 1940. Children arriving in Montreal were transferred by train and bus to the border. There, they entered the United States as quota immigrants, having presented the necessary notarized and documented affidavits while still in England. Nevertheless, the children's rapid entry was barred with unending red tape. Among the delaying procedures was the necessity to obtain notarized affidavits in quadruplicate and proof of sponsors' income and assets. Moreover, as a result of the annual British quota of 65,720, only 5,476 children could enter the country each month. In a scathing article in the *Washington Daily News*, columnist Raymond Clapper attacked Roosevelt and his administration for not changing the laws to eliminate the "red tape."[87]

In response to the article, Roosevelt evaded the charges and blamed not American bureaucracy but difficulties in transportation for the delay in the children's arrive. This problem was easily and rapidly solved. On 13 July 1940, the State and Justice Departments announced that a "simplified procedure" for the entry of British child evacuees had been implemented. Children under sixteen, possessing British citizenship, were permitted to enter the United States with a visitor's visa in order to escape the dangers of war. Thus an unlimited number of children, who at the termination of hostilities would return home, could enter each month.

Next on the agenda were the transportation difficulties. On 17 July 1940 the American Women's Committee for the Release of Ships for European Children (later called the Women's Mercy Ship's Committee) placed a full-page advertisement in the *New York Times* calling for the release of American mercy ships to transport children from the war zone. Simultaneously, Congressmen introduced a neutrality measure permitting mercy ships transporting children to enter the war zone and an amendment requiring a safe-conduct guarantee from Italy and Germany.[88]

While the American Congress continued to debate the neutrality measure, British MP Josiah Wedgwood raised the question in Parliament in July 1940 of including Jewish refugee children among the evacuees. A government spokesman answered that the Dominion did not refuse to take refugee children in the evacuation scheme but gave preference to English children.[89] In August of that year the United States Congress discussed the evacuation plans. During the proceedings of 6 August, it was conclusively stated that Central European (Jewish) refugee children would not be included among the British children in order to preclude the possibility of "infiltration" of Jewish refugee children into the United States under this agreement.[90]

The first group of British children reached the United States during the third week of August 1940, just days before the Mercy Ships Bill was voted into law on 27 August, requiring, as a prerequisite, a safe-conduct guarantee from Germany and Italy.[91] Ironically, the law which so rapidly passed Congress and encountered so little American opposition was now rendered impotent by external forces. Despite American pleas, Germany refused to grant the safe-conduct transit required for the rescue operation, and the Mercy Ships Committee was unsuccessful in forming an organization able to manage the logistics and provide vessels. But the nail in the coffin of the evacuation plan was the German sinking of the *City of Benares*, a ship used to transport evacuated British children to Canada, which caused the deaths of seventy-three British evacuee children.[92]

By December 1940 the evacuation plan was terminated, after 13,702 British children had temporarily migrated to the Dominions and the United States. Refugee children from Continental Europe were all but barred from the scheme, but there was an epilogue to the story, which had bearing on these children's future. In 1941, Lord Halifax, Britain's ambassador to the United States, was appointed temporary guardian for children sent overseas during the war. The bill creating his temporary guardianship was a prototype of the Guardianship Bill of 1944 (see chapter 9) that would apply to refugee children in Britain.[93]

Conclusions

By December 1943, the end of the third wartime period discussed in this section, life for Jewish refugee children in Britain had become routinized. Some of the older refugee children had experienced internment and release. The younger ones had gone through evacuation and reception. Some who had reached age fourteen or sixteen left school and began to look for work. Others who were older joined the British armed forces in an attempt to aid the war effort. While everyone knew that the existing situation would change sharply after the end of the war, that event was still far off. Meanwhile, as the phrase commonly used at that time went, the Jewish refugee children in Britain had "settled down for the duration."

Notes

1. Gruenfeld, *Shefford*, 14.
2. Titmuss, *History of the Second World War*, 103.
3. Ibid., 4.
4. Taylor, *English History*, 535. During the entire Second World War, fewer than these numbers of bombs were dropped on all of Britain.
5. Titmuss, *History of the Second World War*, 28, 33–34; "Information Relating to the General Welfare of Refugees," 19.
6. Titmuss, *History of the Second World War*, 37, 90, 96, 103; Bermant, *Coming Home*, 60.

7. Harris and Oppenheimer, *Into the Arms of Strangers*, 181.
8. Gershon, *We Came as Children*, 88.
9. Birnbaum interview.
10. Harris and Oppenheimer, *Into the Arms of Strangers*, 202.
11. Titmuss, *History of the Second World War*, 111.
12. Bermant, *Coming Home*, 60.
13. *Movement*, 11.
14. *Movement*, 11; Presland, *A Great Adventure*, 5.
15. *Instructions for the Guidance of Regional and Local Committees*, Movement for the Care of Children from Germany, May 1940. Central British Fund Archives, The Wiener Library Microfilm document collection 27/28/155; Presland, *A Great Adventure*, 9–10.
16. Shawyer, "Jewish Refugees in English," 9; *Movement*, 12.
17. Dubrowsky, *Six from Leipzig*, 44.
18. Bekkers and Wiepking, "Generosity and Philanthropy."
19. Titmuss, *History of the Second World War*, 393.
20. Ibid., 121.
21. Freud and Burlingham, *War and Children*, 40; Strachey, *Borrowed Children*.
22. *Movement*, 12.
23. Questionnaires: Ursula H. Mandell, Augusta Shifrin, Hannelore Bergenthal, Klara Scheck.
24. Gruenfeld, *Shefford*, 29–30.
25. Ibid., 14.
26. Gershon, *We Came as Children*, 89.
27. Ibid., 90.
28. Barash interview.
29. Gershon, *We Came as Children*, 86.
30. Ibid., 87.
31. Kleine-Ahlbrandt, *Bitter Prerequisites*, 133–34.
32. Harris and Oppenheimer, *Into the Arms of Strangers*, 229.
33. Freud and Burlingham, *War and Children*, 37.
34. Author's interview Manfred Kirsch, Jerusalem, 9 December 2010.
35. Author's interview with Gertrude Mannheim Kirsch, Jerusalem, 9 December 2010.
36. Gruenfeld, *Shefford*, 74.
37. *The Jewish Chronicle*, 8 September 1939, 16.
38. Titmuss, *History of the Second World War*, 393.
39. Barash interview.
40. CRREC report 1938-48, P/15/9 Munk Archives, Yad Vashem.
41. *The Jewish Chronicle*, 20 October 1939, 21.
42. Titmuss, *History of the Second World War*, 164.
43. *The Jewish Yearbook*, 64.
44. Bermant, *Coming Home*, 60.
45. Dubrowsky, *Six from Leipzig*, 20.
46. Schwartz interview.
47. Steinberg, "Jewish Education in Great Britain during World War II," 53.
48. Hall interview.
49. Fox, *My Heart in a Suitcase*, 66.
50. Drucker, *Kindertransport*, 122.

51. Schwartz interview.
52. *Refugee Children's Movement, Ltd. Second Annual Report,* 1939 –1940, 4. Central British Fund Archives, The Wiener Library Microfilm document collection 27/28/153.
53. Steinberg, "Jewish Education in Great Britain during World War II," 31.
54. Ibid., 38–39; *Contemporary Jewish Record* 4 no. 2 (1941): 182.
55. *The London Times,* 17 February 1940, quoted in Schonfeld, *Jewish Religious Education,* 7.
56. Bermant, *Troubled Eden,* 128.
57. Steinberg, "Jewish Education in Great Britain," 35–41.
58. Titmuss, *History of the Second World War,* 179n1.
59. *Contemporary Jewish Record* 4:2 (April 1941): 182.
60. Extract of the Board of Deputies Meeting, 27 May 1941. Central British Fund Archives, The Wiener Library Microfilm document collection 27/28/153.
61. Religious Teaching Special Committee, 11 June 1941, Central British Fund Archives, The Wiener Library Microfilm document collection 27/28/161.
62. RCM Subcommittee meeting on Religious Education, 14 July 1941. Central British Fund Archives, The Wiener Library Microfilm document collection 27/28/161.
63. RCM Subcommittee meeting on Religious Education, 16 September 1941. Central British Fund Archives, The Wiener Library Microfilm document collection 27/28/161.
64. Marmur, *Reform Judaism,* ix–x.
65. Steinberg, "Jewish Education in Great Britain," 46–47.
66. *The Jewish Chronicle,* 31 December 1943, 12.
67. Memorandum of the Present Position of Jewish Refugee Children in the Country (n.d.), The Munk Archives P/15/9, Yad Vashem; S. Adler-Rudel (OHD) 17(27).
68. Leshem, *Strasse zur Rettung,* 192; 212–13; *Hatzofeh* 13 March 1945, 1.
69. Author's interview with Yitzhak Talmon, Kfar Saba, 11 August 1980 (henceforth: Talmon interview).
70. Author's interview with Chava Markowitz, Tel Aviv, 9 January 1980 (henceforth: Markowitz interview).
71. *Movement,* 12.
72. Association of Jewish Refugees in Great Britain—Untitled Pamphlet, London: AJR, 1942, 7.
73. Author's correspondence with Gerta Katzenstein Kazir, 4 February 1980 (henceforth: Katzenstein Kazir interview). Mr. Kazir worked in the Bedford Children's home run by the Jewish Refugees Committee at Bloomsbury House.
74. Sosnowsky, *The Tragedy of Children,* 183. Figures: 1936—55,511 juveniles caught in crime; 1944—68,069.
75. Talmon interview.
76. By mid-1940, 896 children had left Britain: 761 to the United States, 51 to British colonies, 14 to other countries, and 70 to South America. *Refugee Children's Movement Ltd. Second Annual Report 1939-1940.* Central British Fund Archives, The Wiener Library Microfilm document collection 27/28/153.
77. Bentwich, *They Found Refuge,* 71. The figure for 1943 is erroneously quoted as 38 and not 138 by Herbert Agar, *The Saving Remnant,* 99.
78. Thompson, *Refugees,* 91.
79. *The Jewish Chronicle,* 8 March 1940, 12.

80. *Refugee Children's Movement Ltd. Third Annual Report 1941–1942.* Central British Fund Archives, The Wiener Library Microfilm document collection 27/28/153.
81. Presland, *A Great Adventure,* 14; Wilson, *They Came as Strangers,* 223, Bentwich, *They Found Refuge,* 71.
82. Presser, *Ashes in the Wind,* 8. Presser wrongly states that the date was 10 May 1940. Wijsmuller commented that "if only I could have laid my hands on more cars, I could have saved a good many more people." Presser, 8n2. An oral history source relates that seventy-five children were included in this transport and during the five day trip from Ijmuiden to Liverpool those accompanying the transport listed the children's personal data and it had not been possible to do so previously. Adolphine Bernstein (OHD) 18(27).
83. Barash interview. These children were among the 24,000 Dutch refugees who reached England during the war. Kulischer, *The Displacement of Population in Europe.*
84. Roche, *The Key in the Lock,* 136.
85. *The New York Times,* editorial, 10 June 1940, 110. Memo on State Department conversation on the evacuation of refugee children from France, 14 June 1940 and FDR to Thomas 15 June 1940, both in PPF 4840, Franklin Delano Roosevelt Library, Hyde Park, NY (henceforth: FDRL).
86. *The New York Times,* 21 June 1940, 1.
87. Raymond Clapper, "Let's Save the Children," *Washington Daily News,* 6 July 1940, clipping in OF 3186, FDRL.
88. *The New York Times,* 23 July 1940, 15.
89. *The Jewish Chronicle,* 5 July 1940.
90. "The Evacuation of Refugee Children Our Responsibility," 547.
91. *The New York Times,* 29 August 1940, 2. *Congressional Record* v. 80, 10, 10471-72.
92. Proudfoot, 54.
93. Forbes-Robertson and Strauss, *War Letters from Britain,* 125; "The Temporary Migration of children (Guardianship) Act 1941," in STATUTES (The Public General Acts and Church Assembly Measures of 1941).

Chapter 8

Internment and Deportation

Introduction

"A sovereign state must reserve the right to protect the wellbeing of its citizens against the risks which the uncontrolled entry of foreigners might bring."[1] These words, written by Sir Frank Newsam, Assistant Under Secretary in the Home Office and the man who was to design the system of the aliens tribunals in Britain, echoed the sentiments of many British citizens during the late 1930s.[2] Many of them also agreed that when those aliens, adults or children, were already in Britain, the government was required to take steps in order to secure the country against possible treachery on their part—be it economic, political or in matters of security. This was true in peacetime, during periods of upheaval, and, of course, doubly true in time of war.[3]

What was relegated to the realm of theory during most of the 1930s became a very practical issue at the end of that decade, particularly in view of the tens of thousands of refugees from Nazism who were suddenly permitted into Britain during the early months of 1939 and the general realization that they were on the brink of war. Sometime before the outbreak of the Second World War, the British government decided that there would be no general internment of aliens in Britain at the outbreak of hostilities, only restrictions on their movements and the ownership of arms, cameras, and motor vehicles.[4] Nevertheless, due to growing pressures in view of the large number of aliens entering Britain at that time, on 1 April 1939 a subcommittee of the Committee of Imperial Defense on Control of Aliens in War concurred that if war would break out, general internment would become inevitable at an early date. In order to facilitate that step if it became necessary, a number of sites for possible internment camps were already suggested and listed in order of importance and feasibility.[5]

On 3 September 1939, the day Britain declared war on Germany, there were approximately 69,000 "enemy aliens" in Britain.[6] Similar to the definition used during the First World War, an "enemy alien" was defined as "a person who, not being either a British citizen or a British protected person, possesses the nationality of a state at war with his Majesty."[7]

The day after war was declared, which coincided with his appointment as Home Secretary, Sir John Anderson announced to the House of Commons "an immediate review of all Germans and Austrians in this country."[8] Within days, 120 tribunals were set up across Britain to categorize enemy aliens. Three categories existed: A (to be interned); B (exempt from internment but subject to restrictions); and C (exempt from internment and from restrictions). Stateless persons were to be categorized according to their last country of residence prior to emigration. Most refugee adolescents were included among the 64,200 aliens placed in category C and given the seemingly innocuous name of "friendly enemy aliens."[9]

One of the main tenets of the British legal system is based on the intrinsic connection between legislation and the judiciary application of those laws. In the concise words of prominent educator Sir William Ivor Jennings, an authority on British constitutional law, "the impartiality of laws is not maintained except by the impartiality of their application. The impartiality of the judges is one means by which this is secured."[10] Nevertheless, many chairmen of such tribunals had their prejudices: one against girls working as domestics, another against unemployed young men. Consequently, there were teenagers of the RCM (only aliens over the age of sixteen were examined) who were no different than the rest of their refugee peers but found themselves inexplicably placed in category B and subject to various restrictions.[11] "I never understood what was wrong with me," recalled one young man. "Why was I separated from all my friends and placed into a B and not a C category? Maybe because I had a scar on my cheek and the tribunal thought I looked dangerous? How could they know that it had come from a Nazi blow?!"[12]

The category also had economic implications for both teenagers and adults, as those placed in the B category had to apply to the Home Office for each job permit. The C category aliens were dealt with by the employment exchange but were not permitted to be employed when British labor was available.

The Fall of Western Europe and the Internment of Aliens in Britain

The tribunal system worked well until April 1940, when the fall of Norway released an avalanche of anti-alien sentiment that was expressed both in the press and in Parliament. An example was Colonel Henry Burton, the Conservative MP for Sudbury, who suggested in all seriousness: "Would it not be far better to intern all the lot and then pick out the good ones"?[13] The fall of the Netherlands in

May 1940, which had ostensibly been aided by a "fifth column" in Holland, heralded a second phase of wartime "alien fever." Stories of this "fifth column" were reported extensively in the daily British press, whipping up fear of a possible similar phenomenon inside Britain as well. "Beware the alien kitchen maid!" was the common cry taken up by the masses, as public panic was being shamelessly fed by continuous editorial and columnist propaganda in the popular press, particularly the *Daily Mail*.[14]

One of the first acts of Winston Churchill's government, formed on 10 May 1940, was to create a protected zone along Britain's southern and eastern coasts and to round up and intern all male Germans and Austrians aged sixteen to sixty living in the area, regardless of category. Among them were refugee adolescents, many of whom were Youth Aliyah candidates from training centers in the Kent area.

Fear of a "fifth column menace" in Britain continued to grow. A 1,000-word account thusly entitled, was circulated in Whitehall on 15 May. Written by Sir Neville Bland, British Minister in The Hague, who had participated in the undignified flight from Holland, it widely impressed many government officials and particularly the ministers present at the cabinet meeting on the morning of 15 May at which it was presented. Bland's report, which described the use of the fifth column in Holland, concluded with a call for the internment of all Germans and Austrians in Britain. Following this cabinet meeting and at the urgent recommendation of the Joint Intelligence Committee, Sir John Anderson put into effect provisional instructions formulated on 12 May and ordered the internment of all male category B aliens aged sixteen to sixty to begin on 16 May 1940.[15]

This was only the first stage in the internment of aliens in Britain. Ten days after category B refugee boys were removed directly from boarding schools and taken to internment centers, the government decided to intern category B girls and women as well. As the fear of a fifth column grew once again in late June 1940 after France's defeat, the government decided to intern all Germany and Austrian males in Category C, putting this into effect on 24 June, the day before the armistice between France and Germany went into effect. These were the days when the British fear of a fifth column was reaching its zenith. In a note to General Ismay on 28 June, Prime Minister Winston Churchill wrote: "German parachutists, fifth columnists and enemy motor-cyclists who may penetrate or appear in disguise in unexpected places must be left to the Home Guard reinforced by special squads. Much thought must be given to the (enemy) trick of wearing British uniform."[16]

"What should we really be doing with all these bloody foreigners?" was the true question plaguing many of the officials responsible for alien internment. But until a suitable answer could be found, most agreed that the best that could be done was to cordon them off from the rest of British society, and prevent any possibility of their signaling the enemy. Aliens were therefore sent to camps in various parts of England, notably the Isle of Man, a semi-autonomous province of the United Kingdom that controlled its own domestic policy except in wartime (when this right was partially curtailed), and where enemy aliens had been interned during the First World War.[17] During peacetime, the island was a popular British holiday resort and after war broke out there was a period of time when the island was divided between the internment and vacation sections with a portion still being used as a holiday resort. Refugee boys at Gwrych Castle in Wales were close enough to see the island through binoculars and, in full knowledge that they probably were to be interned there within a few days, wryly regarded newspaper advertisements offering "a peaceful holiday on the Isle of Man."[18]

Even at times of war, in a democracy one cannot just intern aliens without giving some information to the public about the act being carried out. For that reason, Osbert Peake of the Home Office announced four explanations for the government's decision to intern the aliens in Britain:

1. Most refugees were unemployed and were thus a drain on the government.
2. During air raids, aliens would be in danger of violence by local populations who would possibly be severely anti-alien.
3. Many refugees were alarmed by hostilities and had requested to be interned.
4. The military authorities advised internment of aliens.

Once these explanations were made public, it was time for the anti-internment groups to join forces in order to return fire. At this stage, one of the most vocal activists was the British-born Françoise Lafitte (1913–2002), illegitimate son of a young French feminist and an American anarchist. Lafitte was also a former communist turned liberal, thus aware of the topic of Alien civil rights. As a member of the social research organization Political and Economic Planning (PEP), he investigated who the internees really were and what was being done to them. At the end of this investigation, he published an anti-internment pamphlet, entitled "The Internment of Aliens," in which he refuted Peake's arguments. If most refugees were unemployed and a drain on the government, he stated, then why were women, children, and old men who never worked arrested? If fear of unemployment existed, how could it be explained that the internees were kept on government expense, which led to the same monetary drain on government fiscal resources? If the aliens were in danger of being attacked during air raids by the irate civilian population, how is it that only Category C males and not females were interned? Were the women not as vulnerable, if not more so, than the males?[19]

The brief but potent book, which he wrote over a period of less than six weeks, made an impact upon a small but influential minority in Parliament and the liberal press who were outraged at this affront to civil liberties. Copies were even smuggled into the internment camps, producing another round of correspondence. But in truth, its publication accelerated but did not cause a change of approach to the internees, which was already in the making. However, until this change occurred, thousands of aliens, including many older refugee children from the RCM, underwent internment, and in some cases, even deportation.[20]

The Internment Camps

Who were the internees? During the period following the fall of Western Europe, some 28,000 aliens were interned in Britain, among whom were 4,000 women. Approximately 1,000 of the internees were young refugees who were registered with the RCM. As interned mothers were allowed to take younger children with them, there were also children under age sixteen in the internment camps. While some were Nazis or Nazi sympathizers, more than 80 percent were actually Jewish refugees in Britain.[21]

The internees were sent to camps that had been established at Huyton, Liverpool, disused holiday camps, race courses, disused mills, prisons, and camps on the Isle of Man. As it had been a holiday resort, most beds on the Isle of Man were double, and sixteen-year-olds often found themselves sharing a bed with an elderly man or woman.[22] Accommodations in many camps were primitive. In some, no beds existed, no radios were permitted, and letters were held up by the censors for weeks.

The first question the internees asked themselves was how to set up life in these camps to make it possible not only to exist but also to continue life in the most normal way possible. In view of the large number of young children and teenagers in the camps, one of the more important aspects of internee life was the promotion of educational agency, defined as "people actively creating the education they want and need rather than accepting education imposed by others."[23] Under such conditions, education became not just preparation for employment or a means of personal development, but a strategy for survival under precarious circumstances.

In view of the fact that a high percentage of the internees were not dangerous agents from the Third Reich but rather a mixture of distinguished physicians, lawyers, industrialists, scientists, artists, musicians, businessmen, and academics from a variety of disciplines, willing to share their expertise with one another and with the younger internees, the opportunities were endless. Schools were set up in some of the camps to help the boys preparing for matriculation exams or for higher school's certificate examinations. In Huyton, for example, the young men were given six lectures a day both to further their education and to combat boredom.[24]

Gerald Goodwin, a Kindertransport teenager, remembered his internment as a period during which he could make up for some of his lost education.. "You name it and they had someone there who was a professor or an authority on a subject . . . it wasn't recognized by any of the universities or anything, you know. But it was *interesting* . . . it enabled lots of people like myself to catch up on the rest of our education."[25]

With all the German-speaking academics and authorities, there was still one thing lacking in some of the camps: English lessons. When RCM board member Rev. William W. Simpson reported on his visit to the Isle of Man in November 1940, he noted that the young internees were very organized but lacked two things: there seemed to be a food problem for the young internees, and he felt that there was a lack of English influence and particularly language instruction for the refugee youngsters. He also noted that too many refugee boys were still sleeping in double beds with other internees, something considered a problem there as in other internment camps, as the circumstances could be used by homosexuals to prey on young boys. This was one of the reasons that in the Onchan camp the older men encouraged the teenagers to gather in special quarters, where they were provided with supervision and protection from supposedly predatory homosexuals.[26]

The food issue that Rev. Simpson noted seemed to be a problem in a number of camps, not only on the Isle of Man. At the Huyton camp, for example, breakfast consisted of two slices of bread, jam, and bad coffee; lunch was usually soup, a small piece of meat, and two potatoes; and dinner was once again two slices of bread, margarine, a small piece of cheese, and tea.[27] In one camp, a group of Orthodox Youth Aliyah boys were permitted to grow and prepare their own food in order to adhere to Jewish dietary laws. As one of them recalled, "We only wanted to eat kosher, and that's why we prepared our own food and grew almost everything we needed on our own."[28]

At this point the CRREC stepped in. Although Rabbi Schonfeld understood the British government's reasoning behind the internment of the Jewish refugees from Central Europe, he also realized that it would be necessary to make special provisions for Orthodox internees of both sexes, teenagers and adults, to be able to practice their religion while being interned. Within two days of the beginning of the internment scheme, he obtained a pass from the Home Office to visit the various internment camps, and between 16 and 23 July he carried out the first of a number of internment camp tours that he would make over the next few months. During this first tour he even obtained the speedy release of a number of sick internees. Noting the problem of obtaining kosher food, the CRREC set up synagogues and kosher kitchens in the camps, such as that in Huyton where one could buy kosher margarine, matzo, candles, challah, krakower wurst, tinned meat, and kosher soap. Throughout the summer and autumn of 1940, he traveled between the camps, writing detailed reports of the internees' situations and providing a source of moral encouragement and practical assistance. With his assistance, camp rabbis were appointed and he later assisted in securing the release of certain categories of refugee internees, with approximately 1,000 internees being released on the CRREC's sponsorship.[29]

While the refugees, both adults and children, remained grateful to Britain for granting them asylum, they did not adapt to internment easily. Many felt that it was a moral degradation and that the accommodations were primitive. Those who were part of a family group were upset at the fact that families were separated in the camp. Those who fell ill often faced inadequate medical care. There was a lack of cultural facilities in most camps, and the administration did not keep adequate records of the internees. One of the greatest indignities came from the fact that the Jewish refugees and the aliens who were avowed Nazis were placed in close proximity to one another and that the internees were all treated by the guards as Nazis. In fact, until they were enlightened as to the identity of most of the internees—Jewish victims of Nazi persecution—many guards were confused about whom they were guarding and actually thought them all to be Nazis. The following was a typical scene in the internment camps before this issue was explained to the guards in depth. In one of the camps, an internee in the canteen saw an officer brandish a revolver at a sixteen-year-old youth. "Are you Jewish?" the officer asked, "Yes," the boy replied. "Are there many Jews here?" "About eighty percent." "Damn!" the officer explained, "I knew we'd got the wrong lot!"[30]

Deportation

At the Cabinet meeting of 24 May 1940, at which it was decided to intern all female B category aliens, Prime Minister Winston Churchill stated in an aside that he was strongly in favor of removing all internees out of the United Kingdom. This followed the traditional British pattern of deporting undesirables to the colonies, as had been done with prisoners sent to Australia and the American colonies. Until 11 June 1940, no further mention was made of such a scheme but on that day, Neville Chamberlain presented the cabinet with a fait accompli when he announced that Canada had agreed to accept 7,000 internees. In fact, extensive correspondence had passed between Britain and Canada on this subject between 30 May and 10 June when Canada informed Chamberlain that it was willing to accept 4,000 internees and 3,000 prisoners of war. The 4,000 internees, Chamberlain announced to the cabinet, would consist of 5,500 Germans and 1,500 Italians. Alternative solutions were being explored, including shipping the internees to Newfoundland and St. Helena.[31]

Britain continued its search among the Dominions for countries willing to accept internees. On 16 June, Australia cabled its consent to Britain; soon after, Newfoundland agreed to take 1,000 internees. Only South Africa refused to consider the request. Having already interned 2,000 Germans, including a group of South African citizens, it suggested to Britain the possibility of St. Helena and the Falkland Islands. Although the deportation of aliens and prisoner of war was to remain a secret, on 19 June, having been goaded by persistent questioning, Canadian Prime Minister Mackenzie King leaked the story to the press.

Two days later, on 21 June as the Home Office capitulated almost unconditionally to demands for mass internment, Ronald Cross, minister of shipping, announced to the cabinet that the first deportee liner was to leave for Canada that night. The liner in question was the "Dutchess of York," a 20,000-ton passenger liner that carried 2,600 passengers: 500 military prisoners, 1,700 German merchant seamen, and 400 category B and C aliens, including a handful of older teenagers. As the result of a shot fired on board during the course of the journey, panic ensued and was interpreted as mutiny. The incident was reported on at the cabinet meeting of 23 June and strengthened the attitude that internees were dangerous to Britain.

A second deportee ship whose name was to become synonymous with disaster for internees was a 15,000-ton former luxury cruise liner named the *Arandora Star*. The ship was well known to British Jewry, having been advertised extensively in the Anglo-Jewish and general press between 1937 and 1939: "For health shorten your winter. Cruise in sunshine to the Near East . . . spend these weeks amid warm seas and those scenes which are amongst the world's richest in romantic history. Come and live the carefree life in the congenial company, comfort and happiness which distinguishes the world's most delightful cruising liner, *Arandora Star*."[32] This ship, carrying 712 Italian and 478 German internees, sailed from Liverpool to Canada at 4 AM on 1 July 1940. Although there were no precise records of who was on the ship, it is assumed that teenage internees were on board. On the morning of 2 July, the *Arandora Star* was sunk by a German torpedo off the west coast of Ireland. The casualty rate of those on board was 50 percent, and the only message permitted to be sent by survivors was a postcard on which the words "I am safe" had been typed. Many of the people receiving such cards were puzzled by the message, knowing neither of the deportation nor of the torpedoing. However, words of the disaster reached the British public within a few days. In fact, the *Arandora Star* was erroneously referred to as the "Refugee Children's Ship" by some who did not as yet comprehend that this was a deportee chip and not a children's evacuation ship to Canada.[33]

Both the *Ettrick* and the *Sobieski* continued the task of deporting internees to Canada, and by 15 July 1940 some 6,750 internees and prisoner of war, including 2,700 category B and C internees, had reached Canada. Some of the B and C internees were teenage refugee boys both from the RCM and Youth Aliyah. Although there was no precise breakdown of their numbers per deportation country, approximately 400 refugee adolescents were deported both to Canada and Australia, making them 5.5 percent of a total of 7,350 deportees.[34]

Upon reaching Canada, the internees were placed in makeshift camps such as a disused mining camp at Nipigon, a former railway yard near Sherbrooke, Quebec, a sports stadium at Trois-Rivières, Quebec, and finally a purpose built camp at Fredericton, New Brunswick. Conditions were generally better than at British internment camps. Although initially Nazis and Jewish refugees were forced to live in close proximity to one another, they were soon separated. Even after this change, however, a number of very strange incidents stemmed from the fact that some of the Canadian guards did not comprehend the difference between Nazis and Jewish refugees.

In Nipigon, Ontario, for example, when civilian internees asked why they were being guarded so rigorously, they were informed by the guards that this was the treatment deserved by parachutists, spies, and saboteurs. Taking advantage of the opportunity to gain something special from "the enemy," the officer then asked if he could buy some Nazi insignia from them as souvenirs. Realizing the opportunity this afforded them, one Jewish refugee who was on semi-cordial terms with one of the Nazis in the camp, asked to borrow his insignia as a model, copied them, and for a while the entire refugee group, both young and old, were engaged in the wholesale manufacturing of swastikas and Iron Crosses, which they then sold to the Canadian guards as "authentic Nazi insignia."

Simultaneously, the refugees attempted to explain their true identity to the camp commander. These explanations, together with the intervention of Saul Hayes of the United Jewish Refugee and War Relief Agencies in Canada, enabled a change of status for the deportees. In June 1941 they were redefined as refugees and not prisoners of war.[35] When the explanations reached the Canadian government, it reacted with great surprise, having been apprised by Britain that it would be receiving Nazi deportees, prisoners of war, and dangerous enemy foreign nationals, and certainly not Jewish refugees from Nazism. In response, the Canadian government pointed out to Britain that "most of the internees were of the refugee type, and included a large number of schoolboys, college undergrads, priests, rabbis, etc. . . . it is considered that these people should not have been sent to Canada." The British government gave various explanations of why so many category B and C aliens were sent to Canada. One was the sinking of the *Arandora Star* which was carrying mostly A men and the tents of B and C men who were to go to Newfoundland; without these tents no accommodations for the B and C men existed in Newfoundland and the British government was forced to send them to Canada in place of category A men. However the excuses were less than comprehensive and a formal apology was presented to the Canadian government. No such apology, however, was given to the deportees.[36]

As in Britain, educational facilities were organized for the teenage boys in the camp. A technical school in Sherbrooke offered more advanced training for the older boys in mathematics, engineering, chemistry, physics, geometry, machine drawing, and additional subjects. Sherbrooke also offered agricultural courses to train the internees for vital war work in England while also preparing the Zionists for immigration to Palestine.[37] Because of the initial confusion about the internees' origins and intentions, many of the camp commanders initially placed no emphasis on the young internees' education and in some camps formal schooling for the teenagers began a year later than elsewhere. But when such programs did begin, they received significant assistance from groups such as the Canadian YMCA, the Canadian National Committee on Refugees, and the Canadian Hadassah Women's Zionist Organization, which supplied the Youth Aliyah boys with exercise books, literature, and clothing. To free the Youth Aliyah internees in Canada, one needed a $1,000 per head deposit; consequently, the Canadian Hadassah Organization started a drive to raise this sum after the American Hadassah Organization refused to participate.[38]

As in Britain, the young internees in Canada were eager to continue their educations. William Hecksher, a popular schoolmaster at the Farnham Camp near Montreal, remembered that he awoke one morning "and saw ten boys assembled at the foot of my bunk, staring at me with sad eyes. I should have given them a lesson on *Twelfth Night*, and I had overslept my time. It is the dynamic push on the part of the young students which carried along their teachers."[39] In another camp, internees were required to do forestry work during the day, but students studied after evening roll call. As one of them remembered, "We usually disappeared to the toilets. They didn't look in the toilets."[40] The registrar of McGill University worked with the Jewish community to enable students to take the McGill matriculation examinations in Montreal. All in all, dozens of young refugee deportees in Canada took their junior matriculation exams to enter universities.

On the religious level, a problem arose in one of the camps when the office of Internment Operations in Canada issued an order to penalize Jews who refused to work on the Sabbath. Saul Hayes addressed this matter, and it was solved within several weeks. On the most part, internees observed Jewish holidays in the camps and at a 1940 Chanukah party the younger boys were reported as having had "a jolly good time."[41]

In the autumn of 1940, the Canadian government requested that the British government send an official to Canada to deal with the internees. The man chosen was Alexander Patterson, a fifty-six-year-old Home Office Commissioner who arrived in Ottawa on 18 November 1940. By then, the 3,100 civilian internees had been separated from the 3,650 or so merchant seamen and were allocated to five camps.[42] Patterson interviewed the internees and examined the camps. Due to his rapid intervention, the first group of 287 internees, including many refugee boys, sailed from Canada to Britain on 26 December 1940.[43] This group was eligible for release due to a new Home Office White Paper, the second such legislation to deal with the release of internees. After disembarking in England, most of the boys were released almost immediately while the older internees were taken to the Isle of Man pending confirmation of Patterson's decision. Youth Aliyah boys were not included in this transport as it was decided to have them remain in Canada until immigration certificates to Palestine could be procured for them, thus avoiding unnecessary travel.

A second group of 274 deportees returned to Britain in February 1941, and a third group of 330 were sent back in June of that year. Patterson himself returned to Britain in July 1941 and presented a witty account of his work to the new Home Secretary, Sir Herbert Morrison, entitled: "Report on civilian internees sent from the United Kingdom to Canada during the unusually fine summer of 1940." Patterson's only failure was in not receiving permission for the internees with American visas to directly enter the United States from Canada, among them teenage refugee boys whose parents were awaiting them. Many boys were, however, permitted to remain in Canada to continue their. In spite of the difficulties of finding a Canadian sponsor who would assume their financial responsibility for studying at a university in Canada, in early 1943, there were 235 former internees studying at Canadian universities.[44]

By late summer 1943, a total of 1,537 internees had returned to Britain. The others had remained in Canada or had departed for elsewhere. In September of that year, the last refugee camp in Canada was closed.[45]

Simultaneous with the deportations to Canada, the British government sent a large group of refugees to Australia. On 10 July 1940, an 11,000-ton former troopship named the *Dunera* sailed for Australia. Among the 2,543 men it carried on board were 2,100 category C men, including refugee schoolboys, Nazi sailors and 202 Italian survivors of the *Arandora Star*. Aware of the fate of that ship, a group of Youth Aliyah boys debated whether to allow themselves to be included in the Category C men who were to board the *Dunera* the next day, ultimately deciding that it was safer to take their chances on the high seas than to remain in Britain, to be caught by the Nazis if the expected German invasion were successful.[46] As the internees arrived at the Liverpool docks the following morning to board the *Dunera*, they were subjected to a rough search and most of their belongings were stolen. This harsh treatment continued during the two-month journey to Australia; for example, sadistic guards would shatter glass bottles on the decks immediately before the internees, who were forced to march barefooted so as not to dirty the decks, were to have their daily exercise on deck.[47] As a result of the guards' harsh treatment, one internee named Jakob Weiss committed suicide by jumping overboard. Eventually the captain and five of the officers of the *Dunera* were court-marshaled for their treatment of the internees.[48]

Many of the Jewish refugee deportees to Australia, including boys of the RCM and Youth Aliyah (Bachad), were Orthodox and throughout the journey managed to adhere to Jewish dietary law by exchanging food with their nonobservant fellow internees. Some of the more intrepid Orthodox boys managed to salvage a few set of tefillin (phylacteries) from the sailors' looting. The Orthodox boys and men formed queues each morning for the privilege of using them for several minutes in order to pray.

The days aboard ship were both long and monotonous; reveille was at 6 a.m. and lights out at 9 p.m.. The problem was how to fill the hours in between. The younger Bachad boys passed the time in various ways, including with a daily *shiur* (religious learning session) with one of the rabbis on board, playing chess with chessmen formed out of bread remnants, and learning to roll and smoke cigarettes.[49]

At 8:06 a.m. on 12 July 1940, the *Dunera* almost followed the *Arandora Star* to the bottom of the ocean when it narrowly missed being sunk by a German torpedo. When the torpedo was felt grazing the ship's hull most of the deportees, young and old, reacted with relative calm and a fatalistic attitude. Many just lay in their hammocks and waited for the end. However, disaster was averted and the ship continued south to Sierra Leone, where it temporarily anchored on 24 July. By that time there was no doubt among the deportees that they were bound for Australia and not Canada as had previously been thought.[50]

On 3 September 1940, fifty-four days after it had left Liverpool, the *Dunera* docked at Prince's Pier at Melbourne Bay, where the *Arandora Star* survivors disembarked and traveled to an internment camp at Tatura, 110 miles to the north. The *Dunera* then continued on to Sydney, where it docked on 6 September. The remaining 2,100 internees were then taken to their new home, the internment camp at Hay, a railway terminus on the Murrumbidgee River. The internees spent the three-day journey to Hay sleeping, eating, and of course singing the inevitable internee songs that had become popular in Britain shortly before their deportation:

We have been Hitler's enemies for years before the war,
We knew his plans for bombing and invading Britain's shore,
We warned you of his treachery when you believed in peace,
And now we are His Majesties most loyal internees.[51]

The internees at Hay had greater freedom than those in internment camps in Britain. Most of the guards were not professional soldiers but Australian veterans of the First World War, who treated the men with consideration and were almost fatherly to them. Groups such as adolescents and Zionists each had their own hut at Hay. Religious freedom existed—both a synagogue and a church were portioned off for the internees to worship in. The three hundred Orthodox internees ran a kosher kitchen, although there were a few awkward moments such as on Passover Eve, when the boys trying to turn the remaining leaven lit a fire and the guards thought that they were trying to burn down the camp. Some of the religious boys tried to remove the linen labels from the woolen army blankets so as not to transgress the prohibition of *shatnez*, which forbids mixing wool and linen together in any garment.[52]

The adolescents at Hay also had a great deal of freedom. Boys continued to study for their matriculation certificates despite the lack of textbooks, participated in sports groups, and played practical jokes on the other internees. One of their favorite pranks, which the teenage refugees played on the older men, stemmed from the preponderance of internees at Hay with higher academic degrees. A boy would run out of his hut and shout "Hey, Doctor!" and when more than half the camp would turn around and answer "yes?", in reply the boy would continue with the words, "kick you in the pants!"[53] Several departments of the Australian branch of the Women's International Zionist Organization (WIZO) took an interest in the deportees and attempted to alleviate their physical or spiritual discomforts, particularly those of the adolescents. One of these WIZO departments, under the leadership of Ruby Rich, devoted its attention to the Youth Aliyah boys and made great efforts, both in Australia and through the organization's British branch, to secure certificates for them to immigrate to Palestine. After being transferred with most of the internees from Hay to Tatura, six boys of the Youth Aliyah group were sent to Long Bay Camp and then to a third camp near Sidney. This group eventually left for Palestine on a cargo ship that carried only them and six New Zealand doctors as passengers. They arrived in Palestine via boat and train during the intermediate days of Passover 1942, having made a Passover *seder* in the desert out of a few eggs and potatoes.[54]

The remaining internees in Australia were told that they would be permitted to leave as free men only if they were accepted by the Pioneer Corps, the only army corps for which aliens were permitted to volunteer. Many boys of the RCM who had come of age since 1939 volunteered and were accepted as Pioneer Corps recruits. Some left for Britain in June 1941, others in October. Skilled men preferring to remain in Australia were released for vital war work in January 1942, while young men of military age were permitted to join the labor units of the Australian army. Those wishing to leave Australia under the Home Office White Papers would have to travel to the Isle of Man under escort and wait there until their case would be reviewed.[55]

By the end of 1943, a total of 1,141 internees had returned to Britain (47 drowned when their boat was torpedoed en route to Britain), 750 joined the Australian army or were employed in war work, and 150 migrated elsewhere. Apart from the Youth Aliyah youth who left for Palestine, most refugee youth had either returned to Britain under the Home Office White Papers or had joined the Pioneer Corps. Despite their ordeals, all the Jewish deportees had remained Jewish with the exception of two young men who had requested to be baptized by the small group of "non-Aryan" Christians at Hay; they kept separate from the other Jewish internees except for some clashes over the makeshift house of worship.[56]

Release from Internment

By mid-July 1940, some 19,200 men and women had been interned in Britain, 7,350 of whom had been deported and 650 drowned. During June and July 1940, public opinion in Britain had slowly swung from "intern the lot" to "free them now"; there was a growing feeling in the general public that the government may have gone too far in dealing with the refugee aliens.[57] Bowing to public and parliamentary pressures, on 31 July 1940 the Home Office published a White Paper listing eighteen headings under which internees could be released. Headings 1 and 2 applied to refugee youths: 1) Persons under sixteen and over sixty-five years of age, and 2) Young persons under age eighteen who at the time of their internment were resident with British families or were in educational establishments.[58] Children living in hostels were permitted to be released to the heads of the hostels. By the end of August 1940, almost 1,000 internees were released. A second White Paper of August 1940 made it possible for additional adolescents to be released, as did one in October of that year.[59] By December 1940, some 7,800 internees had been freed from captivity and by June 1941 the number had reached 16,694.[60]

As the war years progressed, and no new unaccompanied child refugees entered Britain after 1940, growing numbers of Jewish refugee children in that country came of age and subsequently became independent. A large number of these older adolescents volunteered for the Pioneer Corps, the first branch of the British armed forces to accept refugee volunteers. Boys entering the Pioneer Corps changed their names to avoid being treated as traitors if captured by the Nazis. Cohen became Cunningham or the Welsh Conynghame; Berliner became O'Hara; Marx was turned to Maxton; and Rosenberg became Russell. Various groups lobbied to change the minimum age of enlistment from nineteen to eighteen in order to enable boys who had reached that age to volunteer and thus be eligible for release from the internment camps. Eventually, eight hundred adolescents of the RCM joined the various units of the British armed forces. Only the WRENS (Women's Royal Naval Service) remained closed to alien women throughout the entire war.[61]

Epilogue to Internment

The internment and deportation escapades of 1940 are classic examples of the collective paranoia to which nations are prone at times of stress. Historical research has proven that fears of a fifth column menace in Britain were entirely unfounded. On 12 May 1940, the BBC had to withdraw orders to call up the RAF reservists three hours after they were announced. The false orders were presumed to have been the work of a fifth columnist and were often quoted as proof of a fifth column in Britain. In investigating this story, Louis de Jong has conclusively shown that this was an entirely internal coordination mistake of the BBC.[62]

While loyal aliens had either been under restrictions or interned, the real menace to Britain—fascists such as Sir Oswald Mosley or Sir Barry Domville— were walking around free. Only in June 1940 were such fascists detained, and as early as August 1940, many were released, when it was observed that Britain was "overdoing it." Toward the internees, the only statement that can be interpreted as some form of apology for what had been in most cases unjust internment was that of Sir John Anderson in the House of Commons debate of 22 August 1940, when he said: "I am not here to deny for a moment that most regrettable and deplorable things have happened . . . so far as we can remedy mistakes, we shall remedy them."[63]

Not all mistakes, however, could be remedied. Although the deportees received compensation for the possessions stolen from them during the journey, no such compensation was offered to schoolchildren whose internment forced them to abruptly leave school and job training to which, in many cases, they never returned. There was also never any reaction on the part of the organizations dealing with internees and deportees regarding compensation for education and opportunities lost due to the events of the period. One former youthful internee noted that some internees and deportees refused to accept monetary compensation for possession lost in the course of their incarceration, claiming that what they had lost was irreplaceable and that by accepting compensation they would "morally let Great Britain off the hook."[64] It might be that the refugee organizations took a similar attitude with regard to educational compensation. Another possibility was that they recognized that in the eyes of the British government, the education of one thousand adolescents was a trifling matter compared to the larger issues Britain faced during the war years, or that they realized the futility of such a request in the face of the challenges facing Britain during the postwar period.

How could a country such as Great Britain have let such things happen? One answer, that which summarized the attitude of the general public toward the unfortunate mistakes made during the internment episode, was given by the memorandum issued to the Aliens Tribunals in 1939: "While it is desired to avoid any unnecessary hardship to individuals, nevertheless the interests of the individual cannot in present circumstances be a primary consideration, they must be subordinated to considerations of national security."[65]

Notes

1. Newsam, *The Home Office*, 95.
2. Gillman and Gillman, *Collar the Lot*, 92.
3. This was due to the fear of a fifth column. For American reaction to the fifth column scare, see Friedman, *No Haven*, 113–28.
4. Wasserstein, *Britain and the Jews of Europe*, 83. The precedent for internment of aliens in Britain was the mass internment of aliens in Britain during the first few months of the First World War. Gillman and Gillman, *Collar the Lot*, 8–21.
5. Sub Committee Report of 1 April 1939, HO 144/21262 (700470/2) PRO.
6. Ibid. A second source cites the number as 73,800. Gillman and Gillman, *Collar the Lot*, 45.
7. Fraser, *Control of Aliens*, 194. The definition used in the First World War was "an alien whose sovereign or state is at war with His Majesty the King." Page, *War and Alien Enemies*, 1.
8. 351 HC Deb. 364 (4 September 1939).
9. Maximilian Koessler erroneously cites the number of Aliens tribunals as 112. Koessler, "Enemy Alien Internment," 102.
10. Jennings, *The British Constitution*, 224.
11. According to one source, 528 aliens were initially placed in category A; 8,356 in category B, and some 64,200 in category C. Lafitte, *The Internment of Aliens*, 63.
12. Author's interview with Bernard Kupferman, Jerusalem, 5 December 2010 (henceforth: Kupferman interview).
13. 360 HC Deb. 33, 23 April 1940.
14. de Jong, *The German Fifth Column*, 3, 66–77; *The Daily Mail*, 12 May 1940; 13 May 1940; 14 May 1940. See also *The London Times*, 13 May 1940; *The Observer* 12 May 1940; *The Daily Telegraph*, 14 May 1940; *The Daily Express*, 14 May 1940.
15. Wasserstein, *Britain and the Jews of Europe*, 87, Gillman and Gillman, *Collar the Lot*, 101–05. Gillman portrays Anderson as being opposed to mass internment in comparison with Lafitte, who portrays him as the person behind the scheme. The disparity comes from Gillman's access to sources that had been previously unavailable to Lafitte.

16. Churchill, *The Second World War*, vol. 2, 285.
17. Gillman and Gillman, *Collar the Lot*, 13.
18. Talmon interview.
19. Lafitte, *The Internment of Aliens*, 163–64.
20. Deakin, "Besieging Jericho," retrieved 7 February 2011 from http://cercles.com/n11/deakin.pdf.
21. Historians disagree over the number of internees who were refugees. Kushner and Cesarani suggest that 90 percent of the German and Austrian internees were Jewish; Kushner and Cesarani, "Island of Aliens," *The Jewish Chronicle*, 27 July 1990, 6.
22. Judex, *Anderson's Prisoners*.
23. Seller, *We Built up Our Lives*, 7.
24. Report on Aliens Internment Camp Huyton," 6 Sept. 1940, The Munk Archives, P/15/2 Yad Vashem Archives.
25. Seller, *We Built up Our Lives*, 152.
26. Rev. William W. Simpson, report of his visit to the Isle of Man, 2–6 November 1940; Central British Fund Archives, The Wiener Library Microfilm document collection 27/28/163; Seller, *We Built up Our Lives*, 120.
27. Judex, *Anderson's Prisoners*, 72.
28. "Youth Aliyah Returns from an Internment Camp," Newsletter, n.d., Central Zionist Archives, S75/1638.
29. "Report on Aliens Internment Camp Huyton," 6 Sept. 1940, The Munk Archives, P/15/2 Yad Vashem Archives; Schonfeld reports of visits to internment camp in the Isle of Man, 16–23 July 1940, 23–28 August 1940, 5–7 September 1940, 4–6 November 1940, The Munk Archives, P/15/2, Yad Vashem Archives.
30. Gillman and Gillman, *Collar the Lot*, 107.
31. Ibid., 161.
32. *The Jewish Chronicle*, 21 January 1938, 40.
33. "I think the sinking of the *Arandora Star* (the refugee children's ship) has shaken many parents." Letter from the head of the Math Department of Prior's Field School to an American doctor. Forbes-Robertson and Strauss, *War Letters from Britain*, 71.
34. Presland, *A Great Adventure*, 13.
35. Saul Hayes to Stephany, 30 July 1941, Board of Deputies Archives Acc 3121 C2/3/5/5 quoted in Shatzkes, *Holocaust and Rescue*, 97.
36. Gillman and Gillman, *Collar the Lot*, 239–40.
37. Seller, *We Built up Our Lives*, 164.
38. *Youth Aliyah Magazine*, November 1940, CZA S75/1637; minutes of the meeting of the Executive Committee of Children and Youth Aliyah, 17 December 1941, CZA S75/1640.
39. Cited in Seller, *We Built up Our Lives*, 168.
40. Ibid.
41. Shatzkes, *Holocaust and Rescue*, 98; Spier, *The Protecting Power*, 218.
42. Quebec City, Fredericton, Cochrane, Isle aux Noix, St. Helens Island. United Jewish Refugee and War Relief Agency interview with Brigadier General E. de B. Panet (Director General of Internment Operations), 6 August 1940, P/15/2/ Munch Archives, Yad Vashem.
43. Gillman, *Collar the Lot*, 269.
44. Seller, *We Built up Our Lives*, 169.
45. Letter from Eva Michaelis to Henrietta Szold, 29 November 1940, S75/1637, CZA. Gillman and Gillman, *Collar the Lot*, 269.

46. Talmon interview.
47. Patkin, *The Dunera Internees*, 32; Talmon interview.
48. Dr. Elchanan Hams Blumenthal 03/2384 Yad Vashem Archives; Edgar From 02/473 Yad Vashem Archives.
49. Talmon interview.
50. Gillman and Gillman, *Collar the Lot*, 213, 243, 247.
51. Loewald, "A Dunera Internee at Hay 1940–1941," 513.
52. Talmon interview.
53. Talmon interview. The same was true in certain internment camps in Britain such as Huyton. See Report on Aliens Internment Camp Huyton, 6 September 1940, P/15/2, Munk Archives, Yad Vashem Archives.
54. WIZO also aided German refugees in Australia whose numbers were estimated at 6,500 including "non-Aryan" Christians. Berger, "Australia and the Refugees," 56; Talmon Interview; "Memorandum to Youth Aliyah," 6 January 1941, S75/1639 CZA.
55. Gillman and Gillman, *Collar the Lot*, 280.
56. Patkin, *The Dunera Internees*, 86.
57. Kobler, "From the Activities of the Jews in England," 225.
58. Categories of Persons Eligible for Release from Internment, German and Austrian Internees. London, H.M.S.O. August 1940, Cmd. 6223. The words "or that live with foster or step parents or guardians" were added to heading 2.
59. Civilian Internees of Enemy Nationality; Categories of Persons Eligible for Release from Internment. H.M.S.O. London, October 1940. Cmd. 6233.
60. Tartakower and Grossman, *The Jewish Refugee*, 250.
61. Presland, *A Great Adventure*, 13.
62. de Jong, *The Jewish Fifth Column*, 13, 97.
63. Quoted in Gillman and Gillman, *Collar the Lot*, 129.
64. Talmon interview.
65. Quoted in Gillman and Gillman, *Collar the Lot*, 144.

Chapter 9

The Guardianship

Introduction

"I was in the boarding school in Cornwall until I was sixteen in 1944 and then I left school and went to a hostel in Belsize Park in Hampstead. We were all unhappy there as we knew already what was happening in Europe. The Jewish Refugees Committee found me a job with a leather firm in the East End where I worked for a while. I also worked for the Jewish Refugees Committee for a while and then in the municipality. Reenie was still in school as she was younger than I and then eventually when she finished, she took up nursing and we shared a rented flat in London but she was never there, always at the hospital. No one looked after anyone to make us a home, to find us someone. We learned something important then. If you are on your own and no one makes you a *shidduch* [match], you are without a future."[1]

With these words, Steffi Birnbaum Schwartz continued her wartime reminiscences and noted her worries about what would happen to her and her sister in the years to come. At the time, however, most of the British authorities and Jewish organizations responsible for the welfare of the refugee children in Britain were more concerned about the children's present and immediate situation than their long-term future. This concern became acute during the final wartime phase, which began in December 1943 and was symbolized by the passage of the Guardianship Bill and the religious and social furor surrounding the placement of the Jewish refugee children in non-Jewish homes.

The Final Wartime Phase: The Guardianship

During late 1942, the first details of the "Final Solution" began to reach Britain. As more information was received in 1943, particularly following the fall of the Warsaw ghetto, the fate of European Jewry became clearer. Not only were they being decimated but it was now obvious that many, if not most, of the refugee children in Britain whose parents were still in Continental Europe at the outbreak of war were now orphans. In light of this assumption, the Home Office, after consulting with Refugee Children's Movement officials, decided to reexamine the question of the legal guardianship of all refugee children in Great Britain.[2] There were, at that time, approximately 12,400 such children in Britain, 10,000 who had come through various movements for the rescue of Central European children between 1936 and 1939, some 400 orphans of the Spanish Civil War, and 3,500 British children evacuated from the Channel Islands.[3] Of these children, approximately 8,500 were still minors and thus in need of a legal guardian. Although the RCM was recognized by the Home Office as functioning *in loco parentis*, actual guardianship in the case of each child could only be established by individual application to the High Court. This lack of guardianship created problems for the RCM in various situations, such as when it wanted to receive permission to transfer a child from a certain billet after evacuation.

In response to this worrisome situation, in December 1943 the Home Office sponsored a bill in Parliament that conferred power to a legal guardian over groups of children without parents in Britain.[4] The bill, debated at its second reading,[5] provided that the Home Secretary may appoint a guardian for children who arrived in Great Britain after 1936 because of religious, political, or racial persecution, that being the year in which the first refugee children were brought under the auspices of the Children's Inter-Aid Committee. The children in question had no parents in the United Kingdom and were under age twenty-one, or in the case of females, unmarried and twenty-one or less. The bill also stipulated that if the parent of any child claimed him or her after the war, the guardianship for that child would naturally be null and void.[6]

What, however, was the actual issue at hand? Was it the refugee-orphan children's physical well-being or something much deeper than that? In what ways did the Guardianship Bill rekindle a previously existing internecine war within British Jewry? How did something that was ostensibly portrayed as an issue of caring become a power struggle between various groups in Britain that seemed at times to be using the child refugee issue in order to stake their claim as power brokers both inside and outside the British Jewish community?

At the start of the parliamentary debate, it became obvious that two issues were actually being discussed. The first was the obvious one—the question of protecting orphan children from abuse by providing them with a guardian who would be responsible for their legal issues. However, the underlying issue that was brought up at the same time was that of safeguarding the Jewish refugee children's faith and protecting them from religious proselytizing. This point was brought home several times during the debate by Daniel Lipson, MP for Cheltenham, and Osbert Peake, Parliamentary Under-Secretary for the Home Office (1939–44), who emphasized that special care must be taken to ensure that all Jewish refugee children would have access to Jewish religious facilities.

Although this problem had been brought up time and again by Rabbi Schonfeld of the CRREC and Harry Goodman of Agudath Israel during the early months of 1939, it had basically been pushed aside as a result of the war and the evacuation of hundreds of thousands of British children to the Midlands and other safer areas. Now that the question of appointing a guardian for the refugee children had arisen, Anglo Jewry also reawakened to this problem and to a debate over who this guardian should be.

One of the first people who came to mind was Lord Gorell, Chairman of the Refugee Children's Movement, who was familiar with their status, problems, and the bureaucratic machinery surrounding their resettlement. However, the suggestion of Gorell's candidacy raised a host of other questions: What qualifications should such a guardian have? Was it necessary for him to be of the same religious persuasion as the children in order to best deal with the religious undercurrents that were being brought up? What would be the practical limits of his power vis-à-vis the refugee children? What, in fact, would be the scope of his guardianship?

Although almost ten thousand refugee children from Hitler had entered Great Britain between December 1938 and September 1939, including several thousand "non-Aryan" Christians, the vast majority of the refugee children from Central Europe were Jewish or of Jewish origin. Consequently, and in view of the claim that they needed protection from religious proselytizing, it ostensibly appeared that the Jewish refugee children's guardian should be a major Jewish figure, preferably one sensitive to religious issues, and of sufficient public stature that would engender him general understanding and support when he would have to act upon difficult cases. In the more traditional or religious Jewish circles and particularly those of the CRREC, the general consensus was that the most suitable person for this task was the British Chief Rabbi, Rabbi Dr. Joseph Herman Hertz.

Hertz was a well-accepted public figure not tainted with the intensity of his son-in-law, Rabbi Schonfeld, and was imminently suitable to deal with the issues of proselytizing, refugee children expressing a desire to convert due to pressure from their hosts, and related issues. He was a loyal and patriotic British citizen, upholding national values while not compromising his Jewish beliefs. Finally, the vast majority of underage refugee children in Britain were Jewish. Thus, at first glance, appointing Rabbi Hertz as guardian for the refugee children in Britain appeared to be a suitable solution to the guardianship dilemma.

But what of the non-Jewish refugee children? Wasn't appointing a Jewish religious figure as guardian to non-Jewish children almost as problematic as appointing a non-Jewish guardian for Jewish children? To be fair, almost all of the non-Jewish refugee children from Central Europe had a connection to Judaism, as they were "non-Aryan" Christians, children of mixed marriages who were brought up as Christian but had a Jewish parent, or children of Jewish parents who had converted to Christianity. Nevertheless, appointing a religious Jewish guardian for gentile refugee children might still be considered unsuitable. As a compromise, Hertz suggested creating a dual guardianship: Lord Gorell would be the nominal guardian of all refugee children in Britain, while in practice Hertz would assume sole responsibility for the religious welfare of the Jewish refugee children.

Although at first glance this compromise appeared to solve any potential controversy, not all of those responsible for the welfare of the refugee children in Britain agreed with alacrity to the suggestion. First and foremost among those opposing the idea of Hertz assuming any type of guardianship for the refugee children was Lord Gorell himself. Even before the bill was introduced to Parliament, Gorell penned a note to Hertz in which he stated categorically that he would not accept the claim that Hertz should bear the sole responsibility for the religious welfare of the Jewish refugee children in Britain.[7] In his letter to Hertz, Gorell gave no explanation for his position; however, both correspondents were well aware of the series of events that had led up to its writing. The terse but forceful note was the culmination of the somewhat acrimonious relationship that had developed between Rabbi Hertz and Lord Gorell over the war years regarding the spiritual lives of the Jewish refugee children in Britain. The note was a consequence of the difficult relationship existing between a number of the RCM executive members and Rabbi Shonfeld, Hertz's son-in-law, regarding the placement of Jewish refugee children in gentile foster homes and their resulting religious welfare.

The Public Debate over the Guardianship of Jewish Refugee Children

Long before the actual parliamentary debates over the Guardianship Bill, the issue served to reawaken the religious furor surrounding the placement of Jewish children in non-Jewish foster homes. The 31 December 1943 issue of the Anglo-Jewish weekly, the *Jewish Chronicle*, devoted several articles to a discussion of this problem, describing the close relationships that often developed between gentile foster parents and their Jewish refugee wards. Based on the assumption that the children's natural parents were dead, some foster parents openly stated their intention of raising the children in their care as Christians.[8]

In the same issue, Dayan (religious judge) Dr. Isidore Grunfeld berated the Anglo-Jewish community for its treatment of the refugee children. Most members of the Jewish community, he stated, had donated money to the refugee children's cause, but for various reasons, such as crowded living conditions, locations in dangerous areas, and fear of being reminded of their own refugee past, were reluctant to take children into their homes. Grunfeld noted that the only step that had been thus far been taken in an attempt to safeguard these children's religious observances was the creation of the Joint Committee for Religious Education and Welfare of Jewish Refugee Children in August 1942 by the Central Council for Jewish Refugees. The article concluded with the hope that before the passing of the Guardianship Bill, Jewish refugee children living in non-Jewish homes would be removed to a Jewish environment.[9]

The debate in Anglo-Jewish circles over the religious future of Jewish refugee children in Britain escalated during the early months of 1944. As an answer to Dayan Grunfeld, Mr. G. Berger, president of the Union of Orthodox Hebrew Congregations, reminded the public that it was imprecise to state that Jews did not offer hospitality to Jewish refugee children. Jews indeed did so, in the form of hostels. He also brought to the public's attention a newly published pamphlet by his movement, meant to influence the Home Secretary "to invest guardianship rights in a Jewish body rather than in the interdenominational and tendentious" Refugee Children's Movement and concluded that "Anglo-Jewry must ask him to entrust the guardianship of Jewry's orphans to proper Jewish authorities."[10]

The pamphlet to which Berger referred was *The Child Estranging Movement*, published in January by the Union of Orthodox Hebrew Congregations in Britain, in which the RCM was berated for its placement policies, particularly with regard to Orthodox Jewish refugee children.[11] Taking the position that the RCM knew exactly what it was doing, the booklet's author stated categorically that the organization had a purpose in sending Jewish children to non-Jewish foster homes throughout Britain: "From the outset, representatives of the Movement declared it their intention to make these children forget all their past, to send them as ambassadors into the homes of Christian foster parents where they could assimilate and create Christian–Jewish goodwill."[12]

Initially, the authors wrote, part of the confusion over sending non-Orthodox Jewish refugee children to gentile foster homes also resulted from the discrepancy between denominational labeling in Germany and England. While "Konservative" in Germany was still religious and "Liberal" meant in keeping with certain Jewish traditions, British refugee organization had mistakenly considered any children not classified as Orthodox as freethinking, and thus felt that there would be no religious difficulties resulting from boarding such children with non-Jews. But this was only one expression of the movement's disregard for religious matters. According to this pamphlet, the Refugee Children's Movement placed obstacles in the paths of Orthodox hostels, such as the one in Manchester, wishing to observe the Sabbath.

Additional problems began with the outbreak of the war. According to the booklet, following the evacuation of September 1939, when many children were placed in non-Jewish homes, the Refugee Children's Movement, contrary to its assurances, had given them little or no Jewish education. Part of this stemmed from the exclusion of any Orthodox representatives from the committees of various bodies that dealt with the refugee children. As an example, the booklet stated that other than the selection board dealing with Orthodox boys wishing to learn in yeshivas, throughout the war years no Orthodox representative held any responsible position in the Refugee Children's Movement.

As for Orthodox children, the booklet continued, efforts were made to separate them and send them to non-Orthodox homes. Examples were given to illustrate the depth of the problem. One example was young Frieda Stolberg, who had to be spirited away from her Christian foster home against her householders' will. "Stolzberg, a child from an ultra-Orthodox Jewish home was placed and kept in a non-Jewish home until she was clandestinely transferred to a Jewish hostel."[13] Reminding the readers of the strong conversionist movement that existed in Scotland, the booklet's author stressed how the Refugee Children's Movement had made no efforts to combat the religious influence it was having on Jewish refugee children.

Other claims against the RCM involved their lack of zeal in trying to ameliorate the plight of Orthodox Jewish refugee children who had been placed in non-Jewish foster homes. As the pamphlet's author reminded his readers, in spite of the fact that certain Orthodox children were forbidden by their non-Jewish foster parents to attend religious classes, the Refugee Children's Movement had refused to appoint an official for the purpose of checking into the Orthodox cases it handled. It preferred to push the matter aside and only deal with such cases if someone involved brought it forcefully to their attention. Even then, the solutions were ad hoc and no efforts were made to try to solve the general problem.

At this point in the pamphlet, the author channeled all his arguments into one direction: that of the guardianship issue. Now, it stated, the Anglo-Jewish community was facing the possibility of having a non-Jewish guardian for all Jewish refugee children, Orthodox and Liberal, which would strengthen the resolve of the gentile families wishing to convert their refugee boarders. How could Anglo Jewry let such a thing happen? Having discussed the RCM's unimpressive record regarding the spiritual care of Orthodox children, the pamphlet concluded with the demand that the authority over these children remain in the hands of Anglo Jewry and not in those of a single gentile guardian: "All we ask is the Guardianship of Jewish children should be entrusted to a Jewish body."[14]

The pamphlet's publication underscored not only the dichotomy between the Orthodox and Liberal Jewish refugee cause activists but, in addition, pointed again to the internal divisions among Orthodox Anglo Jewry that existed between the ultra-Orthodox "Adath" and the more mainstream "United Synagogue" congregants and leaders. The authors of this brief but forceful pamphlet, leading members of the Union of Orthodox Hebrew Congregations (the "Adath"), did not refrain at times from attacking their fellow Orthodox Jews for their nonzealous attitude toward the placement, care, and religious upbringing of the Jewish refugee children. This might also explain why the booklet claimed that no Orthodox figures served on any RCM committees while, in fact, there actually was an Orthodox rabbi connected with the United Synagogue movement, Rabbi Maurice Swift, who for a period of time was a member of the RCM Central Committee. However, by late 1943 the more ultra-Orthodox leadership had decided to abandon their internecine wars and consolidate their efforts against the "Progressive" and non-Jewish members of the RCM in the hope of reexamining the placement of various Jewish child refugees presently domiciled with non-Jews.

In view of the accusations that the pamphlet had leveled against the leadership of the Refugee Children's Movement, those at its helm thought it imperative to reply swiftly, convincingly, and publicly to what they considered to be a combination of trumped-up claims, half-truths, and vicious lies about the child refugee organization's policies and goals. The first to reply was Eva Reading, who had been involved for years in acrimonious arguments with Rabbi Shonfeld over RCM placement policies and saw this as an opportunity to publicly set the record straight. As a reply to the pamphlet, the Marchioness of Reading published an article in the *Jewish Chronicle*, recalling her experiences in placing children through the RCM in 1939. At the time, she stated, Jews composed only 1 percent of the British population,[15] making it impossible to accommodate all the Jewish refugee children without assistance from the non-Jewish community. It was therefore imperative to send some children to gentile homes, even if this was considered undesirable by Orthodox refugee activists. This had been the situation in 1939 at the war's outset. Today, she continued, over four years later, the situation had changed. By now, the number of refugee children still in school or living with foster parents had diminished greatly, as many had reached the age of majority, entered the armed forces, married, and so on. Fewer Jewish refugee children of impressionable age remained, limiting the scope of this problem. In fact, at the time of the article's writing in early 1944, Reading reminded her readers that only one thousand refugee children were still under the age of fourteen.[16]

At the same time that Reading was penning her response to the booklet Lord Gorell responded to the issue in a speech delivered in Bloomsbury House in front of the RCM executive and other refugee organization functionaries.[17] Speaking "candidly," as he put it, Gorell first tried to assuage the religious sensibilities of the Jews in his audience who might have some sort of spiritual allegiance to the Chief Rabbi. The real issue, so he began, was not Hertz but his son-in-law, Rabbi Schonfeld. In fact, Gorell continued, Hertz had once said to Gorell privately that "he has not as much authority as does his son-in-law because his son-in-law is a much younger and much more forceful man." Speaking of Schonfeld's attacks on the RCM, Gorell claimed that he had "a letter from the Chief Rabbi mildly disassociating himself from these attacks." Why, then, did he, Gorell, refuse the Chief Rabbi's request to have a representative of the Chief Rabbinate in Britain on the RCM board? In his answer, he now appealed to the broad sense of duty which he assumed that the executive members of the RCM all had: because he felt that Hertz would only be concerned with the religious issues of the refugee children and not the full gamut of issues that each and every member of the RCM Executive was naturally concerned with. With this statement Gorell felled two birds with one stone. Not only did he laud the executive members' universal sense of duty, placing it on a higher moral plane than what he claimed was the Chief Rabbi's religious particularism, but he also laid the groundwork for proving that the Chief Rabbi was unsuitable to act as co-guardian for the Jewish refugee children.

Having painted Hertz with the narrow segregationist brush, he now turned to the Orthodox attitude toward the Guardianship Bill in order to expound upon what their "real" agenda was. Explaining how the bill had given rise to violent attacks on the RCM, he stated that when the Orthodox demanded that Jewish children be taken out of Christian homes and given to Jewish families, in truth they meant to Orthodox homes, something that the Home Office would refuse to do. Ending this part of his talk with righteous anger over the fact that the attackers were giving no credit to the RCM for anything it did or giving thanks for the children's placements, he now tried to portray himself as soothing the ruffled feathers of the Orthodox as if they were part of his audience, just in case they had any sympathizers among his listeners: "I know something of what Orthodox Jewry has suffered on the continent, and how many of them have lost their lives, so that the numbers, therefore, throughout the world are less and I imagine that the pressure on the Chief Rabbi to increase the numbers again is overwhelming. I do sympathize with their view to attract as many back to Orthodox Judaism as possible."

Concluding his talk, Gorell turned to his audience, asking whether they thought that the Home Secretary should go on with the bill already in Parliament or if he should be advised to drop it. In response, the RCM executive warmly endorsed the bill and urged Parliament to proceed with it "in spite of the injustice and inaccurate attacks to which the Movement was being subjected."[18]

All this was, however, a temporary stopgap until a broader written response to the pamphlet could be formulated. The RCM's ultimate response came in the form of a summary pamphlet written under a pseudonym by RCM activist, the author Gladys Bendit, wife of RCM executive committee member Francis Bendit. Published in early 1944, it encapsulated the history and activities of the Movement and listed the steps that had been taken to safeguard Jewish children from proselytizing. "Whenever a Jewish child was placed in a Christian home . . . it was laid down as a principle of the Movement and clearly understood by the host, that there was to be no proselytizing. Further, the child was put in touch with the nearest resident Rabbi, or if there were none with whom direct contact could be made, religious instruction was arranged by correspondence."[19] In fact, an entire third of the pamphlet, which served as the RCM's official history for the next forty-five years, was devoted to the religious aspect of the RCM's activities.

There was, however, a great gap between Bendit's quoted statement in theory and its expression in practice. An examination of a single meeting of a local CRREC branch in Norfolk exemplified just a few examples of this gap. Most of the meeting was devoted to the religious problems of refugee children in the area: the children who had been expected to attend church with their foster families, some of whom were even expected to sing in the church choir; the Christian foster parents who had forbidden their Jewish refugee charges to do homework on Sunday, forcing them to desecrate their Sabbath by writing on Saturday. The committee even discussed the possibility of creating a traveling synagogue that might help combat some of the problems being discussed.[20] And again, all this was from a single meeting of one local branch of the Chief Rabbi's Religious Emergency Council. Multiply it by numerous local branches throughout Britain and one might begin to get a picture of the religious difficulties facing a goodly number of the Jewish refugee children throughout the country. Summarizing what some of the children were facing on a daily basis, the normally mild-mannered Steffi Birnbaum Schwartz recalled the behavior of the gentile headmistress of her boarding school toward the Jewish refugee girls and allowed herself an uncharacteristic and concise epithet: "The headmistress was a bitch and a beast and antisemitic and she wanted to turn us all into Christians."[21]

These, however were only some of the religious problems facing Jewish refugee children. In several public schools, special requests had to be written to the boards of governors, requesting that Jewish boys be excused from their lessons on Saturday.[22] Other children, living with Quaker families, were forced to pray to Jesus before each meal.[23] Children who were adopted into a religious community were at times placed under great social pressure to convert; some could not withstand that pressure and eventually agreed to baptism.[24] It appeared, therefore, that Rabbis Hertz and Shonfeld and the indefatigable but often obstreperous Harry Goodman were correct in their fears for the spiritual welfare of Jewish refugee children in Great Britain.

There was, however, another side to this issue. Despite the CRREC's attempts to place the entire blame for the situation on the RCM and portray itself as a voice continuously crying in the wilderness, this was not the precise or entire truth. It is true that throughout the period in question the CRREC certainly made great efforts to care for the spiritual well-being of the Jewish refugee children. Time and again it held meetings on this subject, in which its activists discussed the fear of proselytizing and made numerous suggestions as to how to combat the rampant phenomenon. And throughout the entire period, the CRREC continuously raised the claim that the RCM was primarily interested in caring for the physical welfare of the refugee children but much less for their spiritual needs.

All this, however, was rhetoric. In practice, a closer look at the CRREC's own activities from the outbreak of war until early 1943 shows that most of its enterprises were those of a sectoral organization caring primarily for its own. Although in theory the CRREC's efforts were directed toward assisting all Jewish refugee children in Britain, in practice the group confined its endeavors to caring for Orthodox refugee children. This stemmed primarily from the group's limited resources and the need to focus on the children they considered most in need of religious assistance. An example was Rabbi Schonfeld's attempts to remove Orthodox Jewish refugee boys from the Jews' Free School for Boys that had been evacuated to Ely, assisting them to transfer to a yeshiva in London, and even offering them finances to cover travel costs and promising them more money upon their arrival in London.[25] However, what this did in practice was to leave the majority of the Jewish refugee children in Britain for most of the wartime period without any group to actively fight for their spiritual welfare.

The results of this neglect were the crux of the arguments between the RCM and the CRREC during the early weeks of 1944.

The Guardianship Bill Is Passed

Despite Chief Rabbi Hertz's efforts to have the Home Office consider him as a candidate for guardianship of the Jewish refugee children in Britain or at least as their special religious legal representative, they rejected these possibilities in view of Lord Gorell's objections. The final bill submitted to Parliament stipulated that only one person would serve as guardian for all the refugee children in the country.[26] During the parliamentary debate, it was also emphasized that this title should not become a "machine guardianship," which was to be assured by the cooperation of the various refugee organizations and religious leaders with the guardian. This last issue was raised in the hope to assuage the Jewish organizations and religious leadership, which had been adamant that Jewish refugee children needed Jewish representation. On 18 February 1944, the bill passed Parliament after its third reading, becoming law upon receiving Royal Assent on 1 March 1944.[27]

In the spring of 1944, Lord Gorell, chairman of the RCM, was appointed guardian for all refugee children in England. This was not only the first time that a group of Jewish children in Britain would have an official non-Jewish legal guardian but also the first time that a group of Roman Catholic children in Britain would have a Protestant legal guardian. Simultaneous with Gorell's appointment, the Rev. Ephraim Levine, minister of the New West End Synagogue in London, was placed in charge of the religious welfare of Jewish children under this guardianship. The choice of a well-known Orthodox rabbinical figure for this purpose was meant to remove the debate from the very personalized Gorell–Hertz sphere in an attempt to assuage those who felt that Jewish refugee children needed a Jewish guardian; they were now provided with a rabbi who was not within the inner circle of the Hertz family. In the eyes of some, the Glasgow-born Rabbi Levine, "Ephie" as he was universally known, was an excellent choice due to both his wit and his excellent rapport with his co-religionists of all branches. However, his appointment did not smooth the path to any kind of religious "cease-fire," as was soon discovered. On his part, when Lord Gorell was asked how he related to the religious aspects of his new task, he recalled that he was asked to give "careful investigation and thought" to any question affecting the life and future of any child, particularly in cases where a Jewish child wished to marry a Christian, a frequent situation in the mid- and late 1940s. Lord Gorell's guardianship continued until all the refugee children attained their majority.[28]

Toward the Future: Facing Intermarriage and Conversion

Throughout 1944, the Refugee Children's Movement held a number of meetings to deal with the religious state of affairs of Jewish refugee children in Britain in general and Orthodox Jewish children in particular. The first group of meetings was internal, with the executive committee attempting to delineate the problem's scope and devise strategies to deal with it. Later in the spring of 1944, Committee members held a number of meetings with the Chief Rabbi to try to reach an understanding about how to proceed. Summarizing these meetings in a note penned on the margin of their minutes, Elaine Blond wrote in her typical understatement: "Not very satisfactory, I'm afraid."[29]

The most common refugee child problem in Britain during the latter war years was that of Jewish children living in Christian households. To the dismay of the Orthodox groups that had raised questions about Lord Gorell's guardianship in the first place, when it came to this issue, Gorell acted just as they had feared. Instead of attempting to remove the Jewish children from non-Jewish households, even in cases of blatant proselytizing and pressuring of the children to convert, he stated categorically that each case was different and had to be decided upon separately.

In practice, Gorell abstained as much as he could from removing the children from non-Jewish foster families unless he was pressured to do so by Jewish religious bodies. In this respect he differed sharply from Rabbi Maurice Swift, a member of the RCM central committee who believed that in all cases Jewish children should be removed from Christian homes and placed either in Jewish foster homes, hostels, or other Jewish institutions.

Almost as if it were a continuation of Gorell's problematic relationship with the Chief Rabbi, Swift now became his chief religious adversary. At an RCM meeting where Swift was asked to give the opening address and mentioned his position on this matter, public controversy erupted between the two. Trying to settle the acrimony between Gorell and Swift and in response to the growing number of cases of Jewish refugee minors asking permission to convert that had been brought to his attention during the year, the Chief Rabbi appealed to Gorell in December 1944 to form a subcommittee that would examine problems of proselytizing among Jewish refuge children. This suggestion was not acted upon.[30]

The question of Jewish children raised in Christian homes during the war was not unique to Britain; it was an integral part of the general postwar difficulties surrounding the care of such children by Jewish organizations wishing to "redeem" them from their non-Jewish foster parents. In many European countries, Jewish children had been hidden by gentiles and were distributed among private households, children's homes, convents, and monasteries. In England, refugee children were not hidden but were openly boarded out. Because they were at an impressionable age, there were children in all countries who were drawn to the warmth and rituals of Christian households and had no objection to joining the Christian faith through baptism. Removal of such children from their immediate environment did not necessarily guarantee their return to the faith of their ancestors; some still believed, even after having physically being "returned to the fold," that their newly baptized souls belonged to the Church.

Taking local nuances into consideration, Jewish organizations in all countries wishing to combat this phenomenon after the war were forced to deal with four different categories of children living with non-Jewish foster parents. The first were those children wishing to return to Judaism and leave their Christian foster parents. One boy recalled how at his first foster home, when he was eleven, his foster mother tried to take him to church. "Just as soon as I realized where we were going I protested strongly shouting loudly 'Jude, Jude.'" Following his protests, he was subsequently removed from the home and sent to a Jewish foster family.[31]

The second involved children who having been influenced by missionaries, their foster parents, or others, now considered themselves as having been "saved" and thus both passively and actively resisted being returned to Judaism. Steffi Birnbaum Schwartz recalled how three girls in her boarding school were actively influenced by the missionary headmistress to convert and would not consider being removed to a different school.[32] Another refugee girl recalled coming to Britain at age nine and being housed at a vicarage with two other Jewish refugee girls. "The Jewish Children's Committee tried on several occasions to remove us to a Jewish hostel. We fought like mad to stay and were eventually left alone. . . . I was fourteen when we were all three baptized."[33]

The third category consisted of children whose non-Jewish foster parents refused to let them be removed from their homes. Among these was a group of children who had been sent to Christadelphians in the Birmingham area.[34] The last category contained children whose desire to convert stemmed from a psychological impulse to escape what they saw as the "collective Jewish fate" and thus took the first step toward Christianity through their own initiative. As one former refugee girl stated about her adolescent urge to be baptized, "This I recognized as . . . a wish to attach myself to a big organization which has endured through the centuries."[35] In this connection there were also cases of children whose parents survived the war and had no objections to their children remaining with gentile foster parents and eventually converting. A refugee girl recalled: "I was twelve years old when I came . . . my father persuaded my sister and myself to be baptized 'for the sake of our children.' I was baptized when I was about sixteen."[36] This was yet another manifestation of an attempt to escape from Judaism as a result of negative wartime experiences.[37]

The first response of the Jewish organizations attempting to deal with these children in liberated Europe was to remove them from their non-Jewish environment. Only after this move could they attempt to reeducate them toward a Jewish and more traditional lifestyle. These were also the two methods proposed by the CRREC in *The Child Estranging Movement* in order to deal with the plight of the Jewish refugee children in Britain. To successfully implement them, it would have been necessary for Orthodox British Jews to maintain a united front, to generate sympathy for the cause among Anglo Jewry and to involve professional educators. But in practice, Anglo-Orthodoxy continued its internal vendettas, there were few professional Jewish educators able to deal with this phenomenon, and the majority of Anglo Jewry remained apathetic to the spiritual plight of Jewish refugee children. Under these circumstances, was it at all realistic to think of implementing the two aforementioned suggestions in Britain of 1944–45?

It would be simplistic to state that in Britain, the cry of Orthodox Jewish organizations to save the souls of the refugee children fell on deaf ears within the majority of Anglo Jewry, and thus nothing was done. In practice, the issues that the CRREC brought up were noted, but in many cases there was actually little that could be done to ameliorate the situation at such a late date. One example was the issue of finding accommodating Jewish refugee children in Britain. Although most of the CRREC's accusations were based on actual cases and surveys, their suggestions were not. Those pointing the accusing finger had not surveyed the number of Jewish households willing and able to care for Jewish refugee children in 1944. Did they have any assurances that more homes would be available then than in 1939? It certainly did not appear so, particularly as the war was still raging and the average British Jewish family's financial situation or living conditions had not changed for the better since the war's outbreak. As for the cry "send them to hostels," this, too, was easier said than done because such a step required unobtainable government financial aid, not to mention the humanitarian outcry that would be raised if thousands of children were forcibly removed from "warm homes" to "impersonal institutions."

There was also no guarantee that at this late date it would still be possible to undo the influences of the previous five years. Many refugee children, victims of racial and religious persecution, had come to Britain at an impressionable age. Once accustomed to the British way of life they clung to it with a tenacious hold, as it was a constant in a world of ever-changing variables. Little was initially more outwardly "British" to the impressionable refugee youngster than the ever-present Yorkshire pudding (originally detested by more than one German Jewish child), scones and cream, high tea, and other national foods and customs. In an attempt to "belong," many refugee children adopted these customs, hoping to erase their refugee past. Above all, the British way of life was epitomized by adherence to the precepts of the Church of England, the bastion of the society to which they aspired to belong. Little wonder that in spite of the lack of precise statistics, intermarriage and conversion rates for this group are assumed to be high.[38]

One refugee girl recalled her gradual transition to the British way of life and with it, to the Church of England: "As a girl of nine I went to foster parents who were members of the Church of England, and from then on my Jewish faith seemed to recede further and further from my mind. They made no attempt to influence me—from an early age I had to decide for myself . . . and over the years I became closer to the C. of E."[39] Another Jewish refugee girl, who had come to a Christian foster family at the age of six, recalled that becoming Christian was for her the natural culmination of life with the family that showed her love and what she considered to be the British way of life: "The transition from being a Jew to being a Christian—and I am now a convinced Christian and a member of a church—was not difficult. My adoptive parents attended church regularly, prayed and taught me at home so that I grew up in this atmosphere and imbibed it."[40] A third refugee girl, who reached England at the age of nine and was baptized in her teens, summarized her reasons for joining the Church in one sentence: "Having at last found some security in our lives we were reluctant to give it up."[41]

A number of British Church personalities turned out to be an unexpected source of religious compassion and tolerance in steering impressionable refugee children away from the church. One was the minister, later to become the Archbishop of Canterbury, who counseled a young Jewish refugee girl with musical inclinations not to attend church services to listen to the choir. He wished, as he told her, neither for her to be influenced by Christianity nor for her actions to be interpreted wrongly by the congregation.[42] Another was the minister who invited an Orthodox refugee boy to a holiday camp for a weekend and prepared a kosher meal, served on new plates, with two candles, two rolls, and an unopened bottle of wine for him to use in ushering in the Sabbath.[43] Yet a third was the Reverend William W. Simpson, member of the RCM executive committee, who was later to become a founding member of the National Council of Christians and Jews. Simpson had long recognized the religious problem and even wrote a memorandum to the RCM, emphasizing what a serious problem the children's baptism was, particularly cases that were now being discovered ex post facto, and he exhorted the RCM to use all its resources to combat this trend.[44] Unfortunately, however such church figures were few and far between.

More common was the behavior of the Barbican Mission to the Jews, a missionary group founded in 1891 that had requested to house and foster Jewish refugee children from Prague. In spite of the fact that as far back as mid-1939 its name had been brought up at RCM meetings as an overt missionary body, its foster home had rarely been inspected during the war years. Only after great pressure did the RCM secretary, Dorothy Hardisty, visit the mission in early 1945, where she learned that most of the Jewish refugee children living on premises had indeed long been baptized. In fact, the Mission's staff was proud of that fact, declaring outright that their mission was to convert as many Jews as possible to Christianity. In the face of Hardisty's protests, the administrators stated that they were in possession of letters from the refugee children's parents, all of whom had agreed to their children's baptism. Hardisty concluded her report by stating that the RCM would now have to attempt to contact the children's parents in order to check the veracity of this story.[45]

One reason for the Jewish refugee children's high rate of intermarriage may have been the general trends related to this issue in twentieth-century Europe in general, in both Continental Europe and Britain. The intermarriage rate of Anglo Jewry had risen significantly since the turn of the century, eventually reaching a zenith in the period following the Second World War, particularly in the smaller towns and rural areas.[46] German Jewish refugee children had come from a country where a high proportion of mixed marriage existed; indeed, some were the products of such marriages.[47] Apart from any pressure from non-Jewish foster parents, or a desire to "fit in," all these were considerations that made an impact on quite a number of Jewish refugee children in Britain and on their attitude toward intermarriage.

This, however, was not the case with regard to the approximated high conversion rate among Jewish refugee children, unparalleled among British Jewry.[48] Here the responsibility for what caused those children to take what they saw as a final step to become totally British appears to have been shared by a number of groups. The first consisted of the missionary societies and communities because of their overt and covert activities to encourage Jewish refugee children to convert. These include the Barbican Mission, certain groups of Christadelphians, and a number of other missionary societies. The second was the Refugee Children's Movement, for its failure to implement the policy of putting all refugee children in touch with a religious leader and by the lax supervision of large numbers of local committees. In certain local committees, the laissez faire attitude they adopted bordered on absolute religious neglect. In a report of a local refugee committee, its secretary stated that their organization had thirty-two Jewish refugee children scattered throughout the county, of which only three were receiving some form of Jewish education and three, backed by their guardians, had declared that they wanted no Jewish education of any kind. As for the rest, the committee's report stated their support for the general tendency to postpone the decision regarding what type of religious education the children should receive in order to enable them to study both Jewish and Christian outlooks. In an ecumenical vein, their report concluded with the following: "Our invariable principle is that each child shall be treated as an individual and that no children's conscience shall become a battle ground."[49]

As for the third group, Anglo Jewry, its contribution to the alienation of the Jewish refugee children came from its spiritual and at times emotional neglect of these children, whom, with few exceptions, it was more convenient to support financially than to care for spiritually. A former Youth Aliyah worker recalled speaking at many fund-raising meetings for Youth Aliyah during the war. Herself a refugee from Germany, she was often struck by the fact that apart from giving donations, the women with whom she spoke seemed unconcerned about the living conditions, emotional state, and spiritual care of the Jewish refugee children in Britain. She recalled: "None of the women visited the hostels housing the young refugees and most assuaged their consciences solely through their pocketbooks."[50] Finally, it is difficult to lightly dismiss the general Anglo-Jewish attitude of treating refugee children as "poor relations," which contributed to their feeling of estrangement and eventual rejection of the Jewish community.

Under the best conditions, as refugee analyst Anna Freud stated, "The child–foster parent relationship has little likelihood of promoting the psychological parent-wanted relationship."[51] All the more so when the relationship was formed in the face of a massive cultural barrier. The politeness of the Jewish refugee child, taken for granted in German or Austrian households, was often viewed at best by foster parents as shyness and at worst as sullenness and aloofness. Their intellectual pursuits were seen as snobbery, their fastidiousness, table manners, and forms of speech often misunderstood. To the average British Jewish family the gracious way of life common to many Central European children was incomprehensible, as was the British way of life, initially, to the refugee children. Cultural barriers usually grew in proportion to the refugee child's age: the older the child, the more European culture they had absorbed, the harder it was for them to adjust in England. Finally, even when they wanted to adjust and tried to with all their might, an allusion to their past always seemed to be waiting for them around the corner. As one former refugee child ironically remarked, summing up what was for him the crux of the refugee experience: "If we had not remembered that we were refugees, there were always others to remind us."[52]

The guardianship furor was in truth a reflection of the battle for the souls of the Jewish refugee children in Great Britain, but not only in the theological sense. It was a battle to make them British. With Home Office officials standing behind the decision of whom to choose as the children's guardian, it was obvious that in the British cultural, political, and at times even xenophobic climate of the mid-1940s the choice would fall on a public figure who was in their eyes "fully British." Whether they were willing to admit it publicly or it only existed in their subconscious, in the eyes of most gentile Home Office officials, a Jew, and an Orthodox one to boot, could not be considered "fully British" even if he were a fourth-generation British citizen. The Jewish refugee children understood this much better than did the Orthodox British Jewish adults who were so concerned about their physical and spiritual welfare. For, as we have seen, to be fully British, the children realized that they would have to relinquish their Judaism, at best converting to Christianity, or at worst, at least intermarrying with British non-Jews. As one converted former refugee girl stated: "Since my girls are older I have told them of their Jewish blood (I am Catholic) and they find it rather interesting, but of course they do not have our attitude. They were very puzzled when I asked them not to tell this to all their friends."[53] Or in the words of a Jewish woman married to a Christian, "My eldest son was baptized when he was twelve. He was a choir boy and he loved it and I thought that anyhow it's already gone to one side. . . . It might do more harm than not if he isn't baptized—in a Christian country. The important thing is that he should feel that he belongs."[54]

Notes

1. Schwartz interview.
2. Michaelis-Stern interview. Simpson interview.
3. 396 Lords Deb. 1976 (6 Feb. 1944).
4. The bill was introduced in the House of Lords on 9 December 1943. 395 Lords Deb. 1943. Several studies, such as Levin, *The Holocaust*, 137, mention a law existing in

The Guardianship 215

Britain that prohibited sending groups or individual children without a guardian to foster homes in Britain. They do not, however, refer to sources. If this is true it is difficult to understand why the British government waited until such a late date to introduce this move.
5. 396 Lords Deb. 1576-1583 (4 February 1944).
6. 396 Lords Deb. 1577 (4 February 1944). In Scotland the "tutorship" was to exist for boys until age fourteen and for girls until age twelve (Statutes). The Guardianship (Refugee Children) Act, 1944, Article 2, Section 1c.
7. Letter Gorell to Hertz, 17 November 1943, Refugee Children's Movement Executive Committee Minutes and Papers, Central British Fund Archives, The Wiener Library Microfilm document collection 27/28/166.
8. *The Jewish Chronicle*, 31 December 1943, 3.
9. Ibid.
10. *The Jewish Chronicle*, 7 January 1944, 3.
11. *The Child Estranging Movement: An Expose on the Alienation of Jewish Refugee Children in Great Britain from Judaism,* Union of Orthodox Hebrew Congregations, January 1944, Central British Fund Archives, The Wiener Library Microfilm document collection 27/29/167.
12. *The Child Estranging Movement*, 1.
13. Ibid., 6.
14. Ibid., 7.
15. In reality, Jews were 0.04 percent of the total British population in 1939. See figures in *TheAmerican Jewish Yearbook* (1945), figures from 1940 yearbook, 262-67.
16. *The Jewish Chronicle*, 14 January 1944, 12.
17. Resume of Lord Gorell's speech in Bloomsbury House in from of the RCM Executive, January 1944. Central British Fund Archives, The Wiener Library Microfilm document collection 27/29/167.
18. Decisions made at the conclusion of Lord Gorell's speech in Bloomsbury House in front of the RCM Executive, January 1944. Central British Fund Archives, The Wiener Library Microfilm document collection 27/29/167.
19. Presland, *A Great Adventure*, 5. Lists of safeguards appear on pages 8-9.
20. Meeting of the Norfolk branch of the CRREC, n.d. P/15/2. The Munk Archives, Yad Vashem, Jerusalem.
21. Schwartz interview.
22. Discussion of religious problems of refugee children, January 1944, P/15/2. The Munk Archives, Yad Vashem, Jerusalem.
23. Questionnaire, Ilsa Schatkin, describing the fate of the Jewish refugee children in her household and several others living with Quaker families in the general area.
24. See, for example, Singer, "My First Year in England," unpublished manuscript in the author's possession. Also documentation found in folder P/15/2, The Munk Archives, Yad Vashem.
25. Dubrowsky, *Six from Leipzig*, 113.
26. 396 Lord Deb. 1579 (4 February 1944). This point was raised by the Solicitor General, Major Sir David Maxwell Fyfe.
27. 397 Lords Deb. 611; 397 Lords Deb. 1476; Legal Guardianship Papers of Lord Gorell, Central British Fund Archives, The Wiener Library Microfilm document collection 27/28/158.
28. Bentwich, *They Found Refuge*, 70.

29. Blond to Gestetner, 20 June 1944. Central British Fund Archives, The Wiener Library Microfilm document collection 27/29/167.
30. Newspaper clipping 24 December 1944, P/15/9, the Munk Archives, Yad Vashem, Jerusalem.
31. Gershon, *We Came as Children*, 61.
32. Schwartz interview.
33. Gershon, *We Came as Children*, 66.
34. Hall interview.
35. Gershon, *We Came as Children*, 157.
36. Ibid., 66.
37. Simpson interview, Michaelis-Stern interview. Typology from Riezel, "The Reeducation of Jewish Child Holocaust victims," 42–77.
38. Association of Jewish Refugees in Great Britain, *Dispersion and Resettlement*, 57.
39. Gershon, *We Came as Children*, 65.
40. Ibid, 66.
41. Ibid.
42. Author's interview with Chava Markowitz, Tel Aviv, 22 January 1980.
43. Talmon interview.
44. Simpson memorandum to RCM, undated, Central British Fund Archives, The Wiener Library Microfilm document collection 27/29/169.
45. Undated report of Dorothy Hardisty's visit to the Barbican Mission on 10 April 1945. Central British Fund Archives, The Wiener Library Microfilm document collection 27/29/167.
46. Freedman, *A Minority in Britain*, 95.
47. See for example the percentage of mixed marriages in Bavaria from the beginning of the century (1901—7.6 percent of all Jewish marriages were mixed; 1910—15.2 percent; 1913—13.7 percent; 1922—18.5 percent; 1923—21 percent; 1924—28.5 percent; 1925—21.8 percent), *Pinkas Hakehilot*, 13. Between 1920 and 1930, 17.5 percent of all marriages of Jews in Germany involved a non-Jewish spouse. Bennathan, "Demographische und wirtschaftliche Struktur," 96.
48. Simpson interview. Michaelis interview.
49. Gershon, *We Came as Children*, 64.
50. Michaelis-Stern interview.
51. Goldstein, Freud, and Solnit, *Beyond the Best Interests of the Child*, 25.
52. Gershon, *We Came as Children*, 155.
53. Ibid., 163.
54. Ibid., 167.

Chapter 10

Epilogue and Memory

Introduction

"I found out about my mother's fate in stages. At a certain point I was working for the Jewish refugees committee at Woburn House and they started getting lists of survivors. I saw the names and knew that people were dead. The social worker who was in charge of me came to me sometime in 1945 and told me the news that my mother had been sent to Auschwitz. I was seventeen at the time . . . the lists that we saw said that my mother was sent to Auschwitz and my grandmother had committed suicide."[1] Within the course of a five-minute interview with a social worker Steffi Birnbaum Schwartz and her sister Reenie found out that they were orphans, that their mother had been murdered in the infamous Nazi death camp in southern Poland and that their mother's beloved mother was also gone. Only later, when they were traced by their uncle who had survived the war in Holland together with his non-Jewish wife, did they learn the tragic details behind the lists of names. Having received her deportation orders, their grandmother asked her non-Jewish daughter-in-law to find her some poison so that she could kill herself before being deported. In spite of the dangers and illegalities involved, the daughter-in-law carried out the request, and, after her mother-in-law's suicide even managed to have her buried in the Jewish cemetery in Berlin.

In a sense, however, Steffi and Reenie were among the lucky ones. Unlike many of the other refugee children who found themselves alone in the world, these two still had family; not only did they have each other but their mother's brother and his wife had survived the war as well. Other refugee children found alternative family groups in the form of Zionist youth movements and were fortunate to be absorbed by a framework that provided them with a feeling of home. Hundreds of refugee children found themselves deep into Zionist youth group activities in movements such as Hashomer Hatzair, Bnai Akiva or Bachad. Some, such as Susi Adler, Chana Gilboa, Chava Laufer, and Mordechai Goldfaden, even eventually made *aliyah* to Palestine in the framework of these movements.

Another type of luck came as a result of geographic and social change. During their late teenage years, large numbers of refugee children received professional training in educational centers far from their foster families. For those children who still felt uncomfortable with their sponsoring families, this juncture afforded them an opportunity to leave these families for a more congenial environment. Some, such as Steffi Birnbaum Schwartz, had their training sponsored by the Jewish refugee movements and remained within a Jewish framework throughout the entire period. Others, however, whose training was sponsored by non-Jewish groups, had little opportunity for any connection with organized Jewish bodies. Coming on the heels of their meager connections with Jewish organizations during the war years and especially after evacuation, these children found themselves at the war's end far removed from their Jewish roots.

From the middle of the war on, various officials in the free world had tacitly alluded to the fact that refugee repatriation was no longer a realistic solution as it was doubtful that there would be somewhere for them to be repatriated. "Compulsory repatriation is out of the question," stated Sir Herbert Emerson, the League of Nations High Commissioner for Refugees and the director of the Inter-government Committee on Refugees in early 1943, echoing these sentiments and giving them finality.[2] Yet for a long time repatriation to Europe was still commonly spoken of by some as a logical solution to the child refugee problem in Britain. At one point, Eva Michaelis-Stern was on a speaking tour in Britain to raise money for refugee children being cared for by Youth Aliyah. The speaker preceding her spoke enthusiastically of repatriating these children to their homes after the war, and Michaelis-Stern was forced in her speech to correct this misapprehension by simply replying "they no longer have homes to be repatriated to."[3]

Immediate Aftermath

By 1945, the Jewish refuge children still in Great Britain were no longer children, no longer refugees, and, in certain cases—no longer Jewish. Almost six years had passed since they had come to Britain, ostensibly as transmigrants. Much had happened during those years. Refugee children who had arrived in 1939 knowing ten words of English now looked, spoke, and acted British, and had even served in the British armed forces. The world that they had left behind in 1939 had been destroyed. Many were orphans, their last memories of their parents often tinged with guilt. In the tension of parting, children had at times responded rudely to their parents and some, angry at being sent away, even refused to say goodbye. These were to be the final memories of their parents that they would carry with them for the rest of their lives and which some of them would still be working through more than seven decades later.

Other children, reunited with their parents after a six-year separation, found that they had no common language. They had forgotten their German, while their parents still knew no English. The culture shock produced by many of these reunions was startling. Orthodox fathers who in 1939 had sent away little boys with caps now often beheld strapping assimilated young men who could barely dredge up half-forgotten memories of prayers. Six years of living in assimilated Jewish or gentile households had taken their toll. Some children had left Orthodoxy as a result of outside pressures; others had taken the first step themselves, some as early as when they left Continental Europe. At one point the trains carrying children from Germany to Holland passed over a river. Yitzchak Talmon recalled how a number of Orthodox boys on his transport availed themselves of this opportunity to rebel against their religious upbringing and threw their tefillin out of the train window and into the icy waters below.[4]

Parents who had parted from preteen children who had been reared in Continental European manners were shocked at how their now British teenage children acted. Looking back, some of the former *Kinder* even surprised themselves by their own reactions at the time. Inge Sadan recalled how she and her siblings heard that their parents had reached Spain, were coming to Britain, and would arrive from London to where they were billeted on a certain train. Afraid to be seen by her schoolmates who were arriving on the same train, Inge left her brother and sister to meet their parents while she waited elsewhere: "We went down to the station to wait, and I couldn't cope with it. So I went back home saying, 'I'm going home. I'm going to put the kettle on. They'll need a cup of tea.' I mean, how English can you get?"[5]

Most hostels and training centers were closing because of a lack of children. Some of the larger centers, such as Whittingehame House, had already closed in 1942 and the remaining children had been moved to smaller centers in the area. Now these underpopulated smaller centers were being threatened with extinction. Some groups proposed to transfer children from non-Jewish foster homes to such hostels or centers, a suggestion made as much to "save" the hostels as to save the children.[6] Consequently, many hostels remained in existence until the late 1940s, by which time most of the refugee teens had grown into adulthood and left either to marry or to settle in other accommodations.

Whether they lived in hostels or with foster families, the refugee children remained under the care of the RCM until they reached age twenty-one, at which time they were considered legal adults. By the time the organization disbanded in June 1948, most refugee children had reached the age of majority and were living independent of any refugee assistance. When the RCM disbanded, the case files of the remaining Jewish refugee children were entrusted to the Jewish Refugees Committee and the files of non-Jewish children were transferred to the Christian Council and affiliated bodies. Twelve cases of baptism pending at the time were also handed over to the Council.[7]

With the passage of time, the refugee child issue began to reach its natural conclusion. By the early 1950s fewer than three hundred Jewish refugee children were still under the age of majority. Their spiritual welfare remained under the care of Rabbi Ephraim Levine, who headed a special religious department set up by the Jewish Refugees Committee. Despite the efforts of the religious Jewish organizations to have all Jewish refugee children removed from their gentile foster homes, in mid-1950 some fifty such children were still living in non-Jewish households. In an attempt to foster a feeling of Jewish solidarity and offer these children a Jewish atmosphere, the Jewish Refugee Committee founded a Jewish club called Achduth ("unity"), to which it hoped the Jewish refugee children would gravitate during their spare time. It seems, however, to have had little effect upon most of these children; few mention it in their memoirs. In the legal sphere, Lord Gorell continued his guardianship until 1959, by which time all refugee children had reached the age of twenty-one.[8]

The First Postwar Period: 1945–65

For the former refugee children in Britain, the first few years after the war's end were characterized by their trying to find their way as young adults in their new home or deciding that they wished to move elsewhere. During the early period, many of these children found themselves grappling simultaneously with issues related to their past, present, and future, making decisions that would affect the rest of their lives.

One of the first issues that occupied the *Kinder* involved dealing with the true impact of the war on their personal future, a worry many of them had put into abeyance during the war years. As one former refugee child wrote, "The end of the war meant that one had suddenly to come to terms with everything one had pushed away while it was going on. The continued anxiety about our families had been partly submerged in the sheer mechanics of coping with every day life. Now the truth was inescapable."[9] For many, this truth involved their parents' often violent deaths and that of many other family members as well. A foster mother of a refugee child remembers having to tell her about her mother's death. "We tried to keep her mother in her mind, thinking that would be the best thing to do, but of course when eventually the news came that they were all killed, we thought we'd better tell her. So I told her one night. She said: 'All my family? My mother and my father and my brother and my grandmother and my cousins and my aunties?' And I said: 'Yes, Felicia, I'm afraid so.' . . . She was then nine years old."[10]

Despite the tragic news that reached England, some children continued to harbor secret hope that the reports were mistaken and for years would try to imagine that their mothers or fathers were alive somewhere and that they would ultimately be reunited. "I still sometimes imagine that it is possible for my mother to be alive somewhere (in spite of first-hand reports to the contrary)," wrote one former refugee child almost twenty years after the war's end.[11]

While large numbers of refugee children learned that they were alone in the world, and fought their feelings of guilt over their own survival, others received news of parents or relatives who had survived the war and faced the question of how to deal with the people from their past. Although almost all such children were initially relieved that their family had survived the war, they often expressed great reluctance to undergo yet another upheaval and leave England, as they had finally managed to settle into their new lives. One former refugee girl recalled her fear of being removed from what had become a comfortable life with her foster parents: "One day when my sister and I got home from school we were told to sit down and were given a letter from our parents. The first news for years! The first intimation that they were still alive. They wanted us home again. It was though the whole house rocked. We were flabbergasted and horrified. No! We didn't want to go. We belong to you, Aunt and Uncle! We can't go! So it was left to Uncle to write this difficult letter to suggest that we finished our education here and did not go through another upheaval. To which they agreed."[12]

One group of children such as Inge Sadan and Bertha Leverton, whose parents had survived the war in Europe, learned that their parents were coming to join them in England. Others, whose parents had found refuge in countries overseas, expected their children to join them now that the war had ended. Greta Marcus from Munich, who had come to Britain at age twelve, recalled how her parents had gotten a visa to Chile and eventually made their way to the United States. "I was excited to think about going to America, but I was also scared. Over the years I had become English, I hadn't gotten on well with my foster family and by the war's end I was living in a hostel in London, had a crowd of friends, and was working at the Jewish Refugees Committee. Even though I was happy to think of joining my parents I wasn't particularly happy at the thought of having to adjust all over again to a new way of life."[13]

A third group whose parents or relatives had survived in hiding wanted their children to rejoin them on the continent. Kurt Fuchel from Vienna, who had come to England at age seven, remembers learning that his parents had been hidden in the south of France and was horrified when told by his foster parents that he would be expected to go back and live with them:

> Uncle Percy persuaded my parents to wait until I finished the English school certificate at age sixteen, and also they needed time to re-establish themselves.... I didn't want to, but the Cohens [his foster family] took me to Paris where I was to meet my parents. I couldn't look at them directly, so I looked at their reflection in the window of a shop as they walked towards me ... we went to dinner in a restaurant and I remember it was difficult because I didn't speak German or French, and they spoke very little English. . . .
> My parents let go of a seven-year-old and got back a sixteen-year-old. My mother, especially, wanted to carry on where she'd left off. But a sixteen-year-old doesn't like to be treated like a seven-year-old.[14]

Yet another group only reunited with their surviving parents or relatives years later. For many in this group, the long years of separation had taken such a toll that there was little real connection, even between parents and children. One former refugee child recalled: "My father returned to Germany from America ten years ago and consequently we are able to see him for ten days or so each year—but by the time we are starting to make any real contact it is time to separate again."[15] Another former refugee girl, who learned after the war that her mother and sister had survived and that she also had a brother, only met her family decades after the war's end: "About two years ago Mutti came to England to visit us, it was the first time in 24 years that we met. Of course we were very happy to see each other and had lots to talk about, but our lives are so far apart—Mother is very Austrian and I'm all English."[16]

For children who returned to their country of origin after the war's end, either to meet their surviving relatives or to go back to live with them permanently, it was not always easy to face the landscape of their childhood, which at times had undergone great devastation due to the war. Steffi and Reenie Birnbaum returned to Berlin for the first time to see their surviving family in 1946; their uncle Gerhard paid for their tickets. Steffi recalled: "It was a trauma seeing Berlin for the first time. We saw our old apartment from the outside but we didn't go in. We went to the Jewish cemetery to our father's grave and to our grandmother's grave. Interestingly, I felt most at ease there at the cemetery."

Initially, communication was problematic. Like many refugee children without relatives in Britain, Steffi and Renee had not spoken German in years. For Steffi, who had left Germany when she was eleven, the language of her childhood eventually emerged from her subconscious: "When I came back to Berlin in 1946 I was British but not English. I barely remembered any German and Renee had forgotten her German completely. But when I started talking with my uncle it all came back to me."[17]

One refugee boy recalled how after speaking no German for several years in order to escape the accusation that he was "the enemy," he was suddenly forced to recall the language: "I renounced my background; I was ashamed of it. I wanted to forget everything. If I was asked where I came from it was tantamount to being accused of a crime. To be reminded that I was Austrian, or worse still, Jewish, and a refugee child, was an insult. But one day I met an elderly man, like myself a refugee from Vienna . . . we spoke, naturally enough, in German; he remembered details and people I had long succeeded in forgetting. And it all came back. I remembered who I was. I was never likely to forget it again."[18]

As opposed to some of the older refugees from Germany who returned to their former homes by choice after the war because it gave them a sense of security and stability, this phenomenon was almost nonexistent among the *Kinder*. Did you ever want to stay in Berlin? I asked Steffi during one of our meetings. Her beautiful amber eyes widened in shock: "*Chas Vechalila!*" (Heaven Forbid!) she answered fervently and instantly in colloquial Hebrew, even though our conversation had been conducted in English.

British but not English, as Steffi described herself, was an apt description for what many of the Jewish refugee children in Britain felt about themselves and their place in British society during the first postwar years. Some felt this way for many years after: British, in the sense that they were no longer German or Austrian, but not English in the true sense of the word. In his study of young Jewish refugees from Nazi Germany, Walter Laqueur summarized the dilemma of many *Kinder:* "They might be holders of British passports, or even local councilors and justices of the peace, but were they accepted as full-fledged Englishmen?" Mentioning that those such as myself who had interviewed the former refugee children in the 1970s and 1980s often found a certain resignation among them regarding this subject, he concluded that in spite of their efforts to become British in their younger years, they had given it up due to unbridgeable differences in mentality and culture. "They tremendously liked the British but felt at the same time that there were differences that could not be overcome, that, whatever their achievements, they were not quite considered part of British society."[19]

Although fully comfortable in the English language, some, particularly among the *Kinder* who had come to Britain as teenagers, had a hybrid cultural frame of reference, neither fully English but no longer fully Continental. In 1948, a group of younger Continental Jewish refugees between the ages of twenty and thirty-five, some of whom had been former unaccompanied refugee children, founded a group called "The Hyphen" in an attempt to find a social framework in which they would feel comfortable. The idea behind the group was to form a cultural, social and welfare group that would engage in activities to make members feel at home in their newly adopted country. The name was chosen because it symbolized the gap between the older generation of refugees who had no intention or desire to integrate into British society, and the aspirations of the younger refugees who wished to become part of British society but had not yet succeeded in realizing that desire.

One of the group's first activities was to set up a study and discussion group to cover topics such as immigration in general, as well as German Jewish immigration into Britain, German Jewish history, and British cultural and political subjects. Its most popular functions were social gatherings and dances. The Hyphen never had more than one hundred members at any time, but between four hundred and five hundred names were usually on its mailing lists. As its members integrated further and further into British society, the group became less active and it folded in 1968. Although the group was marginal in comparison with other German Jewish institutions founded in Britain, it fulfilled a very important function for its members by giving them a sense of belonging during a difficult period of settling in to a new society.

As opposed to the Jewish refugee children who did their utmost to integrate into British society, another group's wartime and immediate postwar experiences strengthened their understanding of the need for their lives to continue outside British soil. While some *Kinder* decided to either return on their own to Continental Europe or make their way to America, the largest group of emigrating *Kinder* were Zionists who made *aliyah* to Palestine or, later, to the State of Israel. As a refugee teenager in London during the war, Chana Gilboa had been active in the religious Zionist youth group Bnai Akiva; she later joined their *hachshara* in Buckingham. "One day right after the war when I was working in a factory making hats, I told some of the women about Palestine. 'Why don't you go there if you are Jewish?' one of them asked. She didn't mean it in an antisemitic way, at least I don't think she did, but rather as a question—you are Jewish, Palestine is the Jewish homeland, so why don't you go there? She got me thinking, and as it was the natural thing to do after I had been so active in Bnai Akiva, I joined the *hachashara* and came to Israel in 1948."[20]

Some *Kinder* came to Israel only later, in an attempt to find what they were missing elsewhere. Steffi Birnbaum Schwartz recalled how she visited Israel almost twenty years after the war's end and decided to make it her home: "I came to Israel on holiday in 1964, while I was working at the public health department in the London municipality and had studied at night for my four-year degree. I really came to break up a bad romance. I visited Israel to see whether it was for me and decided that it was a good fit. We had a relation in Tel Aviv who had come in the 1930s so I wasn't totally alone in the country."[21]

Whether they decided to remain in Britain or settle elsewhere, these were the years when the *Kinder* were beginning their adult lives, finding themselves professionally, and busy forming their own new families. The vast majority of them married and had children. Although at times they grappled with the question of how integrated they actually felt in their adopted homelands, in practice, the majority of their lives during this period involved coping with the daily issues of the present: making a living, caring for their families, creating and retaining friendships, contributing to their communities.

At this early stage when most of the *Kinder* were busy building their new adult lives, it appeared that few had an inclination to record their experiences on paper, either for their young children or for posterity. One of those who was already introspective about how her past was affecting her present was Karen Gershon, pen name of writer and poet Kathleen Tripp (born Kaethe Loewenthal), who had come to Britain from Bielefeld, Germany, on the second Kindertransport. Gershon had initially planned to follow one of her sisters to Palestine but was prevented from doing so by the outbreak of war. Another sister who had come to Britain with a Zionist group, died tragically in 1943, leaving Gershon totally alone in Britain, particularly after she learned of her parents' murder by the Nazis. Forced into a series of menial jobs and domestic service in place of the academic studies which she had desired, in 1948 Gershon married Val Tripp, a non-Jewish art teacher with whom she had four children. Having married in an attempt to escape her unhappy employment station she soon found herself in a loveless marriage.

Gershon had great difficulty in dealing with her Jewish identity in practice and instead found her identity in words, pouring her feelings into poetry and prose. By adopting her father's first name as her own pen name, she was attempting to reconnect with her pre-refugee past while simultaneously preserving her own anonymity in the present. Never having felt at home in England, Gershon immigrated to Israel in 1969. Although three out of her four children remained there, she returned to Britain in the mid-1970s where she resided until her death in 1993.[22]

In 1963, at the time of the twenty-fifth anniversary of the Kindertransports, Gershon was motivated to explore the story of the child refugee scheme. Having turned to the Jewish refugee organizations to obtain documentation, she was erroneously told that most of the documents had been destroyed. Turning to the scheme's protagonists and activists, she realized that many no longer remembered the events clearly and that others were no longer alive. Consequently, she decided to try to contact former *Kinder* to obtain their recollections in order to put together some type of collective memoir for future generations. In response to her request for information, which appeared in all the major British newspapers, more than three hundred people contacted her, of whom she interviewed about thirty. A total of 234 former *Kinder* contributed to her book, most of whom were at the time in their thirties and forties.

At first she thought of asking them to write an outline about their refugee lives; later, she decided to question them about a number of topics that she felt best summarized the refugee children's collective history: the transports, reception camps, new homes, institutions, schooldays, internment, experiences of older children, death and survival, and facing past and future. In summing up their experiences, they were asked about their present lives, relationships with surviving family members, former sponsors and foster parents, and their definitions of the terms *refugee* and *home*. The result was a book entitled *We Came As Children: A Collective Autobiography*, published in 1966 with the dedication "For Our Children." In it, the *Kinder* were allowed to speak anonymously, which enabled them to express themselves without fear of being identified and criticized by their surroundings. And although the book was dedicated to the *Kinder*'s "second generation," many had yet spoken of their experiences to their children and were grateful for the anonymity that Gershon afforded them.

"A refugee is a person without a country and as soon as he can grow roots and create a home in a new country and accept this country it becomes a part of his life," wrote a former refugee child to Gershon. "I feel that England is my home, although the English will never accept me as one of themselves," he concluded.[23] "I am still a refugee because my roots are where I am not," wrote another.[24] "Home is the first place one knows. One can be happier later on, one can live in a house much superior to the one in which one grew up. But home is the place in which one is neither privileged nor resented; one just belongs there," wrote yet another.[25] "My home is a house not a home. What I remember is a dream of home," wrote a respondent.[26] "Home is where one can live with a feeling of permanency," stated yet one other.[27] "You cannot ever really be happy again when your parents have been killed in concentration camps," was the way one of them summed up the refugee child experience.[28]

The Second Postwar Period: 1967–87

During the years following the publication of Gershon's book, it appeared as if the child refugee issue in Britain had disappeared or had at least gone into deep hibernation. Apart from a handful of former *Kinder*'s memoirs, there were no books, articles, or collections published about the Kindertransports during this period. Those few that did appear received little or no recognition and publicity.[29] At first glance, the waning of interest in the topic of wartime child refugees seemed to be part of the *Kinder*'s natural progression into a more normal existence. Most were in their forties and fifties, their children were growing up and marrying; toward the end of this period, some were already becoming grandparents. Those who had not spoken to their children about their wartime experiences rarely opened up to them during these years, having few outside triggers to help them do so. And those who were to ultimately speak to their grandchildren about their past would only do so in the future as these grandchildren began to grow older and ask questions about their grandparents' former lives.

Routine may be the backbone of life, but it is often the liquidator of initiative. During these years quite a number of the *Kinder* had settled in professionally and were deeply involved with their daily routine of supporting their growing families. Some of the younger *Kinder* who at the beginning of this period were still "searching for themselves" began to settle down and entered a stage during which they devoted all their time and energy to the present. There were no public events that brought the Kindertransports to the headlines, something which could also explain the lack of press and media exposure regarding the topic.

Digging somewhat beneath the surface of the events of those years, we can nevertheless find a number of junctures that ultimately influenced future publicity which the refugee children's issue would receive. The first was the Israeli Six-Day War of 1967, a turning point for large numbers of Diaspora Jews regarding their own Jewish identity. The overwhelmingly positive publicity that the Jewish State received following its military victory was for some a catalyst to reexamine their own attitudes toward Judaism. As a result of the new emphasis on "Jewish Pride," some former *Kinder* began to come to terms with their Jewish roots after having hidden them for years.

Another milestone of this period was the opening of British and American government archival collections that dealt with the prewar and wartime period. With twenty-five and thirty-year statues mandating the closure of various national archival collections coming to an end in the late 1960s and early 1970s, researchers, historians, and publicists began analyzing the data that came to light. Among the topics that emerged were governmental attitudes toward the rescue of refugees from Nazism, including the rescue of children prior to and during the Holocaust. The results were a number of studies, most of which blasted the British and American governments of the Hitler era for what appeared to be a very complex and reluctant attitude toward rescuing Jews from Europe both before and during the Second World War.

While in the United States journalist Arthur Morse laid the groundwork for future books on this topic with his pathbreaking study entitled *While Six Million Died,* soon followed by studies by David Wyman, Saul Friedman, and Henry Feingold. In Britain, historians Alan Joshua Sherman and later Bernard Wasserstein took up the gauntlet and exposed the shortcomings of British government policy toward the rescue of European Jewry.[30] And while the British government was sharply criticized for its policy of barring the entry of Jewish refugees to Palestine during this period, the Kindertransport scheme was described as one of its shining moments, despite reminders that the entire scheme was basically conceived of in order to lessen American pressure over Britain's refusal to allow Jewish refugees from Hitler into Palestine following *Kristallnacht.* In this vein, the only focus was on the ultimate physical rescue of the *Kinder* with no attention given to the operation's religious, social, or emotional costs. This was a continuation of what Jennifer Norton called the "dominant triumphant narrative" that had begun in the official summaries of the refugee organizations and memoirs of their protagonists, such as books by Presland or Bentwich, where any devastating results of the Kindertransport were glossed over in the desire to paint a rosy picture of rescue and resettlement.[31]

At this early stage, no studies were devoted entirely to the child refugee issue or to the Kindertransports, but within the next decade one scholarly study was written on that topic: my master's thesis in 1981, devoted to the story of Jewish refugee children in Great Britain between 1938 and 1945. Because I began research on the topic during the late 1970s, quite a number of the child rescue scheme and refugee organization protagonists were still alive and happy to share their recollections with me, either in person or through correspondence. These included Elaine Laski Blond, Eva Michaelis-Stern, Arieh Handler, Bertha Kahn, and Norbert Wollheim all of whom not only added to my general knowledge about the Kindertransports but could also give me inside stories of human and historical interest that only such major players would have been aware of. One of my most interesting meetings, which showed me both sides of the rescue experience, was with RCM activist Rev. William W. (Bill) Simpson and his wife Ruth Weyl, a former Jewish refugee whom he married long after the war.

In response to newspaper requests that appeared in the Anglo, American, Canadian, Australian, South African Jewish presses, and Israeli newspapers, several hundred *Kinder* contacted me and I eventually interviewed or sent in-depth questionnaires to more than sixty of them, most of whom were around fifty years old at the time. Their responses, together with British government files, refugee organization archives, private collections, and newspaper surveys from the period, served as the basis for my study and for a number of articles that I published at the time, based on my Kindertransport research.

A third factor emerging during this period was a growing interest in the Holocaust throughout the Western world. In 1978, Gerald Green's four part miniseries *Holocaust* was broadcast in the United States and later in other countries, including West Germany. The critically acclaimed drama about two families under Hitler, which later won eight Emmy awards, heralded an awakening of public interest in the topic and was even credited with persuading the West German government to repeal the statute of limitations on Nazi War Crimes. This growing interest in the Holocaust generated results not only in the legal sphere but in the cultural, academic, and plastic ones as well. Holocaust memorials were erected in dozens and later hundreds of cities, often funded by money that Holocaust survivors had donated. The same held true for the Holocaust chairs and research institutes that began to be established in universities worldwide to promote the academic study of the topic.

As public interest in the Holocaust swelled, publishing houses realized that they had a golden goose at their fingertips and actively began seeking out Holocaust-related manuscripts written by journalists, Holocaust survivor memoirs, first-person stories, and academic studies. The timing was right—the new postwar generation that had finally reached maturity provided fertile ground for such publications and for the avalanche of Holocaust films being released. Producers and script writers were snowed under with work as Holocaust related films appeared in an almost never-ending stream. Claude Lanzmann's nine-hour-and-thirty-six minute opus *Shoah* (1985) drew vast audiences throughout the world while *Sophie's Choice* (1982) based on William Styron's novel of a Polish Auschwitz survivor who had to choose which of her two children to save when she arrived at that camp, became a household expression.[32]

Holocaust survivor memoirs hit the bookstands at the rate of several a week, and academic studies of the Holocaust followed at a somewhat slower rate. Although I had set aside my research on the British Kindertransports after having completed my master's thesis, I continued with a doctoral study of other Kindertransport children, the OTC (One Thousand Children) operation in the United States during the same period, of which my own older half-brother and sister, born in Germany, had been part. Unlike my master's thesis, which sat untouched on the shelf in my office for years, my doctoral dissertation was soon published as part of the plethora of Holocaust studies released to the public in the 1980s and early 1990s.[33]

This unexpected publication and media explosion surrounding the Holocaust had other expressions as well. During these years, a growing body of Holocaust memorials was being erected throughout the world, reminding the general public of the cataclysm, the victims, and the survivors. A large selection of Holocaust courses was being offered even in American colleges and universities where no other courses in Jewish studies were even being taught. All this activity cemented an ongoing interest in anything even remotely related to the Holocaust and received a form of public homage, consecration, and canonization. Although this process enabled and encouraged previously reticent Holocaust survivors to recount their experiences, either publicly or for their immediate families, it had another side, particularly for many of the *Kinder*. In view of the horrific experiences of those who had survived camps and ghettos, living in hiding or under false identities in occupied Europe during the war, how could they even consider their stories of rescue and wartime experiences in free Britain worthy of note? How could evacuation and adjustment to sponsors and foster families compare to one day in the Warsaw ghetto or one hour in an extermination camp? In what way could they even think they were similar to Auschwitz survivors or to those in hiding who had lived in constant fear of being captured by the Nazis? There had been no Nazis in their daily lives, and although many had lost parents and other relatives to the Nazis, they had never even experienced one day of occupation, ghettoization, deportation, expropriation, or potential extermination.

"We weren't survivors," stated Steffi when asked where the *Kinder* had located themselves within the Holocaust hierarchy, "and yet what we had been through was not negligible."[34] It would take, however, a very special event to elicit a public reckoning by the *Kinder* of their place within the public story of the Holocaust and its protagonists. This event would only take place in 1989, as the fiftieth anniversary of the Kindertransports drew near.

The Third Postwar Period: 1989 and Onward

"One evening I was watching a boring television programme and my eyes were wandering around the room and they fell on the photographs of my lovely grandchildren. One of them was exactly the same age I was when I left Germany . . . my grandchildren knew I'd come from Germany, they knew little bits of the story, but they never really knew what we went through. Well I'm a very impulsive person so I jumped up, went to the telephone and phoned up the only friend I'd kept in touch with from my school-days. I said, 'Ilse, I'm going to make a get together, a reunion of the *Kinder* from fifty years ago. Do you realize it's forty-nine years we've been in this country and nowhere in the *Jewish Chronicle* or anywhere in the press is any mention of the Kindertransport?'"[35]

Bertha Leverton (b. 1923) likes to recall that she conceived of the Kindertransport reunion due to the combination of a boring British television program and her grandchildren's pictures, but in fact it was an idea that had been long in the making. The growing awareness of anything even remotely connected to the Holocaust from the late 1970s on served as fertile background for the *Kinder* to begin ruminating about their own past, although initially their experiences paled in comparison with those who had survived in occupied Europe. However, as the decade progressed and the Holocaust hierarchy broadened to include refugees from Hitler, many of the former child refugees began to experience a sense of belonging to a larger story. The reunion-in-making was an outgrowth of this feeling, and an expression of the *Kinder*'s need to understand their present and shape the place that the story of the Kindertransports would have in their future by connecting it with a larger body of former *Kinder* who had shared their past.

At the time Leverton conceived of the idea of the Kindertransport reunion, she knew little about the numbers behind or mechanism surrounding the transports, and initially she thought she would hire a local synagogue hall and at most gather together one hundred participants. But as time passed and more and more former *Kinder* heard of the upcoming reunion, she began hearing from people living on several continents and realized that it was going to be a massive undertaking. "It was absolutely the right time for a reunion, because any earlier we were busy making a living and bringing up our children. Nobody wanted to think back. It was too raw, too soon. Now the time was right and the idea struck a chord."[36]

After months of planning, the first Kindertransport reunion in Britain was held in June 1989 beginning in Harwich, at the site of the reception center where the boats bringing the children to Britain docked. The British reunion was an event that changed the lives of hundreds of former *Kinder*. Writing about the Kindertransports on her blog, former refugee child Ester Golan from Israel wrote: "For decades the word did not ring a bell. Hardly anybody who did not come with a Kinder Transport knew what was meant by that word. Even many of the refugee children themselves could only remember their own personal experience, but little else about the wider aspect of it and how it all came about. The great change came when in 1989 there was a reunion in London organized by Bertha Leverton."[37]

Although Leverton and the other organizers kept no precise statistics, it appears that more than one thousand *Kinder*, primarily from Britain, the United States, and Israel, but also from Canada, Australia, and as far as Nepal, attended the three-day reunion, which culminated with a one-day affair held in Albert Hall in London. The event received enormous media attention and launched the story of the Kindertransports into the public consciousness on an international scale.[38]

The fiftieth-anniversary Kindertransport reunion was an opportunity for the *Kinder* to legitimize their Holocaust-related experiences, an experience of collective identity. It was also an opportunity to created collective memory and commemoration as a response to their feelings of dislocation, isolation, and atomization. This first reunion gave birth to a number of endeavors and organizations that cemented the group's existence in the international public mind. The first was a documentary film that directors Sabine Bruening and Peter Merseburger made of the reunion, entitled: *Als sie nicht mehr deutsche sein durfen. Ueber die Kindertransporte nach England*. The second was the creation of the Reunion of Kindertransports (ROK) organization, founded by Leverton, which became the national organization for all *Kinder* in England. In addition to sending out a regular newsletter, the ROK initiated additional *Kinder*-related projects such as soliciting *Kinder* memoirs that became the basis for the book *I Came Alone*.[39] The organization was eventually coopted by the Association of Jewish Refugees (AJR) in Britain and became its Kindertransport section. The AJR continues the tradition of sending out quarterly Kindertransport newsletters that are available on the organization's website.[40]

The British reunion was also the springboard for *Kinder* worldwide to organize similar Kindertransport reunions and organizations in their own countries. The first to do so was Inge Sadan (b. 1930), Bertha Leverton's sister who lived in Jerusalem. During the winter of 1989–90, Sadan organized the first such country-specific reunion in Israel at Kibbutz Lavi, where a number of *Kinder* had made their homes. As I was the only historian at that time who had written about the Kindertransports in detail, I was asked to deliver the keynote address. During a rainy weekend that winter, more than one hundred Israeli *Kinder* and their families gathered and reconnected at the kibbutz. Sadan created an Israeli Kindertransport association, similar to the British ROK, and held a second reunion in 1994. Annual Kindertransport reunions in Netanya have occurred since that time. Like her sister in Britain, Sadan collected *Kinder* testimony in Israel and published a collected volume of their memoirs, entitled *No Longer a Stranger*.[41] The *Kinder* of Scotland also set up a separate organization at that time and groups of *Kinder* from specific countries such as Czechoslovakia or those who were raised at specific hostels remain in contact and still hold periodic meetings.

Edward Behrendt (1930–2005) from Danzig was one of the *Kinder* who attended the London reunion. On the flight back to the United States, where he had made his home since age seventeen, he asked himself why the 2,500 American and Canadian *Kinder* should not establish their own organization. Funding the initial administrative and public relations steps from his own pocket, he ultimately involved the ADL and the Wiesenthal Center in Los Angeles in the project. In late 1989, he founded the Kindertransport Association (KTA) in America and in November 1990 the American and Canadian *Kinder* held their first reunion at the Fallsview Hotel in Ellenville, New York, attended by more than five hundred *Kinder* and their families.[42] Like the British organization, the KTA also put out a newsletter, entitled the *Kinderlink,* and established a website detailing the history, exhibits, events, voices, and resources connected to the Kindertransports.[43]

The British reunion was also a catalyst for quite a number of *Kinder* to put pen to paper and record their experiences. Olga Levy Drucker wrote: "The 1989 reunion in London . . . was a turning point in my life. The idea to write a book about my childhood, *for children*, first came to me there. I looked around the huge gym hall where the speeches were held, prayers offered, meals served, concerts given, and saw a roomful of elderly and aging people. Most of us were still agile and vigorous. But how many years did any of us have left? I needed to tell my story and tell it now."[44]

As stories from the Kindertransports became more widely known, public interest in the topic grew, resulting in a number of commemorative and spinoff projects. These included plays, poems, and documentary films about the Kindertransports, collective memoirs, and the Kindertransport memory quilt project by the KTA.[45] In June 1999, the ROK held a sixtieth anniversary reunion in London and in November 2008, a year earlier than originally planned, it held a seventieth anniversary celebration at the Jewish Free School in North London. Billed as the "last Kindertransport reunion," it was moved up by a year as so many of the former refugee children had already died, a fact that was obvious to anyone seeing the growing necrology sections of the various Kinderstransport newsletters and bulletins. Attended by more than six hundred *Kinder* and their families, the participants were greeted by Charles, Prince of Wales, who spoke of how proud he was that his paternal grandmother, Princess Alice of Greece, had sheltered a Jewish family during the war. In another speech at the gathering, Sir Martin Gilbert summarized the Kindertransports from a seventy-year perspective: "Today we celebrate your lives and your achievements—your survival. But we who know your stories and recount them, also know your pain."[46]

Alongside the gatherings and the newsletters were commemorations. In June 1999, in honor of the sixtieth anniversary, House of Commons Speaker Betty Boothroyd unveiled a bronze plaque at the Palace of Westminster in a first public act of remembering the Kindertransports. In September 2003, a memorial sculpture at Liverpool Street Station was unveiled—the "suitcase memorial" by Flor Kent, which included a glass suitcase in which *Kinder* could place artifacts of memory. The artifacts' disintegration led to the dismantling of the memorial in late 2005; the artifacts were given to the Imperial War Museum and were joined to the Holocaust collection. Soon after, in 2006 a new memorial by artist and former *Kind* Frank Meisler was unveiled in Hope Square outside the station, as part of a memorial sculpture series. The bronze sculpture includes five children, two boys and three girls, waiting with their suitcases, and a violin case gazing in different directions, some standing, others sitting at the end of train tracks. Two additional sculptures commemorating the departure and journey of the Kindertransport were erected in Berlin and Gdansk in 2008 and 2009.[47] Finally, a plaque commemorating the Kindertransports was erected on the dock at Harwich where the children had arrived.

One of the most poignant forms of Kindertransport commemoration was a reenactment of the Winton rescue train. Nicholas Winton had been the force behind the rescue of 669 mostly Jewish refugee children from Czechoslovakia. During the war, his humanitarian efforts faded into obscurity while he served in the British armed forces. After the war Winton married but never mentioned his prewar deeds to his wife Greta. In 1988, however, she found a detailed scrapbook in the attic, containing lists of the children's names, including their parents' appellations and the names and addresses of the families that took them in. Greta Winton contacted Elizabeth Maxwell, who organized an emotional meeting on a BBC television program between Winton and several of the children he had saved. All in all it was estimated that there were some five thousand people around the world who owed their lives to Winton—the children he saved and their descendants.

From then on, Winton was a celebrity. In 1998 Czech president Václav Havel awarded him the Order of T. G. Masaryk, and students from a high school in the Czech town of Koncak collected 53,000 signatures on a manifesto calling to award him the Nobel Peace Prize. In 2002, he was knighted by Queen

Elizabeth II in recognition of his work on the Czech Kindertransports. A minor planet was named in his honor by Czech astronomers, and to celebrate his hundredth birthday he was flown in a microlight piloted by the daughter of one of the children he saved.

The most striking commemoration of his deeds was a three-day recreation of the Kindertransport journey from Prague by rail and ferry. Beginning on 1 September 2009, it was timed to mark the seventieth anniversary of the intended last Kindertransport, which had been due to set off on 3 September 1939 but was canceled because of the outbreak of war. A total of 170 people participated in the recreated journey that began with a train ride from Prague on an original locomotive and carriages used in the 1930s, continued by ferry to England, and culminated with a train ride to London in a refurbished British steam train. Two dozen of the passengers were former *Kinder* whom he had saved; the rest were members of their families. Winton greeted them under the sprawling canopy of the Liverpool Street Station where some of the *Kinder,* now over eighty years old, gave him flowers. "It is wonderful to see you all after 70 years," he stated, shaking hands with former child refugees as they stepped off the train. "Don't leave it quite so long until we meet here again."[48]

Only two decades earlier, the *Kinder* had been a few thousand sixty-year-old individuals scattered throughout the world who had once shared a Continental past and a prewar transfer to England. Since that time, they began to be conceived of as a cohesive group referred to by a collective noun. Now it was time once again to locate the individuals within the collective and examine the variations existing within the group. To do so, in 2007 the AJR initiated a survey among large numbers of surviving Kinder, questioning them about their origins, wartime experiences, postwar lives, relationship to the religion, country of origin, and adopted homeland. A request for cooperation elicited 1368 replies, some 14 percent of the total number of *Kinder.* All in all, 1,025 of them filled out full questionnaires, amounting to 11 percent of all *Kinder.* The results were then entered into a data base that could be accessed by researchers and has been utilized for this book.

Most of the *Kinder* answering the questionnaires were of German origin, and 66 percent of them later took British citizenship. Over 40 percent of the respondents originated in Berlin and Vienna. Nineteen percent of the respondents were Orthodox Jews. Girls outnumbered boys by 6 percent and the median age of their arrival in Britain was twelve. Almost a third of the *Kinder* answering had arrived with at least one sibling. Close to 40 percent of the respondents were evacuated during the war and 10 percent were deported. A total of 30 percent served in the British armed forces. The *Kinder* were often highly educated: 16 percent had university degrees and 22 percent had received some type of higher education, often in night school. Theo Vered (Verderber) recalled the importance education held for many of the *Kinder*: "Our childhood in Germany was not a happy one, it was suppressed and often impoverished. Yet, when we came to the UK and freedom, many of us relied on what we remembered from 'home' and realized that we had to have an education in order to support oneself."[49]

Surprisingly, only 60 percent of the respondents lost their parents during the war, while the others were often reunited with them at a later date. A total of 94 percent of the respondents married, 84 percent of them had children, and 81 percent have spoken with their children or grandchildren about their early lives.[50]

If the second postwar period was characterized by a general reticence among many of the *Kinder* to speak with their children about their prewar and wartime experiences, it appears that this phenomenon slowly began to reverse itself during the third postwar period following the fiftieth anniversary reunion. Slowly, because after years of silence and in view of many of the *Kinder*'s rather reserved British upbringing it was difficult to break a pattern that had existed for years. At the second British Kindertransport reunion held in 1999, there was even a special workshop offered to try to get the first- and second-generation *Kinder* to talk about these experiences and "to break down the wall of silence that still existed between parents and children in the early 1990s."[51]

For many of the *Kinder* it was a combination of the reunions, the heightened awareness of the importance of their experiences, and the age-related desire to leave testimony for the past that brought them to finally want to speak to their children and grandchildren about their experiences. Among a small group there was no change. Cita Bental from Leipzig recalled how her sons were not particularly interested in knowing much about her prewar and wartime life: "They didn't ask much and I didn't say much about it. I never spoke to them about it on my own initiative. When one of my grandchildren was writing a 'family roots' paper she asked me some questions but that was about it. Even today when something happens in current events that connects to that time, I may mention something about it, but on the most part my grandchildren are not that interested, unfortunately!"[52]

This group, however, was not the majority. Others experienced just the opposite and found the period following the first reunions to be an opportunity to connect their descendants to their past. "It was as if all of a sudden they—my children and grandchildren—wanted to know everything about my life during the war," recalled Chana Gilboa. "When they were younger my children weren't interested in hearing about it, they were busy with their friends and I wasn't that eager to speak about it either. I was busy. But now as we got older it comes up more. Then I didn't find a need to speak, everyone went through something, I went through nothing special. But now I know that it was special nonetheless."[53]

Steffi Birnbaum Schwartz agreed. "I had spoken to my daughter about my wartime life somewhat before but I definitely spoke to her more about my experiences after the first reunion we had here in Israel," she recalled. There was quite a difference in my attitude towards speaking about it thirty years ago and today." Could it be a result of growing older, I asked? "To be sure," Steffi agreed, "But many of us still needed some kind of outside catalyst to get that ball rolling and those were the reunions."[54]

Chava Laufer, originally from Breslau, agreed. "I was lucky, I spoke to my children about my past when they were younger and then to my grandchildren when they were working on their 'family roots' project. But I know that for friends of mine here in Israel that first reunion at Kibbutz Lavi and those that followed helped them open up and tell their grandchildren about what they had gone through before and during the war."[55] Chedva Tipperberg Ben-Yashar, who reached England from Cologne via Zbąszyń, also felt that her children "knew my whole story, but only in the past years, when my grandchildren were interested in family history because of their school projects, did I open up more. One granddaughter who had interviewed me when she was twelve ended up writing her high school history thesis about me last year and it even received a number of prizes."[56]

How did the second and third generations respond to learning about their parents' past? Anita Grosz, whose father had come to England from Czechoslovakia at age fifteen with his thirteen-year-old brother, recalls knowing a bit about her father's past as a child but only having a sketchy picture of the events, as he didn't talk about it generally. "It wasn't until I was in my late twenties when I started exploring about the Kindertransport. Through my working with others and helping to start up the USA Kindertransport Association, my father started opening up more about his past." To what extent did her father's wartime history affect her, I asked? "I always felt I was different. But I don't know how much of it is attributed to the Kindertransport versus living in a place where there are very few foreigners. My mother is Danish. So I had two foreign parents. It wasn't until I moved to NYC in my thirties that I finally felt comfortable."[57]

Similar to large numbers of children of *Kinder*, Grosz stated that she felt most comfortable with what she termed 2GKT—Second generation of Kindertransport children. "I helped organize the first 2G Kindertransport group in New York back in the 1980s. We met regularly for more than a year. It was through this group that Melissa Hacker made her film *My Knees were Jumping*. We still get together when there is a KTA reunion." My final question referred to the connection between her father's experiences as a Jewish refugee child and various decisions she made regarding her own life. Did learning about her father's past affect her own sense of moral choice, I asked? "Yes," she responded. "I have always felt obliged to my fellow man. I have a strong social sense of responsibility and equality. And I have tried to use these ethos in some of my work and volunteer choices."[58]

Other 2GKT felt differently. Avner Gilboa recalled how his mother Chana would speak little about her experiences during his childhood. Did he ever ask her about her past? "No," he responded, "we children didn't feel any need to ask. We had full lives of our own and there were other things that interested us and connected us as a family such as opera and the love of music. What had happened to my mother before and during the war was so long ago. For us it was if it was a story from beyond the black hills." When did the change occur, I asked? "When we got older we began to ask questions about her experiences and for my mother it had also become more important to tell us about her past." Gilboa stressed that his mother's experiences never caused him to feel different from any of his contemporaries, that they had no connection to his sense of moral choice. Nor did they arouse in him any desire to be in contact with other 2GKT's to share experiences.

For Chana Gilboa, like for many others, the transition from wanting to forget her past and live in the present to wanting to preserve her experiences for future generations came primarily through her grandchildren. In several conversations, she spoke animatedly about how she could finally open up to her grandchildren about her experiences and how they responded in kind. Her son Avner, however, presented a different picture. "Not all of the grandchildren were interested," he recalled in a separate conversation. "Some were more interested and some less. In fact, most weren't the type of children who really wanted that kind of connection to her through these stories."[59]

Is the clash between the two descriptions of how grandchildren responded to their grandmothers' Kindertransport stories a rashomon caused by an elderly *Kind*'s wishful thinking? We will never know. However, the need that many of the *Kinder*'s children felt to connect with others from a similar background was definitely real. So real, in fact, that in 1985, three years before Bertha Leverton came up with the idea of a Kindertransport reunion, a group of 2GKT in Britain decided to establish the ACJR—the Association of Children of Jewish Refugees in Britain—as an offshoot of the Association of Jewish Refugees. The group aimed to promote social, cultural, and intellectual activities for its members, all of whom were children of refugees from Nazi persecution. As the group's website states: "Those who may not feel entirely at home in the mainstream Anglo-Jewish environment often find that, at the ACJR, they can discover common links and a sense of kinship."[60]

Over time this sense of kinship has developed many varied expressions. During the quarter of a century since its founding, the group has created an ongoing repertoire of social events to unite its members, including communal meals and holiday celebrations, talks and discussion groups, visits to theater, concerts, and films, a second-night Passover Seder, visits to places of Jewish and general interest, and a summer barbecue. These shared activities were at first an expression of a desire to be together with other 2GKT's in order to commune with them about a shared past. As the ACJR website states, "Although the link that binds us is our common continental heritage and our parents' refugee backgrounds, a wide range of outlooks is to be found within this shared framework in attitudes to Germany, to our Central and East European culture and in religious observance and belief (or lack of it). This may simply reflect the diversity of our parents' experiences: from the luckier ones who escaped relatively lightly with their immediate families intact, to those who left on the Kindertransports and those who survived the camps. In one member's view: 'It is only to be expected that our parents' histories have been such a strong influence on our lives: the ACJR allows people to share their thoughts and feelings with others who seem to understand almost before a word has been uttered.'"[61]

At the same time, however, it was also a place for the *Kinder*'s children to create a present and future separate from that of their parents but with their experiences accompanying them as an ongoing background melody. By following the almost three hundred issues of the ACJR Newsletter that the group has put out since its inception, one can see how ACJR members have developed a dynamic of their own. Over the years, the group's membership has grown and evolved; the chairman, vice chairman, membership and events secretaries, newsletter editor and acting treasurer have changed several times. When asked about the group's present composition, newsletter editor Anne Salinger emphasized that the fluidity in ACJR membership is something to be expected: "Lots of members left us for no reason other than that they 'moved on' in their lives. I myself wasn't involved much from about 1996 until 2003, when I took over editing the newsletter. That was simply due to family commitments." Emphasizing that the ACJR is purely a social group, she explained that "people who are interested in serious discussion tend to go to '2nd Generation,'" in other words, those groups dealing primarily with children of Holocaust survivors.[62]

Many years ago, when I first began receiving the ACJR newsletter, Oliver Walter, one of the active members of the ACJR, had written me that a major impetus for the organization's creation was the search for identity. Just as the first generation of *Kinder* seemed to be seeking their true identity—British? Continental? Hybrid?—at the time, their children were looking for their own identity as members of something bigger than themselves that had either liminally or subliminally left its mark on their childhood and, consequently, on their adulthood. To understand what that "something" was, however, and how it actually had affected their lives, it would be necessary for them to better understand what their parents had really gone through, including painful incidents that may have been kept from them or which they would actually have preferred not to hear about.

For years the official refrain had been that the Jewish refugee children who had reached Britain before the war were the lucky ones and in spite of going through the hardships of refugeeism, evacuation, and at times even internment, their resettlement had ultimately been successful. From the time that Gladys Bendit had written the RCM's "official history" in 1944 under the pseudonym John Presland, through Norman Bentwich's *They Found Refuge* in 1956 and even up to the first study dealing with Great Britain and the Jews of Europe by Wasserstein in 1979, Britain's role in saving almost ten thousand refugee children from Central Europe was described as a benevolent deliverance in view of what was portrayed as the unavoidable separation of parents and children. The English sponsors were cast as "welcoming," the children as "adapting," and the rescue as "almost miraculous." As Jennifer Norton states, while it was understandable that anyone involved in the rescue scheme had a reason to "skew the narrative towards the redemptive and the celebratory," these publications propagated the myth that "the children's rescue nullified the suffering they had experienced after being torn from their parents."[63] This "triumphant narrative," appearing in many of the *Kinder*'s own early memoirs, was also reinforced by their children in many of the articles appearing in the ACJR newsletter over the years.[64]

In truth, however, as Norton has shown in her fascinating thesis, there was at times another, darker side to the story. The first had to do with the young refugees' experiences. In her story of a group of refugee children in the Manchester area, Gertrude Dubrowsky writes about having interviewed an Orthodox refugee girl who had been repeatedly raped by her host over the years.[65] Other *Kinder* experienced hunger, molestation, and various physical and mental tortures at the hands of their sponsors. How many went through such experiences? No one will ever know. But as Dubrowsky writes in a footnote in which she documents her interview with this former *Kind*, "this was not an isolated incident."[66]

Then there was the side of the British government. Until recently, while most studies of Britain during the Holocaust took the British to task for its Palestine policy of the time, the rescue of ten thousand mostly Jewish refugee children from the Reich was portrayed as its redeeming act. Only in the past few years did historians and political scientists raise the question of why the British government allowed the children to be rescued without saving their parents as well. And while Karen Gershon's book allowed those *Kinder* who even in the 1960s could not buy fully into the triumphant narrative to express their feelings on the matter, most autobiographies that the *Kinder* continued to write for the next three or even four decades continued spouting the official thankful version of the Kindertransport narrative. It appears that there was something too compelling in the version which painted British benevolence with bright cheery colors for them to pose difficult and painful questions about the British government's inaction in trying to save their parents, questions that would possibly be interpreted as lack of gratitude toward those who saved their lives. The monuments erected in commemoration of the Kindertransports and the plaques dedicated to the children's rescue reinforce an unambiguous triumphant narrative of rescue through memorials that honor what Norton terms "the British self-image of generosity and exceptionalism."[67]

Did the second generation of Kindertransport children support this triumphant narrative in their own writings because of their inability to hear painful and difficult truths about their parents' lives during their first years in Britain? Were they even aware of a parallel narrative, one that did not speak only of gratitude toward the British government and the British people but viewed the events surrounding the Kindertransports through a different and less positive prism? Did their parents continue supporting that triumphant narrative because it was too difficult for them to speak about issues like molestation and worse? Do their autobiographies usually support that narrative because it was expected of them or because it was easier than facing the truth of their own past experiences? After all, only recently did the first serious study of sexual violence against women during the Holocaust appear, a topic long ignored by mainstream Holocaust research and even gender research.[68] Could it be that similar to the process which certain Holocaust survivors had recently undergone in which they were able to open up and talk about experiences that they had pushed aside in their minds for years? Now could some of the *Kinder*, and with them, their own children, be able to face the other side of the story? Or is it possibly more important in the long run for the triumphant narrative to remain paramount in order to allow the *Kinder* to live with themselves and their losses?

Meanwhile, at least, the triumphant narrative appears to live on and even flourish. Chana Gilboa still speaks of the fact that today, more than seventy years after she arrived in England and thirty years after I first interviewed her, she sees things in a different perspective even than she had three decades ago and believes today that God was very kind to her, guiding her to good places. "It wasn't always great in England but it also wasn't terrible. My perspective is that in general the British were pretty good to us."[69]

While I was preparing the manuscript for this book, Joe Haberer, who had given the project its start, sent me a New Year's correspondence that he had received from an old friend, Theo Vered (Verdeber), who had shared his Kindertransport experiences. Summing up their lives from a vantage point of more than seventy years after their arrival in England, Vered writes: "We are like a forgotten seed left dormant for years in the corner of a dark shed. When the shed was cleaned out the seed was left on the damp earth and germinated producing a beautiful plant spreading out in all directions carrying fruit on its branches.[70] A final, beautiful, positive and hopeful picture in which memories of the dark shed, the rot, the mold, and the crawling creatures in the dark were left far behind to ultimately vanish in the black hole of oblivion.

What has changed in the past thirty years? I asked Steffi. "Does the Kindertransport experience look any different from the vantage point of eighty than it did from that of fifty? "Oh, my dear," she answered in her usual ironic manner, "don't you know that age only exaggerates everything that one was before? Things are often the same, there is just more of it! Those who were grateful are even more grateful. Those who were not are even more bitter, and those who feel guilty about having survived when their parents did not, feel even more guilty. The only way for some of us to survive was to never look back." "And what of this 'triumphant narrative'?" I asked her. "Do you think that people realized they might be painting things a bit too cheery?" "Some of us always realized that, you know," she responded, "and so did you thirty years ago when you wrote your first pieces about the *Kinder*."[71]

Pondering Steffi's words, I went back to my original master's thesis that I had written in the spring of 1981. She was correct. Even before some of the *Kinder* dared to express their mixed feelings and experiences in writing, they had begun to share them with me in our interviews and discussions. Their stories had shaped my conclusions about the Kindertransport experience, conclusions that have remained unchanged, even in the light of the plethora of sources that have since become available. I will therefore end my saga of the Jewish refugee children in Great Britain with the words I used to conclude my thesis more than three decades ago:

> One clear cut fact emerges from this study—from the beginning, nothing was as it seemed on the surface. Britain's motivation in permitting the entry of refugee children was primarily not a humanitarian one, but one of political pragmatism. Numerically speaking, Great Britain had permitted more refugee children to enter than had any other country. The care of their physical welfare was on the most part, satisfactory. The same cannot always be said for their emotional and spiritual welfare. Anglo Jewry, who had repeatedly promised the British government since 1933 to "care for their own," had managed, within six years to alienate a substantial portion of the Jewish refugee children in Great Britain by their condescending and intolerant attitudes towards them.
>
> In his *Ethics*, Aristotle states: "Virtue [is] of two kinds, intellectual and moral. Intellectual virtue derives both its origin and its growth mainly from teaching, wherefore it requires experience and time, while moral virtue is the fruit of habit."[72] While one might expect compassion to be the chief emotion surfacing among those dealing with frightened and vulnerable children, this was not always so. It was the moral virtue of those who did treat them with compassion that distinguished them from the shapeless mass to which the refugee children in Britain were at best a curiosity and at worst a nuisance.
>
> Leo Baeck once related that, shortly before the outbreak of war, he saw a poster on a bus in England on which the psalm "God is a refuge" was written. One day an anonymous pen added an "e," making it "God is a refugee." It was a sign of the times. From one day to the next children, parents, teachers, pupils, entire communities had become refugees. Unlike the refugees of the French Revolution, being an émigré in Britain of 1939 was not a status symbol but a liability. The assimilation process of refugee children was often long and arduous; even decades after their departure from Central Europe there were Jewish refugee children who still had no true sense of belonging or "home."
>
> The "open door" policy of the Western world towards child refugees which has become more and more evident in each decade since the Second World War is in part a continuing attempt to exonerate the guilt connected with the fateful period during which refugees, both young and old, were a surplus commodity, and where innocent children were put in the position of exchanging their birthright for a place to lay their heads."[73]

Where Are They Today (July 2011)?

What became of the *Kinder* and those involved in their rescue? Of the roughly ten thousand refugee children who came to Britain before the war, only about half stayed in Britain. About a thousand of them immigrated to Israel, others to the United States and additional countries. In his *Generation Exodus*, Walter Laqueur states that the choice of profession was largely accidental and varied widely, bringing the story of one refugee boy who ended up in charge of a herd of six thousand Canadian reindeer in the Arctic Circle, another who ran a health ranch in Mexico, walked through the Gobi Desert, ran Buddhist meditations courses in Australia, and now lives in a twelve-by-twelve-foot mud and rock house near Katmandu. "Most of the others opted for more humdrum careers as teachers, businessmen, engineers and housewives."[74]

Some tried to hide their origins, and many changed their names, although this was often done to be able to serve in the British army or in Israel where many new immigrants were encouraged to Hebraicize both their personal and family names. Others, as we have seen, changed their religion in order to fit in with their surroundings. For the majority of the younger *Kinder*, the German language was neither a home nor an emotional pillar, although some continued to speak it with relatives after the war.

Are there any generational characteristics with common features for all the Jewish refugee children who escaped Central Europe, to a variety of countries, before the war? Laqueur poses this question and comes up with some very interesting answers. One was the traditional Central European Jewish belief in higher education that remained an ideal even for *Kinder* who were forced to terminate their studies due to the war. Another was an exaggerated respect for the upper class of their new country, and particularly for their self-assurance and command of the language. A third was a general thirst for knowledge, leading quite a number of *Kinder* to strive to become professionals. Laqueur notes that quite a number of those he studied were workaholics and overachievers, and one wonders whether this came from the young refugees' knowledge that they were alone in the world, that no one owed them a living, and that it was a question of sinking or swimming.[75]

A number of *Kinder* went on to become prominent figures in public life. They include Baron Alfred Dubs from Czechoslovakia, a British politician; Walter Kohn from Austria, an American physicist and Nobel laureate; Otto Newman from Austria, a British psychologist; Arno Penzias from Germany, an American physicist and Nobel laureate; Sir Erich Reich from Austria, a British entrepreneur; Joe Schlesinger from Austria, a Canadian journalist and author; Sir Guenter Treitel from Germany, a British law scholar; and Rolf Decker from Germany, an American Olympic hero and international soccer player.

By the time I completed my original thesis about the Jewish refugee children in Great Britain in 1981, many of the activists who had been involved in the refugee scheme were no longer alive. In 1944, Sir Herbert Samuel became the head of the Liberal Party in the House of Lords and was the first British politician to deliver a party political broadcast on television. In his later years, he was concerned with the future of humanity and science and wrote several books on the subject. Sir Herbert Samuel died in 1963 at the age of ninety-two.

During the war, Sir Norman Bentwich served in the British Ministry of Information and Air Ministry. He later chaired a number of organizations including the International Peace Council, the Jewish Committee for Relief Abroad, the United Restitution Office, and the Friends of the Hebrew University. For the last thirteen years of his life he was president of the London North Western Reform Synagogue. Bentwich died in 1971 at the age of eighty-eight.

Lord Gorell remained the official guardian of the refugee children in Britain until the last of them reached their majority. Both during and after the war, he continued writing detective stories, his main passion, and was co-president of the Detection Club with Agatha Christie from 1956 to 1963. All in all he wrote fourteen works of fiction. Lord Gorell died in 1963 at age seventy-seven.

Anna Essinger remained at Bunce Court, writing and staying in touch with her former charges until her death at age eighty-one in 1960.

When I interviewed the *Kinder* for the first time around 1980, most were in their fifties, working and busy raising families. Some of the younger refugee activists were still alive at the time. After our interviews or correspondence, we remained in touch until their deaths.

The rescue activities of Nicholas Winton only became known after I wrote my thesis. He is the only one of the activists still alive at the time of writing.

After the war, Rabbi Solomon Schonfeld continued the CRREC's activities among the She'erit Hapleta, the Jewish Displaced Persons in Europe. He remained "an individualist," forceful, impulsive, and driven, as Chanan Tomlin continuously described him, involved in his community.[76] At the time I wrote my thesis, Schonfeld was already unwell and thus not able to meet with me, In 1984, he died. His personal papers were made available to several historians and are now at the University of Southampton. Copies of many of the important documents involving his rescue activities may be found in the Munk collection at Yad Vashem.

Norbert Wollheim returned to Germany after bringing several Kindertransports to Britain, was caught by the Nazis and sent to Auschwitz where he lost his wife and son. After the war, he sued the I.G. Farben company where he had been a slave laborer during the war and in addition to winning his case he was involved in a global settlement awarding several thousand former slave laborers of the Farben company a settlement of 30 million DM. In 1951, he immigrated to the United States where he studied accounting and later worked as a tax advisor. A family friend, as he and my father had been incarcerated together in the Auschwitz-Buna (Monowitz) camp for several years, he freely shared his Kindertransport and wartime experiences with me. Norbert Wollheim died in New York in 1998 at the age of eighty-five.

The Reverend William W. (Bill) Simpson was one of the founders of the International Council of Christians and Jews, dedicated to fostering understanding between the two groups. Simpson later married Ruth Weyl, a former Jewish refugee child from Berlin whose family found refuge in Palestine in 1948. Ruth and Bill were an incredible couple, working together in the Council. What I best remember from my meetings with them was Bill Simpson's ironic but understated British sense of humor when describing some of his fellow refugee activists. Bill Simpson passed away in 1987 and his wife continues his work in the International Council of Christians and Jews.

Eva Michaelis-Stern returned to Palestine after the war, where she remained active in Youth Aliyah until 1952. She then founded an organization to promote civic improvement projects in Jerusalem. She became active in AKIM, the National Association for the Habilitation of the Mentally Handicapped, and founded a memorial fund at the Hebrew University to help train social workers to work with the handicapped. Eva Michaelis-Stern died in Jerusalem in 1992 at the age of eighty-eight.

Arieh Handler, one of the founders of the British Bachad, lived in London after the war and was active in many Israeli government and British Zionist institutions. For many years he was the president of the British Mizrachi Zionist movement and was involved in the British Labour Party. Handler was the last person alive to have been present at the Israeli Declaration of Independence. In 2006 he returned to Israel and lived in Jerusalem. Arieh Handler died in 2011, a week short of his ninety-seventh birthday.

And what of the *Kinder*? When I tried to contact my entire original list of *Kinder* with whom I had corresponded and interviewed thirty years ago, I was dismayed to learn how many of them were no longer alive. Those whom I reached were almost all in their eighties, many still active and involved with causes and their families. The fortunate ones whose parents survived the war spoke of reunited families and parents who lived to see great-grandchildren. Others were now involved with their own grandchildren and great-grandchildren.

After organizing the fiftieth reunion of the Kindertransports in 1989, Bertha Leverton began editing a *Kinder* Newsletter and arranged for the sixtieth reunion in London in 1999. In 2009, she immigrated to Israel from London at age eighty-seven to join her daughter's family on the settlement of Kedumim.

Lore Grossman Segal attended the women's division of the University of London and in 1951 moved to the United States, where she became a writer. Her mother, Franzi Groszmann, was the last survivor of the parents who sent their children to England on the Kindertransports. Until age ninety-five, Franzi had breakfast with her daughter every day. In 1995, Franzi Groszmann died in New York at the age of one hundred.

After the war, Joseph Haberer moved to the United States where he studied history and political science. He taught at Rutgers and then at Purdue University until his retirement. He was the founding editor of *Shofar: An Interdisciplinary Journal of Jewish Studies,* and continues to act as its book review editor. Haberer lives with his wife in West Lafayette, Indiana.

Chana Gilboa and her husband came to Israel in 1948. Today they live on the Massuot Yitzchak Moshav on Israel's coastal plain. She spends time with her three children and her grandchildren.

After the war, Reenie Birnbaum trained as a nurse and worked for years in London. After retiring, she immigrated to Israel in 2010 to join her older sister Steffi and her family in Jerusalem.

Steffi Birnbaum Schwartz moved to Israel in 1964, married, and had a daughter. She remains in close contact with her relatives who survived the war and especially her uncle and aunt's family in Holland. In 1993, she retired from the Institute of Contemporary Jewry at the Hebrew University of Jerusalem. Steffi Birnbaum Schwartz has written two booklets of poetry including a large number of poems dealing with the Kindertransport experience and its aftermath. Today she lives in Jerusalem near her daughter Raya, her son-in-law, and four grandchildren. Throughout the writing of this book Steffi gave me unstintingly of her time and encouragement. When I told her that I had almost completed the manuscript and was concerned how it would be received she told me that she was sure it would be an important and significant book. "The stories speak for themselves," she reminded me in her matter-of-fact German British way, "as for the rest, one tries to do one's best and that's that; I'm sure it will be fine."

I hope that she is correct.

Notes

1. Schwartz interview.
2. Emerson, "Postwar Problems," 219.
3. Michaelis-Stern interview.
4. Talmon Interview.
5. Harris and Oppenheimer, *Into the Arms of Strangers*, 229.
6. *The Jewish Chronicle*, 9 February 1945, 5.
7. Report on Jewish Refugee Children brought to England, May 1950, Refugee Children's Movement, Correspondence, Central British Fund Archives, The Wiener Library Microfilm document collection 27/29/169.
8. Report on Jewish Refugee Children brought to England, May 1950, Refugee Children's Movement, Correspondence, Central British Fund Archives, The Wiener Library Microfilm document collection 27/29/169; Bentwich, *They Found Refuge*, 50.
9. Gershon, *We Came as Children*, 113.
10. Ibid., 113–14.
11. Ibid., 113.
12. Ibid., 114.
13. Author's interview with Grete Marcus, New York, 7 May 2008.
14. Harris and Oppenheimer, *Into the Arms of Strangers*, 233–34.
15. Gershon, *We Came as Children*, 116.
16. Ibid.
17. Schwartz interview.
18. Gershon, *We Came as Children*, 87–88.
19. Laqueur, *Generation Exodus*, 211.
20. Author's telephone interview with Chana Gilboa, 15 May 2011 (henceforth: Gilboa interview).
21. Schwartz interview.

22. Gershon, *A Lesser Child*; Gershon, *A Tempered Wind*.
23. Gershon, *We Came as Children*, 150.
24. Ibid., 160.
25. Ibid., 152.
26. Ibid., 153.
27. Ibid., 160.
28. Ibid., 152.
29. For example, Singer, *Children of the Apocalypse*; Zurndorfer, *The Ninth of November*.
30. Morse, *While Six Million Died*; Wyman, *Paper Walls*; Feingold, *The Politics of Rescue*; Friedman, *No Haven for the Oppressed*; Sherman, *Island Refuge*; Wasserstein, *Britain and the Jews of Europe 1939–1945*.
31. Norton, "The Kindertransport."
32. Styron, *Sophie's Choice*.
33. Baumel, *Unfulfilled Promise*.
34. Schwartz interview.
35. Harris and Oppenheimer, *Into the Arms of Strangers*, 252.
36. Ibid., 253.
37. Ester Golan, Entry for Friday October 5, 2007, Youth Aliya and Kinder Transport.
38. Reunion of Kindertransport Documents, 1987–2002, The Wiener Library microfilm document collection, 1368/2/7/ ABC.
39. Leverton and Lowensohn, *I Came Alone*.
40. http://www.ajr.org.uk/kt-newsletters.
41. Sadan, *No Longer a Stranger*, 1999.
42. http://www.kindertransport.org/history08_FoundingKTA.htm.
43. http://www.kindertransport.org/default.aspx.
44. Drucker, *Kindertransport*, 144.
45. Films: Mark Jonathan Harris (dir.), *Into the Arms of Strangers: Stories of the Kindertransport* (2000); Melissa Hacker (dir.) *My Knees Were Jumping* (1997); Sue Read and Jim Goulding, *The Children Who Cheated the Nazis*, British documentary film shown first on channel 4 (2000); Kate Kranz (dir.), *Maybe I Was Lucky*" (2002); *Holocaust Day: A Haven in Wales*, a BBC documentary broadcast on BBC2 Wales on Holocaust Day 2005; *All My Loved Ones (Vsichni moji blzci)* (1999); *The Power of Good: Nicholas Winton (Sila lidskosti—Nicholas Winton)* (2002). Plays: *Kindertransport* (1993); *Memory* (2006); *My Heart in a Suitcase* (2006); *The End of Everything Ever* (2008). The Kindertransport memory quilt project started in 1996 by Anita Grosz, daughter of a *Kind* from Czechoslovakia; on each square people wrote a page describing his or her experiences in the Kindertransport. The Memory Quilt Book presents each square and is available through the KTA. The originals are housed at the Holocaust Memorial Center at Farmington Hills near Detroit. An Amish woman did the quilting and in 2008 the project had sixty-five squares made into three large quilts and two smaller ones. http://www.kindertransport.org/exhibits_MQ.aspx.
46. http://www.ajr.org.uk/documents/Kindertransport_talk_-_Sir_Martin_Gilbert_-_Nov_08.pdf.
47. "Journey to Survival," 54.
48. "Elderly Jews re-create kindertransport trip."
49. Personal correspondence Theo Vered (Verderber) to Joseph Haberer, 30 August 2010, in the author's possession (henceforth cited: Vered correspondence).
50. AJR *Kinder* database, http://www.ajr.org.uk/kindersurvey. Original questionnaires are housed at the Wiener Library. http://www.ajr.org.uk/documents/KinderTrans-

port_Survey_2007_Final_Databases_21Aug2009_-clean_results_deduped_renumbered.xls.
51. AJS Kindertransport newsletter, April 2006.
52. Author's telephone interview with Cita Bental, 10 June 2011.
53. Gilboa interview.
54. Schwartz interview.
55. Author's telephone interview with Chava Laufer, 10 June 2011.
56. Author's telephone interview with Chedva Tipperberg Ben-Yashar, 10 June 2011.
57. Author's correspondence with Anita Grosz, 24 January 2011.
58. Ibid.
59. Author's telephone interview with Avner Gilboa, 12 June 2011.
60. http://www.owalter.co.uk/acjr/index.htm.
61. http://www.owalter.co.uk/acjr/index.htm.
62. Author's correspondence with Anne Salinger, 15 June 2011.
63. Norton, 193.
64. Sharples, "Reconstructing the Past," 40–62.
65. Dobrowsky, 130.
66. Ibid., 132.
67. Norton, "The Kindertransport," 202.
68. Hedgepeth and Saidel, *Sexual Violence against Jewish Women during the Holocaust*.
69. Gilboa interview.
70. Vered correspondence.
71. Schwartz interview.
72. Warrington, *Aristotle's Ethics*, 28.
73. Baumel, "The Jewish Refugee Children in Great Britain," 190.
74. Laqueur, *Generation Exodus*, 198.
75. Ibid., 296.
76. Tomlin, *Protest and Prayer*, 227.

Timeline

1932	Establishment of Aliyat Hanoar in Germany
1933 (April)	Establishment of the Central British Fund
1933 (April	Establishment of the Jewish Refugees' Committee
1933 (April)	Bunce Court School founded by Anna Essinger
1934 (Sept.)	Boys' School for refugees founded at Elgin
1936 (March)	Council for German Jewry Founded
1936	Inter-Aid Committee Founded
1937	3,800 Spanish Civil War orphans arrive in England
1938 (March)	Chief Rabbi's Religious Emergency Council founded
1938 (12 March)	German takeover of Austria (*Anschluss*)
1938 (May)	Coordinating Committee for Refugees founded
1938 (1 Oct.)	German invasion of the Sudetenland
1938 (9–10 Nov.)	*Kristallnacht*
1938 (15 Nov.)	Chamberlain meets with deputation from the Council for German Jewry about the refugee problem
1938 (21 Nov.)	House of Commons debate on the refugee problem. Public announcement of scheme to permit transmigrant children to use Britain as a temporary refuge.
1938 (22 Nov.)	First official meeting of the Movement for the Care of Children from Germany
1938 (23 Nov.)	House of Commons announces the waiving of visa requirements for transmigrant children
1938 (25 Nov.)	Norman Bentwich leaves for the Netherlands to arrange for the transfer of transmigrant children
1938 (2 Dec.)	First group of children arrive from Germany
1938 (8 Dec.)	Lord Baldwin makes appeal for refugees. Lord Baldwin Fund launched
1938 (late Dec.)	Pakefield reception camp evacuated of refugee children due to cold

TIMELINE

1939 (Feb.)	Bloomsbury house purchased as a center for all refugee organizations
1939 (5 Feb.)	First group of children arrive from Zbąszyń
1939 (1 March)	£50 clause for sponsors of refugee children goes into effect
1939 (March 15)	German takeover of Czechoslovakia
1939 (March)	Movement for the Care of Children from Germany incorporates. Lord Gorell and Sir Charles Stead co-chairmen
1939 (15 May)	Meeting of Jewish Educational Organizations formulating plans for Jewish education after evacuation
1939 (July)	Lord Baldwin Fund closes with over half a million pounds sterling having been collected for refugees
1939 (1 Sept.)	Evacuation of school children and others from major centers to the Midlands and protected areas
1939 (1 Sept.)	Last prewar transport arrives via the Netherlands
1939 (3 Sept.)	Britain declares war on Germany
1940 (11 May)	Creation of a protected area on the eastern and southern coasts of Britain
1940 (14 May)	Last transport of children arrives from the Netherlands
1940 (16 May)	Roundup and internment of Category "B" males
1940 (27 May)	Roundup and internment of Category "B" females
1940 (21 June)	First deportee ship *Duchess of York* leaves for Canada
1940 (24 June)	Roundup and internment of Category "C" males
1940 (2 July)	Deportee ship *Arandora Star* sunk by German torpedo
1940 (July)	First White Paper releasing internees
1940 (Aug.)	Second White Paper releasing internees
1940 (Nov.)	Third White Paper releasing internees
1942 (Aug.)	Joint Committee for Religious Education of Jewish Refugees founded
1944 (1 March)	Guardianship Act passed into law
1944 (March)	Lord Gorell appointed guardian of refugee children in Britain
1948	Refugee Children's Movement disbanded

Glossary

1938–45. The major portion of this book focuses on the period between *Kristallnacht*, the night between 9–10 November 1938, which was considered the turning point in the British attitude toward refugee children, and May 1945—the end of the war in the European theater, heralding the arrival of the next major group of refugee children in Great Britain. These were young survivors who had been liberated from concentration camps, who have been described in other studies such as Martin Gilbert's *The Boys*. Chapter 2 provides a brief introduction to this period.

Children. With the exception of chapter 8 (dealing with "Internment and Deportation"), a child is defined as anyone between the ages of birth and seventeen inclusive, this being the British government's legal definition of a refugee child for immigration purposes. In chapter 8 "childhood" is extended to age eighteen inclusive, as sixteen-to-eighteen year olds were listed as a separate category in the internment orders. Late- and post-teenage Jewish refugee children are mentioned in connection with service in the Royal Pioneer Corps, the only branch of the British armed forces for which, initially, aliens were permitted to volunteer.

Great Britain. By definition Great Britain comprises England, Scotland, and Wales. I therefore deal primarily with children who settled in those countries. In chapter 6, on Youth Aliyah, I make brief mention of agricultural training centers (*hachsharot*, singular: *hachshara*) in Northern Ireland.

Jewish. Although this is not the accepted Orthodox definition of a Jew, for the purposes of this study my definition of a Jewish child is one with a Jewish mother or father (who did not convert to Christianity) or both of whose parents were Jews. This study does not deal with children whom the Nazis defined as "non-Aryan Christians" (i.e., converts to Christianity, or first- and second-degree *Mischlinge*—children of mixed marriages or those with one Jewish grandparent) if they did not identify themselves as Jews.

Refugee. Anyone who left Continental Europe as a result of the rise of Nazism is considered a refugee for purposes of this study.

Foreign Terms

Aliyat Hanoar. Youth Aliyah

Anschluss. The German invasion of Austria on 15 March 1938 (lit. in German: unification)

Auslandhachshara. Agricultural training outside Germany

Austrittsgemeinde. The ultra-Orthodox separatist community founded by Rabbi Samson Raphael Hirsch in nineteenth-century Germany

Auswanderungsabteilung. Immigration department

Begleiter. Escorts (of transports)

Chas Vechalila. Heaven Forbid (colloquial Hebrew)

Dayan. Religious judge

Hachshara. Pioneering settlement (pl., *Hachsharot*)

Heder. Small schoolroom in which Jewish studies were taught (lit. in Hebrew: room)

Kiddush. Blessing over the wine on Saturdays and festivals, used also to describe the Saturday morning meal

Kinder. Refugee children (lit. in German: children), singular, *Kind*

Kristallnacht or *Reichskristallnacht* The Nazi pogrom in the Third Reich on the night between 9–10 November 1938 (lit. in German: "crystal night," named for the broken glass that littered the streets following the pogrom)

Kultusgemeinde. Jewish community offices (Vienna)

Madrichim. Group counselors (singular: *madrich*)

Mapai. Eretz Yisrael Worker's Party (Labor)

Metaplot. Caretakers

Mischlinge. Children of mixed marriages or those with one Jewish grandparent, in the Third Reich

Mittelschule. Middle school

Mittlernhachshara. *Hachshara* for middle school students

Mutti. Mother

Numerus clausus. Quota legislation in schools and universities in the Third Reich

Pikuach nefesh A life-threatening situation in which one is permitted by Jewish law to do anything necessary to survive as long as it is not immoral

Reichsmark. Nazi currency in Germany

Schiffschul. Orthodox Jewish synagogue in Vienna

Shabbat. Saturday

Shaliach. Zionist emissary

She'erit Hapleta. Jewish Displaced Persons in Europe after the Second World War (lit. in Hebrew: Surviving Remnant)

Shtiblach. Small Hasidic prayer houses (lit. in Yiddish: small home)

Taubschen. Little dove

Va'ad Haleumi. The National Council in Palestine

Wehrmacht. German military forces of the Third Reich

Yishuv. Pre-State Jewish community in Palestine

Discussion Questions

1. What were the major prewar Jewish organizations in Great Britain? How did they respond to the growing refugee crisis during the late 1930s?
2. Can you think of the advantages and disadvantages of moving entire schools from Germany to Britain, along with their pupils, as part of the refugee child scheme?
3. What were the advantages and disadvantages of having several organizations deal simultaneously with rescuing Jewish refugee children from the Third Reich? How did the organizations approach this situation?
4. How was the British announcement of November 1938, to allow refugee children from greater Germany into Britain, connected to the existence of the British Mandate for Palestine?
5. What common denominators can you find among the individuals who started rescue schemes to save refugee children from Germany independent of the existing major refugee child-rescue organizations?
6. List the advantages and disadvantages of placing refugee children in private homes as opposed to hostels. Why was it necessary for so many refugee child hostels to be opened in Britain?
7. What principles guided Rabbi Solomon Schonfeld in his rescue endeavors for refugee children? In what sense did the battle over the guardianship of these children serve as the climax of his organization's efforts?
8. Why did the British government intern Jewish refugee teenagers from Germany? How could they not understand that these children were enemies of Nazi Germany and treat them accordingly?
9. What were the most difficult adjustments for most of the Jewish refugee children coming to Britain?
10. What is meant by the phrase "triumphant narrative" that is used to describe many of the former *Kinder*'s memoirs and the early books dealing with the rescue of Jewish refugee children to Britain? What parts of their experiences were often missing in these descriptions of their rescue and later lives? Why were these parts missing?

Bibliography

Primary Sources

Archives

American Friends Service Committee Archives, Philadelphia, USA
AFSC general file—Relief General

The Wiener Library, London, England
Central British Fund Archives
21/1/20 Council for German Jewry Executive Committee Minutes
27/28/153 Refugee Children's Movement, Annual Reports
27/28/154 Refugee Children's Movement, Bunce Court School
27/28/155 Refugee Children's Movement, Instructions for the Guidance of Regional and Local Committees
27/28/156 Refugee Children's Movement, John Presland, *A Great Adventure*
27/28/158 Refugee Children's Movement, Lord Gorell—Legal Guardianship, Deed of Apprenticeship
27/28/161 Refugee Children's Movement, Religious Teaching Sub/committee minutes,11 June 1941–June 1949
27/28/163 Refugee Children's Movement, Report on a Visit to the Isle of Man, Internee Camps
27/28/164 Refugee Children's Movement, Memoranda and Articles of Association
27/28/166 Refugee Children's Movement, Executive Committee Minutes and Papers, 1940–1943
27/29/167 Refugee Children's Movement, Executive Committee Minutes and Papers, 1944–1958
27/29/169 Refugee Children's movement, Correspondence

Kindertransport Reunion Documents

1368/2/7/ ABC Reunion of Kindertransport Documents, 1987–2002

The Central Zionist Archives, Jerusalem, Israel

S7—782 Palestine Office (London) Hachshara 1938–1939
S 75—1173 Jewish Refugee Children in London
S 75—1174 Refugees Correspondence with Mordechai Shattner
S 75—1638 Correspondence with London Youth Aliyah Offices
S 75—1639 Correspondence with London Youth Aliyah Offices
S 75—1640 Correspondence with London Youth Aliyah Offices
S 75—1643 Correspondence with London Youth Aliyah Offices
S 75—1644 Correspondence with London Youth Aliyah Offices
S 75—1645 Correspondence with London Youth Aliyah Offices
S 75—1646 Correspondence with London Youth Aliyah Offices
S 75—1647 Correspondence with London Youth Aliyah Offices

Franklin Delano Roosevelt Library, Hyde Park, NY, USA

FDR—President's Personal File (PPF 4840)
OF 3186—Clippings

Heichal Yahaduth Wohlyn, Yad Vashem Givatayim, Israel

1895/127 Ervin Lichtenstein (Interview in German)

Imperial War Museum, London, England

Poster exhibit at the "Women at War" exhibition, the Imperial War Museum, London (15 October 2003–18 April 2004). http://www.iwm.org.uk/upload/package/41/women/displays.htm

Labor Party Archives, Beit Berl, Moshav Tzofit, Israel

38/23(1938) Mapai Central Committee Minutes

The Leo Baeck Institute Archives, New York, USA

AR A.1068/3686, Unterrichts Anstalten Gross-Breesen

Public Record Office, Kew, London, England

HO 144/21262 (1939)
HO 213/1627 (1933)
CAB 24/239 (1933)
CAB 23/96 (1938)
PREM 1/326 (1938)
FO 371/22527 (1938)
FO 371/22536, W 15037/104/98 (1938)
FO 371/24085 (1938)

Bibliography

Religious Kibbutz Archives (RKA), Kevutzat Yavneh, Israel

933.68 (42)—1, 7, 11 Hachshara Centers in Britain
15—83   Hachshara Centers in Britain
15—84   Hachshara Centers in Britain

Yad Vashem Archives (YVA), Jerusalem, Israel

The Munk Archives P/15/2; P/15/9
E/188 Hanna Bergas (Testimony)
03/2384 Dr. Elchanan Hans Blumenthal (Testimony)
02/473 Edgar From (Testimony)
Wiener Library Series: 02/626 Gertruida Wijsmuller-Meijer

The Public General Acts and The Church Assembly Measures (Statutes)

1914 The Aliens Restriction Act
1919 The Aliens Restriction Act (Amendment)
1926 The Adoption of Children Act
1930 The Adoption of Children (Scotland)
1941 The Temporary Migration of Children (Guardianship) Act
1944 The Guardianship (Refugee Children) Act

United Kingdom Parliamentary and Command Papers

Hansard, 5th Series, Parliamentary Debates, House of Lords, House of Commons:
395 Lords Deb. (1943)
396 Lords Deb. (1944)
397 Lords Deb. (1944)
341 HC Deb. (1938)
342 HC Deb. (1938)
351 HC Deb. (1939)
360 HC Deb. (1940)
The Home Office, Categories of Persons Eligible for Release from Internment: German and Austrian Civilian Internees (London, HMSO, July 1940) Cmd. 6217.
The Home Office, Categories of Persons Eligible for Release from Internment: German and Austrian Civilian Internees (London, HMSO, August 1940) Cmd. 6223.
The Home Office, Civilian Internees of Enemy Nationality: Categories of Persons Eligible for Release from Internment (London, HMSO, November 1940), Cmd. 6223.

United States Government Publications

Congressional Record v. 80 (1939–40).
FRUS diplomatic papers, general: 1938 I Washington: US Government Printing Office, 1938.

Reports of Refugee Organizations

Association of Jewish Refugees in Great Britain—Untitled Pamphlet, London: AJR, 1942.
Association of Jewish Refugees in Great Britain, *Britain's New Citizens: The Story of Refugees from Germany and Austria 1941–1951*, London: AJR, 1952.
Bulletin of the Co-ordinating Committee for Refugees, April 1939, London 1939.
The Caring for Child Refugees, London: Christian Council for Refugees from Germany and Central Europe, 1939.
The Child Estranging Movement: An Expose on the Alienation of Jewish Refugee Children in Great Britain from Judaism. London: Union of Orthodox Hebrew Congregations, 1944.
Movement for the Care of Children from Germany, Ltd. *First Annual Report*, n.d. London 1940.
Movement for the Care of Children from Germany, Ltd. *Second Annual Report*, n.d. London 1941.
Refugee Children's Movement Ltd. *Third Annual Report 1941–1942*.
Whittingehame Farm School, Ltd. First Annual Report, 31 January 1940.

Author's Interviews

Joan Barash, Tel Aviv, 22 March 1980.
Cita Bental (telephone), 10 June 2011.
Chedva Tipperberg Ben-Yashar (telephone), 10 June 2011.
Avner Gilboa (telephone), 12 June 2011.
Chana Gilboa (telephone), 15 May 2011.
Edgar and Marjorie Hall, Tel Aviv, 30 April 1980.
Arieh Handler, Tel Aviv, 21 June 1980, 16 July 1980.
David Heinemann, Jerusalem, 22 December 2010.
Gertrude Mannheim Kirsch, Jerusalem, 9 December 2010.
Manfred Kirsch, Jerusalem, 9 December 2010.
Lillian Klein, Tel Aviv, 16 January 1980, 22 January 1980.
Bernard Kupferman, Jerusalem, 5 December 2010.
Chava Laufer (telephone), 10 June 2011.
Grete Marcus, New York, 7 May, 2008.
Gerda Margulies, Tel Aviv, 16 December 1979.
Chava Markowitz, Tel Aviv, 9 January 1980, 22 January 1980.
Hilda Matzdorf, Jerusalem, 3 December 1981.
Freida Mertzbach, Tel Aviv, 22 January 1980.
Eva Michaelis-Stern, Jerusalem, 2 February 1980, 18 February 1980.
Steffi Birnbaum Schwartz, Jerusalem, 5 August 2010.
Hilda Schmerler, Ramat Gan, 18 July 1980.
Rev. William W. Simpson, Jerusalem, 22 June 1980.

Prof. Daniel Sperber, Ramat Gan, 22 April 1981.
Yitzhak Talmon, Kfar Saba, 11 August 1980.
Norbert Wollheim, New York, 11 April 1981.
Boaz Wreschner, Ramat Gan, 5 December 1979.

Correspondence

Author's correspondence with Elaine Laski Blond, July 1980.
Author's correspondence with Edith Bloomberg, 22 May, 1980.
Author's correspondence with Fred Dunston (formerly Fritz Deutsch, *madrich* at the Great Engham Farm), 20 June 1980.
Private correspondence between Dr. Leonore Goldschmidt and Dr. Joseph Walk, 20 January 1967.
Author's correspondence with Anita Grosz, 24 January 2011.
Author's correspondence with Bertha Kahn, sister of Anna Essinger, May 1980.
Author's Correspondence with Gerda Katzenstein-Kazir, February 1980.
Author's correspondence with Eva Michaelis-Stern, February 1980.
Author's correspondence with Anne Salinger, 15 June 2011.
Author's correspondence with Nachman Schaeffer, 22 May 1980.
Private correspondence between Theo Vered (Verderber) and Joseph Haberer, 30 August 2010.
Author's correspondence with Woburn House Archives, February 1980.

Newspapers and Periodicals

AJS Kindertransport newsletter
Chayenu (Bachad Bulletin)
Contemporary Jewish Record
The Daily Express
The Daily Herald
The Daily Mail
The Daily Telegraph
Dapim Lamadrich: For the Education of the Hachsharat Hanoar
Ha'aretz
Hatzofeh
The Jewish Chronicle
The Jewish Weekly
The London Times
The New York Times
The Observer

Oral History Division, Institute for Contemporary Jewry, The Hebrew University of Jerusalem

Solomon Adler-Rudel, OHD), 17(27)
Yocheved Bar Rachel (OHD) 38 (27)
Adolphine Bernstein OHD 18(27)
Joseph Heinemann (OHD) 52(27)
Giora Lotan (OHD) 49 (27)
Raanan Malitz (OHD), 21(27)
Eva Michaelis (OHD) 16 (27)
Henry Pels, OHD, 35(27)
Kathe Rosenheim,OHD 63(27)
Herta Souhami, OHD 50(27)

Questionnaires

Ellen R. Alexander
Joachim L. Auerbach
Gabrielle Ben-Ron
Hannelore Bergenthal
Ruth Berkley
Zeev Berkley
Harry Curtis
Betty Edr
Henny Eva Einstein
Ruth L. Finch
H.G.
G.G.
Hanna Gilboa
Ruth Golan
Mordechai Goldfaden
Noemi Kalisch
Ruth Kirschbaum
Sonja Kupferschmid
Tanya Lester
Eva Levy
Binyamin Malachi
Chava Markowitz
Nehemia Markowitz
Ursula H. Mendell
Naomi Peritz
Tova Perlow
Klara Pipel

Getty Batya Rabin
Hetty Raz
Nachman Schaeffer
Ilsa Schatkin
Klara Scheck
Augusta Shifrin
Miriam Spielman
Henry Stein
Gertrude Urman
Ernst Valfer
Edith H. Visni
Ruth Weinbach

Encyclopedias, Almanachs, Yearbooks

Whittaker's Almanach (1938–1946)
The Jewish Yearbook, London (1939–1946)
American Jewish Yearbook, New York: American Jewish Committee (1939–1946)

Films

Mark Jonathan Harris (dir.), *Into the Arms of Strangers: Stories of the Kindertransport* (2000)
Melissa Hacker (dir.), *My Knees Were Jumping* (1997)
Sue Read and Jim Goulding, *The Children Who Cheated the Nazis*, British documentary film shown first on channel 4 (2000)
Kate Kranz (dir), *Maybe I Was Lucky* (2002)
Holocaust Day: A Haven in Wales, a BBC documentary broadcast on BBC2 Wales on Holocaust day 2005
All My Loved Ones (*Vsichni moji blzci*) (1999)
The Power of Good: Nicholas Winton (*Sila lidskosti—Nicholas Winton*) (2002)

Plays

Kindertransport 1993
Memory 2006
My Heart in a Suitcase 2006
The End of Everything Ever 2008

Secondary Sources

Articles and Books

Abella, Irving, and Harold Troper. *None Is Too Many: Canada and the Jews of Europe 1933-1948*. Toronto: Lester and Orpan Dennys, 1982.

Adler-Rudel, Solomon. "The Evian Conference on the Refugee Question." *Leo Baeck Institute Year Book* 13 (1968), 235-73.

Agar, Herbert. *The Saving Remnant: An Account of Jewish Survival since 1914*. New York: Viking Press, 1960.

Alderman, Geoffrey. *Modern British Jewry*. Oxford: Clarendon Press, 1998.

Angell, Norman, and Dorothy F. Buxton. *You and the Refugee: The Morals and Economics of the Problem*. Harmondsworth: Penguin, 1939.

Angress, Werner T. "Auswanderlehrgut Gross-Breesen." *Leo Baeck Institute Yearbook* 10 (1965), 170-79.

Ansbacher, Mordechai. "Rescue and Return: Post-Kristallnacht 'German-Jewish' Refugee Children in Belgium and Their Return to Germany in 1941." In *Belgium and the Holocaust: Jews, Belgians, Germans*, edited by Dan Michman, 433-43. Jerusalem: Yad Vashem, 1998.

Apfel, Roberta J., and Bennett Simon (eds.), *Minefields in their Hearts: The Mental Health of Children in War and Communal Violence*. New Haven, CT: Yale University Press, 1996.

Arbabzadah, Nushin (ed.), *From Outside In: Refugees and British Society—an Anthology of Writings by Refugees on Britain and Britishness*. London: Arcadia Books, 2006.

Association of Jewish Refugees in Great Britain. *Dispersion and Resettlement: The Story of the Jews from Central Europe*. London: AJR, 1959.

Bailey, J. E. Brenda, *A Quaker Couple in Nazi Germany: Leonhard Friedrich Survives Buchenwald*. York: William Sessions, 1994.

Baker, Leonard. *Days of Sorrow and Pain: Leo Baeck and the Berlin Jews*. New York: Macmillan, 1978.

Barnard, Jacqueline. *The Children You Gave Us*. New York: Jewish Care Association, 1973.

Barnett, Ruth. "The Other Side of the Abyss: A Psychodynamic Approach to Working with Groups of People Who Came to England as Children on the Kindertransporte." *British Journal of Psychotherapy* 12 (1995): 175-94.

Bartrop, Paul R. "Not a Problem for Australia: The *Kristallnacht* viewed from the Commonwealth, November 1938." *Australian Jewish Historical Society Journal* 10, no. 6 (1989): 489-99.

Bauer, Barbara, and Waltraud Strickhausen (eds.). *"Fuer ein Kind war das anders": Traumatische Erfahrungen juedischer Kinder und Jugendlicher im nationalsozialistischen Deutschland*. Berlin: Metropol Verlag, 1999.

Bauer, Yehuda, *My Brother's Keeper: A History of the American Jewish Joint Distribution Committee 1929-1939*. Philadelphia: JPS, 1974.
Baumel, Judith Tydor. "The Adoption Plan of Children from Germany 1938" (Heb.). In *Dappim Leheker Tekufat Hashoah* 3 (Haifa University/Ghetto Fighters House, 1985), 212-29.
———. "Great Britain and the Jewish Refugee Children," *European Judaism* 15 (Winter 1981): 19-25.
———. "Strange Bedfellows: The Revisionist Movement and Agudath Israel during the Holocaust" (Heb.). *Iyunim Betikumat Yisrael* 12 (2003): 465-92.
———. "Twice a Refugee: Jewish Refugee Children in Britain during Evacuation 1939-1943." *Jewish Social Studies* 45 (Spring 1983): 174-84.
———. *Unfulfilled Promise: Rescue and Resettlement of Jewish Refugee Children in the United States 1934-1945*. Juneau, AK: Denali, 1990.
——— (ed.). *Loving and Beloved: The Diary of Susi Adler, a Child of the Kindertransport* (Heb.). Jerusalem: Yad Vashem, 2004.
Bekkers, René. "Its Not All in the Ask: Effects and Effectiveness in Recruitment Strategies Used by Nonprofits in the Netherlands." Paper presented at the 34th Arnova Annual Conference, Washington DC, 18 November 2005.
———. "Traditional and Health-Related Philanthropy: The Role of Resources and Personality." *Social Psychology Quarterly* 69, no. 4 (2006): 349-66.
Bekkers, René, and Pamala Weipking. "Generosity and Philanthropy: A Literature Review" (28 October 2007), available at SSRN http://ssrn.com/abstract=1015507.
———. "To Give or Not to Give ... That is the Question." *Nonprofit and Voluntary Sector Quarterly* 35, no. 3 (2006): 533-40.
Bennathan, Esra. "Die demographische und wirtschaftliche struktur der Juden." In *Entscheidungsjahr 1932: zur judenfrage in der endphase der Weimarer Republik*. Edited by Werner E. Mosse. Tuebingen: Mohr (Siebeck), 1966.
Bentwich, Norman. *Jewish Youth Comes Home*. London: Victor Gollancz, 1944.
———. *My 77 Years*. London: Routledge and Kegan Paul, 1962.
———. *The Refugees from Germany*. London: G. Allen and Unwin, 1936.
———. *The Rescue and Achievement of Refugee Scholars*. The Hague: M. Nijhoff, 1953.
———. *Wanderer between Two Worlds*. London: K. Paul Trench and Trubner, 1941.
———. *Wanderer in War 1939-4*. London: Victor Gollancz, 1946.
Benz, Ute. "Traumatization through Separation: Loss of Family and Home as Childhood Catastrophes." *Shofar* 23, no. 1 (2004): 85-99.
Benz, Wolfgang, Claudia Curio, and Andrea Hammel. *Kindertransports 1938/39- Rescue and Integration*. A special edition of *Shofar* 23, no. 1 (Fall 2004).
Berger, George M. "Australia and the Refugees." *The Australian Quarterly* 13, no. 44 (December 1941): 52-60.
Bermant, Chaim. *Coming Home*. London: Allen and Unwin, 1976.

———. *The Cousinhood: The Anglo-Jewish Gentry.* London: Eyre and Spottiswoode, 1971.

———. *Troubled Eden: An Anatomy of British Jewry.* London: Vallentine Mitchell, 1969.

Bielefeld, Wolfgang, Patrick Rooney, and Cathy Steinberg. In *Gifts of Time and Money in America's Communities*, edited by Arthur Brooks, 127–58. Lanham, MD: Rowman and Littlefield, 2005.

Blond, Anthony. *Jew Made in England.* London: Timewell Press, 2007.

Blond, Elaine, with Barry Turner. *Marks of Distinction: The Memoirs of Elaine Blond.* London: Vallentine Mitchell, 1988.

Bolchover, Richard. *British Jewry and the Holocaust.* Cambridge: Cambridge University Press, 1993.

Boyarin, Jonathan (ed.). *Remapping Memory: The Politics of Timespace.* Minneapolis: University of Minnesota Press, 1994.

Bradman, Tony. *Give Me Shelter: An Asylum Seeker's Anthology.* London: Frances Lincoln Children's Books, 2007.

Brody, David. "American Jewry, the Refugees and Immigration Restrictions (1932–1942). In *The Jewish Experience in America*, vol. 5, edited by Abraham J. Karp, 339–44. Waltham, MA: American Jewish Historical Society, 1969.

Brotman, Adolph G. "Jewish Communal Organizations." In *Jewish Life in Modern Britain*, edited by Julius Gould and Shaul Esh, 5–17. London: Routledge and Kegan Paul, 1964.

Brown, Eleanor. "College, Social Capital and Charitable Giving." In *Gifts of Time and Money in America's Communities*, edited by Arthur Brooks, 185–204. Lanham, MD: Rowman and Littlefield.

Bryant, W. Keith, Haekyung Jeon-Slaughter, Hyojin Kang, and Aaron Tax. "Participation in Philanthropic Activities: Donating Money and Time." *Journal of Consumer Policy* 26 (2003): 43–73.

Butler, Judith. *Gender Trouble: Feminism and the Subversion of Identity.* New York: Routledge, 1990.

Buxton, Dorothy Frances, and Sir Norman Angell. *The Economics of the Refugee Problem.* London: The Focus Publishing Company, 1939.

Carroll, James, Siobhan McCarthy, and Carol Newman. "An Econometric Analysis of Charitable Donations in the Republic of Ireland." *The Economic and Social Review* 23, no. 3 (2006): 229–49.

Castendyck, Elsa. "Refugee Children in Europe." *Social Service Review* (Chicago) (December 1939): 587–601.

Chang, Wen-Chun. "Determinants of Donations: Empirical Evidence from Taiwan." *The Developing Economies* 43, no. 2 (2005): 217–34.

Chappell, Connery. *Island of Barbed Wire.* London: Robert Hale, 1984.

Chodorow, Nancy. *The Reproduction of Mothering: Psychoanalysis and the Sociology of Gender.* Berkeley: University of California Press, 1978.

Churchill, Winston S. *The Second World War: Their Finest Hour*, vol. 2. Cambridge: Cambridge University Press, 1949.
Clapper, Raymond. "Let's Save the Children." *Washington Daily News*, 6 July 1940.
Cohen, Joseph L. *Salvaging German Jewry: A Guide to Those Who Wish to Help*. London: The Jewish Chronicle, 1939.
Curio, Claudia. *Verfolgung, Flucht, Rettung: Die Kindertransporte 1938/39 Nach Grossbritannien*. Berlin: Metropol, 2006.
Deakin, Nicholas. "Besieging Jericho: Episodes from the Early Career of Françoise Lafitte (1931–1945). *Cercles* (occasional paper series, 2004, 28p.). Accessed 7 February 2011 from http://cercles.com/n11/deakin.pdf.
Drucker, Olga Levy. *Kindertransport*. New York: Henry Holt and Company, 1992.
Drucker, Peter F. *Management: Tasks, Responsibilities, Practices*. Oxford: Butterworth Heinemann, 1974.
Dubrowsky, Gertrude W. *Six from Leipzig: Kindertransport and the Cambridge Refugee Children's Committee*. London: Vallentine and Mitchell, 2003.
Echt, Samuel. *Die Geschichte der Juden in Danzig*. Leer: Rautenberg, 1972.
Elath, Eliahu, Norman Bentwich, and Doris May (eds.). *Memories of Sir Wyndham Deedes*. London: Gollancz in association with the Anglo-Israel Association, 1958.
"Elderly Jews Re-create Kindertransport Trip." *Ha'aretz*, 4 September 2009.
Emanuel, Muriel, and Vera Gissing. *Nicholas Winton and the Rescued Generation*. London and Portland, OR: Vallentine Mitchell, 2001.
Emerson, Herbert. "Postwar Problems of Refugees." *Foreign Affairs* 21, no. 2 (January 1943): 219.
Endelman, Todd M. *The Jews of Georgian England 1714–1830: Tradition and Change in a Liberal Society*. Philadelphia: JPS, 1979.
Essinger, Anna. *Bunce Court School 1933–1943*, pamphlet, n.p., n.d.
"The Evacuation of Refugee Children Our Responsibility." *Social Studies Review* (1940): 547.
Fast, Vera. *Children's Exodus: A History of the Kindertransport*. London: Taurus, 2011.
Feidel-Mertz, Hildegard. "Integration and Formation of Identity: Exile Schools in Great Britain." *Shofar* 23, no. 1 (2004): 71–84.
———. *Schulen im Exil: Die verdraengte Paedagogik nach 1933*. Reinbek bei Hamburg: Rowohlt Verlag, 1983.
Feingold, Henry L. *The Politics of Rescue: The Roosevelt Administration and the Holocaust, 1938–1945*. New Brunswick, NJ: Rutgers University Press, 1970.
Fishman, Isidore, and Harold Levy. "Jewish Education in Great Britain." In *Jewish Life in Modern Britain*, edited by Julius Gould and Shaul Esh, 67–92. London: Routledge and Kegan Paul, 1964.
Forbes-Robertson, Diana, and Roger W. Jr. Strauss (eds.). *War Letters from Britain*. New York: Putnam, 1941.

Fox, Anne L. *My Heart in a Suitcase*. London: Vallentine Mitchell, 1996.
Fraser, Charles F. *Control of Aliens in the British Commonwealth of Nations*. London: The Hogarth Press, 1940.
Freedman, Maurice (ed.). *A Minority in Britain: Social Studies of the Anglo-Jewish Community*. London: Vallentine and Mitchell, 1955.
Friedenfeld, Gerard. "Lola Hahn-Warburg: My Successful Guardian Angel." *The Jewish Chronicle*, 29 March 2010.
Friedenson, Joseph. *Heroine of Rescue: The Incredible Story of Recha Sternbuch Who Saved Thousands from the Holocaust*. New York: Artscroll/Mesorah, 1984.
Friedman, Edie, and Reva Klein. *Reluctant Refuge: The Story of Asylum in Britain*. London: British Library Publishing Division, 2008.
Friedman, Saul S. *No Haven for the Oppressed: United States Policy towards Jewish Refugees, 1938-1945*. Detroit: Wayne State University Press, 1973.
Freud, Anna, and Dorothy T. Burlingham. *War and Children*, edited by Philip R. Lehrman. Westport, CT: Greenwood Press, 1973 [originally 1943].
Fry, Helen. *The King's Most Loyal Enemy Aliens: Germans Who Fought for Britain in the Second World War*. Stroud: Sutton Publishing, 2007.
Gainer, Bernard. *The Alien Invasion: The Origins of the Aliens Act of 1905*. London: Heinemann Educational Books, 1972.
Gannon, Franklin Reid. *The British Press and Germany, 1936-1939*. Oxford: Clarendon, 1971.
Gartner, Lloyd P. *The Jewish Immigrant in England, 1870-1914*. Detroit: Wayne State University Press, 1960.
Gelber, Yoav. "Zionist Policy and the Fate of European Jewry (1939-1942)." In *Yad Vashem Studies* 13 (1979), edited by Livia Rothkirchen: 169-210.
Genizi, Haim. "American Non-sectarian Refugee Relief Organizations." *Yad Vashem Studies* 11 (1976): 164-220.
Gershon, Karen. *A Lesser Child*. London: Peter Owen, 1994
———. *A Tempered Wind (Jewish Lives)*, edited by Phyllis Lassner and Peter Lawson. Evanston, IL: Northwestern University Press, 2010.
———. *We Came as Children: A Collective Autobiography*. London: Papermac, 1966.
Gilbert, Martin. *The Boys*. London: Holt, 1998.
Gilbert, Martin, and Richard Gott. *The Appeasers*. London: Weidenfeld and Nicolson, 1963.
Gilligan, Carol. *In a Different Voice*. Cambridge, MA and London: Harvard University Press, 1982.
Gillman, Peter, and Leni Gillman. *Collar the Lot: How Britain Interned and Expelled Its Wartime Refugees*. London: Quartet Books, 1980.
Goepfert, Rebekka. *Der Juedische Kindertransport von Deutschland nach England 1938/39, Geschichte und Errinerung*. Frankfurt a/m and New York: Campus Verlag, 1999.

——— (ed.) . *Ich Kam Allein: die Rettung von Zehntausend juedischen Kindern.* Munich, Dtv, 1994.
Goldstein, Joseph, Anna Freud, and Albert J. Solnit. *Beyond the Best Interests of the Child.* New York: The Free Press, 1973.
Goldwyn, Robert M., "The Indestructible Bacillus Bureaucraticus." *Plastic and Reconstructive Surgery: Journal of the American Society of Plastic Surgeons* 114 (Oct. 2004): 46–48.
Gottlieb, Amy Zahl. *Men of Vision: Anglo-Jewry's Aid to Victims of the Nazi Regime, 1933–1945.* London: Weidenfeld and Nicolson, 1998.
Graves, Robert, and Alan Hodge. *The Long Weekend: A Social History of Great Britain, 1918–1939.* New York: Macmillan, 1940.
Grunfeld, Judith. *Shefford: The Story of a Jewish School Community in Evacuation, 1939–1945.* Essex: The Anchor Press, 1980.
Guske, Iris. Trauma and Attachment in the Kindertransport Context: German-Jewish Child Refugees' Account of Displacement and Acculturation in Great Britain. Newcastle upon Tyne: Cambridge Scholars Publishing, 2009.
Gutman, Yisrael et al. (eds.), *Rescue Attempts during the Holocaust: Proceedings of the Second Yad Vashem International Holocaust Conference, Jerusalem, April 1974.* Jerusalem. Yad Vashem, 1977.
Habbas, Bracha. *Sefer Aliyat Hanoar* (Heb.). Jerusalem: Aliyat Hanoar, 1941.
Harris, Mark Jonathan, and Deborah Oppenheimer. *Into the Arms of Strangers: Stories of the Kindertransport.* London: Bloomsbury, 2000.
Hasson, Nir, and Yehuda Lahav, "Jews Saved by U.K. Stockbroker to Reenact 1939 Journey to Safety," *Haaretz*, 9 September 2009 http://www.haaretz.com/jewish-world/news/jews-saved-by-u-k-stockbroker-to-reenact-1939-journey-to-safety-1.283126.
Hedgepeth, Sonja M., and Rochelle G. Saidel (eds.). *Sexual Violence against Jewish Women during the Holocaust.* Waltham, MA: Brandeis, 2010.
Homa, Bernard. *Orthodoxy in Anglo-Jewry 1880–1940: The Story of Machzike Adath.* London: Vallentine and Co., 1953.
Hurewitz, J. C. *The Struggle for Palestine.* New York: Schocken, 1976.
Information Relating to the General Welfare of Refugees from Nazi Oppression. Pamphlet, London, May 1980, p. 19.
Jackson, Harold. "Anna's Children." *The Guardian*, July 18, 2003.
Jackson, Robin. "The Camphill Movement: The Vision of Karl Koenig." *Encounter: Education for Meaning and Social Justice* 19, no. 3 (2006): 45–48.
Jennings, W. Ivor. *The British Constitution.* 3rd edition. Cambridge: University Press, 1950.
"Jewish Children in Vienna." *The Jewish Frontier*, New York, January 1939, p. 10.
Jones, Michael, and Michael McKee. "Feedback Information and Contributions for Not-for-Profit Enterprises: Experimentational Investigations and Implications for Large-Scale Fund Raising." *Public Finance Review* 32, no. 5 (2004): 512–27.

Jones, Rufus M. *A Service of Love in Wartime: American Friends Relief Work in Europe, 1917-1919.* London: Macmillan, 1920.
Jong, Louis de. *The German Fifth Column in the Second World War.* Chicago: University of Chicago Press, 1956.
"Journey to Survival." *Atmosphere*, August 2010, p. 54.
Judex. *Anderson's Prisoners.* London: Gollancz, 1940.
"Jüdisches Hilfswerk in England." *Jüdisches Nachrichtenblatt* 3, May 1939, p. 1.
Judt, Tony. "Words." *The New York Review of Books* 57, no. 12 (July 15–August 18, 2010): 4.
Kadosh, Sara. "Jewish Refugee Children in Switzerland, 1939–1950." In *Remembering for the Future: The Holocaust in an Age of Genocides*, edited by John K. Roth et al. New York: Palgrave, 2001, 281–97.
Kaplan, Marion. *German-Jewish Refugees in England: The Ambiguities of Assimilation.* New York: St. Martins Press, 1984.
Karbach, Oskar. "The Liquidation of the Jewish Community of Vienna." *Jewish Social Studies* 2 (1940): 255–78.
Kaye, Lucie. *Burning for the Cause—the Centenary Celebration of Lola Hahn-Warburg, 1901–1989.* Oxford: First Edition, 2001.
Kershen, Anne J., and Jonathan A. Romain. *Tradition and Change: A History of Reform Judaism in Britain, 1840–1995.* London and Portland, OR: Vallentine Mitchell, 1995.
Kessler, Edward. "Claude Montifiore and Liberal Judaism." *European Judaism* 34 (2001): 17–32.
Kindertransport: A Special Interest Group of the Association of Jewish Refugees, April 2010, p. 10. http://www.ajr.org.uk/documents/KT_Newsletter_Ap_2010.pdf. (accessed 18 September 2011).
Kleine-Ahlbrandt, Wm. Laird. *Bitter Prerequisites: A Faculty for Survival from Nazi Terror.* West Lafayette, IN: Purdue University Press, 2001.
Kley, Stefan. "Hitler and the Pogrom of November 9–10, 1938." *Yad Vashem Studies* 28 (2000): 87–112.
Kobler, Franz. "From the Activities of the Jews in England 1933–1943" (Heb.). *Metzudah* (Book 2), December 1943, p. 225.
Koch, Eric. *Deemed Suspect.* Toronto: Methuen, 1980.
Kochan, Lionel. *Pogrom, 10 November 1938.* London: Andre Deutsch, 1957.
Koessler, Maximillian. "Enemy Alien Internment." *Political Science Quarterly* 57, no. 1 (March 1942): 98–127.
Kranzler, David. *Holocaust Hero: Solomon Schonfeld.* Jersey City, NJ: Ktav, 2004.
Kranzler, David, and Gertrude Hirschler. *Solomon Schonfeld: His Page in History.* New York: Judaica, 1982.
Kroeger, Marianne. "Child Exiles: A New Research Area?" *Shofar* 23, no. 1 (2004): 8–20.
Kulischer, Eugene M. *The Displacement of Population in Europe.* Montreal, International Labor Office, 1943.

———. *Europe on the Move*. New York: Columbia University Press, 1948.
Kushner, Tony, *The Persistence of Prejudice: Anti-Semitism in British Society during the Second World War*. Manchester: Manchester University Press, 1989.
Kushner, Tony, and David Cesarani. "Island of Aliens." *The Jewish Chronicle*, 27 July 1990, p. 6.
Lafitte, Françoise. *The Internment of Aliens*. London, Penguin, 1940.
Landry, Craig E., Andreas Lange, John A. List, Michael K. Price, and Nicholas G. Rupp. "Towards an Understanding of the Economics of Charity: Evidence from a Field Experiment." *The Quarterly Journal of Economics* 121, no. 2 (2006): 747–82.
Laski, Neville. *Jewish Rights and Jewish Wrongs*. London: Soncino, 1939.
Laqueur, Walter. *Generation Exodus: The Fate of Young Refugees from Nazi Germany*. Hanover, NH and London: Brandeis University Press, 2001.
Latané, Bibb, and John M. Darley. *The Unresponsive Bystander: Why Doesn't He Help?* New York: Appleton-Century Crofts, 1970.
Leshem, Peretz. *Strasse zur Rettung 1933–1939: aus Deutschland vertrieben–Bereitet sich Juedische Jugend auf Palestina vor*. Tel Aviv: Histadrut, 1973.
Leverton, Bertha, and Shmuel Lowensohn. *I Came Alone: The Stories of the Kindertransports*. London: Book Guild, 1990.
Levin, Nora. *The Holocaust*. New York: Schocken, 1968.
Liberlas, Robert. "The Origins of the Reform Movement in England." *AJS Review* 1 (1976): 121–50.
Lichtenstein, Erwin. *Die Juden der Freien Stadt Danzig unter der Herrschaft des Nazionalsozialismus*. Tuebingen: Mohr, 1973.
Lipman, Vivian D. *A History of the Jews in Britain since 1858*. New York: Holmes and Meier, 1990, 204–205.
Loewald, K. G. "A Dunera Internee at Hay 1940–1941." *Australian Historical Studies* 17, no. 69 (October 1977): 512–21.
London, Louise. *Whitehall and the Jews: 1933–1948*. Cambridge: Cambridge University Press, 2000.
Machover, Jonah. *Towards Rescue: The Story of Australian Jewry's Stand for the Jewish Cause 1940–1948*. Jerusalem: Institute of Contemporary Jewry, 1972.
Mandel, George. *In Memory of F. M. Friedmann*. 1978 (n.p.).
Marcus, Jacob R. *The Rise and Destiny of the German Jew*. New York: Ktav, 1971.
Margaliot, Abraham. "The Problem of the Rescue of German Jewry during the Years 1933–1939: The Reasons for the Delay in Their Emigration from the Third Reich." In *Rescue Attempts during the Holocaust*, edited by Yisrael Gutman et al., 247–65. Jerusalem: Yad Vashem, 1977.
Marks, Lara. "'Dear Old Mother Levy's: The Jewish Maternity Home and Sick Room Helps Society, 1895–1939." *Social History of Medicine* 3, no. 1 (1990): 61–88.

Marmur, Dow (ed.). *Reform Judaism: Essays on Reform Judaism in Britain*. London: Reform Synagogues of Great Britain, 1973, 16–41.
Martin, Douglas. "Ernst Bulova, 98, Founder of Camp with a Free Spirit." *The New York Times*, 28 January 2001.
Mazey, Mary Ellen, and David R. Lee (eds.). *Her Space, Her Place: A Geography of Women*. Washington DC: Association of American Geographers, 1983.
Mikula, Maja (ed.). *Women, Activism and Social Change*. Milton Park: Routledge, 2005.
Moorehead, Caroline. *Human Cargo: A Journey among Refugees*. London: Vintage, 2006.
Morse, Arthur D. *While Six Million Died: A Chronicle of American Apathy*. New York: Random House, 1967.
Mowat, Charles Loch. *Britain between the Wars, 1918–1940*. Chicago: University of Chicago Press, 1955.
Newman, Aubrey. "German Jews in Britain: A Prologue." In *Second Chance: Two Centuries of German Speaking Jews in the United Kingdom*, edited by Werner Eugen Mosse, Julius Carlebach, Gerhard Hirschfeld, Aubrew Newman, Arnold Paucker, and Peter Pulzer, 31–36. Schriftenreihe wissenschaftlicher Abhandlungen des Leo Baeck Instituts volume 48, Tuebingen: J.C.B. Mohr (Paul Siebeck), 1991.
———. *The United Synagogue 1870–1970*. London: Routledge and Kegan Paul, 1985.
Newman, Jacob. *Kinder Transporte: A Study of Stresses and Traumas of Refugee Children*. Self-published, 1992.
Newsam, Sir Frank. *The Home Office*. London: George Allen and Unwin, 1954.
Ofir, Baruch Zvi. *Pinkas Hakehilot, Bavaria* (Heb.). Jerusalem: Yad Vashem, 1973.
Oldfield, Sybil. "'It is Usually She': The Role of British Women in the Rescue and Care of Kindertransport Kinder." *Shofar* 23, no. 1 (2004): 57–70.
Page, Arthur. *War and Alien Enemies: The Law Affecting Their Personal and Trading Rights and herein of Contraband of War and the Capture of Prizes at Sea*. 2nd. ed. London: Steven and Sons, 1915.
Palmer, Glen. "Seventeen Children: Australia's Response to German Jewish Refugee Children, 1933–1945." *Australian Jewish Historical Society Journal* 13, no. 1 (1995): 88–96.
Papanek, Ernst, and Edward Linn. *Out of the Fire*. New York: Morrow, 1975.
Patkin, Benzion. *The Dunera Internees*. Melbourne: Benmir Books, 1979.
Pearce, Robert D. *The Turning Point in Africa: British Colonial Policy 1938–48*. London: Frank Cass, 1982.
Peter, Laurence J. (ed.). *Peter's Quotations: Ideas for Our Times*. New York: Bantam Books, 1977.
Piliavin, Jane Allyn, and Hong-Wen Charg. "Altruism: A Review of Recent Theory and Research." *Annual Review of Sociology* 16 (1990): 27–65.

Presland, John [Gladys Bendit]. *A Great Adventure*. London: Bloomsbury House, 1944.
Presser, Jacob. *Ashes in the Wind: The Destruction of Dutch Jewry*. New York: Dutton, 1969.
Proudfoot, Malcolm. *European Refugees 1939-1952: A Study in Forced Population Movement*, London: Faber and Faber, 1957.
Reading, Eva Isaacs. *For the Record: The Memoirs of Eva, Marchioness of Reading*. London: Hutchinson, 1973.
Reed, Paul B., and L. Kevin Selbee. "Is There a Distinctive Pattern of Values Associated with Giving and Volunteering? The Canadian Case." Paper presented at the 32nd Arnova Conference, Montreal, Canada, 14-16 November 2002.
Roche, Thomas W. E. *The Key in the Lock: A History of Immigration Control in England from 1066 to the Present Day*. London: Murray, 1968.
Roehrs, Hermann (ed.). *Bildung als Wagnis und Bewaehrung: eine Darstellung des Lebenswerks von Kurt Hahn*. Heidelberg: Verlag Quelle & Meyer, 1966.
Rosenblatt, Roger. *Children of War*. Garden City, NY: Anchor, 1983.
Rosenthal, Erich. "Trends of the Jewish Population in Germany, 1870-1939." *Jewish Social Studies* 6 (1944): 233-74.
Roth, Cecil. "Economic Life and Population Movements." In *The World History of the Jewish People: The Dark Ages*, edited by Cecil Roth. Tel Aviv: Masada, 1966.
———. *History of the Jews*. New York: Schocken, 1961.
Rozien, Ron. "Herschel Grynszpan: The Fate of a Forgotten Assassin." *Holocaust and Genocide Studies* 1, no. 2 (1986): 217-28.
Rutter, Jill. *Refugee Children in the UK*. Milton Keynes: Open University Press, 1999.
Sadan, Inge. *No Longer a Stranger*. Inge Sadan: Jerusalem, 1999.
Saenger, Gerhart. *Today's Refugees, Tomorrow's Citizens*. New York: Harper and Brothers, 1941.
Samuel, Herbert Louis (1st Viscount Samuel). *Memoirs*. London: The Cresset Press, 1945.
Schewe, Donald B. (ed.). *Franklin D. Roosevelt and Foreign Affairs: Second Series, January 1, 1938-August 31, 1939*. New York: Clearwater, 1979.
Schimansky, Stefan K. "Refugee Children in England." *Contemporary Jewish Record* 2 (July-August 1939): 27.
Schonfeld, Solomon, *Jewish Religious Education*. London, CRREC, 1943.
Schroeder, David A., Louis A. Pennar, John F. Dovidio, and Jane Allyn Piliavin. *The Psychology of Helping and Altruism: Problems and Puzzles*. New York: McGraw-Hill, 1995.
Schwartz, Shalom H. "The Justice of Need and the Activation of Humanitarian Norms." *Journal of Social Issues* 31, no. 3 (1975): 111-36.
Schwarz-Bart, Andre. *The Last of the Just*. New York: Bantam, 1960.

Seller, Maxine Schwartz. *We Built up Our Lives: Education and Community among Jewish Refugees Interned by Britain in World War II*. Westport, CT and London: Greenwood Press, 2001.

Shamir, Haim. *Before the Holocaust: The Persecution of German Jewry and Public Opinion in Western Europe* (Heb.). Tel Aviv: Sifriyat Hapoalim, 1974.

Sharf, Andrew. *The British Press and Jews under Nazi Rule*. London: Oxford University Press, 1964.

Sharot, Stephen. "Reform and Liberal Judaism in London, 1840–1940." *Jewish Social Studies* 41, no. 3:4 (1979): 211–28.

Sharples, Caroline. "Reconstructing the Past: Refugee Writings on the *Kindertransport*." *Holocaust Studies: A Journal of Culture and History* 12, no. 3 (Winter 2006): 40–62.

Shatzker, Chaim. "The Jewish Youth Movement in Germany in the Holocaust Period (II): The Relations between the Youth Movement and Hechalutz," *Leo Baeck Institute Yearbook* 33, no. 1 (1988), 301–325.

Shatzkes, Pamela. *Holocaust and Rescue: Impotent or Indifferent? Anglo-Jewry 1938–1945*. London: Palgrave, 2002.

Shawyer, A. "Jewish Refugees in England" (Heb.). *Hagalgal* 1, no. 11 (3 Feb. 1944): 9.

Shepherd, Naomi. Introduction to *Wilfred Israel: German Jewry's Secret Ambassador*. London: Weidenfeld and Nicolson, 1984.

Sherman, Alan J. *Island Refuge: Britain and Refugees from the Third Reich, 1933–1939*. Berkeley: University of California Press, 1973.

Sherman, Alan J., and Shatzkes, Pamela. "Otto M. Schiff (1875–1952), Unsung Rescuer." *The Leo Baeck Institute Year Book* 54, no.1 (2009), 243–71.

Sichel, Freida H. *From Refugee to Citizen*. Capetown and Amsterdam: A. A. Balkema, 1966.

Simpson, Sir John Hope. *The Refugee Problem: Report of a Survey*. London: Institute of International Affairs, 1939.

———. *Refugees: A Review of the Situation since September 1938*. London: Royal Institute of International Affairs, 1939.

Singer, Elisabeth. *Children of the Apocalypse*. London: Hodder and Stoughton, 1967.

Smith, David Horton. "Voluntary Action and Voluntary Groups." *Annual Review of Sociology* 1 (1975): 247–70.

Solantus, Tytti. *Mental Health of Young People and the Threat of Nuclear War: Socioepidemiological and Activity Theoretical Studies*. Helsinki: Department of Public Health, Helsinki University, 1990.

Sompolinsky, Meir. *Britain and the Holocaust: The Failure of Anglo-Jewish Leadership*. Brighton: Sussex, 1999.

Sosnowsky, Kiryl. *The Tragedy of Children under Nazi Rule*. Warsaw: Zachodnia Agencja Prasowa, 1962.

Spier, Eugene. *The Protecting Power*. London: Skeffington and Sons, Ltd., 1951.

Stahl, Rudolph. "Vocational Retraining of Jews in Nazi Germany, 1933-1938." *Jewish Social Studies* 1, no. 2 (1939): 169-94.
Stein, Joshua B. *Britain and the Jews of Europe*. Ph.D. diss., St. Louis University, 1972. Ann Arbor: University Microfilms, 1972.
———. "Great Britain and the Evian Conference of 1938." *The Wiener Library Bulletin* 29 (London, 1976): 40-52.
Stein, Leonard, and C. C. Aronsfeld (eds.). *Leonard G. Montefiore in Memoriam*. London: Valentine, 1964.
Steinberg, Bernard. "Jewish Education in Great Britain during World War II." *Jewish Social Studies* 29 (1967): 27-63.
Stent, Ronald. *A Bespattered Page*. London: A. Deutsch, 1980.
Stevens, Austin. *The Dispossessed*. London: Barrie and Jenkins, 1975.
Stewart, Barbara M. *United States Government Policy on Refugees from Nazism 1933-1940*. Ph.D. diss., Columbia University, 1969.
Stoessinger, John George. *The Refugees and the World Community*. Minneapolis: University of Minnesota Press, 1956.
Strachey, Amy St. Loe. *Borrowed Children*. London: John Murray, 1940.
Styron, William. *Sophie's Choice*. New York: Random House, 1979.
Sylfield, Brian. "Earl Winterton: 47 Years Our MP." *The Horsham Society*, September 2007, http://www.horshamsociety.org/history/winterton.htm (accessed 22 August 2010).
Szajkowski, Zosa. "The Attitude of American Jewry to Refugees from Germany in the 1930s." *American Jewish Historical Quarterly* 61 (1971-2): 101-143.
Tartakower, Arieh, and Jurt R. Grossman. *The Jewish Refugee*. New York: Institute of Jewish Affairs, 1944.
Taylor, A. J. P. *English History 1914-1945*. Oxford: Clarendon, 1965.
Templewood, Viscount (Samuel John Gurney Hoare). *Nine Troubled Years*. London: Collins, 1954.
Thompson, Dorothy." "Refugees: A World Problem." *Foreign Affairs* (16 April 1938): 375-87.
———. *Refugees: Anarchy or Organization*. New York: Random House, 1938.
Thompson, Gertrud H. "The Dr. Leonore Goldschmidt Schule (1935-1941)." *Leo Baeck Institute Yearbook* 50 (2005): 301-352.
Tomlin, Chanan. *Protest and Prayer: Rabbi Dr. Solomon Schonfeld and Orthodox Jewish Responses in Britain to the Nazi Persecution of Europe's Jews 1942-1945*. Oxford: Peter Lang, 2006.
Turner, Barry. *And the Policeman Smiled: 10,000Children Escape from Nazi Germany*. London: Bloomsbury, 1990.
———. *One Small Suitcase: The True Story of how 10,000 Children Escaped the Nazi Holocaust*. London: Puffin 2003.
Umansky, Ellen M. "Liberal Judaism in England: The Contribution of Lily H. Montague." *Hebrew Union College Annual* 55 (1985): 309-322.

Walk, Joseph. *The Education of the Jewish Child in Germany: The Law and Its Implementation* (Heb.). Jerusalem: Yad Vashem, 1975.
Warrington, John (ed.). *Aristotle's Ethics*. London: Dent, 1963.
Wasserstein, Bernard. *Britain and the Jews of Europe, 1939–1945*. London: Institute of Jewish Affairs, 1979.
Wedgewood, Cicely Veronica. *The Last of the Radicals*. London: Jonathan Cape, 1951.
Weyl, Ruth. "W. W. Simpson, a Pioneer in Dialogue." *Jewish Christian Relations* 20, no. 3 (1987): 22–34.
Wheeler Bennett, John. *John Anderson: Viscount Waverly*. London: St. Martin's Press, 1962.
Wilson, Francesca. *They Came as Strangers*. London: Hamish Hamilton, 1959.
Wischnitzer, Mark. *To Dwell in Safety: The Story of Jewish Migration since 1800*. Philadelphia: JPS, 1948.
Wolfenden, Barbara. *Little Holocaust Survivors and the English School that Saved Them*. Oxford and Westport, CT: Greenwood, 2008.
Wyman, David. *Paper Walls: America and the Refugee Crisis, 1938–1941*. Amherst: University of Massachusetts Press, 1968.
Yahil, Leni. *The Rescue of Danish Jewry: Test of a Democracy*. Philadelphia: JPS, 1969.
———. "The Wanderings of the Jews from Germany, Austria and Czechoslovakia during the Years 1933–1939: Basic Problems and General Lines (Heb.). *Lectures of the 15th Historical Conference, Migration and Emigration in Jewish History and in World History*. Jerusalem: Mercaz Shazar, 1973, 103–123.
Zurndorfer, Hannele. *The Ninth of November*. London: Quartet Books, 1983.
Zuroff, Efraim. Response of Orthodox Jewry in the United States: The Activities of the Vaad Ha-Hatzala Rescue Committee, 1939–1945. Newark, NJ: Ktav, 2000.

Unpublished Manuscripts

Rothwell, Sidney. "Marianne Rothwell—A Victim of the Holocaust."
Singer, Charlotte. "My First Year in England: The Diary of a Refugee."

Unpublished M.A. and Doctoral Dissertations

Baumel, Judith. "The Jewish Refugee Children in Great Britain 1938–1945." M.A. thesis, Department of Jewish History, Bar-Ilan University, 1981.
Hill, Paula. "Anglo Jewry and the Refugee Children 1938–1945." Ph.D. dissertation, Royal Holloway College, University College London 2001.
Michman, Dan. "The Jewish Refugees from Germany in Holland between 1933 and 1940" (Heb.). Ph.D. dissertation, Hebrew University of Jerusalem, 1978.

Norton, Jennifer. "The Kindertransport: History and Memory." M.A. thesis presented to the History Department of the California State University at Sacramento, Fall 2010.

Riezel, Arieh. *The Reeducation of Jewish Child Holocaust victims in Belgian Live-In Educational Institutions* (Heb.) . M.A. thesis, Department of Jewish History, Bar Ilan University, Ramat-Gan, Israel, 1976.

Internet Sites

http://www.gwrychtrust.co.uk/html/operation_kindertransport.html (accessed May 29, 2011).

http://www.gordonstoun.org.uk/about/school-history (accessed August 22, 2010).

Ester Golan, Entry for Friday October 5, 2007, Youth Aliya and Kinder Transport. http://golanes.blogspot.com/2007/10/kinder-transport-kinder-transport.html (accessed 2 June 2011).

http://www.kindertransport.org/default.aspx (accessed 2 June 2011).

http://www.ajr.org.uk/kt-newsletters (accessed 2 June 2011).

http://www.kindertransport.org/history08_FoundingKTA.htm (accessed 2 June 2011).

http://www.kindertransport.org/exhibits_MQ.aspx (accessed 2 June 2011).

http://www.ajr.org.uk/documents/Kindertransport_talk_-_Sir_Martin_Gilbert_-_Nov_08.pdf (accessed 3 June 2011).

AJR *Kinder* database. http://www.ajr.org.uk/kindersurvey (accessed 3 June 2011).

http://www.ajr.org.uk/documents/KinderTransport_Survey_2007_Final_Databases_21Aug2009_-clean_results_deduped_renumbered.xls (accessed on 3 June 2011).

http://www.owalter.co.uk/acjr/index.htm (accessed 12 June 2011).

Index

Aberdeen, 30, 31
Abergele, 137, 146
Achduth, 220
Acland-Troyte, Gilbert John, 94
Adler, Hermann, 52
Adler, Susi, 124, 218
Adler-Rudel, Solomon, 56, 139
AFL, 61
Agudah Youth, 172
Agudath Israel World Organization, 28, 79
AKIM, 243
Alice, Princess of Greece, 232
Allard, Lorraine, 156, 158
Altman, Rabbi Alexander, 147
American Jewish Joint Distribution Committee, 36, 92
American Women's Committee for the Release of Ships for European Children, 175
Anderson, John, 144, 165, 182, 183, 194, 195
Anglo-Jewish Association, 35
Arctic Circle, 241
Aristotle, 240
Ashford, Kent, 144
Association of Jewish Refugees, 129, 230, 236
Astfalck, Nora, 32

Auschwitz, 217, 228, 229, 242
Australia, 3, 13, 34, 41, 46, 102, 110, 122, 131, 187, 188, 191, 192, 193, 227, 230, 241
Austria, 2, 3, 31, 41, 42, 43, 47, 49, 54, 56, 64, 67, 68, 73, 74, 78, 80, 81, 86, 87, 88, 90, 98, 108, 109, 121, 125, 129, 130, 174, 182, 183, 214, 222, 223, 241
Avrays, Harry, 15

Bachad, 138, 140, 145, 146, 147, 152, 172, 191, 217, 243
Baeck, Rabbi Leo, 105, 240
Bakstansky, Lavy, 37, 39
Baldwin, Stanley Earl, 63, 92, 93
Balfour, Arthur James, 141
Balfour, Robert Arthur Lytton (Viscount Traprain), 141
Balzac, Honoré de, 95
Baram, Myra, 15
Barash, Rae, 174
Barbican Mission to the Jews, 88, 212, 213
Battersea, 78
Behrendt, Edward, 231
Bekkers, René, 8, 37, 39, 40, 89, 159
Belfast, 146
Belgium, 5
Bell, Ernest, 84
Belsize Park, 3, 199

277

Beltane School, 31
Bendit, Francis, 37, 206
Bendit (Skelton, Williams), Gladys, 37, 40, 41, 56, 57, 206, 237
Ben-Gurion, David, 62
Bental, Cita, 234
Bentwich, Helen Caroline, 35, 40, 55, 56, 57
Bentwich, Norman De Mattos, 11, 35, 37, 39, 40, 67, 77, 84, 142, 237, 242
Ben-Yashar, Chedva Tipperberg, 235
Benz, Wolfgang, 14
Berger, G., 203
Berger, J. A., 113
Berghahn, Marion, 11
Berlin, 1, 23, 31, 42, 50, 52, 53, 58, 66, 67, 86, 90, 99, 101, 103, 104, 105, 106, 107, 110, 112, 122, 125, 130, 138, 144, 145, 162, 217, 222, 232, 233, 242
Berlin, Isaiah, 9
Bielefeld, 224
Birmingham, 24, 78, 111, 117, 158, 210
Birnbaum, Reenie, 1, 2, 3, 4, 23, 26, 28, 101, 102, 107, 112, 122, 123, 126, 157, 199, 217, 222, 244
Black, Martin, 86. 89
Bland, Neville, 183
Blend, Martha, 15
Blond, Bernard, 77
Blond, Elaine (Laski), 76, 77, 147, 169, 209, 227
Bloomsbury, 17, 36, 85, 91, 150, 158, 159, 205
B'nai Brith, 35, 40, 49, 73, 74, 88, 119
B'nai B'rith Council for Refugee Children, 73
Board of Guardians, 24, 34
Board of Jewish Deputies, 24, 169
Board of Shechita, 26
Bolchover, Richard, 12
Boothroyd, Betty, 232
Bournmouth, 144
Bowers, Klaus, 15

Bowlby, John, 14
Boyarin, Jonathan, 9
Bracey, Bertha, 31, 58, 89
Brand, Gisele, 15
Breslau, 113, 235
Bristol, 78, 117
Brith Kodesh, 145
British Movement for the Care of Children, 75
British Zionist Federation, 39
Brotman, Adolf, 169
Bruening, Sabine, 230
Bulova Ernst, 31
Bulova, Ilse, 31
Bunbury, Henry, 84
Bunce Court School, 30, 32, 33, 116, 242
Burlingham, Dorothy T., 11, 160, 162
Burton, Henry, 182
Buxton, Charles Roden, 65
Buxton, Dorothy Frances, 65
Bydown, 145, 147

Cambodia, 15
Cambridge, 78, 158, 159, 165
Camp Hill House, 31
Canada, 3, 34, 85, 122, 174, 176, 187, 188, 189, 190, 191, 230
Canadian National Committee on Refugees, 189
Canadian YMCA, 189
Canossa, 43
Caputh, 145
Cardiff, 26, 45, 145, 158
Catholic Committee for Refugees from Germany, 84
Central British Fund for German Jewry, 9, 12, 36, 49
Central Committee for Jewish Education, 167
Central Committee for Refugees, 173
Central Council for Jewish Refugees, 170, 172, 202
Chadwick, Trevor, 86, 87, 88, 89, 9697, 109

Index

Chamberlain, Neville, 43, 52, 60, 187,
Channel Islands, 200
Chappell, Connery, 13
Charles, Prince of Wales, 232
Chase, Valerie Jean, 15
Cheltenham, 63, 94, 200
Chief Rabbi's Religious Emergency Council (CRREC), 3, 7, 10, 13, 14, 57, 64, 74, 78, 79, 80, 81, 82, 96, 109, 113, 118, 121, 130, 161, 164, 165, 168, 170, 171, 186, 201, 206, 207, 208, 210, 211, 242
Children's Inter-Aid Committee, 37, 49, 73, 74, 200
Children's Overseas Reception Board, 174
Chile, 221
Christian Council for Refugees, 35
Christian-Jewish Alliance, 83, 84
Christie, Agatha, 242
Church of England Committee for Non-Aryan Christians, 84
Churchill, Winston, 183, 187
Clapper, Raymond, 175
Claydon, 117
Cleve, 130
Clonin Castle, 146
Cohen, David, 67
Cohen, Dennis M., 35
Cohen, Lee, 15
Cohen, Leonard, 38
Colijn, Hendrikus, 67
Cologne, 130, 235
Comité Israelite pour les Enfants venant d'Allemagne et de l'Europe Centrale, 51
Comité Suisse d'aide aux Enfants d'émigrés, 51
Coordinating Committee for Refugees, 83, 125
Cornwall, 3, 4, 166, 167, 168, 174, 199
Council for German Jewry, 11, 36, 37, 40, 49, 52, 55, 56, 57, 58, 60, 78, 81, 82, 91, 92, 114, 130, 143, 147, 148,
Crerar, Thomas Alexander, 174
Croatia, 15

Cross, Ronald, 187
Cuba, 15
Cuffley, 156
Curio, Claudia, 14
Czechoslovakia, 2, 13, 43, 44, 54, 60, 67, 76, 84, 85, 86, 87, 88, 90, 97, 105, 109, 121, 129, 143, 231, 232, 235, 241,

Danzig, 110, 111, 231
David, Ruth, 15
Davidson, Bernard, 35
Dawson, Geoffrey, 66
De Jong, Louis, 194
Decker, Rolf, 241
Deedes, Wyndham Henry, 37, 39, 40, 56, 74, 75
Denmark, 139
Dominican Republic, 43, 102
Domville, Barry, 194
Donnington, 146
Dorset, 87
Dovercourt, 30, 93, 113, 114, 115, 116, 117, 118, 157
Drucker, Olga Levy, 107, 166, 231
Drucker, Peter F., 73
Dubrowsky, Gertrude, 159, 238
Dubs, Alfred, 241
Dundonald, Lord, 145

Ealing, 82
Edgeware, 25
Edinburgh, 141, 142, 143, 158, 168
Edward I, 24
Eichmann, Adolf, 41, 67, 80, 109
Einstein, Albert, 61
Eisenhower, Dwight D., 76
Elizabeth II, Queen, 233
Ellenville, New York, 231
Emanuel, Muriel, 13
EMIG-Direct, 36
Epstein, Hedy, 50
Essinger, Anna, 29. 30, 32, 116, 242
Evian, France, 42, 43, 53, 91, 94, 102

Falkland Islands, 187
Fast, Vera, 14
Faversham, 30
Federation of Synagogues, 26, 27
Feingold, Henry, 227
Fox, Anne, 15, 105, 166
France, 5, 42, 52, 65, 139, 165, 174, 183, 221
Frankfurt, 27, 35, 38, 40, 92, 106
Fredericton, New Brunswick, 188
Freier, Recha, 138
Freud, Anna, 11, 160, 162, 213
Friedman, Saul, 227
Friedmann, Fridolin M., 145
Friends of the Hebrew University, 242
Friends Service Committee, 35
Fry, Helen, 13
Fuchel, Kurt, 221
Fürth, 156, 158

Galilee, 5
Gaster, Moses, 38, 40
Gdansk, 232
General Zionists, 145
Genizi, Haim, 75
Germany, 2, 5,8, 9, 11, 14, 23, 24, 28, 29, 30, 31, 32, 33, 34, 35, 36, 41, 42, 44, 49, 50, 51, 52, 53, 55, 56, 57, 60, 61, 62, 64, 67, 68, 72, 74, 75, 80, 81, 84, 86, 89, 90, 91, 103, 104, 105, 106, 107, 108, 109, 110, 112, 114, 115, 116, 117, 119, 121, 112, 123, 124, 125, 126, 128, 129, 138, 139, 140, 143, 145, 156, 162, 175, 176, 182, 183, 203, 213, 219, 222, 223, 224, 228, 229, 233, 236, 241, 242
Gershon, Karen (Kathleen Tripp, Kaethe Lowenthal), 15, 224, 225, 226, 238
Gestetner, Sigfreid, 121
Giessen, 27
Gilbert, Martin, 232
Gilboa, Avner, 235
Gilboa, Chana, 218, 224, 234, 236, 239, 246

Gillman, Leni, 13
Gillman, Peter, 13
Gissing, Vera, 13, 15, 105, 156
Givatayim, 10
Glasgow, 23, 26, 208
Gloucester, 158
Goepfert, Rebekka, 13
Golabek Mona, 15
Golan, Ester, 230
Golders Green, 25
Goldfaden, Mordechai, 218
Goodman, Harry, 10, 28, 57, 77, 78, 79, 81, 82, 169, 171, 201, 207,
Goodwin, Gerald, 185
Gordon, Alexander, 108, 114, 116
Gordon, Robert, 30
Gordonia, 144
Gordonstoun School, 30, 76
Gorell, Lord (Ronald Gorell Barnes), 3, 64, 75, 76, 77, 120, 201, 202, 205, 206, 208, 209, 220, 242
Gottlieb, Amy Zahl, 9, 12, 39, 57
Green, Gerald, 227
Greene, Ben, 58
Grosz, Anita, 235
Groszman, Franzi, 107, 243
Gruenfeld, Judith, 82, 163
Grunfeld, Isidore, 78, 202, 203
Guske, Iris, 14
Gwrych Castle, 130, 137, 138, 145, 146, 184

Haberer, Joseph, 6, 162, 239, 243
Habonim, 121, 140, 172
Hadassah Women's Zionist organization, 189
Hague, 183
Hahn, Kurt, 30, 76
Hahn-Warburg, Lola, 56, 76, 139, 147, 169
Hailey, Lord William Malcolm, 84
Halifax, Lord, 55, 176
Hall, Edgar, 128
Hall, Marjorie, 128

Index

Hamburg, 113
Hammel, Andrea, 14
Hampstead, 25, 123, 199
Hampstead Synagogue Ladies Aid Society, 141
Handler, Arieh, 227, 243
Hannam, Charles, 15
Hanoar, 172
Hardisty, Dorothy, 75, 76, 77, 83, 169, 212
Harvey, Thomas, Edmund, 59
Harwich, 110, 111, 113, 130, 139, 230, 232
Hashomer Hatzair, 138, 144, 172, 217
Haslemere, 31
Havel, Vaclav, 232
Hay, 192, 193
Hayes, Saul, 189, 190
Hechalutz, 121, 138, 171, 172
Hechalutz BeAnglia 139,
Hecksher, William, 190
Heidelberg, 30
Heinemann, Hans, 147
Herrlingen school, 29
Hertz (Schonfeld), Judith, 79, 81
Hertz, Joseph Herman, 3, 26, 28, 78, 79, 81, 113, 114, 165, 170, 171, 201, 202, 205, 206, 207, 208
Heyman, Eva, 15
HIAS, 36
HICEM, 36
Hill, Paula, 14
Hirsch, Otto, 104, 105
Hirsch, Samson Raphael, 27
Hitler, Adolph, 12, 25, 28, 29, 31, 34, 35, 41, 43, 50, 53, 54, 86, 103, 111, 125, 126, 146, 159, 192, 201, 226, 227, 228, 229
Hoare, Jean, 85, 89
Hoare, Sir Samuel, 11, 53, 54, 58, 59, 64, 85
Hoek van Holland, 110, 111, 130, 139
Holland, 67, 105, 109, 110, 111, 130, 139, 174, 183, 217, 219, 244
Hoover, Herbert, 61
Hutman, Ruth, 64

Huyton, 185, 186
Hyphen, 223

ICA, 36
Iden, Thea, 15
Ijmuiden, 174
Ilford, 25
Initiation Society, 26
Innisfallen, 24
Inter-Aid Committee for Children Coming from Germany, 37, 41, 49, 56, 58, 59, 73, 74, 75, 84, 93, 131, 200
International Peace Council, 242
International Student Service, 84
Ipswich, 117
Isle of Man, 183, 184, 185, 186, 190, 193
Israel, 10, 137, 139, 146, 224, 225, 226, 227, 230, 231, 234, 235, 240, 241, 243, 244
Israel, Wilfred, 9, 13, 52
Italy, 35, 43, 139, 175, 176

Jacoby, Ingrid, 15
Jennings, William Ivor, 182
Jerusalem, 1, 10, 132, 231, 243, 244
Jesus, 3, 166, 207
Jewish Agency, 39, 43, 54, 60, 62, 143,
Jewish Agricultural Committee, 121, 122
Jewish Committee for Relief Abroad, 242
Jewish Day Nursery, 40
Jewish Labor Committee, 62
Jewish Refugees Committee, 9, 35, 36, 49, 67, 78, 117, 159, 164, 167, 174, 199, 217, 219, 220, 221
Jewish Religious Education Board, 167
Jewish Secondary School, 27, 79, 82, 161, 164, 169
Jews' Free School for Boys, 207
Jews' Temporary Shelter, 34, 35, 38
Johannesburg, 114
Joint Committee for Religious Education and Welfare of Jewish Refugee children, 170, 202

Joint Emergency Committee for Jewish Education, 168, 170
Joint Emergency Committee for the Religious Education of Jewish Evacuated Children, 169
Judt, Tony, 13

Kashrut Commission, 26
Katmandu, 241
Kelley, Mr., 156, 166
Kelley, Mrs., 156, 166
Kent, 30, 115, 121, 122, 143, 144, 145, 183
Kent, Flor, 232
Kevutzat Yavneh, 10
Kibbutz Lavi, 5, 231, 235
King, Mackenzie, 187
Kirsch, Manfred, 162
Kitchener Camp, 122, 170
Koch, Eric, 13
Koenig, Karl, 31
Kohn, Walter, 241
Korman, Gerd, 15
Korobkin, Freida Stolzberg, 15
Kramer, Lotte, 15
Kranzler, David, 13
Kushner, Tony, 12
Kynnersley, 146

Lafitte, Françoise, 184
Langdon, Geoffrey, 56
Lanzmann, Claude, 228
Laqueur, Walter, 9, 124, 223, 241
Laski (Blond), Elaine, 76, 77, 83, 147, 169, 209, 227
Laski, Cissie (Phina Emily), 35, 40, 56
Laski, Neville Jonas, 34, 38, 40
Laufer, Chava, 218, 235
Lawrence, A. Levay, 49
Lazarus, Frank, 35
League of Nations, 36, 42, 54, 94, 218
Leeds, 24, 25, 110, 114, 116, 118, 119, 122, 158
Leipzig, 159, 234,

Leven, Louise, 32
Leverton, Bertha, 50, 106, 115, 221, 229, 230, 231, 236, 243
Levine, Ephraim, 208, 220
Levy, Berthold, 107
Levy, Charlotte, 107
Levy, Ernie, 29
Levy, Hans, 107
Levy, Olga, 15
Liberal Jewish Synagogue, 27
Lichtenstein, Fritz (Peretz Leshem), 143
Lincoln, 158
Lion, Hilde, 331, 32
Lipson, Daniel Leopold, 63, 94, 200
Liverpool, 112, 147, 174, 185, 188, 191, 192, 232, 233
Lloyd, Geoffrey, 59, 91, 94
London, 1, 2, 3, 4, 6, 9, 15, 24, 25, 26, 27, 31, 34, 36, 38, 40, 41, 56, 60, 64, 65, 66, 74, 75, 80, 81, 84, 86, 92, 100, 102, 104, 105, 110, 111, 112, 114, 116, 117, 118, 119, 122, 123, 126, 127, 128, 130, 139, 140, 142, 146, 147, 150, 155, 156, 157, 158, 161, 162, 168, 169, 170, 171, 199, 207, 208, 219, 221, 224, 230, 231, 233, 242, 243, 244
London Metropolitan Archives, 10
London Women's Society, 141
London, Louise, 12, 60
Lord Baldwin Fund, 63, 92
Lowestoft, 113, 114
Luxembourg, 139

Maccabi, 172
Maccabi Hatzair (Young Maccabi), 138, 140
MacColl, James, 56
Macdonald, James G., 36
MacDonald, Malcolm, 54
Machover, Jonah, 110
Mainz, Ernest, 35
Manchester, 24, 25, 38, 75, 78, 82, 117, 118, 119, 147, 158, 174, 203, 238

Mapai (Palestine Labor Zionists), 62
Marcus, Grete, 221
Margate, 171
Margulies, Gerda, 143
Marks, Simon, 38
Marley, Lady, 114
Marley, Lord, 114
Massuot Yitzchak, 243
Maxwell, Elizabeth, 232
Maxwell, R. C., 141
Meisler, Frank, 232
Menashe ben Israel, 24
Merseburger, Peter, 230
Mertzbach, Freida, 123
Mexico, 102, 241
Michaelis-Stern, Eva, 139, 218, 227, 243
Middlesex, 156
Midlands, 2, 3, 121, 126, 159, 201
Millisle Farm, 146
Milton, Edith, 15
Mishmar, 172
Mizrachi, 79, 80, 110, 243
Model, Alice, 35, 40
Montagu, Lily Helen, 26, 27, 169
Montagu, Samuel, 26, 27
Montefiore, Claude Joseph Goldsmid, 26, 27
Montefiore, Leonard Nathaniel Goldsmid, 35, 38, 39
Montefiore, Moses, 27
Montreal, 175, 190
Moravia, 76
Morrison, Herbert, 64, 190
Morse, Arthur, 227
Mosley, Oswald, 194
Movement for the Care of Children from Germany, 56, 57, 62, 67, 73, 74, 75, 84, 115, 116, 125
Munster, 23
Murrumbidgee River, 192

Nacken, Hanna, 32
Nantclwyd, 146

National Archives, 10
National Council of Churches, 61
Nepal, 230
Netherlands, 5, 51, 62, 67, 68, 104, 109, 165, 173, 182
New Herrlingen school, 29
New Liberal Jewish Association (Social Youth Group), 172
New York, 10, 25, 26, 231, 235, 242, 243
New Zealand, 192
Newcastle Under-Lyme, 63
Newfoundland, 187, 188
Newman, Otto, 15, 241
Newsam, Frank, 181
Nigeria, 87
Nipingon, 188
Nitra, Slovakia, 79, 80
Noel-Baker, Philip, 58, 85
Northampton, 162
Northern Ireland, 78, 146
Norton, Jennifer, 14, 227, 237
Norway, 182
Norwich, 117
Nottingham, 158

Ormerod, Mary, 85, 86
Ormerod, S., 84
OSE (Oeuvre de Secours aux Enfants), 51, 115
Ottawa, 190
Otto Hirsch Youth, 172
Oxford, 9, 30, 158

Pakefield, 113, 117
Palestine, 5, 12, 27, 33, 36, 38, 39, 40, 43, 49, 52, 53, 54, 55, 60, 61, 62, 93, 102, 110, 121, 122, 131, 138, 139, 140, 141, 142, 144, 145, 146, 147, 148, 149, 150, 173, 189, 190, 192, 193, 218, 224, 227, 238, 242, 243
Papanek, Ernst, 115
Paris, 41, 43, 221
Patkin, Benizon, 13

Patterson, Alexander, 190
Peake, Osbert, 184, 200
Pels, Henry, 80
Penzias, Arno, 241
Petronius, 97
Pioneer Corps, 193, 194
Polish Refugee Fund, 109, 110
Portugal, 173
Prague, 43, 85, 86, 87, 88, 89, 96, 109, 212, 233,
Pressburg, 27
Presland, John, 41, 227, 237

Quakers, 7, 35, 52, 85, 86, 109, 112, 128,

Ramler, Sigfried, 15
Rath, Ernst vom, 44
Rawson, E. L., 35
Reading, Eva, 11, 205
Refugee Children's Movement (RCM), 3, 9, 10, 30, 41, 64, 75, 76, 77, 78, 80, 82, 83, 87, 88, 91, 92, 94, 95, 96, 102, 103, 105, 109, 111, 112, 113, 116, 117, 118, 119, 120, 121, 122, 123, 130, 131, 138, 139, 141, 143, 147, 148, 149, 150, 157, 158, 161, 162, 164, 165, 166, 167, 168, 169, 170, 172, 173, 182, 184, 185, 188, 191, 193, 194, 200, 201, 202, 203, 204, 205, 107, 208, 209, 212, 213, 219, 227, 237
Reich, Erich, 241
Reichsvertretungder Juden in Deutschland (Central Organization of Jews in Germany), 32, 67, 86, 96, 103
Reti, Irene, 15
Reunion of Kindertransports (ROK) Organization, 230, 231
Richborough, 122, 170
Robbins, Thomas, 84
Roosevelt, Eleanor, 175
Roosevelt, Franklin Delano, 42, 51, 175
Rosen, Yaakov Kopul, 147
Rosenfeld, Ursula, 51

Rosenheim, Jacob, 78, 81
Rosner, Bob, 15
Roth, Milena, 15
Rothschild, Anthony de, 35, 147
Rothschild, Lionel de, 38
Rothschild, Yvonne de, 147
Royal Institute of British Architects, 85
Rublee, George S., 43
Ruthin, 146

Sacramento, 14
Sadan, Inge, 162, 219, 221, 231
Salisbury, 144
Salinger, Anne, 237
Samuel, Col. F.D., 84
Samuel, Herbert, 11, 35, 37, 38, 40, 52, 56, 58, 65, 66, 75, 77, 78, 91, 241
Save the Children Fund, 37, 75, 93
Schacht, Hjalmar, 34
Schiff, Jacob, 35
Schiff, Otto M., 34, 38
Schlesinger, Bernard, 2, 3, 4, 101, 112, 122, 123, 166,
Schlesinger, Joe, 241
Schloss Salem School, 31
Schonfeld, Avigdor, 27
Schonfeld, Solomon, 3, 10, 12, 13, 27, 28, 57, 64, 77, 79, 80, 81, 88, 88, 96, 97, 109, 113, 120, 164, 169, 186, 201, 205, 206, 242
Schroeder, David, 8
Schwab, Anna, 35, 40
Schwartz, Shalom, 8
Schwartz, Steffi Birnbaum, 1, 2, 3, 4, 15, 23, 26, 28, 51, 101, 102, 107, 112, 123, 156, 157, 166, 167, 199, 207, 210, 217, 218, 222, 223, 224, 229, 234, 239, 244
Schwartzman, Jacob, 142
Schwarz-Bart, Andre, 29
Schwerte, Westphalia, 170
Scotland, 23, 24, 26, 30, 31, 76, 78, 121, 141, 146, 155, 156, 204, 231
Sealand, 146

Segal, Lore Grossman, 15, 107, 114, 243
Seligman, Eliezer (Erwin), 146
Seller, Maxine, 13
Serbia, 15
Shatzkes, Pamela, 13
Shefford, 161, 163, 164, 169,
Shepherd, Naomi, 9
Sherbrooke, 188, 189
Sherman, Alan Joshua, 12, 227
Sieff, Rebecca, 56, 57, 121, 147
Sierra Leone, 191
Simpson, William W. (Bill), 35, 83, 185, 186, 212, 227, 242, 243
Singer, Dorothy, 167
Singer, Elisabeth, 128
Slobodka, 79
Smith, David Horton, 8
Society for the Protection of Science and Learning, 84
Society of Friends, 32, 58, 84, 85, 109
Sompolinsky, Meir, 12
Souhami, Herta, 104
South Africa, 34, 187, 227
South East London Refugee Children's Committee, 141
Southgate, 25
Southport, 117, 156
Spain, 34, 173, 219
Sperber, Rabbi Samuel, 146, 147
St. Asaph, 146
St. Helena, 187
St. John's Wood, 27
Stamford Hill, 25, 27, 82
Stead, Charles, 75
Steiner, Rudolph, 31
Steinfeld, Julius, 80, 109
Stent, Ronald, 13
Stephany, Meyer, 37, 39, 147
Stern, Eva Michaelis, 189, 213, 227, 243
Stoatley Rough School, 31, 32, 33
Stolberg, Freida, 203
Strachey, Amy St. Loe, 160
Strasser, Charles, 15

Styrone, William, 228
Sudbury, 182
Sudetenland, 43
Surrey, 31
Sweden, 5, 139
Swift, Maurice, 204, 209
Switzerland, 5, 33, 42, 51, 52, 86, 92, 102, 139

Talmon, Yitzchak, 171, 219
Talmud Torah Trust, 167
Tatura, 192
Taylor, Myron, 43
Templewood, Lord, 11
Thompson, Dorothy, 173
Titmuss, Richard, 157, 160, 164
Tomlin, Chanan, 11, 13, 242
Trades Union Congress and Labour Party (the International Solidarity Fund), 84
Transylvania, 146
Treitel, Guenter, 241
Tripp, Val, 224
Trois-Rivieres, 188
Trumpeldor, Joseph, 40
Tunbridge Wells, 158
Turk, Eric, 35
Turlough O'Briain, 24
Turner, Barry, 14, 15

Ulm, 29
Union of Hebrew and Religious Classes, 167
Union of Orthodox Hebrew Congregations, 27, 79, 203, 204
United Palestine Appeal, 37
United Restitution Office, 242
United States, 5, 12, 14, 15, 31, 37, 41, 42, 43, 55, 60, 61, 62, 63, 75, 83, 85, 93, 96, 120, 173, 174, 175, 190, 221, 227, 228, 230, 241, 242, 243
United States Committee for the Care of European Children (USC), 175
United Synagogue, 26, 27, 79, 204

Unterman, Isser Yehuda, 147
Uruguay, 34, 46

Vaad Hatzala, 96
Vered, Mordechai (Theo Verdeber), 110
Vietnam, 15
Villingen, 162

Waley-Cohen, Charles, 121
Walter, Oliver, 237
Walton, 117
Warburg, Felix, 37
Warburg, Max, 76
Wasserstein, Bernard, 12, 227, 237
Weber, Hanus, 15
Wedgewood, Josiah, 63
Weimar, 32
Weiner Library, 10
Weiss, Jakob, 191
Weissmandel, Michel Dov Ber, 79, 80
Weizmann, Chaim, 38, 53, 54, 55, 139
Weizmann, Vera, 139
Weyl, Ruth, 227, 242
Whitechapel, 25, 110
Whiteman, Dorit, 15
Wiepking, Pamala, 8, 37, 38, 40, 89, 159
Wiesenthal Center, 231
Wijsmuller-Meijer, Gertruida, 67, 109, 111, 132, 173, 174
Willesden, 82
Wimbledon, 31
Winterton, Lord (Edward Turnour), 42
Winton, Greta, 232
Winton, Nicholas, 13, 86, 87, 88, 89, 96, 97, 109, 232, 233, 242
Wishnick Dubrovsky, Gertrude, 15
Woburn House, 9, 35, 36, 83, 217
Wohlmann, Ingeborg, 109
Wolff, Emmy, 32
Wollheim, Norbert, 50, 104, 105, 106, 227, 242
Women's Appeal for German and Austrian Women and Children, 74

Women's International Zionist Organization WIZO, 76, 192
Women's Mercy Ships' Committee, 175
Woodside, Queens, 31
World Movement for the Rescue of Children from Germany, 75
WRENS (Women's Royal Naval Service), 194
Wreschner, Boaz, 117
Wyman, David, 227

Young Maccabi (*Maccabi Hatzair*), 138, 140
Youth Aliyah, 7, 9, 10, 14, 36, 49, 76, 88, 121, 130, 132, 136, 138, 139, 140, 141, 142, 143, 144, 145, 146, 147, 148, 149, 150, 161, 183, 186, 188, 190, 191, 192, 213, 218, 243
Yugoslavia, 139

Zbąszyń, 108, 109, 110, 139, 235
Zeller, Fredric, 15
Zeytlyn, Elsley, 11
Zurndorfer, Hannle, 15
Zyl, Werner Van der, 170

www.ingramcontent.com/pod-product-compliance
Lightning Source LLC
Chambersburg PA
CBHW070019010526
44117CB00011B/1633